SHARI`A LAW AND MODERN MUSLIM ETHICS

SHARI`A LAW AND MODERN MUSLIM ETHICS

Edited by Robert W. Hefner

Indiana University Press

Bloomington and Indianapolis

This book is a publication of

Indiana University Press
Office of Scholarly Publishing
Herman B Wells Library 350
1320 East 10th Street
Bloomington, Indiana 47405 USA

iupress.indiana.edu

Library of Congress Cataloging-in-Publication Data

Names: Hefner, Robert W., 1952–, editor.
Title: Shari`a law and modern Muslim ethics / edited by
    Robert W. Hefner.
Description: Bloomington, Indiana : Indiana University Press, 2016. |
    Includes bibliographical references and index.
Identifiers: LCCN 2016021951 (print) | LCCN 2016022780 (ebook) |
    ISBN 9780253022479 (cloth : alk. paper) | ISBN 9780253022523
    (pbk. : alk. paper) | ISBN 9780253022608 (ebook)
Subjects: LCSH: Islamic law—Philosophy. | Law and ethics. | Islamic
    ethics.
Classification: LCC KBP444 .S43 2016 (print) | LCC KBP444 (ebook)
    | DDC
    297.5—dc23
LC record available at https://lccn.loc.gov/2016021951

1 2 3 4 5 21 20 19 18 17 16

Contents

Section III: New Ethical Imbrications

Acknowledgments

THIS VOLUME WAS the product of a two-year project organized at the Institute on Culture, Religion, and World Affairs at the Pardee School of Global Affairs at Boston University. The project was funded by the Luce Foundation and an anonymous donor. I thank the Luce Foundation and Religion Program Director Toby Volkman for their generous support and institutional vision. No foundation I know has done more to address the importance of religion in contemporary global affairs.

I also thank Dean Adil Najam of the Pardee School for his continuing support of programs on religion and world affairs at the Pardee School.

Finally, I thank Dee Mortensen, editorial director at Indiana University Press, for her care and skill in ushering this volume through the production process in an engaging and productive manner.

A Note on Transliteration

As THE CASE studies in this book indicate, the contributors to this volume draw on a broad array of languages, each with its own conventions of transliteration and spelling of Arabic and local-language words. In the interest of consistency, we have kept the transliteration of non-English terms to a minimum. With the exception of the ` to indicate the Arabic letter `ayn` (as in shari`a) and ' to indicate the *hamza* (as in Qur'an), we have dispensed with diacritical marks in this volume. The *hamza* is, moreover, indicated within words (as in Qur'an) but not at their ends.

Arabic-derived words are rendered in different ways in non-Arabic languages; indeed, in some languages, such as Malay and Indonesian, the rendering can appear quite different from the Arabic original. Our preference throughout the volume has been to render words used in all of the book's chapters, such as shari`a, in a uniform manner, but in some cases (as in the chapter on Malaysia), we have deferred to the wishes of the author when retaining a local spelling was important for conveying the word's local colorings. Except when discussing `ulama (singular: `alim), we have also usually indicated the plural form of Arabic terms by adding an *s* to the singular form—thus *fatwas* rather than *fatawa* and *madrasas* rather than *madaris*. Finally, Arabic words that occur frequently throughout the volume are not italicized.

SHARI`A LAW AND MODERN MUSLIM ETHICS

1   Shari`a Law and the Quest for a Modern Muslim Ethics

Robert W. Hefner

IN RECENT YEARS many Muslim-majority societies have undergone complex and difficult political transitions. As in Indonesia and Tunisia, some of these passages have been from authoritarian rule to a significant measure of democracy and citizen rights. As in Egypt, Libya, and Syria, however, other transitions began with hope but soon gave rise to a barrage of state and societal violence that left the national landscape anything but civil or democratic.

Whatever the precise course of events, common to all these transitions has been heightened debate over the role of shari`a law and Islamic ethics in politics and social life. Across the world today, prominent Muslim democrats invoke shari`a and Islamic values to justify calls for democracy, pluralist tolerance, and gender equality (see Abou el Fadl 2001, 2004; Moosa 2001; Ramadan 2009). At the same time, however, radical movements such as the Islamic State in Iraq and the Levant (ISIL) and Boko Haram in West Africa cite what they insist are shari`a principles to legitimize rejection of democracy, enslavement of non-Muslim women, and mass killing of so-called apostates. Two generations ago, the idea that disputes over the forms and meanings of Islamic law and ethics might figure prominently in Muslim politics would have struck most observers as unthinkable—but no longer. The pervasiveness of appeals to shari`a in today's upheavals, as well as the existence of conflicting interpretations of Islamic values, shows that understanding the struggles of the Muslim world requires a coming to terms with the varied meanings and uses of Islamic law and ethics.

The chapters in this book aim to provide just such an understanding. They are the product of a two-year collaboration that began in March 2013 with a workshop at Boston University's Institute on Culture, Religion, and World Affairs and that ended in early 2015.[1] The collaborators in this project came together in response to modern changes in politics and ethics in the Muslim world. In early 2011, the transitions collectively known as the "Arab Spring" had just gotten under way. Notwithstanding initially encouraging events, reform-minded proponents of democracy and citizenship in many lands soon found themselves challenged by rivals who dismissed democracy as being incompatible with Islam and who called for a new order based on their own understandings of shari`a law. By the time of our workshop, events in Syria and Libya no longer instilled springtime optimism but instead cast dark shadows of concern.

The quickened pace of developments did not end there. The first months of 2014 saw an explosion of killing, rape, and enslavement on the parts of Boko Haram and ISIL (Hanne and Flichy de la Neuville 2014). Mali, once known for its robust democracy, remained mired in an ethnic and Islamist insurgency (see chapter 9, Schulz). The Pakistani government, a beacon of modernist progressivism only two generations earlier, had difficulty recruiting clerical allies for its antiradical campaigns (see chapter 8, Zaman). Turkey, until recently seen as a model of democracy for the Muslim Middle East, saw its once moderate Islamist leadership impose draconian restrictions on the press as well as on opposition groups (see chapter 7, Kuru).

But not all news from Muslim lands was dire. In the 2010s, an international coalition of Muslim feminists known as Musawah had established branches in dozens of Muslim-majority countries, invoking Islamic values in the cause of gender-equity reform (see chapter 3, Mir-Hosseini). In Morocco, the astonishingly open public debate surrounding a young woman's rape, marriage, and subsequent suicide revealed that new ideas of gender dignity had taken hold among a broad swath of Moroccan youth (see chapter 4, Salime). Moreover, over the course of 2014, Tunisian parliamentarians succeeded in crafting a boldly democratic constitution (see chapter 5, Zeghal). Indonesia in the 2010s was well into in its second decade of impressive democratic reform, with women's groups helping lead the way (see chapter 11, Hefner). However, what made the course of Muslim-world developments so perplexing was that actors and movements on all sides regularly invoked Islamic law and ethical values to justify vastly different positions.

In light of these developments and controversies, the contributors to this volume felt it imperative that they revisit the question of the varied meanings and uses of Islamic legal and ethical traditions today.[2] The authors come from a variety of disciplines, including Islamic studies, political science, legal studies, and anthropology, but they share one conviction: that one of the keys to understanding Islamic law and ethics lies in exploring their imbrications with the various ethical projects and "social imaginaries" (Arkoun 2003; Taylor 2004) at play in the transitions under way in the contemporary Muslim world. In highlighting transitions, we do not limit our attention to the regime changes seen in the Middle East and North Africa (MENA) in the aftermath of the so-called Arab Spring. Rather, our cases extend well beyond the MENA region, involving disputations and transitions more varied than those of state-level politics alone and focusing on matters related to law and women as well as to governance. Our inquiries are also as much concerned with the "epistemological crisis" affecting Islamic ethical traditions—in philosopher Alasdair MacIntyre's (1984; 1988) sense of the term (see later this chapter)—as they are with state-related politics.

Three theoretical premises inform our aims: First, to understand Islamic ethics and law today, we must put aside narrowly instrumentalist approaches to Muslim politics, which see appeals to ethics as cloaks for more "real" political–economic interests. Rather than dismissing legal and ethical arguments, the contributors to this volume recognize that the varied ethical aspirations to which actors dedicate themselves are key features of Muslim society and politics. In adopting this perspective, the authors build on new approaches to ethics and morality that have emerged over the past ten years in fields as varied as anthropology, political ethics, Muslim feminist theory, and Islamic studies (see later this chapter). With regard to Islamic studies in particular, these approaches share the conviction that to understand contemporary events we must recognize "the continuing commitment of today's Muslims to the central domain of the moral" (Hallaq 2013, 169) even as the details of Islamic morality remain a point of contention.

Second, a proper assessment of Islamic ethicolegal traditions requires that we recognize that the latter are "in practice . . . various, not homogeneous" (Hooker 2008, 1; see also Abou el Fadl 2014, xxxii; Moosa 2001, 7), being subject to widely divergent interpretations in different times and places. Much as ISIL and Boko Haram do, many among today's radical proponents of shariʿa claim that its meanings are unitary, clear, and unquestionable. Muslims who suggest otherwise they deem fools or apostates. But the overwhelming majority of the world's Muslims adamantly reject these absolutist claims. More generally, history shows that Muslim understandings of Islamic law and ethics have always been varied. Rarely has that variation been more politically consequential, however, than it is today.

This, in turn, raises a third issue vital to a discussion of the matters addressed in this book. To understand how and why cultural understandings of Islamic law and ethics vary over time and space, merely probing the scriptures or textual commentaries to which some actors refer as the source for Islamic values is not sufficient. However authoritative such sources might be, Muslim ethical understandings vary because the achievement of those understandings is contingent and conjunctural. Ethical understandings are not hermetically sealed from the world but rather emerge from the efforts of real human actors who engage Islamic traditions even as they are involved in other life projects and influenced by other ethical norms. As a result of these "entanglements" (Lempert 2013), Muslims' understandings of shariʿa and ethics can change over time and can differ from or contradict those of other believers (see Lempert 2013; Simon 2009, 265; Zigon 2008; 2014, 753; cf. Masud 2002; Metcalf 1984).

This last point is, analytically speaking, the most critical, and it raises the larger question of how we are to understand the relationship of Islamic law and ethics to the diverse ethical currents that flow through all Muslim societies. In recent years, scholars of comparative law have come to recognize that all societies are characterized by legal plurality, defined as "a situation in which two or more legal systems coexist in the same social field" (Engle Merry 1988, 870; see also Tucker 2008, 9). This plurality is important because coexistent bodies of law "may make competing claims of authority; they may impose conflicting demands or norms; they may have different styles and orientations"; moreover, the plurality "poses a challenge to the legal authorities themselves, for it means that they have rivals" (Tamanaha 2008, 375; cf. Modood 2009; Turner 2011, 151–74).

Legal plurality is, however, but one part of the larger *ethical* plurality that characterizes all human societies. As highlighted in the anthropology of Islam and the new anthropology of morality (Clarke 2014; Laidlaw 2014; Lambek 2010; Robbins 2007; Schielke 2010a; 2010b; Simon 2009; Soares 2005; Zigon 2014), all societies make a variety of moral registers available to their members, each associated with a particular social field or fields and sustained by a distinctive interplay of actors, institutions, and powers. As is most notably the case with moral registers identified as "law" or "religion," some moral registers may be discursivized—which is to say performed, produced, and reproduced in explicit cultural terms by actors and institutions who have been endowed with authority and power. Contrary to the tendency of some authors to extend the notion of "discourse" to any and all normative forms, however, not all ethical registers that operate in society achieve such an explicit and authoritative standing. Other moral currents might be less formal or articulate or may not be officially recognized or publicly discursivized at all (see Laidlaw 2014, 82; Lambek 2010; Robbins 2007; Schielke 2010a; 2010b; Simon 2009; Zigon 2014). Notwithstanding their less public standing, these "ordinary" (Das 2012; Lambek 2010) moral registers may exercise a powerful influence on actors' subjectivities and aspirations. No less important, they influence the ways that actors understand more formalized moral discourses—including, for example, Islamic law. To borrow a notion from Zakia Salime (this volume, chapter 4), one often sees a web of exchanges among movements and across moral registers in a society, mutualistic imbrications that take on fuller meaning when linked to particular time-events (see also Lempert 2013; Simon 2009). Only by exploring this entanglement of moral registers and projects can we begin to understand the varied forms and meanings of Islamic ethicolegal traditions and their implications for the three concerns at the heart of this book: government, public law, and gender roles.[3]

Having presented a few additional remarks on this framework, I turn in the second part of this introduction to the chapters themselves. I then conclude by making several general observations about what the ethical variety operative in contemporary Muslim societies says about the prospects for a democratic and pluralist Islamic ethics in years to come.

Islamic Law amid Ethical Plurality

To begin to understand Islamic legal and ethical traditions, one must dispense with the idea that the latter are a fixed and finished body of normative regulations, derived from sacred texts and uniform across time and space, an essentialist understanding of Islamic law and ethics once common among Orientalist scholars of Islamic law. In recent years, such a view has found a second lease on life among conservative Islamists and even among some mainstream Muslim scholars, particularly those who have sought to embed what they describe as "shari`a" in the positive law of the modern nation-state (see Hooker 2008; Musallam 2005; Zubaida 2003, 135). Ironically, an essentialized understanding of shari`a has also figured in the imaginations of anti-Muslim activists in the West. The "antishari`a movement" that emerged in the United States and Western Europe in the 2000s portrayed shari`a as uniform and unchanging while claiming, in the words of former House Speaker Newt Gingrich, that shari`a is "a moral threat to the survival of freedom . . . in the world as we know it" (Shane 2011; see Center for Security Policy 2010; this volume, Emon, chapter 2; and Uddin and Pantzer 2012).

Rather than viewing Islamic legal and ethical ideals as being unitary and unchanging, we come closer to their living reality when we recognize that their understanding is always mediated through an array of popular and elite ethical imaginaries, as well as media of representation and organized practices of transmission, performance, and discipline. Rather than scriptural texts' generating a single and unchanging truth, ethical meaning emerges from "diverse and often far-flung materials" linked in ongoing and multisited "entanglements" (Lempert 2013, 373; cf. Simon 2009; Zigon 2014, 753). To borrow a phrase from Fredrik Barth's (1993, 177–236) anthropology of knowledge, the interplay of these elements may well bring about "criteria of validity" with sufficient internal consistency, social resonance, and public authority to allow a stable understanding of Islamic law and ethics in a particular time and place. Precisely because ethical understandings and practices emerge from this imbrication, however, the specific "corpus of assertions" (ibid.) inspired by what is regarded as shari`a or any other ethical tradition can vary, sometimes in contradictory ways (see also Dupret 2012; Mir-Hosseini 2003; Moosa 2001).

While recognizing their situated and conjunctural nature, we must take care not to deconstruct Islamic law and ethics so thoroughly as to assume that they have always been entirely relative from one time and place to another. In a manner most directly comparable to Judaism's ethical traditions (Neusner and Sonn 1999, 1–17), a concern for God's commands and ethical guidance has been central to Islamic civilization from the first. Moreover, one of the great achievements of that civilization in its third to fifth centuries of existence (the tenth to twelfth centuries CE) was to put in place an educational and political "assemblage" (Latour 2005) for the enduring production and reproduction of the knowledge that came to be regarded as Islamic law. Until the great political transformations of the nineteenth and twentieth centuries (when much would change; see later this chapter), the institution at the heart of this ethicolegal assemblage was the *madrasa*, a boarding school for intermediate and advanced study in the Islamic sciences (Berkey 1992; Chamberlain 1994; Hefner 2007; Makdisi 1981). *Madrasa* curricula varied, and in some times and places they included training in Islamic spirituality, mathematics, and astronomy or even in the Greek-influenced "sciences of the ancients" with their natural science and humanistic philosophy (Arjomand 1999; Grandin and Gaborieau 1997). In most pre-twentieth-century Muslim lands, however, the subject matter at the heart of *madrasa* curricula was fiqh, or Islamic jurisprudence.

Meaning, literally, "understanding," and referring to the efforts of religious scholars to understand God's commands, fiqh was the scholarly specialty *par excellence* responsible for the derivation of legal and ethical "rules" (Ar. *ahkam*, sing. *hukm*) from shari`a (Berkey 1992; 2003; Hefner 2009; Makdisi 1981; see also this volume, Emon, chapter 2, and this volume, Mir-Hosseini, chapter 3). In the premodern period, fiqh was neither codified nor rendered as positive statutory law.[4] From the ninth century onward, different schools of Islamic jurisprudence (four Sunni and three Shi'a) each had a measure of "ijtihadic plurality" (Hallaq 2009, 449) that allowed scholars considerable leeway in legal judgment. Viewed from a comparative perspective, then, Islamic fiqh was in every respect a rich ethical "tradition" in philosopher Alasdair MacIntyre's sense of the term (MacIntyre 1988, 12, 350). Rather than a settled list of positive laws, Islamic legal commentary was "an argument extended through time in which certain fundamental agreements are defined and redefined," having its own standards of rational justification and inquiry through which actors come to understand "[their] own commitments or those of others . . . by situating them within those histories which made them what they have now become" (1988, 12–13).

Contemporary academic commentators on Islamic legal traditions have been so impressed by what is, from a comparative perspective, the textual tradition's richness and coherence (see Glenn 2000) that some have identified the fiqh tradition and, behind it, shari`a as the fount from which all Muslim ethical values flow.[5] But this assumption unwittingly reproduces a textualist and unitary bias in the study of Islamic law and ethics, overlooking the myriad ways in which these latter traditions have always interacted with and been altered by other moral registers and social projects, including some whose proponents see them as being every bit as Islamic as fiqh-based law is.

How, then, are we to understand the meaning and importance of Islamic law and values without losing sight of the ethical plurality that marks all Muslim societies? Answering this question has long proved challenging, not least because there is still no agreed framework in the social sciences and humanities for studying ethical and legal plurality within or across cultures. In the study of Islamic law and ethics, this shortcoming has been compounded by a lack of analytic consensus on how the "ordinary ethics" (Lambek 2010; Lempert 2013; Zigon 2014; see also Holmes Katz 2008) that operates in everyday life relates to the more formal and discursivized normative assemblages regarded as "Islamic law."

In light of recent developments in comparative law, gender studies, and the anthropology and sociology of morality, however, today we are in a better position to understand the plurality and contingency of ethics in Muslim-majority societies. We can begin by remembering, first of all, that in premodern times, mastery of Islamic legal traditions was a thoroughly specialized affair reserved almost exclusively for male scholars (Ali 2006; Holmes Katz 2008; but see also Abou-Bakr 2003). In the premodern Middle East, most Muslims—indeed, by some estimates, upward of 98 percent of residents in North Africa and the Levant (Findley 1989)—were illiterate, although the figure was certainly lower in major urban centers (Berkey 1992; see also Guigay 2013, 112). As the celebrated medieval historian Ibn Khaldûn (d. 1406; see Khaldûn 1969) reminds us, across the vast expanse of the Middle East and North Africa during the Muslim Middle Ages, multiethnic urban communities lived alongside pastoralist tribes and peasant communities, each having its own customs, political hierarchies, and varied ethical cultures. Even when a community claimed allegiance to shari'a, its members' understanding of the law bore the imprint of diverse moral entanglements—including, for example, deeply gendered tribal traditions of honor, status, and moral shame.

In her now classic study of Bedouin populations in the Western Desert of Egypt in the late 1970s, anthropologist Lila Abu-Lughod (1986) showed that the imbrications of Islamic and tribal moral registers regarding gender and sexuality were not by any means a thing of the distant past. Similarly, in studying gender and Islamic law in coastal Kenya, anthropologist Susan Hirsch has demonstrated that the interplay of jurisprudential discourses with "Swahili ethics" has a pervasive influence on gender discussions in Islamic courts (Hirsch 1998, 20; see also Peletz 1996; Tucker 1998).

The gendered nature of law and ethics in Muslim societies has long been a point of discussion in Islamic studies, but one additional observation bears mention here. As Kecia Ali (2006; 2010) has demonstrated in two important studies of classical Islamic jurisprudence on marriage and slavery (see also Tucker 2008), when dealing with questions of family and gender, many of the most distinguished jurists drew not just on scriptural sources for their rulemaking but also on deep-seated cultural assumptions about the nature of male and female, freeman and slave, and social hierarchy. Reread from the perspective of contemporary studies of Islamic thought, some of the gender premises of classical jurisprudence seem more firmly rooted in local custom than in systematic engagement with Qur'anic ethics (see also Holmes Katz 2006; Mir-Hosseini 2003).[6]

If the first key to understanding Muslim legal and ethical plurality lies with understanding the specialized culture of scholarly elites, the second situates itself squarely in popular society. In premodern times as today, "ordinary Muslims" (Peletz 1997) from outside the ranks of the scholarly class honed their understanding of God's commands not in *madrasas* but in an array of less law-minded ethical performances that included daily prayer (see Simon 2009); listening to entertaining stories from *adab* ("letters") literature, with their wry accounts of virtue and hypocrisy (Kelsay 2013, 2810; Metcalf 1984); participation in state, calendrical, and life cycle rituals (Holmes Katz 2008); pilgrimage to the shrines of Islamic saints, an activity in which women figured prominently (Pemberton 2010); visits with Islamic healers, among whom women also often played leading roles (Flueckiger 2006); and the devotional activities of diverse Sufi orders (see, for example, Sanders 1994; Shoshan 1993, 67–78). This range of ethical practices again reminds us that Muslim ethics has never been derived from any single discourse or practice but from activities and ethical imaginaries sustained in diverse social fields.

Modern scholars of Islamic ethics sometimes summarize this ethical plurality by observing that popular ethics was broadly Sufi-spiritualist in nature, a contrast to scholarly ethics' fiqh-grounded legalism. Although the contrast correctly highlights certain tensions in Muslim ethical life, it is important to add that for most of Muslim history, the relationship between fiqh-oriented scholars and Sufi leaders was not by any means oppositional. Many Sufi masters were also trained legal scholars, and some promoted strict varieties of shari'a reform, particularly during the early modern period (Berkey 2003; Bruinessen and Howell 2007). Rather than being sociologically accurate, then, the Sufi-fiqh contrast points to a more general truth: Before the rise of the modern state, mass education (Eickelman 1992), and modern Islamic reform movements, many popular varieties of Islamic ethical practice drew on ontologies and epistemologies more varied than those of shari'a or jurisprudence alone (see De Jong and Radtke 1999; Karamustafa 2007).

It is no less important to recognize that the diversity of Muslim moral registers and epistemologies was not just a matter affecting unlettered commoners. As Wael Hallaq has argued, in different times and places religious scholars shared a strong "epistemic consensus" premised on an agreed-on "epistemic hierarchy of the legal sources" (Hallaq 2001, 127). However, nonscholars—including even rulers and religious notables—brought significantly different epistemologies and aspirations to their ethical learning. As A. Azar Moin has demonstrated in an important new study of kingship and sainthood in early modern Iran and South

Asia, less legal-minded but no less Islamic traditions often received an enthusiastic hearing even in the commanding heights of Muslim societies, in which, not uncommonly, "'heretical' conceptions of sacred authority attracted a Muslim sovereign more than 'orthodox' notions of Islam" (Moin 2012, 6).

These last observations point to a third key to understanding ethical plurality in Muslim societies in earlier times and today. Even as diverse ethical currents flowed through society, performative bridges connected at least some of the knowledge and values of jurists and the general population as a whole. One of the most important involved state officials' preparation of edicts said to be consonant with fiqh principles and enforced in state-sponsored courts (Vikor 2005, 207; see also Vogel 2007). Another centered on the issuing of nonbinding legal opinions, or *fatwa* (pl. *fatawa*), by qualified religious scholars on matters deemed subject to shari'a norms. These opinions were typically provided in response to a question from a lay individual on some aspect of the law. Where *fatwa* questioning and answering was common, as in medieval Egypt or contemporary Yemen, the practice provided a point of epistemological contact between jurists' normative work and popular ethical imaginaries (Berkey 2003; see also Messick 1996; Skovgaard-Petersen 1997).

A fourth and final lesson here is vital to an understanding of the ways in which the diverse ethical currents flowing through society actually influenced each other in a manner that allowed even highly discursivized traditions, such as Islamic law, to come under the influence of less formalized ethical currents and, in so doing, to take on new meanings. In his pioneering study of Islam and economic ethics in contemporary Mali, anthropologist Benjamin Soares (2005) observes that the diverse moral registers found in that modern African society often stand in juxtaposition with each other, neither merging nor hybridizing but remaining apart. Like Canadian anthropologist Michael Lambek (2010) and British anthropologist Magnus Marsden (2005), Soares underscores this point so as to take exception to the view, still widespread in Western academic circles (especially those influenced by Kantian or Durkheimian approaches to ethics; on this, see Cassaniti and Hickman 2014, 256; Laidlaw 2014, 18), that a society's moral traditions are unitary and rule-based, without significant internal contradiction. In a thoughtful essay highlighting the moral registers operating in contemporary Egyptian society, anthropologist Samuli Schielke offers a related insight, observing six "key moral registers" available to the young Cairene men among whom he worked, each of which had "values, terminologies, discourses, and fields of [its] own" (Schielke 2010a, 29). The registers comprise "not a coherent system, but an incoherent and unsystematic conglomerate of moral registers that exist in parallel and often contradict each other" (ibid.). As noted above, Lila Abu-Lughod's (1986, xvii) study of romantic poetry among the Awlad 'Ali Bedouins of the Western Desert of Egypt anticipated this insight years ago. In her remarkable study, she highlighted the coexistence of two discourses of self and sentiment, the less public of which stood in tension with the core (and "more Islamic") ethical premises of the other.

How, then, are we to make sense of an ethical plurality that allows for inconsistency and even contradiction? We can begin by recognizing that in all societies, the moral subjectivities of actors may be characterized by "a coexistence of various motivations . . . that can and often do conflict but do not constitute exclusive opposites" (Schielke 2010a, 28). This insight is consistent with the realization, now widespread in cultural psychology and psychological anthropology, that human subjectivity is never seamlessly integrated but rather is marked by ambivalence and inconsistency (Ewing 1990; Gregg 1998; Shore 1990; Simon 2009; Wikan 1995). As Schielke and Soares' insights into Salafiyya activism make clear (see also Masquelier 2007 and this volume, Schulz, chapter 9), however, in some societies and in some religious traditions, actors may at some point be so seized by the truth of one especially authoritative moral register that they aspire to extend its principles and discipline to all other social fields. As Max Weber emphasized almost a century ago in his celebrated study of the Calvinist ethic and capitalism, when such world-building ethical projects gain ascendance, once separate moral fields may be reconstructed and realigned under the value-rationalizing influence of a totalizing ethical discourse (see Hefner 1993; Keyes 2002).

Inevitably, however, the latter ambition never succeeds at bringing all ethical thought and practice under its fold. As with the adherents of the so-called Islamic State of Iraq and the Levant today, movements dedicated to the imposition of a single ethicolegal standard inevitably attract actors whose values, interests, and political entanglements radically differ from those of a moral tradition's founders or custodians. As ISIL's brutal actions with regard to slavery and apostasy tragically illustrate, the proponents of an ostensibly unchanging shari'a may become the unwitting agents of its transformation and degradation.

Modernity, Rupture, Revival

A recurring theme in the historical study of Islamic ethics and law—and one vital for understanding the conflict of interpretations over Islamic law and ethics today—is that in the nineteenth and twentieth centuries, the state-supported legal systems of most Muslim-majority societies experienced a radical rupture. The most widely noted aspect of this change was a great narrowing of the jurisdictional scope and influence of Islamic legal traditions. Challenged by the European powers, Egyptian and Ottoman rulers concluded that they needed not more Islamic law but rather a centralized and state-authorized legal code similar to that of the Europeans (Anderson 1976; Imber 2002; Vikor 2005, 230). When European powers intervened directly in Muslim societies, the new rulers found the scope of Islamic legal traditions an impediment to their imperial ambitions. At times, as in British India, Nigeria, and Malaya, Europeans tolerated a selective synthesis of European and Islamic laws (Anderson 1996; Zaman 2002, 23), but the narrowing of the scope of Islamic legal traditions continued apace.

In the aftermath of colonial rule, rulers in most Muslim-majority states continued these restrictive policies (Brown 2000, 119). In one of the boldest of state-mandated secularizations, in 1956, Egyptian president Gamal Abdel Nasser (1918–70) did away with most of the country's Islamic legal institutions (Brown 1997, 85; Lombardi 2006, 110–16). In other countries, ruling elites retained only those elements of Islamic law that dealt with family affairs (marriage, divorce, inheritance) and such specialized religious matters as pious endowments (Ar. *awqaf,* sing. *waqf*; see Kahf 1995).

The nationalist heyday was not the end, however, of the shariʿa story. In the 1970s and 1980s, Muslim lands witnessed the emergence of new social movements calling for the state to implement what its proponents called shariʿa. The Islamic awakening (Ar. *sahwa*) of which these movements were part had multiple genealogies and aspirations. But some among its enthusiasts were convinced that the only guarantee of justice and decency in society was state implementation of a standardized and codified shariʿa.

As has been widely observed, there was an irony to these movements' core ambition. The "shariʿa" advocated by most activists was supposed to be enacted by state legislatures, codified as positive statutes, and enforced by the administrative powers of the modern state. In all these respects, this "Islamic law" was unlike any previously seen in history (see also this volume, Emon, chapter 2). One of the contributors to this volume, Clark Lombardi (2006, 64), has observed that an additional irony of this version of Islamic law was that "the judges who applied the code would simply apply the rule as written, and would not need to have any knowledge of how the law had been derived. Thus, moving to a system of codified law meant that people without classical legal training could serve as judges" (see also Peters 2002). In their classical form, Islamic laws were neither codified, nor were they the exclusive preserve of state authorities; rather, they were "placed *between* state and civil society" (Vikor 2005, 254). More generally, as Sami Zubaida (2003, 135; see also Layish 2004) has remarked, the *étatization* and codification of Islamic legal traditions represented the "triumph of European models" over classical Islamic legal traditions.

Notwithstanding these ironies, in the aftermath of the Islamic awakening, many activists concluded that the ethical plurality seen in society was not an inevitable feature of modern social living, nor an example of the ethical plurality for which classical Islamic traditions had always made room (Shabana 2010), but rather an obstacle to piety and social justice. Animated by this conviction, activists sought to extend the reach of what they called shariʿa norms into public and private life (see Hasyim 2011; Shaikh 2008, 593–609; Tibi 2013, 2–3, 70–74). Some among these shari'a movements operated in a grassroots manner and, as in the piety movement so vividly described by Saba Mahmood (2005), abjured any interest in the seizure and "Islamization" of the state. In other instances, however, as with Zia ul-Haq's Islamization programs in Pakistan in the late 1970s (Zaman 2002, 89; and this volume, Zaman, chapter 8), the projects were tightly tethered to the ambitions of high-ranking state leaders and powerful social movements (see Bayat 2007, 147).

Whatever their precise political genealogy, these movements' demands for conformity to an ostensibly divine law put Muslim proponents of customary ethical traditions (*'urf, 'ada*) and otherwise "ordinary" (Peletz 1997) varieties of Islamic ethics on the defensive. Especially when untrained in the Islamic sciences, many people found themselves unable to legitimize their social customs or everyday behaviors in authoritative religious terms. "Repertoires of public reasoning" (Bowen 2003) once deemed sufficient to justify local practices on Islamic grounds lost credibility in the face of state authorities and movements claiming a definitive, authentic, and unitary understanding of God's commands.

It is from this historical conjuncture that the chapters in this volume begin their stories. Why? The ethical contention surrounding shari'a did not end with Islamist claims of a monopoly understanding of the law. The force of this claim merely deepened debate over just what Islamic law is and who has the right to decide its meanings. The contention was so great that eventually it caused an "epistemological crisis" akin to that in classical Greece and the modern West, analyzed by Alasdair MacIntyre (1988): The tradition appears no longer capable of resolving key ethical challenges in a manner consistent with long-established methods of rational justification (see also Arkoun 2003 and this volume, Mir-Hosseini, chapter 3).

Crises within ethical traditions typically trend toward a set of opposed positions, and exactly this has happened during contemporary Islamic ethical controversies. Debates over shari'a and Islamic ethics have come to settle, in most communities, on several deeply consequential questions: Who has the right to define Islamic ethics and legal traditions (see Anwar 2001; Esposito and Mogahed 2007)? By what methods and authorities are these traditions to be derived and enforced? And are shari'a regulations *really* like positive law, finished in their form? Or, as Tariq Ramadan (2009, 59–76), Ebrahim Moosa (2001), Muhammad Hashim Kamali (2008), and Muhammad Khaled Masud (2005) argue, building on Abu Ishaq al-Shatibi's (d. 1388) scholarship (see Masud 2005; al-Raysuni 2005)—and as Muslim feminists such as Kecia Ali (2006) and Ziba Mir-Hosseini (1999; 2003; 2009) have also observed—does a proper derivation of shari'a norms require a holistic determination of the "spirit of God's law" or the law's "higher aims" (*maqasid al-shari'a*)? Such questions show that rather than diminishing the ethical diversity of the contemporary Muslim world, movements for the "shari'atization" of state and society have only deepened it.

Muslim legal scholars will continue to debate whether *maqasid*-based approaches are technically compatible with the broader heritage of Islamic legal theory (*usul-al fiqh*, lit. "sources of the law"; Auda 2008; Hallaq 1997, 153; Johnston 2007; Moosa 2001, 17–22). But the chapters in this volume are not concerned with passing judgment on the details of any single legal methodology. Rather, they aim to show that a variety of shari'a understandings exist in all Muslim societies and then to explore the political and ethical processes that make one variety ascendant over others. In modern times, one critical influence on the latter outcome has been whether movements or authorities are able to scale their versions of Islamic law and morality to suit the purposes of the legislative, educative, and disciplining apparatuses of the state.

Even when such state-based programs are put in place, however, they unleash diverse and sometimes contradictory ethical aspirations and practices. As in contemporary Jordan, Mali, or Indonesia, programs of girls' religious education created with an eye to fostering identification with official gender and religious ideals might draw young women into exercises of self-formation and personal achievement unlike those to which they previously had access (Adely 2012; Masquelier 2007; Smith-Hefner 2005; 2007). In so doing, such programs may sow the seeds of hopes and ethical aspirations different from those intended by state and religious authorities. In these and other examples, one is reminded that for real and existing social actors, the "rationality of traditions" (MacIntyre 1988, 349) depends not only on the techniques of learning, rational justification, and subject formation interior to an ethical tradition but also on the life experiences and aspirational projects actors bring from outside to their learning encounter. The latter is a theme that has been highlighted in Muslim feminist commentaries on Islamic ethics, but it applies to all varieties of ethical practice (see, for example, Hammer 2012; Holmes Katz 2006; Wadud 1999).

Recent events in the Middle East and West Africa also remind us that shari'a contests can work in horizon-narrowing as well as horizon-broadening ways. As Boko Haram in Nigeria and the Islamic State in Iraq and the Levant illustrate, late modern radicals often justify their reading of God's law with reference not to the rich legacy of Islamic ethical traditions but rather to a mobilizational imaginary that represents the central moral struggle of our age as a unitary "Islam" battling an equally monolithic "West." Rather than being grounded in Islamic civilizational legacies, this narrative has emerged from circumstances similar to those that gave rise to the right-wing populism and vicious antisemitism that ravaged Europe in the 1930s and 1940s—elements of which may be getting a second lease on life today. As Samuli Schielke (2010b, 8) has noted, populism is a modality of political discourse and mobilization "that turns a diffuse and often implicit moral 'gut feeling' into simple slogans and personified distinctions of good and evil, us and them" (see also Betz 1994). In so doing, it also legitimizes the truth claims of its own leaders while discrediting those of its rivals. As one careful observer of Islamist militias in Indonesia during the early 2000s commented, for radical populists, "piety is . . . defined in opposition to demonised outsiders rather than constituting something to be actively pursued through study, instruction, or routine fulfillment of religious obligations" (Wilson 2008, 197; see Hefner 2005). The radical ethic shows the imprint, then, not of the civilizational legacies of Islamic learning but of the zero-sum strategies of modern populist mobilization.

On the Rationality of a New Ethical Reform

In these and other examples, we thus see striking evidence of the fact that Islamic moral values, including those informing understandings of shari'a and Islamic ethics, change over time in a manner that reflects their imbrications and entanglements with a complex assemblage (Latour 2005) of media, practices, and powers. The chapters in this volume bear witness to the complex nature of these conjunctures, as well as to the social circumstances that favor the ascendance of one ethical variety over another.

One cautionary theme emerges from the chapters: When, as is the case in some parts of the world today, a Muslim ethical imaginary is animated by the conviction that the law is unitary and unchanging, and that a true Islamic ethics can do no more than implement that law in *sensu stricto*, it will seem impious to suggest that the pursuit of new forms of knowledge, such as those associated with the natural and social sciences, and new ethical projects, such as those promoting democracy and gender equality, are consistent with an authentic profession of the faith. When an unreformed shari'a is the very essence of the divine good, on what religious grounds can one advocate anything else?

In recent years, one solution to this ethical and epistemological impasse has been that proposed by Swiss-born Muslim intellectual and grandson of Hassan al-Banna (d. 1949), Tariq Ramadan (2009, 101–12). Moreover, South African–born scholar Ebrahim Moosa has provided a philosophically sustained variation on the same reformist theme (Moosa 2001), as have Kecia Ali (2006) and Ziba Mir-Hosseini (1999; 2003; 2009; Mir-Hosseini et al. 2013) in their writings on modern Muslim sexual ethics. For ease of presentation, my discussion here uses Ramadan's proposals as its core referent (see also this volume, Kuru, chapter 7).

In his call for a "radical reform" of Islamic law and ethics, Ramadan argues that an Islamic ethics capable of meeting the challenges of the modern age will be impossible without the cooperation, as equals, of *ulama an-nusus* ("text scholars") and *ulama al-waqi'* ("context scholars"). In Ramadan's model, the *ulama al-waqi* are primarily scholars working in the natural and social sciences. They are as important as scholars of the Islamic sciences are, Ramadan explains, because "the world, its laws, and areas of specialized knowledge not only shed light on scriptural sources but also constitute a source of law on their own" (Ramadan 2009, 83).

Here, then, is a model for a most remarkable epistemological imbrication. Its appeal for an integration of knowledge of the law with the sciences of nature and society recalls the efforts of great Islamic philosophers such as Ibn Rushd (Averroes, d. 1198; see Freamon 2008, 344) or late nineteenth-century pioneers of Islamic reform such as Muhammad Abduh. In Ramadan's view, an ethical life consistent with shari'a is not merely a matter of conformity to a fixed and finished body of legal rules (*ahkam*). The struggle for the good also requires that believers grasp the higher aims of the law (*maqasid al-shari'a*) and then go one step further to develop the empirical knowledge of society and nature required to solve ethical problems in an empirically effective manner consistent with the full truth of the divine message (see Auda 2008; Johnston 2007).

What relation might such sophisticated reform proposals as those of Ramadan, Moosa, Ali, or Mir-Hosseini have with the day-to-day struggles of ordinary reformists, many of whom lack the religious training required to devise sophisticated religious rulings? As I discuss in chapter 11, on Indonesia, historical studies show that movements that advocate a reformed practice of Islamic ethics in fields such as public health, education, and care for the poor often promote their aims by declaring their efforts consistent with the higher aims of God's commands— even when the reformists themselves have not yet devised sophisticated legal rationales to justify their actions in more detailed jurisprudential terms. This situation can give rise to ethical tensions or even conflict in the broader Muslim community. However, as reformist initiatives in fields such as education, public health, and Islamic finance move forward, their practices and organization may begin to have a striking performative effect. Namely, they provide a visible alternative to the claims of those who insist that a proper Islamic ethics involves no more and no less than conformity to unchanging "shari'a" rules. In short, movements of Islamic ethical reform gain momentum as much through their demonstration effects as they do through their intellectual rationales. The effort works best when it offers a real-world counterpoint to the unempirical idealizations of absolutists who claim that an essentialized version of Islamic law is a panacea for all social ills irrespective of its degree of consistency with what other commentators insist is the full truth of the divine message.

There is a related sociological feature to this process of generating new Islamic understandings of the good through in-the-world endeavors. The creation of modern schools, clinics, banks, and cooperatives—which is to say, sites where Muslim actors put new forms of knowledge and ethical action into daily practice—allows believers who have technical training and life-world skills to acquire a social and ethical influence that may come to rival that of activists committed to a reified understanding of Islamic law. These and other activities can work to convince a growing number of believers that the moral challenges of the age require ethical action more complex than simple conformity to unchanging rules or to the dictates of religious authorities who claim an exclusive right to voice their truth.

If the educational and associational initiatives discussed in the chapters on Indonesia, Pakistan, Tunisia, and Egypt illustrate some of the sociological changes that can spur a desire for a reformulated law and ethics, they also illustrate that such actions may not themselves be sufficient to make the new ethics sustainable. If the ideal of unchanging and positive shari`a commands respect among believers, then ethical proposals that are not justified in these terms will be dismissed as inauthentic and un-Islamic. For this reason, among others, Anver Emon appeals in chapter 2 for "an ethics of shari`a discourse that does not avoid the inherited tradition but rather works through it" (see also this volume, Mir-Hosseini, chapter 3; and Mir-Hosseini 2003; 2009).

There is a practical as well as an epistemological rationale for taking such a tack. Even when religious authorities agree with proposed reforms, a dissenting minority may reject the new consensus and work to mobilize discontent under the banner of a more "authentic" understanding of Islamic law. The pluralization and fragmentation of authority that is a hallmark of late modern Muslim cultural politics (especially Sunni Muslim politics; see Anderson and Eickelman 2003; Eickelman and Piscatori 1996, 71, 131–35; Mandaville 2007) make challenges of this sort not only possible but probable. The vulnerability underscores the second ingredient needed for any long-term reworking of Islamic law and ethics: the mobilizations of actors and movements having the desire and ability to scale up new Islamic ethics behind reform-oriented collaborations in state and society. In short, sustainable ethical reform requires serious normative work by qualified authorities, followed by the scaling up of those intellectual labors through their dissemination and "hegemonization" in state and society (Hefner 2000, 25, 226n32).

Contentions such as these give urgency to the questions at the heart of this book. The chapters herein provide insight into the mix of circumstances and aspirational projects that favor the emergence of pluralist, gender-equitable, and democratic understandings of Islamic ethicolegal traditions. In an age in which Boko Haram and ISIL claim to profess the sole authentic variety of Islam, it may seem absurd to suggest that ethical reforms of this sort are possible, let alone well under way in countries around the world. But they are. Notwithstanding the tragic devastation wrought by certain self-appointed Islamist commanders, ours is an age of remarkable—and, yes, hopeful—educational advance and ethical renewal across the breadth of the Muslim world.

Transition, Coimbrication, and Consonance

The transitions with which the chapters in this book are concerned are, again, as much ethical and epistemological as they are legal and political. Although all were written in the aftermath of the Arab Spring, the locales explored are also not limited to MENA settings. All are also concerned with the ways in which legal and ethical debates have "gone public," making their way well beyond the horizons of judges, jurists, and legislators to a broad range of actors and movements.

In chapter 2, Toronto-based legal scholar Anver M. Emon juxtaposes shari`a traditions to the contemporary enterprise of governance as captured in the popular phrase "the rule of law." Scholars of Islamic legal traditions have for the most part paid little heed to the latter notion, but Emon demonstrates the importance of the concept, which points to an interaction of ideals at play when Islamist parties and constitution writers propose to introduce what they see as shari`a traditions into the programs and policies of a modern state. The invocation, Emon explains, requires that analysts attend to the depth of the contrast between a classical fiqh crafted for an earlier Muslim imperial polity and "the technologies of modern geopolitically delimited states in which parties invoke those premodern doctrines to give Islamic content to the workings of the state." Rather than discarding the inherited legacy of fiqh ethics and politics, Emon calls for "an ethics of shari`a discourse that does not avoid the inherited tradition but rather works through it." To do so requires that we examine not only texts but also the "conditions of intelligibility" of legal doctrines, as well as the distinctive "claim spaces" through which they are understood and enacted.

In developing this comparison, Emon also sheds light on shari`a talk in less familiar parts of the world, including Western Europe and North America, where various antishari`a movements suffer their own (mis)understandings of Islamic ethics and law. Emon also examines a different variety of shari`a talk in the Republic of the Maldives, where shari`a ideas are invoked to enforce the claim that non-Muslims may not become citizens. In these and other examples, the juxtaposition Emon recommends requires that analysts pay close attention to the legal and ethical conditions consonant with modern governance and society. This latter recognition illustrates why recent efforts by groups such as ISIL to impose punitive restrictions on non-Muslims show an utter misrecognition not just of the rights and dignity of non-Muslims but also of the legacy of Islamic law and ethics themselves.

In chapter 3, one of our generation's most distinguished Muslim feminist scholars, Ziba Mir-Hosseini, picks up Emon's theme of working through rather than against Islamic ethicolegal traditions and projects it forward into efforts to reform Muslim family laws in gender-equitable ways. Mir-Hosseini grounds her analysis on two premises: first, that "gender equality is a modern ideal" but one also consistent with the higher aims of Islamic ethics and Qur'anic revelation, and second, that the idea of gender equality has created a MacIntyrean epistemological crisis in Islamic traditions, the resolution of which requires efforts from within the tradition to legitimize and integrate gender-equitable ideals.

Mir-Hosseini provides an overview of Islamic legal reforms since the late nineteenth century, outlining why such an integration has thus far proved difficult. The reform and codification of state-sanctioned fiqh led to the creation of a legal hybrid "that was neither classical fiqh nor Western." Moreover, deprived of the authority to implement an earlier assortment of Islamic legal traditions, Muslim jurists came to regard family law as "the last bastion of Islam." This led some jurists to retreat to what Mir-Hosseini calls a "neofiqh" conservatism, opposing gender equality on the grounds that it is an alien Western value (see also al-Sharmani 2013). Ironically, however, the harnessing of such neoconservative declarations to movements for the "Islamization" of the state has had the unintended effect of bringing fiqh texts out of the scholarly closet and into public scrutiny—at exactly the same time when religious study and higher education have allowed growing numbers of women (as well as reform-minded men) to critically engage Islamic ethical traditions from within.

Mir-Hosseni has been involved with, and provides a narrative history of, one of the most remarkable of Muslim feminist organizations working to reform Islamic law around the world, the Musawah ("equality") movement. Although it now has branches in dozens of countries, Musawah's establishment in 2009 was spearheaded by the Malaysia-based Sisters in Islam, one of the earliest and most prominent Muslim feminist organizations (estab. 1988; see Anwar 2001; 2013). In the course of their campaigns to reform family laws, Musawah activists have encountered opposition from leading officials in various religious establishments. However—a point that must be emphasized for non-Muslim Western readers— Musawah's efforts have also been handicapped by Western, and especially American, governments' appropriation of the women's rights banner to justify ill-conceived interventions in Afghanistan and Iraq. "As scholars and activists, many of us found ourselves in the crossfire," Mir-Hosseini observes. All this has complicated Musawah's efforts to "break down the perceived dichotomy between 'Islam' and 'human rights.'"

In chapter 4, Moroccan-born sociologist Zakia Salime takes the book's discussion of ethics and law beyond courtrooms and houses of legislature and into the brave new world of Moroccan social media. Salime (2011) is the author of a celebrated study of the feminist, progressive, and royal coalition that united in 2004 to bring about a far-reaching reformation of Morocco's Islamic family law, known as the *mudawana*. In her chapter, Salime shifts her analytic gaze away from formal lawmaking to the public discussion that raged in March and April 2012 in the aftermath of the suicide of a young Moroccan women named Amina, who had taken her life one year after her court-ordered marriage to her rapist. The marital arrangement, which had been in keeping with article 20 of the Moroccan Family code, caused a storm of controversy both in social media and in the political public sphere.

The controversy was compounded because one feature of Morocco's Arab Spring was the rise to power, in November 2012, of the moderate Islamist Justice and Development (JD) Party. Proreform protests continued in the aftermath of the JD's election and in fact escalated as it became clear that the JD had misperceived the public's outrage over Amina's suicide. Social media–based critics of the law that had mandated Amina's marriage invoked a justice-based discourse that, by comparison with the women's movement of the 1990s, seemed willing to dispense with fiqh rationales in formulating its ethical arguments. More remarkably, even many supporters of the Islamist government were inclined to shift the debate into a register that was "more nuanced, less legalistic, and more grounded in the plurality of real and existing marriage practices." In all this there was evidence of a relative marginalization not just of conventional shari`a talk but also of legalism and court-based procedures themselves.

In chapter 5, Harvard-based scholar of Islam and politics Malika Zeghal provides this volume's most comprehensive analysis of Islamic law and constitution-making. Her case study focuses on Tunisia, the one Arab country to emerge from Arab Spring upheavals with its democratic hopes intact. As in Egypt, Zeghal notes, the political transition was marked by extensive debates about what it means for the state to be both Muslim and democratic. Tunisia, though often mischaracterized as being thoroughly "secular," saw Islam made the religion of state in its 1959 constitution while guaranteeing freedom of creed "within the limits of 'public order.'" After the fall of President Ben Ali in January 2011, Tunisia transitioned to an electoral and democratic system. After a National Constituent Assembly (NCA) was established in October 2011, NCA debates revealed strong agreement across parties on the importance of maintaining a state-based religious establishment. However, deep disagreement surfaced over the proper extent of that establishment, the role of shari`a in legislation, and whether freedom of conscience included the right to criticize or even leave a religion.

Despite these differences, the drafters of the 2014 constitution reached a historic compromise. Although many in the ruling al-Nahdha party (moderately Islamist, but with a significant conservative lobby) had hoped to see shari`a recognized as a source—or even the solitary source—of legislation, references to shari`a were notably absent in the new constitution. No less significant, article 6 of the new constitution affirmed a principle of freedom of conscience that was seen by its proponents as counterbalancing the designation of the state as the custodian of Islam. Zeghal's analysis shows us a powerful example of a democratic state that prescribes close collaboration between religious and state authorities (an arrangement once the norm, of course, in Western Europe; see Stepan 2011) while protecting citizens from more invasive forms of religious coercion. Whether this hopeful balance can be maintained in the face of the wave of ISIL terror spreading across North Africa remains to be seen.

If Tunisia offers an example of a hopeful accommodation of Islamic traditions and democratic forms, post-Mubarak Egypt offers an example of a less happy outcome. For the indefinite future, democratic freedoms in Egypt remain on hold. As legal scholars Clark B. Lombardi and Connie J. Cannon remind us in chapter 6, in their discussion of "forbidding wrong" in pre–Arab Spring Egypt, the sheer scale of the tumult in the country today tempts us to forget that promising ethicolegal imbrications took place up through the end of the Mubarak regime. The most remarkable of these involved Islamist litigants' efforts to use lawsuits to fulfill the Qur'anic ethical injunction known as hisba: "to command right and forbid wrong" (see Cook 2001). Classical fiqh on forbidding wrong makes no reference to the possibility of doing so by filing lawsuits, but in the final years of the twentieth century, legal liberals in Egypt had begun to look to the country's courts and lawsuits as a counterweight to Egypt's strong executive. Having witnessed the success of these initiatives, and having been quietly encouraged by some officials in the judiciary, Islamists soon came to share the legal liberals' hope that the power of the courts might be used to check executive power.

Unlike the legal liberals, however, the Islamists also turned to the courts to strike down "un-Islamic" laws and take action against private citizens such as Nasr Hamid Abu Zayd, a liberal scholar whom Islamist litigants accused of apostasy for his poststructuralist approaches to classical Prophetic narratives. "The attorneys here," Lombardi and Cannon observe, "were asking courts to enforce private laws with the goal of stopping the activities of *private citizens*" (see also Rutherford 2013, 69). Notwithstanding these illiberal challenges, their combined effect was to create a "semi-liberal faction within the community of Islamist lawyers," one that began to view democratic governance and constitutional courts positively. Unfortunately, the 2013 military coup against a freely elected Islamist government, and the subsequent suppression of the Muslim Brotherhood, have resulted in the judiciary's forfeiture of its reputation as an arbiter of legal or political affairs.

If Egypt has always been something of democratic long shot, Turkey for many years has been regarded as the Near Eastern country most likely to integrate Islamic principles with democratic governance. The author of chapter 7, Ahmet T. Kuru, an internationally regarded scholar of secularity and democracy, was for many years among those analysts who cautiously described Turkey in just such hopeful terms. As he explains in his chapter, he had good reasons for optimism. In the early years of the twentieth century, religious scholars such as Bediuzzaman Said Nursi (d. 1960) had developed a detailed and articulate alternative to formalist understandings of Islamic law, emphasizing the importance of reason in textual exegesis and favoring "individual inner experience of Islam rather than top-down 'Islamization' of public institutions." Nursi never repudiated politics outright, but he laid the foundation for a reorientation of Islamic ethics away from etatist dirigisme and toward renewal of civil society.

In the 1960s and 1970s, these same ideas were developed further by Turkey's powerful Hizmet ("service") movement, especially by the wing under the leadership of the charismatic reformist Sufi leader Fethullah Gülen (see also Tittensor 2014). Gülen and his followers favored an ethics-based understanding of shari`a and viewed the idea of an "Islamic state" as a self-defeating illusion. Like Ramadan, Moosa, Masud, Ali, and Mir-Hosseini today, Gülen also promoted an understanding of shari`a based largely on the higher aims (*maqasid*) of the law. No less significant, Gülen and his followers called for far-reaching reforms in Islamic family ethics, arguing, for example, that polygyny was never intended to be any more than a "special dispensation" in the time of the Prophet.

For reasons that have more to do with the bitterly factionalized nature of Turkish politics than with the intellectual shortsightedness of Muslim scholars, the varied currents that had once united behind the Justice and Development Party (AKP) fell into bitter dispute in the 2010s. The AKP-led government launched a fierce public attack on the Gülen wing of the Hizmet movement, and many existing checks on executive power collapsed. The downturn leads Kuru to conclude that Turkey can no longer be seen as a model for the harmonious integration of Islamic and democratic principles. The example offers an even more general lesson, he suggests, not least with regard to the principle of checks and balances in government: Without respect for these general principles of civil politics, a Muslim democracy is unlikely to flourish.

In chapter 8, Princeton-based scholar of South Asian Islam Muhammad Qasim Zaman provides an intellectual and political history of one of the more influential of contemporary Muslim ethical amalgams, Islamic modernism. Zaman defines modernism as the effort "to rethink Islamic norms, reinterpret foundational Islamic texts, and reform particular Muslim institutions in ways that serve . . . to align them with the 'spirit' of Islam and . . . what are taken to be 'modern' needs and sensibilities"—the latter typically including the ideals of democracy, pluralism, and gender equality.

Although contemporary news reports may obscure the fact, Pakistan was once a major center for modernist Muslim thought. Muhammad Ali Jinnah, Pakistan's founder, regularly voiced modernist sentiments, rejecting formalistic understandings of Islamic law. However, from early on, the "elements of incoherence" seen in documents such as the 1949 Objectives Resolution had an unhelpful effect on state religious policy. More worrying, opposition to modernist principles on the part of the network of `ulama associated with the country's *madrasas* led many modernist intellectuals to succumb to the temptation of resorting to state coercion to advance their programs. Even much-celebrated reformist intellectual Fazlur Rahman drifted toward a "statist vision" premised on "close regulation of the religious sphere." In this sense, the authoritarian reformism promoted by General Pervez Musharraf after the 9/11 attacks, in alliance with the United States, has a more troubled genealogy than is recognized in many contemporary commentaries on Pakistan. "And," Zaman concludes, "the authoritarianism frequently buttressing modernist ethical sensibilities in Pakistan has not done much to broaden their appeal."

Chapter 9 presents a different perspective from the rest of the volume on the meanings and popular appeal of Islamic law, showing how in certain settings, unreformed understandings of the law can come to be seen as a welcome instrument of ethical uplifting. German anthropologist Dorothea E. Schulz explores this theme in the context of the West African country of Mali. Although since 2012 Mali has been widely known for being afflicted by the activities of al-Qa'ida–inspired rebels, for most of the preceding twenty years, it was a darling of Western governments for having effected a successful transition to multiparty democracy.

In an account that combines careful social history with intimate ethnography, Schulz demonstrates that the favorable resonances that "shari`a" measures generated in the 2000s were the culmination of a long and steady growth in movements of moral renewal, including those having special appeal among youth and women. In the 1970s, the movements had benefited from an influx of funds provided by Saudi Arabia–based *da`wa* organizations. But "Islam" also served as a rallying cry for the young male migrants who, returning from centers of learning in Libya and Algeria, came to blame their social marginalization on the alleged capture of the state by "unbelievers." Schulz observes that the "shari`a" to which movement activists rallied lacked programmatic detail and was thus a shifting, elusive signifier. For its proponents, however, this idealized law had the benefit of being not a matter of tradition or religious elders but one of personal conviction and youthful responsibility *in opposition to* established authorities. In an era of economic hardship and neoliberal disciplines, "shari`a" reforms were also seen as prescribing a sober and spare lifestyle consistent with the realities of the urban poor if not the aspirations of the educated middle and upper classes.

The Muslim-majority country of Malaysia provides a decidedly more buttoned-down and corporatized variation on the theme of modern shari`a imaginaries (see also Peletz 2002). Using the Malay spelling for the Islamic judiciary system, chapter 10, "Syariah, Inc.," examines the continuities, changes, and cultural politics in Malaysia's syariah judiciary over the past forty years. A leading anthropologist of Southeast Asian Islam at Emory University, Michael G. Peletz demonstrates that although competition between the ruling party and the Islamist opposition contributed to the government's selective promotion of Islamic legal traditions, the social forces bearing on syariah and ethics are of wildly disparate provenance and have less to do with debates over the intricacies of belief, worship, and doctrine than with questions about how best to discipline and control the nation's citizenry. A key feature of the government strategy is "lawfare"—the government's use of rules and penal codes to impose a sense of order on citizens.

When he turns to examine the changes that have taken place in the Islamic judiciary during the past fifteen years, Peletz discovers that the main features of such change—greater reliance on written evidence and precedent, the introduction of lawyers and adversarial hearings, and snappy new courtrooms and judicial robes—show that rather than becoming more self-reliantly "Islamic," the syariah courts have increasingly modeled themselves on the country's far more prestigious civil courts. The syariah courts have also brought in all manner of technological gadgets for "e-governance"—high-end information and communication technologies intended to facilitate efficient governance on the e-commerce model. The Islamic judiciary's "E-Syariah Portal," for example, provides information on statutory laws and links to passages from the Qur'an and *hadith* that officials regard as providing authoritative rationales for state statutes.

Moreover, there is a distinctive tack to the syariah judiciary's normative preoccupations. Foremost among them is the policing of the boundaries of acceptable sexual practice, as evidenced in everything from the penalizing of acts of "illicit proximity" (*khalwat*) to the prosecution of men who pose as women. In these and other regards, the main developmental current in Malaysian syariah has not been a liberalization and pluralization of religious sensibilities but rather a "relatively successful" program of state-enforced religious homogenization.

In chapter 11 I close the book by also adopting a historical perspective, tracing the role of Islamic social and religious movements in the construction and reform of women's roles in Indonesia from the late nineteenth century to today. Although the high standing of women in public life in Indonesia was once explained away by the claim that "Indonesians aren't very Islamic," the real cause is more complex and has much to do with Islam. Societies across the Indonesian archipelago underwent a far-reaching process of Islamic conversion from the thirteenth to the nineteenth centuries. However, the "Islam" to which most Muslims were drawn was not fiqh-minded but rather a Sufi-inflected traditionalist variety. Until the late nineteenth century, the institution responsible in most of the Middle East for the production and dissemination of legal knowledge, the *madrasa*, was notable in the archipelago simply for its rarity. The situation changed in the late nineteenth century with the rapid spread of Islamic boarding schools (known locally as *pesantren*; see Azra, Afrianty, and Hefner 2007) for study in the intermediate and advanced Islamic sciences. During the first years of the twentieth century, then, movements for the implementation of a more or less unreformed variety of fiqh gained momentum. No sooner had such movements arisen, however, than their ethical aims were challenged by new varieties of Islamic reform that promoted general as well as religious education, being dedicated to the pursuit of *maslahah*-based notions of the public good (see Opwis 2007) rather than the implementation of set legal rules (*ahkam*).

Women's movements dedicated to girls' education and family health also rose to prominence during these years. Although its members agreed on many issues, the movement split into Islamic and secularist factions over the issue of reforming the country's marriage laws. During the 1950s and early 1960s, an escalating rivalry between Islamic political parties and the country's even larger nationalist and communist parties pushed women's issues to the margins and eventually resulted in the annihilation of the communist party and the evisceration of the country's most prominent women's associations. Although the "New Order" government that arose in the aftermath of the anticommunist bloodshed promoted patriarchal models of female domesticity, the state's programs of mass education and industrialization brought a new class of well-educated middle-class women into existence. Some made their way through the country's impressive system of state Islamic universities. By the 1990s, a new generation of Muslim feminists had emerged—among the most politically influential in the entire Muslim world. Although they have not yet reformed their country's Islamic marriage laws, their movement has had great success in promoting a variety of educational and welfare programs. No less important, movement leaders have joined the alliance of Muslim movements and intellectuals, laying the foundation for a sustainable program of Islamic and democratic ethical reform.

Conditions of a Modern Ethical Possibility

Looking across the world of the early twenty-first century, neoconservative movements for the implementation of Islamic legal traditions can be seen as having unintentionally created something of a civilizational learning curve. The earliest proponents of state-enforced shari`a promoted an unreformed and narrowed "Islamic law" that they claimed was divine and unchanging (An-Na`im 2008). What these proponents did not anticipate was that many Muslim publics brought a more expansive and contemporary set of hopes to bear on their aspiration to develop a new and truly relevant practice of Islamic ethics. This was perhaps most strikingly the case for a new generation of believing Muslim women (Badran 2009; Mernissi 1991; Wadud 1999). Education and the desire to practice their religion more faithfully encouraged many to yearn for a more learned and participatory profession of their faith. As they took steps to do so, however, many women discovered that other believers had different ideas about just what God prescribes. More alarming yet, some among the latter did not hesitate to use violence to enforce their normative claims. The resulting clash of aspirations has been so great that it has led growing numbers of Muslims to ask, *Is what* they *call shari`a really God's law?* This simple question is at the heart of the Muslim legal and ethical debates that rage across the world today.

Although often overlooked in accounts of contemporary Muslim politics, the conviction that Islamic ethical traditions can and should be forces for human dignity, gender equality, and social justice is socially pervasive and powerful. It goes without saying that this is not the only understanding of Islamic values in our world. Indeed, wherever political events and narrative frames create crisis, oppression, and victimization—all grimly pervasive across broad swaths of today's Middle East and North Africa—we should not be surprised to see that the religious ideals to which some rally may be zero-sum and exclusivist. But this outcome reflects the deadly logic of fight-to-the-finish mobilizations more than it does any enduring ethical legacy peculiar to Islam. Indeed, non-Muslim Westerners would do well to remind themselves that there is nothing uniquely Muslim about this latter development. In the early decades of the twentieth century, Western Europeans saw their own varieties of lock-step exclusivism and zero-sum populism. Supporters of these Western extremist movements justified their programs in ethnonationalist rather than religious terms, of course. But that is precisely the point. In circumstances of vicious-circle competition and violence, all variety of ethical imaginaries can be redeployed toward direly destructive ends.

The tragic chaos that is now devastating large swaths of the Muslim Middle East, as well as the violence inflicted at times in the name of shari`a law, guarantees that questions of shari`a and Muslim ethics will remain the focus of bitter contention for many years to come. The core lesson to keep in mind, however, is that Muslim ethics other than those of an absolutist sort are at work in our world—ones aspiring to new practices of participation, dignity, and equality. Most proponents of these visions of ethical renewal seek to work within a broadened framework of Islamic ethicolegal traditions. Their aspiration reminds us that, as Badran (2009, 9) has noted with regard to Islamic feminism, the ethical imaginary under construction here is not by any means a simple derivative of Western liberalism: It is Islamic. However, the new reformists do not operate merely within the horizons of long-established ethicolegal doctrines. Rather, they bring new social and educational aspirations to bear on Islamic legal and ethical traditions (Freamon 2008; Ramadan 2009). In this sense, and as was earlier the case with religious values in the modern West, higher education and new opportunities for self-expression will remain at the heart of this quest for a modern religious ethics. Antireform radicals in groups such as Boko Haram and ISIL, all too aware of this fact, have adjusted their targets for attack accordingly.

The great majority of the world's Muslims clearly hope that the civilizational devastation unleashed by these latter movements will at long last be contained. When it is—and it undoubtedly will be—the great transformation of knowledge and authority at the heart of the new ethical reform will accelerate and deepen in most Muslim lands. However dark the clouds may appear today, a reformed Muslim ethics is taking hold across broad expanses of our world. Its precise meanings and achievements will inevitably vary in time and place. Of this much, however, there should be no question: The Muslim world has entered a new era of ethical reform, and its spirit has become one of the driving forces of our age.

References

Abou-Bakr, O. 2003. "Teaching the Words of the Prophet: Women Instructors of the *Hadith* (Fourteenth and Fifteenth Centuries)." *Hawwa: Journal of Women of the Middle East and the Islamic World* 1 (3): 306–28.

Abou el Fadl, Khaled. 2001. *Speaking in God's Name: Islamic Law, Authority and Women.* Oxford: One World.

———. 2004. *Islam and the Challenge of Democracy.* Edited by Joshua Cohen and Deborah Chasman. Princeton, NJ, and Oxford: Princeton University Press.

———. 2014. *Reasoning with God: Reclaiming Shari'ah in the Modern Age.* Lanham, MD: Rowman and Littlefield.

Abu-Lughod, Lila. 1986. *Veiled Sentiments: Honor and Poetry in a Bedouin Society.* Berkeley and Los Angeles: University of California Press.

Adely, Fida. 2012. *Gendered Paradoxes: Educating Jordanian Women in Nation, Faith, and Progress.* Chicago: University of Chicago Press.

Ali, Kecia. 2006. *Sexual Ethics and Islam: Feminist Reflections on Qur'an, Hadith, and Jurisprudence.* Oxford: One World.

———. 2010. *Marriage and Slavery in Early Islam.* Cambridge, MA: Harvard University Press.

al-Raysuni, Ahmad. 2005. *Imam al-Shatibi's Theory of the Higher Objectives and Intents of Islamic Law.* London and Washington, DC: International Institute of Islamic Thought.

al-Sharmani, Mulki. 2013. "*Qiwâma* in Egyptian Family Laws: 'Wifely Obedience' between Legal Texts, Courtroom Practices and Realities of Marriages." In *Gender and Equality in Muslim Family Law: Justice and Ethics in the Islamic Legal Tradition,* edited by Ziba Mir-Hosseini, Kari Vogt, Lena Larsen, and Christian Moe, 37–55. London and New York: Tauris.

Anderson, J. S. 1976. *Law and Reform in the Muslim World.* London: Athlone.

Anderson, Michael R. 1996. *Occasional Paper No. 7: Islamic Law and the Colonial Encounter in British India.* London: Women Living under Muslim Law.

Anderson, Jon W., and Dale F. Eickelman, eds. 2003. *New Media in the Muslim World: The Emerging Public Sphere.* Bloomington: Indiana University Press.

An-Na'im, Abdullahi Ahmed. 2008. *Islam and the Secular State: Negotiating the Future of Shari'a.* Cambridge, MA: Harvard University Press.

Anwar, Zainah. 2001. "What Islam, Whose Islam? Sisters in Islam and the Struggle for Women's Rights." In *The Politics of Multiculturalism: Pluralism and Citizenship in Malaysia, Singapore, and Indonesia,* edited by Robert W. Hefner, 227–52. Honolulu: University of Hawaii Press.

———. 2013. "From Local to Global: Sisters in Islam and the Making of Musawah: A Global Movement for Equality in the Muslim Family." In *Gender and Equality in Muslim Family Law: Justice and Ethics in the Islamic Legal Tradition,* edited by Ziba Mir-Hosseini, Kari Vogt, Lena Larsen, and Christian Moe, 107–24. London and New York: Tauris.

Arjomand, Said Amir. April 1999. "The Law, Agency, and Policy in Medieval Islamic Society: Development of the Institutions of Learning from the Tenth to the Fifteenth Century." *Comparative Studies in Society and History* 41 (2): 263–93.

Arkoun, Mohammed. 2003. "Rethinking Islam Today." *American Academy of Political and Social Science* 588:18–39.

Auda, Jasser. 2008. Maqasid al-Sharia *as Philosophy of Islamic Law: A Systems Approach.* London and Washington, DC: International Institute of Islamic Thought.

Azra, Azumardi, Dina Afrianty, and Robert W. Hefner. 2007. "*Pesantren* and *Madrasa*: Muslim Schools and National Ideals in Indonesia." In *Schooling Islam: The Culture and Politics of Modern Muslim Education,* edited by Robert W. Hefner and Muhammad Qasim Zaman, 172–98. Princeton, NJ: Princeton University Press.

Badran, Margot. 2009. *Feminism in Islam: Secular and Religious Convergences.* Oxford: One World.

Barth, Fredrik. 1993. *Balinese Worlds.* Princeton, NJ: Princeton University Press.

Bayat, Asef. 2007. *Making Islam Democratic: Social Movements and the Post-Islamist Turn.* Stanford, CA: Stanford University Press.

Berkey, Jonathan. 1992. *The Transmission of Knowledge in Medieval Cairo: A Social History* of Islamic Education. Princeton, NJ: Princeton University Press.

———. 2003. *The Formation of Islam.* Cambridge, UK: Cambridge University Press.

Betz, H. G. 1994. *Radical Right-wing Populism in Western Europe.* Basingstoke, UK: Macmillan.

Bowen, John R. 2003. *Islam, Law and Equality in Indonesia: An Anthropology of Public Reasoning.* Cambridge, UK: Cambridge University Press.

Brown, Carl. 2000. *Religion and State: The Muslim Approach to Politics.* New York: Columbia University Press.

Brown, Nathan. 1997. *The Rule of Law in the Arab World: Courts in Egypt and the Gulf.* Cambridge, UK: Cambridge University Press.

Bruinessen, Martin van, and Julia Day Howell, eds. 2007. *Sufism and the "Modern" in Islam.* London and New York: I.B. Tauris.

Burak, Guy. 2013. "The Second Formation of Islamic Law: The Post-Mongol Context of the Ottoman Adoption of a School of Law." *Comparative Studies in Society and History* 55 (3): 579–602.

Cassaniti, Julia L., and Jacob R. Hickman. 2014. "New Directions in the Anthropology of Morality." *Anthropological Theory* 14 (3): 251–62.

Center for Security Policy. 2010. *Shariah: The Threat to America.* Washington, DC: Center for Security Policy.

Chamberlain, Michael. 1994. *Knowledge and Social Practice in Medieval Damascus, 1190–1350.* Cambridge, UK: Cambridge University Press.

Clarke, Morgan. 2009. *Islam and New Kinship: Reproductive Technology and Shariah in Lebanon.* New York and Oxford: Berghahn Books.

————. 2014. "Cough Sweets and Angels: The Ordinary Ethics of the Extraordinary in Sufi Practice in Lebanon." *Journal of the Royal Anthropological Institute* 20 (3): 407–25.

Cook, Michael. 2001. *Commanding Right and Forbidding Wrong in Islamic Thought*. Cambridge, UK: Cambridge University Press.

Das, Veena. 2012. "Ordinary Ethics." In *A Companion to Moral Anthropology*, edited by Didier Fassin, 133–49. Malden, MA: Wiley-Blackwell.

De Jong, Frederick, and Bernd Radtke, eds. 1999. *Islamic Mysticism Contested: Thirteen Centuries of Controversies and Polemics*. Leiden and Boston, MA: Brill.

Dupret, Baudouin. 2012. *La Charia aujourd'hui: Usages de la référence au droit Islamique*. Paris: La Découverte.

Eickelman, Dale F. 1992. "Mass Higher Education and the Religious Imagination in Contemporary Arab Societies." *American Ethnologist* 19 (4): 643–55.

Eickelman, Dale F., and James Piscatori. 1996. *Muslim Politics*. Princeton, NJ: Princeton University Press.

Engle Merry, Sally. 1988. "Legal Pluralism." *Law and Society Review* 22 (5): 869–96.

Esposito, John L., and Dalia Mogahed. 2007. *Who Speaks for Islam? What a Billion Muslims Really Think*. New York: Gallup Press.

Ewing, Katherine P. 1990. "The Illusion of Wholeness: Culture, Self, and the Experience of Inconsistency." *Ethos* 18 (3): 251–78.

Findley, Carter Vaughn. 1989. "Knowledge and Education in the Modern Middle East: A Comparative View." In *The Modern Economic and Social History of the Middle East in Its World Context*, edited by Georges Sabagh, 130–54. Cambridge, UK: Cambridge University Press.

Flueckiger, Joyce Burkhalter. 2006. *In Amma's Healing Room: Gender and Vernacular Islam in South India*. Bloomington: Indiana University Press.

Freamon, Bernard K. 2008. "The Emergence of a New Qur'anic Hermeneutic: The Role and Impact of Universities in West and East." In *The Law Applied: Contextualizing the Islamic Shari`a*, edited by Peri Bearman, Wolfhart Heinrichs, and Bernard G. Weiss, 342–71. London and New York: I.B. Tauris.

Glenn, H. Patrick. 2000. *Legal Traditions of the World: Sustainable Diversity in Law*. New York: Oxford University Press.

Grandin, Nicole, and Marc Gaborieau, eds. 1997. *Madrasa: La transmission du savoir dans le monde Musulman*. Paris: Éditions Arguments.

Gregg, Gary. 1998. "Culture, Personality, and the Multiplicity of Identity: Evidence from North African Life Narratives." *Ethos* 26 (1): 120–52.

Guigay, Caroline. 2013. "L'enseignement élémentaire dans le monde de l'Islam (XI–XV siècle)." In *Lumières de la Sagesse: Écoles médiévales d'Orient et d'Occident*, edited by Eric Vallet, Sandra Aube, and Thierry Kouame, 111–17. Paris: Publications de la Sorbonne et Institut du Monde Arabe.

Hallaq, Wael B. 1997. *A History of Islamic Legal Theories: An Introduction to Sunnî Usûl al-Fiqh*. Cambridge, UK: Cambridge University Press.

————. 2001. *Authority, Continuity and Change in Islamic Law*. Cambridge, UK: Cambridge University Press.

————. 2009. *Sharî`a: Theory, Practice, Transformations*. Cambridge, UK: Cambridge University Press.

————. 2013. *The Impossible State: Islam, Politics, and Modernity's Moral Predicament*. New York: Columbia University Press.

Hammer, Juliane. 2012. "Painful, Personal, Particular: Writing, Reading, and Representing (Her) self." In *A Jihad for Justice: Honoring the Work and Life of Amina Wadud*, edited by Kecia Ali, Juliane Hammer, and Laury Silvers, 17–28. Akron, Ohio: 48HrBooks.

Hanne, Olivier, and Thomas Flichy de la Neuville. 2014. *L'État islamique: Anatomie du nouveau Califat*. Paris: Bernard Giovanangeli.

Hasyim, Syafiq. 2011. *The Council of Indonesian Ulama (Majelis Ulama Indonesia, MUI) and Religious Freedom*. Bangkok: IRASEC.

Hefner, Robert W. 1993. "World-Building and the Rationality of Conversion." In *Conversion to Christianity: Historical and Anthropological Perspectives on a Great Transformation*, edited by Robert W. Hefner, 3–44. Berkeley and Los Angeles: University of California Press.

———. 2000. *Civil Islam: Muslims and Democratization in Indonesia*. Princeton, NJ: Princeton University Press.

———. 2005. "Muslim Democrats and Islamist Violence in Post-Soeharto Indonesia." In *Remaking Muslim Politics: Pluralism, Contestation, Democratization*, edited by Robert W. Hefner, 273–301. Princeton, NJ: Princeton University Press.

———. 2007. "Introduction: The Culture, Politics, and Future of Muslim Education." In *Schooling Islam: The Culture and Politics of Modern Muslim Education*, edited by Robert W. Hefner and Muhammad Qasim Zaman, 1–39. Princeton, NJ: Princeton University Press.

———. 2009. "The Politics and Cultures of Islamic Education in Southeast Asia." In *Making Modern Muslims: The Politics of Islamic Education in Southeast Asia*, edited by Robert W. Hefner, 1–54. Honolulu: University of Hawaii Press.

Hirsch, Susan F. 1998. *Pronouncing and Persevering: Gender and the Discourses of Disputing in an African Islamic Court*. Chicago: University of Chicago Press.

Holmes Katz, Marion. 2006. "The 'Corruption of the Times' and the Mutability of the Shariʿa." *Cardoza Law Review* 28 (1): 171–85.

———. 2008. "Women's '*Mawlid*' Performances in Sanaa and the Construction of 'Popular Islam.'" *International Journal of Middle East Studies* 40 (3): 467–84.

Hooker, M. B. 2008. *Indonesian Syariah: Defining a National School of Islamic Law*. Singapore: Institute of Southeast Asian Studies.

Imber, Colin. 1997. *Ebu's-suʿud: The Islamic Legal Tradition*. Stanford, CA: Stanford University Press.

———. 2002. *The Ottoman Empire, 1300–1600: The Structure of Power*. New York: Palgrave Macmillan.

Inhorn, Marcia. 2003. *Local Babies, Global Science: Gender, Religion and In Vitro Fertilization in Egypt*. New York: Routledge.

Johnston, David L. 2007. "Maqâṣid al-Shariʿa: Epistemology and Hermeneutics of Muslim Theologies of Human Rights." *Die Welt des Islams* 47 (2): 149–87.

Kahf, Monzer. 1995. "*Waqf*." In *The Oxford Encyclopedia of the Modern Islamic World*, vol. 4, edited by John L. Esposito, 312–16. New York: Oxford University Press.

Kamali, Mohammad Hashim Kamali. 2008. *Shariʿah Law: An Introduction*. Oxford: One World.

Karamustafa, Ahmet T. 2007. *Sufism: The Formative Period*. Berkeley and Los Angeles: University of California Press.

Kelsay, John. 2013. "Islamic Ethics." In *The International Encyclopedia of Ethics*, edited by Hugh LaFollette, 2801–13. London: Blackwell.

Keyes, Charles F. 2002. "Weber and Anthropology." *Annual Review of Anthropology* 31:233–55.

Khaldūn, Ibn. 1969. *The Muqaddimah: An Introduction to History*. 3 vols. Princeton, NJ: Princeton University Press.

Laidlaw, James. 2014. *The Subject of Virtue: An Anthropology of Ethics and Freedom*. Cambridge, UK: Cambridge University Press.

Lambek, Michael. 2010. "Introduction." In *Ordinary Ethics: Anthropology, Language, and Action*, edited by Michael Lambek, 1–36. New York: Fordham University Press.

Latour, Bruno. 2005. *Reassembling the Social: An Introduction to Actor-Network Theory*. Oxford: Oxford University Press.

Layish, Aharon. 2004. "The Transformation of the Sharî`a from Jurists' Law to Statutory Law in the Contemporary Muslim World." *Die Welt des Islams* 44 (1): 85–113.

Lempert, Michael. 2013. "No Ordinary Ethics." *Anthropological Theory* 13 (4): 370–93.

Lindsey, Tim. 2012. *Islam, Law and the State in Southeast Asia*, vol. 1, *Indonesia*. London and New York: Tauris.

Lombardi, Clark B. 2006. *State Law as Islamic Law in Modern Egypt: The Incorporation of the Shari`a into Egyptian Constitutional Law*. Leiden, MA: Brill.

MacIntyre, Alasdair. 1984. *After Virtue: A Study in Moral Theory*, 2nd ed. Notre Dame, IN: University of Notre Dame Press.

———. 1988. *Whose Justice? Whose Rationality?* Notre Dame, IN: University of Notre Dame Press.

Mahmood, Saba. 2005. *Politics of Piety: The Islamic Revival and the Feminist Subject*. Princeton, NJ, and Oxford: Princeton University Press.

Makdisi, George. 1981. *The Rise of Colleges: Institutions of Learning in Islam and the West*. Edinburgh: University of Edinburgh Press.

Mandaville, Peter. 2007. "Globalization and the Politics of Religious Knowledge: Pluralizing Authority in the Muslim World." *Theory, Culture, Society* 24 (2): 101–15.

Marsden, Magnus. 2005. *Living Islam: Muslim Religious Experience in Pakistan's North-West Frontier*. Cambridge, UK: Cambridge University Press.

Masquelier, Adeline. 2007. "Negotiating Futures: Islam, Youth, and the State in Niger." In *Islam and Muslim Politics in Africa*, edited by B. F. Soares and R. Otayek, 243–62. New York: Palgrave MacMillan.

Masud, Muhammad Khalid. 2002. "The Scope of Pluralism in Islamic Moral Traditions." In *Islamic Political Ethics: Civil Society, Pluralism, and Conflict*, edited by Sohail H. Hashmi, 135–47. Princeton, NJ: Princeton University Press.

———. 2005. *Shâtibî's Philosophy of Islamic Law*. Kuala Lumpur: Islamic Book Trust.

Mernissi, Fatima. 1991. *Women in Islam: An Historical and Theological Enquiry*. Oxford: Basil Blackwell.

Messick, Brinkley. 1996. "Media *Muftis*: Radio *Fatwas* in Yemen." In *Islamic Legal Interpretation: Muftis and Their Fatwas*, edited by M. K. Masud, B. Messick, and David Powers, 310–20. Cambridge, MA: Harvard University Press.

Metcalf, Barbara Daly, ed. 1984. *Moral Conduct and Authority: The Place of Adab in South Asian Islam*. Berkeley and Los Angeles: University of California Press.

Mir-Hosseini, Ziba. 1999. *Islam and Gender: The Religious Debate in Contemporary Iran*. Princeton, NJ: Princeton University Press.

———. 2003. "The Construction of Gender in Islamic Legal Thought and Strategies for Reform." *Hawwa: Journal of Women of the Middle East and the Islamic World* 1 (1): 1–28.

———. 2009. "Towards Gender Equality: Muslim Family Laws and the Shari`ah." In *Wanted: Equality and Justice in the Muslim Family*, edited by Zainah Anwar, 23–63. Petaling Jaya, Malaysia: Musawah.

Mir-Hosseini, Ziba, Kari Vogt, Lena Larsen, and Christian Moe. 2013. *Gender and Equality in Muslim Family Law: Justice in the Islamic Legal Tradition*. London: I.B. Tauris.

Modood, Tariq. 2009. "Muslims, Religious Equality and Secularism." In *Secularism, Religion and Multicultural Citizenship*, edited by Geoffrey Brahm Levey and Tariq Modood, 164–85. Cambridge, UK: Cambridge University Press.

Moin, A. Afzar. 2012. *The Millennial Sovereign: Sacred Kingship and Sainthood in Islam*. New York: Columbia University Press.

Moosa, Ebrahim. 2001. "The Poetics and Politics of Law after Empire: Reading Women's Rights in the Contestation of Law." *UCLA Journal of Islamic and Near Eastern Law* 1:1–46.

Musallam, Adnan A. 2005. *From Secularism to Jihad: Sayyid Qutb and the Foundations of Radical Islamism*. Westport, CT: Praeger.

Neusner, Jacob, and Tamara Sonn. 1999. *Comparing Religions through Law: Judaism and Islam*. London and New York: Routledge.

Njoto-Feillard, Gwenaël. 2012. *L'Islam et la réinvention du capitalisme en Indonésie*. Paris: Karthala.

Opwis, Felicitas. 2007. "Islamic Law and Legal Change: The Concept of *Maslaha* in Classical and Contemporary Islamic Legal Theory." In *Shari'a: Islamic Law in the Contemporary Context*, edited by Abbas Amanat and Frank Griffel, 62–82. Stanford, CA: Stanford University Press.

Osella, Filippo, and Caroline Osella. 2009. "Muslim Entrepreneurs in Public Life between India and the Gulf: Making Good and Doing Good." *Journal of the Royal Anthropological Institute* 15 supp. 1: S202–S221.

Peletz, Michael G. 1996. *Reason and Passion: Representations of Gender in a Malay Society*. Berkeley and Los Angeles: University of California Press.

———. 1997. "'Ordinary Muslims' and Muslim Resurgents in Contemporary Malaysia: Notes on an Ambivalent Relationship." In *Islam in an Era of Nation-States: Politics and Religious Renewal in Muslim Southeast Asia*, edited by Robert W. Hefner and Patricia Horvatich, 231–72. Honolulu: University of Hawaii Press.

———. 2002. *Islamic Modern: Religious Courts and Cultural Politics in Malaysia*. Princeton, NJ: Princeton University Press.

Pemberton, Kelly. 2010. *Women Mystics and Sufi Shrines in India*. Columbia: University of South Carolina Press.

Peters, Rudolph. 2002. "From Jurists' Law to Statute Law or What Happens When the Shari'a Is Codified." *Mediterranean Politics* 7 (4): 82–95.

Ramadan, Tariq. 2009. *Radical Reform: Islamic Ethics and Liberation*. Oxford and New York: Oxford University Press.

Robbins, Joel. 2007. "Between Reproduction and Freedom: Morality, Value, and Radical Cultural Change." *Ethnos* 72 (3): 293–314.

Rudnyckyj, Daromir. 2010. *Spiritual Economies: Islam, Globalization, and the Afterlife of Development*. Ithaca, NY: Cornell University Press.

Rutherford, Bruce K. 2013. *Egypt after Mubarak: Liberalism, Islam, and Democracy in the Arab World*. Princeton, NJ: Princeton University Press.

Salime, Zakia. 2011. *Between Feminism and Islam: Human Rights and Shari'a Law in Morocco*. Minneapolis: University of Minnesota Press.

Sanders, Paula. 1994. *Ritual, Politics, and the City in Fatimid Cairo*. Albany: State University of New York Press.

Schielke, Samuli. 2010a. "Being Good in Ramadan: Ambivalence, Fragmentation, and the Moral Self in the Lives of Young Egyptians." In *Islam, Politics, Anthropology*, edited by Filippo Osella and Benjamin Soares, 23–38. Hoboken, NJ: John Wiley.

———. 2010b. "Second Thoughts about the Anthropology of Islam, or How to Make Sense of Grand Schemes in Everyday Life." Working Papers no. 2. Berlin: Zentrum Moderner Orient.

Shabana, Ayman. 2010. *Custom in Islamic Law and Legal Theory: The Development of Concepts of `Urf and `Adah in the Islamic Legal Tradition*. New York: Palgrave.

Shaikh, Farzana. 2008. "From Islamisation to Shariatisation: Cultural Transnationalism in Pakistan." *Third World Quarterly* 29 (3): 593–609.

Shane, Scott. 2011. "In Islamic Law, Gingrich Sees a Moral Threat to U.S." *New York Times*, December 21, 1.

Shore, Bradd. 1990. "Human Ambivalence and the Structuring of Moral Values." *Ethos* 18 (2): 165–79.

Shoshan, Boaz. 1993. *Popular Culture in Medieval Cairo*. Cambridge, UK: Cambridge University Press.

Simon, Gregory M. 2009. "The Soul Freed of Cares? Islamic Prayer, Subjectivity, and the Contradictions of Moral Selfhood in Minangkabau, Indonesia." *American Ethnologist* 36 (2): 258–75.

Skovgaard-Petersen, Jakob. 1997. *Defining Islam for the Egyptian State: Muftis and Fatwas of the Dâr al-Iftâ*. Leiden and Boston, MA: Brill.

Smith-Hefner, Nancy J. 2005. "The New Muslim Romance: Changing Patterns of Courtship and Marriage among Educated Javanese Youth." *Journal of Southeast Asian Studies* 36 (3): 441–59.

———. 2007. "Javanese Women and the Veil in Post-Soeharto Indonesia." *The Journal of Asian Studies* 66 (2): 389–420.

Soares, B. F. 2005. *Islam and the Prayer Economy: History and Authority in a Malian Town*. Ann Arbor: University of Michigan Press.

Stepan, Alfred. 2011. "The Multiple Secularisms of Modern Democratic and Non-Democratic Regimes." In *Rethinking Secularism*, edited by Craig Calhoun, Mark Juergensmeyer, and Jonathan Van Antwerpen, 114–44. Oxford: Oxford University Press.

Tamanaha, Brian Z. 2008. "Understanding Legal Pluralism: Past to Present, Local to Global." *Sydney Law Review* 30:375–411.

Taylor, Charles. 2004. *Modern Social Imaginaries*. Durham, NC: Duke University Press.

Taylor, Christopher Brennan. 2015. "Islamic Charity in India: Ethical Entrepreneurism and the Ritual, Revival, and Reform of *Zakat* among a Muslim Minority." PhD thesis. Boston: Department of Anthropology, Boston University.

Tibi, Bassam. 2013. *The Shari`a State: Arab Spring and Democratization*. London and New York: Routledge.

Tittensor, David. 2014. *The House of Service: The Gülen Movement and Islam's Third Way*. New York: Oxford University Press.

Tucker, Judith E. 1998. *In the House of the Law: Gender and Islamic Law in Ottoman Syria and Palestine*. Berkeley and Los Angeles: University of California Press.

———. 2008. *Women, Family, and Gender in Islamic Law*. Cambridge, UK: Cambridge University Press.

Turner, Bryan S. 2011. *Religion and Modern Society: Citizenship, Secularisation and the State*. Cambridge, UK: Cambridge University Press.

Uddin, Asma T., and Dave Pantzer. 2012. *A First Amendment Analysis of Anti-Sharia Initiatives*. Washington, DC: Institute for Social Policy and Understanding.

Vikor, Knut S. 2005. *Between God and the Sultan: A History of Islamic Law*. Oxford: Oxford University Press.

Vogel, Frank E. 2007. "Siyasa." In *Encyclopedia of Islam*, new ed., vol. 9, 694–96. Leiden and Boston, MA: Brill.

Wadud, Amina. 1999. *Qur'an and Woman: Rereading the Sacred Text from a Woman's Perspective.* Oxford: Oxford University Press.

Wikan, Unni. 1995. "The Self in a World of Urgency and Necessity." *Ethos* 23 (3): 259–85.

Wilson, Ian Douglas. 2008. "'As Long as It's *Halal*': Islamic *Preman* in Jakarta." In *Expressing Islam: Religious Life and Politics in Indonesia,* edited by Greg Fealy and Sally White, 192–210. Singapore: Institute of Southeast Asian Studies.

Zaman, Muhammad Qasim. 2002. *The 'Ulama in Contemporary Islam: Custodians of Change.* Princeton, NJ, and Oxford: Princeton University Press.

Zigon, Jarrett. 2008. *Morality: An Anthropological Perspective.* New York: Berg.

———. 2014. "An Ethics of Dwelling and a Politics of World-Building: A Critical Response to Ordinary Ethics." *Journal of the Royal Anthropological Institute* 20 (4): 746–64.

Zubaida, Sami. 2003. *Law and Power in the Muslim World.* London: I.B. Tauris.

Notes

1. The 2013–15 project was the sequel to an earlier one-year project, also sponsored by CURA, carried out during 2008: "Shari'a Politics in Muslim-Majority Countries." The results of that project were presented in a volume published in 2011 by Indiana University Press, *Shari'a Politics: Islamic Law and Society in the Modern World.*

2. My concern in this chapter is with the relationship of what is typically called shari'a or Islamic law to the other legal and moral registers on which Muslim actors draw in everyday and institutional settings. Although in some contexts the terms "shari'a" and "Islamic law" are useful (and I will use them several times in this chapter), some scholars, recognizing that many people hear both terms as implying the existence of a fixed, finished, and unitary body of positive law, avoid both terms in favor of the less positivistic phrase "Islamic legal traditions" (see, for example, Lindsey 2012). The latter phrase signals that the traditions in question are plural, subject to historical and sociological variation. Because in this chapter I am also concerned with a variety of ethical registers, I will also speak of "Islamic ethical and legal traditions" or "Islamic ethicolegal traditions," with apologies to readers for the phrases' inelegance.

3. Although this volume focuses on governance, public law, and gender, Islamic traditions are interacting with late modern sciences in other spheres as well to create novel reformulations of Islamic law and ethics—Islamic education being one such sphere (see Adely 2012; Hefner 2007; 2009). Another sphere is the field of Islamic economics, which has seen, in everything from management training to charities, new and expansive reinterpretations of Islamic ethical traditions (see Njoto-Feillard 2012; Osella and Osella 2009; Rudnyckyj 2010; Taylor 2015). One of the most unusual domains of innovative thought within an Islamic ethicolegal perspective, however, is in the quickly growing field of infertility and reproductive technologies (Clarke 2009; Inhorn 2003).

4. As Guy Burak (2013) has recently demonstrated, however, from the late fifteenth century on, state officials in the Ottoman empire regularized and centralized Islamic legal traditions more extensively than had earlier Muslim polities. In promoting these centralizing reforms, the Ottomans anticipated some of the *étatizing* reforms of the nineteenth and twentieth centuries (see also Imber 1997, 244; Tucker 2008, 19; Vikor 2005, 207–9). The Ottoman example also reminds us that, contrary to some historical accounts, the standardization and centralization of Islamic law was not just a consequence of the Muslim encounter with the West.

5. One of our most gifted academic scholars of Islamic legal traditions, Wael Hallaq, skates dangerously close to just such a conclusion when he writes, "It is a salient feature of that

[premodern Muslim] society that it *lived* legal ethics and legal morality, for these constituted the religious foundations and codes of social praxis" (Hallaq 2013, 55–56).

6. Ebrahim Moosa (2001, 39) makes a similar point in even broader terms: "A closer scrutiny would reveal that these 'authentic' and 'pure' texts [of commentaries on the law] are actually hybrid constructions of ideas and practices that emanate from multiple origins in their medieval and premodern contexts."

SECTION I
Shari`a Pluralities

2   Shari`a and the Rule of Law

Anver M. Emon*

THE TITLE OF this chapter might cause the reader to wonder why and in what sense "shari`a" and "rule of law" can be juxtaposed—and, moreover, what such a juxtaposition contributes analytically to the study of shari`a. In the fields of legal theory and law and development, "rule of law" resonates with a weight that seems to need neither explanation nor justification. Though use of the term is nearly omnipresent in scholarly fields, little consensus holds on what "rule of law" means or requires. Some years ago, Lon Fuller put forth a series of principles intended to give moral content to the "enterprise of law" (Fuller 1973). Similarly, David Dyzenhaus reads into "rule of law" principles of justification that are internal to "the practice of public reason" and whose use allows evaluation of a legal outcome (Dyzenhaus 1993). In the context of development studies, "rule of law" often refers to the institutional conditions of effective and efficient state governance. However, in developmental contexts, rule of law discussions often ignore the more informal mechanisms of dispute resolution that prevail when the formal state is less than effective—if not completely failed.[1] Moreover, as Stephen Humphreys has notably shown, rule of law development projects are often covers for neoimperial projects loosely based on, and justified by, the very theories that tend to avoid precise definitions of the term (Humphreys 2010).

Scholarship on Islamic law does not seem particularly attuned to the idea of rule of law, for various reasons. For instance, such scholarship occurs in fields and disciplines that do not often intersect with the university nexes where Islamic law is taught or studied (for example, religious studies or area studies). Additionally, rule of law discourse in Muslim-majority contexts is usually framed by development policies and development funding and thereby imports the politics that come with international support and preconditions for domestic legal

* I thank Robert W. Hefner and the authors of this volume, whose comments on an earlier draft of this chapter proved invaluable. In particular, Robert Hefner has provided excellent leadership as an editor, and his comments and vision for this volume have helped me clarify various aspects of the argument herein. I also thank the faculty of UC Berkeley Law School for their comments on an earlier version of this essay. Furthermore, I thank Nataliya Horodetsky, Hon. Derek Green, Hon. Marc Richard, and the Department of Judicial Affairs of the Maldives for their support and engagement during the course of my research on the Maldives.

reform (Humphreys 2010). But, and perhaps more to the point, the idea of bringing together shari`a and rule of law is problematic when each term of art remains highly contested and thereby subject to dispute.[2]

Yet, as events have unfolded in the Middle East since 2011, both shari`a and rule of law have become inescapable features of the political terrain, with draft constitutions invoking shari`a within the institutions of government in new and highly contested ways. Even in the case of the Islamic State in Iraq and al-Sham (ISIS), the terms of political debate on all sides increasingly invoke shari`a as either salve or specter (see also this volume, chapter 1). Events in the Arab world since 2011 have offered a welcome opportunity to reflect on the place of shari`a in Muslim-majority states, whatever may ultimately result from the tumult that exists in that region. More to the point, the invocation of shari`a in a modern state requires heightened attention to the relationship between premodern doctrines (fiqh) crafted for an (often imagined) Islamic imperial polity and how those premodern doctrines are used to give Islamic content to the workings of the state.

Though some might simply wish to wave away the inherited legacy of fiqh as outdated, antiquated, or otherwise inapposite, this chapter suggests that to do so artificially and undemocratically fashions a public ethics of subordination. No matter one's position on Islam and Islamic law, the historical doctrines of Islamic law inform in various ways what Charles Taylor (2003) might call a "social imaginary" in the Muslim world. The fiqh tradition and other sources of the Islamic tradition give content to a social imaginary in the Muslim world that also includes ethical norms of more modern vintage (for example, human rights norms, development norms, and the norms of multilateralism). This condition of normative pluralism calls out for an ethics of shari`a discourse that does not avoid the inherited tradition but rather works *through* it. Working through shari`a requires a deepened appreciation of the profound legal pluralism in Muslim-majority states today.

This chapter proceeds in two parts. The first illuminates the way in which shari`a discourse operates in different "social imaginaries" that cannot simply be waved away, avoided, or worked around. The second offers an account of what it would mean to *work through* the Islamic tradition as part of a public ethics in modern Muslim-majority societies. Specifically, the second part examines the issue of religious freedom in light of the premodern dhimmi rules, which are of considerable relevance for the status and future of religious minorities in Islamist-led governments in the Middle East.

Shari`a in Competing Social Imaginaries

To suggest that shari`a informs a social imaginary that contributes to a public debate on law and governance implies that excising it from an ethics of public debate in Muslim-majority politics would be both undemocratic and fundamentally illusory. To illustrate, this section explores different vignettes involving "shari`a talk" to reveal the political work that social imaginaries do, as well as to suggest that waving away shari`a entirely is artificial at best—and ethically violent at worst.

Certainly the Arab Spring featured much in the way of shari`a talk, especially in the wake of major electoral victories by Islamist parties such as En-Nahda in Tunisia and the Muslim Brotherhood in Egypt—notwithstanding the subsequent ejection of President Morsi from office in Egypt. But, in fairness, the Arab Spring is not itself the fount of shari`a talk. Shari`a talk has been with us for a long time. It was with us when the Swiss electorate constitutionally banned minarets, when the French government banned *niqabs* and *burkas*, and when the European Court of Human Rights decided against covered Muslim women in *Dahlab v. Switzerland* and *Sahin v. Turkey* on the grounds that covering was contrary to privileged secular democratic commitments. Shari`a talk was also on the minds of those who debated shari`a family arbitration in Ontario, Canada, in 2004–5, as well as those who called for the ouster of then Archbishop Rowan Williams in 2007 after his speech to members of the legal profession in the United Kingdom about shari`a arbitration tribunals. Indeed, shari`a talk has been with us since well before the Arab Spring.

It is important to note that the sites of all this shari`a talk were not in Muslim-majority contexts but in the West: Europe, Canada, and the United States. This is not to suggest that there is no shari`a talk in the Muslim world. Of course there is; indeed, it is very much on the rise. But in each context, what shari`a signifies depends on the underlying norms that animate public debate. Indeed, examining and contrasting whether and how shari`a is embedded in these different contexts will further reveal how in Muslim-majority contexts, shari`a talk is built on an already existing normative worldview that cannot simply be avoided or relegated to the "private" and "personal."

This section presents a series of vignettes that illuminate the social imaginaries within which shari`a talk occurs. Shari`a talk in the North Atlantic world often aims to oust shari`a from the public sphere in contrast to the Muslim-majority world. Recognizing this contrast is important, for doing so reveals why proposals to bypass shari`a or otherwise remove it from public discourse in the Muslim world are illusory at best. The contrast contributes to the broader argument of this chapter: that contending with shari`a in Muslim societies in transition will require working *through* the historical tradition and not around it.

This analysis begins with legislative efforts in the United States to ban shari`a, then turns to the outpouring of comments that attended the now infamous speech of then Archbishop of Canterbury Rowan Williams. From there the analysis reflects on the shari`a talk of the Islamic feminist group Musawah, which confounds the all-too-neat dichotomy between secularism and religion. I conclude with a final vignette on the Maldives, a country in the Indian Ocean whose transition to democracy in 2008 has been anything but smooth. The Maldives conditions citizenship on being Sunni Muslim and defines its entire population of less than 500,000 as uniformly Muslim.

"Shari`a" in the United States: Legislative Theater in a Time of Crisis

The 2010 midterm elections in the United States put various state legislatures into Republican hands. In what seemed like an amazing coincidence over a two-week period in January 2011, nearly a dozen states introduced legislation to ban shari`a, whether expressly or through implication—as a type of "foreign law." The number of states that have proposed such legislation has since climbed, and although many such bills have become mired in judiciary committees, others have passed and become state law (see, for example, legislation passed in Tennessee, discussed hereafter). What explains these bills and their almost verbatim language across the various states?

Arguably, the story started earlier in 2010 with the release of a report from the Center for Security Policy (CSP), *Shariah: The Threat to America*. In this report, a team of security experts pilloried official government policy on Muslims and Islam for being naive and foolishly politically correct. The team comprised nineteen security specialists and retired military personnel, led by Lt. Gen. William Boykin (ret.) and Lt. Gen. Harry E. Soyster (ret.). The authors of the report clearly indicated that the report's purpose was not to understand shari`a. Rather, they aimed to apply official US threat assessment doctrine to shari`a. That doctrine requires US officials to analyze those of an enemy's precepts and beliefs that justify its attacks. Whether such an assessment is "accurate, appropriate, or even identifiable with 'genuine' Islam is wholly irrelevant" (CSP 2010, 84). For securocrats such as those on the Boykin-Soyster team, if an enemy who attacks and kills Americans "refers to and relies on this doctrine to guide and justify his actions, then that is all that matters in terms of the enemy threat doctrine US civilian[,] and military leaders must roughly understand and orient upon for the purpose of defeating such foes" (CSP 2010, 84–85). In other words, the study is not necessarily—nor does it aim to be—an accurate depiction or representation of shari`a. Rather, the study adopts a doomsday lens through which to consider the implications of certain aspects of the historical tradition on US security policy.

Certainly few would argue against the importance of knowing what one's enemy thinks and how the enemy justifies attacks against "us," whoever "we" are. Were that the only aim of the study, I myself would be hard pressed to find fault with its approach. However, the report goes further. The Boykin-Soyster team concluded that because US enemies cite doctrines from within the tradition of shari`a, adherence to shari`a is the litmus test for assessing whether someone poses a threat: "Shariah is the crucial fault line of Islam's internecine struggle" (CSP 2010, 2). In a particularly striking passage, the report proclaims: "7th Century impulses, enshrined in shariah, have reemerged as the most critical existential threat to constitutional governance and the freedom-loving, reason-driven principles that undergird Western civilization" (CSP 2010, 11).

The troubling implication of this position is that if the Boykin-Soyster version of shari`a poses an existential threat to US constitutional governance, and if Muslims within the United States adhere to shari`a—albeit their own versions—enemies are necessarily hidden among "us." But how do "we" identify the enemy among "us" without simultaneously casting indiscriminate aspersions on all Muslims in America? The Boykin-Soyster team proposes to examine any given Muslim's attitude toward shari`a. Indeed, the report states baldly that "conformance to shariah in America constitutes as great a threat as any enemy the nation has ever confronted" (CSP 2010, 11). The greatest enemy to America thus is no longer the ever-elusive al-Qaeda, nor the Taliban. Rather, the greatest enemy to the United States consists of Muslim neighbors who adhere to shari`a.

If this threat assessment is right, then what follows? As various Republican state legislators demonstrated in January 2011, one response is to legislatively prohibit recourse to shari`a in the legal system. For instance, a Tennessee bill introduced by state senator Bill Ketron and state representative Judd Matheny initially proclaimed, "The knowing adherence to sharia . . . is prima facie evidence of an act in support of the overthrow of the United States government . . . by the likely use of imminent criminal violence and terrorism with the aim of imposing sharia on the people of [Tennessee]."[3] The Tennessee bill has since been amended to remove all references to shari`a, but legislative and statutes that have targeted foreign law, international law, and shari`a share an animating characteristic: They all seek to prevent the onset of "other" legal traditions from threatening the ongoing existence of the American spirit as found in its legal tradition. The titles of these bills evince a crisis of existential proportion—witness Oklahoma's "Save Our State Amendment."[4]

Bills that expressly ban shari`a also ban other foreign and international laws. States that have considered such bills include Arizona, Missouri, Oklahoma, Tennessee, and Wyoming. In many cases, such bills have identified international law with institutions of global reach and significance, such as the United Nations, the European Union, the International Monetary Fund, or the World Bank. Other such bills have not specifically mentioned shari`a, but instead refer to "foreign religious or moral" codes or "religious or cultural law." However, comments made by the bills' sponsors, such as by Texas legislator Leo Berman, evince a fear of shari`a at the heart of the matter.[5]

When paired with references to international law in such bills, talk of shari`a serves as rhetorical emphasis for a more substantive debate about the well-being and vibrancy of American democracy and popular sovereignty. In his book *Political Theology*, Paul Kahn observes that Americans remain reluctant to make domestic space for international law, especially if that might mean displacing their own law. As Kahn writes, "Americans have a problem imagining international law: if law is an expression of popular sovereignty, how can a system of norms that has no source in that sovereign constitute law?" (Kahn 2011, 10). Kahn's observations resonate with the well-known dispute between US Supreme Court justices Anthony Kennedy and Antonin Scalia, now deceased, about the role of foreign law in constitutional interpretation. For Scalia, introduction of international law into American courts betrayed the popular, representative, and democratic enterprise of governance (Toobin 2005). That ideal of popular sovereignty is a form of political theology, a pious commitment stemming from America's founding and requiring the purity of America's legal order. Indeed, Kahn writes, the "state creates and maintains its own sacred space and history" (Kahn 2011, 19). If we accept that the American enterprise of governance is based on a notion of popular sovereignty that informs what the law is and can be, it necessarily follows that recognition and enforcement of a foreign legal tradition (whether shari`a or international law) is a stain, impurity, or danger that must be removed lest the founding principles of the state be violated from within. For the sponsors of these bills, international law is such an impurity. When juxtaposed with international law, shari`a appears simply as a more extreme case of that threat. By banning shari`a and international law through legislation, legislators use the rituals of domestic law to exorcise the nation.[6]

Shari`a in the West: Commenting on the Archbishop of Canterbury's Commenting on Shari`a

In 2008, then Archbishop of Canterbury Rowan Williams lectured the Royal Courts of Justice in London on law and multiculturalism. Addressing members of the legal profession, he asked "whether there should be a higher level of attention to religious identity and communal rights in the practice of the law, and . . . something like a delegation of certain legal functions to the religious courts of a community" (Williams 2010, 296–97, para. 8). More specifically, he advocated a limited accommodation of traditions such as shari`a to evince a commitment to multiculturalism in Britain.

His speech was the subject of considerable commentary and even vitriol. Of particular interest here is a volume of essays published in 2010 entitled *Sharia in the West* (Ahdar and Aroney 2010). The essays' commentary on the Archbishop's speech falls into two categories: (1) situation of the speech in light of contemporary debates about law and multiculturalism and (2) consideration of the place of Islamic law (politically, legally, and institutionally) within a liberal democratic polity such as Britain. This second category of articles is of particular interest here for what its "shari`a talk" reveals. These articles' characterization of and antagonism toward shari`a implicitly reveal a commitment to an underspecified set of values that are presumed to be fundamental to liberal democratic polities such as the United Kingdom and that would be threatened by any proposed accommodation of shari`a.

That the sovereign primacy of liberal democratic values is at stake is obvious by the authors' utter failure to address the narrow issue of Williams's speech. Williams carefully remarked that the issue was about delegation of "certain legal functions" and recognized that this inquiry affected not just Muslims but others, such as the Orthodox Jewish community in its use of Beth Din courts to resolve issues of divorce (for example, through the *get*) (Williams 2010, 297). Williams was well aware, however, that designating and demarcating the scope and limits of that delegation was a tricky issue—an issue that he expressly dodged. Indeed, in the question-and-answer period that followed his speech, he admitted that he was not "postulating a detailed scheme." Rather, he stated that his goal was to raise "a question about what the most fruitful kinds of relationship might be between the law of the state and what I have been calling 'supplementary jurisdiction.' But I think were there to be . . . further forms of accommodation, then there would need to be I think, some element of transparency of monitoring which expressed a cooperative relationship rather than just parallel tracks" (Williams 2010, 305).

In his speech, Williams aimed to spur a conversation about intricate and complex issues of legal ordering, institutional design, and multicultural accommodation of minority groups within the prevailing legal order. He did not endorse parallel tracks of law, nor a wholesale incorporation of a religious legal tradition (whether Islamic or Rabbinic) into the British legal system. Nonetheless, many of the commentaries on his speech ignored the legal intricacies of what he was proposing. Instead they recharacterized Williams's contribution as if his question posited a zero-sum game in which the very preservation of liberal democratic values *en toto* was at stake.

For instance, Michael Nazir-Ali, an Anglican Bishop of Pakistani origin, relies on anecdotal personal experiences as a Christian in Pakistan to substantiate his authority as a commentator on Islamic law (Nazir-Ali 2010). He addresses various issues in Islamic law, such as its sources, the status of women, apostasy, blasphemy, its treatment of non-Muslim minorities, finance, and even *jihad*—most of which have nothing to do with the narrow issue Williams addressed. Nazir-Ali concludes that although Muslims should be free to order their lives according to the tenets of their faith, "there should be no recognition of Shari`a in terms of public law since the assumptions of the latter are quite different from the former" (Nazir-Ali 2010, 71). But what are the assumptions of "public law," according to Nazir-Ali? Nazir-Ali argues that public law in Western countries is derived from the Judeo–Christian tradition as filtered through the Enlightenment. The shari`a, he argues, is based on quite different assumptions. Without explaining anything more about these conclusions, he then says that shari`a's "recognition or incorporation into public law could cause not only confusion, but an undermining of the fundamental assumptions undergirding the general law" (Nazir-Ali 2010, 87). In almost religious overtones, he issues statements about fundamental rights, access to courts, and so on to conclude that there is no real possibility for incorporating one into the other (as if that were what Williams had been suggesting).

Likewise, Kolig's existential concern for the sovereign primacy of liberal democratic values is revealed when he presumes the relevant inquiry is whether or not the "*total* application and recognition of shari`a *in all its consequences*" (emphasis mine) is feasible in a liberal democracy—a straw-man argument to say the least (Kolig 2010, 260). James Skillen posits a similar argument by suggesting that because Muslims presumably understand shari`a as an all-or-nothing system, there is no way of extracting pieces of Islamic law for use within a modern liberal democratic state system (Skillen 2010). He uses this presumptively pious ideal of shari`a to transform Williams's more nuanced suggestion into a zero-sum game in which nothing less than the foundational values of a liberal democratic policy are at stake. Skillen writes: "To the extent that religions such as Islam and Christianity are ways of life and not merely modes of worship, they will require public access and expression in many if not all areas of life" (Skillen 2010, 100). Moreover, he holds that Islamic law does not have the internal mechanisms to tolerate other religions or ensure equal treatment of all faiths in diverse contexts. Notably, however, Skillen holds that Christianity does have a basis for equal treatment of the "other" in public life. Thus not only is Islamic law a holistic tradition that seeks "omnicompetent authority for the government," but it also lacks the resources to compete with the Christian tradition for purposes of effective governance in a diverse British polity (Skillen 2010, 101).

These essays ignore the technical legal points in Williams's speech and instead situate shari`a at the center of nothing less than a civilizational conflict. Their antagonism toward shari`a begs the question of what is on the other side of shari`a. For those living in Britain, where the Anglican Church is the official state church, it is not enough to simply suggest that on the other side of shari`a is some vague notion of a liberal democratic polity. Rather, the essays hint at what only John Milbank argues expressly in one of his two essays in the volume: "only a hegemonically Christian outlook, and not a secular one, can accord to Islam respect *as Islam*" (Milbank 2010, 138).

For Milbank, that Christian outlook is exactly what makes British society and its laws fair and impartial, as well as closed to the idea of accommodating a tradition such as shari`a. Relying on unspecified anecdotes as if they were data, Milbank writes, "It is apparent from the reactions of many British Muslims to the Archbishop's speech . . . that they not only welcome the detached fairness of British civil law, but also the political establishment of Christianity in the United Kingdom" (Milbank 2010, 138). Christianity provides the level playing field that Islam and Islamic law cannot. Milbank goes further, however, and raises the existential stakes. He argues that to make space for an Islamic tradition within a Christian British legal order would turn the tables on Britain's fundamental values, which he proudly acknowledges are substantive and hegemonic: "We cannot treat Islam in terms of full liberal pluralist equality without abandoning the principles of *both* Christianity *and* the Enlightenment. We can only accommodate Islam on our own terms . . . [T]here is *never* any truly 'neutral,' procedural ground . . . Something always rules, and this something is always substantive" (Milbank 2010, 146).

Whatever Williams was trying to address in his speech, commentators have ignored it in their shari`a talk. They have instead recharacterized Williams's argument to address existential concerns about nothing short of the sovereign primacy of a value system that has been so deeply embedded as to be taken for granted. These authors consider shari`a to be ground zero of a zero-sum game. To decide the winner, they rely on normative resources and ideas that have always been assumed to be true but that have never needed detailed explanation, let alone justification—at least, not until now.

Shari`a and the Pluralist Social Imaginary in a Transitional MENA Region

Shari`a in US and UK debates is seen as the "other" against which always available and prevailing liberal democratic values are given shape, content, and primacy. In the Middle East and North Africa (MENA), the political polarity is reversed. Shari`a informs public debate and, in doing so, inverts the assumptions that inform shari`a talk in the United States and the United Kingdom. For instance, consider Egyptian activist and scholar Dr. Rabab al-Mahdi comments on secularism, Islamist politics, and the law in 2011 Egypt during an interview for *Middle East Law and Governance*'s Arab revolutions issue:

> Let us first agree that "secularism" is a historical and social construct tied to time and place. Hence, both the U.S. and France, for example[,] are considered secular states, but what this label means and its implications in the two contexts are quite different. So even though I believe in separating religion from politics, I do understand that political Islamism is an important current in Egypt, and that it comes in different forms—some of which are more progressive than others. (Emon, Lust, and Macklin 2011, 227)

In other words, political Islam (and its shari'a talk) allowed al-Mahdi to prob-
lematize the all-too-common assumptions that, at least in North Atlantic political thinking, distinguish between the "religious" and the "secular" without
problematizing one in relation to the other.[7] Whether in the case of the al-Nahda
party in Tunisia, the Muslim Brotherhood in Egypt, or even the more "secular"
trends often associated with the military, shari'a talk is not excluded from both
political and legal reflection, dialogue, and considerations. Islam and Islamic law
give content to the social imaginary that undergirds the politics of these regions.
Indeed, the shari'a talk in these regions is the diametric opposite to that which
prevailed in the US and UK debates already discussed. In the foregoing cases,
shari'a talk made plain the cultural resources that gave content to the US and
British social imaginary—Christianity, for example, or the Enlightenment. In
the MENA, shari'a talk is indicative of the corpus of value and tradition that
invariably informs the content of any public discourse on governance and order,
regardless of whether shari'a is invoked expressly or implicitly.

In the early days of the revolution in Egypt, the Islamists were relatively
cautious and even reticent, as Carrie R. Wickham has noted. Though younger
Brotherhood members were present and even played key roles in coordinating
protests, the Brotherhood's "senior leadership maintained a low profile" (Wickham 2011, 212). Though members of the Brotherhood might have lain low, the
more interesting point is that people knew to look for them—and that people
assumed that Islamist politics and Islamic legal issues would become part of any
future transition. For example, writing for *Foreign Affairs* only months after the
revolution in Tahrir Square, Middle East policy analyst Shadi Hamid predicted
that after the protests settled down, "[i]f truly democratic governments form in
their wake, they are likely to include significant representation of mainstream
Islamic groups. Like it or not, the United States will have to learn to live with
political Islam" (Hamid 2011, 40).

This is not to suggest that what shari'a means and how it fits into the larger
political and legal context of the region is uncontested. Shari'a is certainly contested. But the language used in contests over what is and is not shari'a is fascinating by taking for granted the relevance of Islam and Islamic law as traditions
of value that contribute to debates about the future of the MENA. In a particular
and notable difference, however, considering the postcolonial condition of the
peoples and countries in the MENA, shari'a talk in these regions must account
for how colonial penetration, and now multilateral intervention, informs what
counts as legitimate law and governance in the modern state. As much as the
relevance of Islamic ideas is obvious, if not taken for granted, in the MENA,
those ideas are arguably *less* taken for granted or unquestioned than Enlightenment ideals in the United States and the United Kingdom, not least because of
the relatively recent history in the MENA of colonialism, the modern state, and
globalization, together with all that they imply for law and governance.

The work of the Islamic feminist group Musawah illustrates Islamic thought as a normative framework providing ready content that is not taken for granted in the way that liberal democratic values are in the United States and the United Kingdom. The reflections of one of its founders, Ziba Mir-Hosseini (a contributor to this volume), on shari`a when addressing gender equality are of particular interest. Though the group was founded in Malaysia and is international in its scope, much of its research arises from the MENA or focuses on the MENA.

In her essay describing the group's foundation and its framework for reform, Mir-Hosseini argues that Musawah and its *Framework for Action* "herald a new phase in the encounter between Islamic and international human rights law" (Mir-Hosseini 2012, 291). After outlining the basic features of "classical rulings" of Islamic family law and the politics that surround debates on Islam and human rights, Mir-Hosseini describes the Moroccan 2004 family law reforms as having been inspiration for Musawah. Indeed, the example of Morocco illustrated how scholarship and activism could contribute to change in domestic family law.[8]

Musawah's signature difference from other women's equality groups is its unabashed and unflinching engagement *with* the Islamic tradition. Mir-Hosseini acknowledges that for most of the twentieth century, religion, especially Islam, was commonly linked with oppression of women. Consequently, any feminist or gender equality agenda must be framed using materials external to the religious tradition of Islam. However, she notes, this narrow notion of feminism has been used in the service of colonial projects and has thus been discredited in the minds of many in the Muslim world. Indeed, Mir-Hosseini makes similar arguments about the human rights movement. Consequently, the Musawah model works from *within* the Islamic legal tradition toward a tradition of gender equality. Only in this fashion, she argues, "could [we] free ourselves from an apparent choice between the devil of those who want to impose patriarchal interpretations of Islam's sacred texts, and the deep blue sea of those who pursue a neo-colonialist hegemonic global project in the name of human rights and feminism" (Mir-Hosseini 2012, 299).

This turn to the Islamic tradition is of particular interest for the purpose of this chapter. It is a turn that recognizes shari`a as an always ready resource that when ignored or cast aside renders the external critique (whether from the feminist or the human rights perspective) suspect if not an outright threat. In other words, shari`a gives content to a social imaginary of its own. But the turn to these resources is not without its critical edge—an edge that draws on different resources that also inform that same social imaginary. As Mir-Hosseini writes elsewhere, "by advocating a brand of feminism that takes Islam as the source of its legitimacy, the new discourse (in other words, Musawah's gender equality approach) can challenge the hegemony of orthodox interpretations and question the legitimacy of the views of those who until now have spoken in the name of Islam" (Mir-Hosseini 2003, 21). The challenge is possible, critical, and legitimate because it draws on the languages and conceptual vocabularies of a complex, pluralist social imaginary without succumbing to the grammar of any single variety.

This short vignette about Musawah contrasts with shari`a talk in the US and UK contexts. There, shari`a is a threat, an external normative order that has no business being part of any domestic North Atlantic legal system. More to the point, shari`a talk is used to define and distinguish "us" and "them." The rhetoric of shari`a in the North Atlantic region is thus about threat and security; it is invoked to identify and demarcate the line across which stands the enemy. The Musawah model reveals, ironically, a similar rhetoric arising from shari`a talk. Adopting a postcolonial critique of feminism and human rights, Mir-Hosseini turns to shari`a in order to reinstantiate an "us" as opposed to a "them." Shari`a talk, in the case of Musawah, is the point from which any conversation, *among Muslims and for Muslims,* must start. What it actually stands for is less relevant. Certainly Musawah's advocates argue for a fundamental change in doctrine out of deference to gender justice considerations. But even so, shari`a, whatever it might be, offers a resource, taken for granted, that permits demarcation between "us" and "them."

The Maldives: Normative Pluralism at Sea?

I conclude this section by examining the Maldives, an island archipelago located in the Indian Ocean just south of India and Sri Lanka. If shari`a talk in the Muslim world reflects a social imaginary that is the inverse of the social imaginary in the United States and the United Kingdom as already described, the Maldives offers an important example by which we can appreciate the further implications of this inverted polarity.

The Maldives claims to be 100 percent Muslim. It also participates in the international community, is an international tourist destination, and, most recently, has been undergoing massive democratic turmoil since the passage of its 2008 constitution. A nation-state of mostly uninhabited islands, the Maldives is strategically tempting to regional powers (among them India, Pakistan, and China) that are keen to protect the trade routes in the Indian Ocean.[9] This is the context in which we must appreciate the assumptions, taken for granted, that animate shari`a talk in the country.

The Maldives is an island archipelago of more than 1,000 islands, of which only 191 are inhabited. Another 60 have resorts built on them for the benefit of international tourists—and about forty more resorts are in various stages of construction at the time of this writing. Tourism is a significant feature of the Maldives' economy, accounting for roughly 28 percent of GDP and more than 60 percent of foreign exchange receipts (Central Intelligence Agency 2013). The growth of the tourism industry in the Maldives has been dramatic: "From just

42000 tourists in 1980, numbers grew close to 800,000 in 2010. This is despite the government's plan in the 1980s to cap tourist arrivals at 160,000 annually" (Scheyvens 2011, 151). The rapid growth of tourism in the country has been managed by the Quality Tourism Strategy put in place in 1978 under then president Maumoon Abdul Gayoom:

> The Quality Tourism Strategy was in part a response to the haphazard style of development of the sector prior to this time, which included independent tourists on extended holidays in India and Sri Lanka turning up on islands to "hang out" for a while. Their behavior, including their standards of dress and their partying, was seen as disrespectful of local customs and religion in this Islamic state. (Scheyvens 2011, 152)

The Quality Tourism Strategy aimed, then, to prevent "cultural pollution" (Scheyvens 2011, 152), a phrase that captures the complex tension that arises between pursuing an aggressive tourist-based economy and ensuring the stability and integrity of what Maldivians consider to be their culture, religion, and traditional value system. To find a balance between supporting the economy and protecting local culture and traditions, tourist resorts are built on uninhabited islands only, a key consideration in the Quality Tourism Strategy.[10]

Despite efforts to keep Maldivians and tourists apart, the two populations cannot be hermetically sealed off from each other. In an extreme case, the 2007 Sultan Square bombing claimed the lives of foreign tourists. For many, the bombing was a sign of an Islamic extremism that could undermine the economic well-being of most Maldivians. Considering the country's reliance on the tourism sector, many Maldivians feared that the bombing could adversely affect the country's tourism industry (Niyaz 2010). In 2010, in a less violent but provocative and highly publicized event, a foreign couple seeking to renew their wedding vows took part in a special ceremony on one of the resort islands. A Maldivian who helped run the resort conducted the ceremony using both local traditions and the local language. The couple thought they were being regaled in Dhivehi, the local language, with words of great sentiment and cultural significance, but the officiant actually directed vulgar and unpleasant remarks at them instead. When the videotaped ceremony was uploaded to YouTube,[11] Maldivians connected to social media outlets immediately responded. Some condemned the officiant. Others tried to explain the incident away by describing it as a natural result of the cultural and societal challenges associating with bringing the Maldives into the community of nations, international trade, and a global tourist economy (Henderson 2008; Shakeela and Weaver 2012).

Global trade and tourism also fuel debates about Islam and shari`a. The international dimension of religious debate in the Maldives pits a local Islam that is open, flexible, and open to pragmatic considerations against an international

Islam (such as that originating in Pakistan or Afghanistan) that advocates a more austere form of religious purity (Wright 2012). Viewed in such a light, the clamor around then President Mohammad Nasheed's proposal to allow guest homes to be opened on inhabited islands should have come as no surprise. Although the guest house measure responded to the demands of locals who wanted to participate in the international tourist economy, Nasheed reversed his position in the face of strong opposition. Opponents of the plan argued that such a move would taint local traditions and values by introducing low-cost tourist packages to the region.[12]

Even more painful was the October 1, 2012, murder of parliamentarian and Islamic scholar Afrasheem Ali, a man routinely criticized by religious conservatives and extremists. On the day of his death, he publicly defended the legitimacy, from an Islamic viewpoint, of his positions on local television. On returning home, he was brutally attacked and killed (Sruthijith 2012). Many speculated that the four suspects arrested for the murder sought vengeance on behalf of their ousted leader, ex-president Mohamed Nasheed. Others, however, feared that his death was prompted by his more moderate views of Islam. Indeed, former president Nasheed reportedly condemned the murder and "called for people to embrace the moderate Islamic views of the murdered religious scholar" (BBC News 2012; Robinson 2012). Though the murderers' motives remain unknown, Ali's murder worried many who feared the onset of an extremist version of Islam.

This context of intra-Muslim conflict about Islam frames the pluralist dimension of shari`a talk in the Maldives. So, too, does the constitutional presumption that the Maldives is an Islamic country and that the nearly four hundred thousand citizens of the Maldives are Muslim. Under article 2 of the 2008 constitution, the Maldives is deemed to be a "sovereign, independent, democratic republic based on the principles of Islam." Article 10 declares that the religion of the Maldives is Islam, and that "Islam shall be the [sic] one of the basis [sic] of all the laws of [t]he Maldives." It further states that "[n]o law contrary to any tenet of Islam shall be enacted in [t]he Maldives" (article 10[b]). These constitutional provisions supply some framing for an Islamic social imaginary, just as similar provisions do in other Muslim-majority countries (Emon 2008). The Maldivian constitution is interesting, however, for saying, in article 9(d), that a "non-Muslim may not become a citizen of [t]he Maldives." Coupled with the constitutional silence on religious freedom,[13] these constitutional provisions offer a silent presumption about what being Maldivian implies about one's religious identity. Indeed, to be Maldivian is to infuse citizenship in a state with specific religious commitments.

This elision of national and religious identity is evident in various regulatory regimes that oversee the Maldives' legal sector. For example, the Judicial Services Commission (JSC), a constitutionally created body that hires, transfers, and disciplines judges, comprises ten members who must satisfy various qualifications, including being Muslim (Judicial Services Commission Act, s. 5). When members of the JSC are sworn into office, they state, as part of their oath, "I . . . do swear in the name of Allah that I will respect the religion of Islam, that I will uphold the Constitution of the Republic of [t]he Maldives, that I will bear true faith and allegiance to [t]he Maldives, that I will uphold the fundamental rights of the Maldivian citizens" (Judicial Services Commission Act, s. 13). The JSC's code of conduct for judges instructs judges to decide matters pursuant to the constitution and the prevailing law. If neither provides guidance, they have recourse to "Islamic shari`ah" (Code of Conduct for Judges, s. 1.1; The Judges Act of the Maldives, Law no. 13/2010, s. 5[a]). Indeed, the Judicature Act provides that "[a]ll matters adjudicated before the courts of The Maldives shall be decided upon in accordance with the Constitution, the laws, and the Islamic shari`ah" (Judicature Act of the Maldives, Act no. 22/2010, s. 3.).

Deciding the content of shari`a in [t]he Maldives, however, is a process framed by the presumption of Sunni Muslim homogeneity.[14] Shari`a talk in the Maldives is animated less by worries about the religious other than such talk might be in places such as Egypt or Lebanon, which feature significant Christian minority populations.[15] The Maldives, however, countenances a different concern with religious difference. Amid a presumptively homogenous population of Sunni Muslims, shari`a talk is animated by debates that increasingly pit "moderate" Muslims against a more conservative variety (Helios Life Association 2012, 1). In a manner analogous to those proposing bans on Islamic law in the United States, the latter worry about the implications of globalization and foreigners on the purity of Maldivian values.

Shari`a as Rule of Law: A Case Study on Religious Freedom and the Dhimmi Rules

The vignettes already discussed reveal how a shift in polarity between competing social imaginaries can have distinct implications for the meaning and significance of shari`a talk in a particular polity. Acknowledging the significance of these shifts, can help us appreciate just why attempts to work around or obviate shari`a in the MENA's transitional climate will fail. Shari`a can no more be eliminated from the politics of transition in the MENA than Enlightenment or Christian ideals can be removed from the political imagination in the United States and the United Kingdom. Such a statement does not mean everyone must situate his or her respective positions in terms of some historical norm that has its pedigree from a premodern Islamic legal source. Rather, one cannot avoid thinking about or contending with variations of shari`a in places such as the MENA.

However one might define shari`a, on issues such as minority rights and religious freedom, a historical fiqh tradition (the dhimmi rules) remains part of the contemporary imagination. That tradition demands addressing, for its rules alarm non-Muslims when they consider Muslim attitudes toward religious others. Certainly in the North Atlantic world, these rules have led researchers, policy analysts, and polemicists to proclaim the inherent intolerance of Islam and Muslims. In the Muslim world, these rules find expression in schools and informal settings and have informed the ways in which Muslims understand their place in the world amid the non-Muslim other. The rules themselves are rarely applied in legal systems; indeed, their formal application is more the exception than the rule.[16] But they continue to inform Muslim discourse about community, difference, and tolerance of the other, whether in the form of school textbooks[17] or Islamist political platforms. To cite another example, in the 2007 Draft Political Party Platform of Egypt's Muslim Brotherhood, certain provisions limit key posts to Muslims only, as Kristen Stilt writes:

> The Platform requires that the president be a male Muslim . . . Under the heading of "civil state," the Platform says that there are basic religious positions in the state and the officials who hold them are responsible for protecting and encouraging religion. In Egypt, these officials are the President and the Prime Minister . . . Further, decisions concerning war are decisions governed by Islamic law, and cannot be made by a non-Muslim. (Stilt 2010, 101)

Stilt acknowledges that this provision, perhaps among the most controversial in the platform, must be couched within the larger context of dissent *within* the Brotherhood (Brown and Hamzawy 2008; Stilt 2010, 85)—a context of dissent that has increased since the ouster of Hosni Mubarak.

The persistence of shari`a talk in the Muslim-majority world demands that we think *through* the historical tradition and modern legal statecraft rather than work around the tradition entirely. As I have addressed at greater length elsewhere (see Emon 2012a), one approach is to think of shari`a as rule of law. To view shari`a as rule of law will permit a more robust appreciation of how, to what extent, and in relation to what other legal norms (both formal and informal) Islamic law is embedded in the modern state. Shari`a as rule of law offers a lens through which to appreciate the long, deep transition from the Islamic empire to the modern state, as well as the often informal implications of that early transition for the more formal role that shari`a-based discourses can have going forward in today's transitional states in the MENA region.

Rule of Law as Bounded Claim Space

The phrase *rule of law* is used in a variety of disciplines, from law and philosophy to development economics. Rule of law, for many, has become the panacea for good governance, the promotion of human development, and vibrant market economies. At minimum, rule of law implies that governing officials are no less held to the law than are those who are subjects of a particular ruling regime.

Moreover, it is invoked as an alarm against the threat of arbitrary discretion (Raz 1994). Beyond that, it can refer to legal institutions, regulatory frameworks, constitutional design, and rights regimes (Dworkin 2004; Tamanaha 2004; Vermeule 2006).

Thinking through rule of law in a comparative *diachronic* perspective—moving from the premodern to the modern—reveals the rhetorical function of rule of law. As I suggest hereafter, rule of law might be better appreciated as a *claim space within which arguments of justice are made.* However, to imagine rule of law as a claim space about governance presumes that the space is bounded in such a way as to render arguments of justice distinctively and intelligibly legal in nature. In this sense, the rule of law approach is not prescriptive but rather rhetorically analytic, offering a standpoint from which to examine the different features of a legal system to better appreciate the conditions that make legal arguments intelligible as distinctively legal. Whether a given legal argument is a dissenting opinion or binding precedent, legal arguments of different weight and persuasion offer insights into the underlying conditions or boundaries that define the claim space of what counts as legal for a particular rule of law system.

An example will suffice to explain the metaphor of boundary and how it helps define the claim space of a given rule of law tradition. In *Baker v. Canada*, a 1999 Supreme Court of Canada decision, a foreign-born woman residing in Canada and having Canadian-born dependents applied for permanent residency. Pursuant to the relevant immigration law provisions, she could apply for permanent residence only from outside Canada. Faced with deportation, she sought an exception on "humanitarian and compassionate" grounds in view of the needs of her children. The Supreme Court of Canada considered, among other things, whether "humanitarian and compassionate" grounds might be informed by international law, specifically the Convention on the Rights of the Child. At the time of the case, Canada was a signatory to the convention, but Parliament had not legislatively implemented the convention into Canadian law. Consequently, the question before the court was whether a convention signed by Canada's executive could inform the Supreme Court's interpretation of domestic immigration law even though the legislature had not legislated the convention into domestic law in any way. The Supreme Court answered affirmatively, with the majority interpreting the purpose of the *Immigration Act* as being the reuniting of families, which it took to be in the "best interests" of the children—a principle enshrined in the ratified but unimplemented convention. In a concurring opinion, Justices Iacobucci and Cory agreed with the result but took issue with the majority's resort to the ratified but unimplemented Convention:

> It is a matter of well-settled law that an international convention ratified by the executive branch of government is of no force or effect within the Canadian legal system until such time as its provisions have been incorporated into domestic law by way of implementing legislation. I do not agree with the

approach adopted by my colleague wherein reference is made to the underlying values of an unimplemented international treaty in the course of the contextual approach to statutory interpretation and administrative law because such an approach is not in accordance with the court's jurisprudence concerning the status of international law within the domestic legal system. In my view we should proceed with caution in deciding matters of this nature lest we adversely affect the balance maintained by our parliamentary tradition, or inadvertently grant the executive the power to bind citizens without the necessity of involving the legislative branch. (*Baker* 1999, 865)

As the concurrence notes, though the executive may have signed the convention, a commitment to parliamentary sovereignty requires that Parliament implement the convention into domestic law. For a court to refer to ratified but unimplemented international conventions is tantamount to allowing the executive to perform an end-run around Parliament. Justices' Iacobucci and Cory's concurrence raised fundamental concerns about the boundaries of Canada's rule of law system.

Rule of law as a claim space turns our attention to the constituent features that define and delimit that space. The judicial debate in *Baker v. Canada* about the status of international legal instruments reveals the boundaries (for example, parliamentary sovereignty) that give content, legitimacy, and intelligibility to a claim of justice made from within Canada's rule of law claim space. Indeed, the debate in *Baker v. Canada* can be recast as being boundary-setting for Canada's rule of law claim space. Rule of law as claim space focuses our attention on the various presumptions about the considerations, doctrines, and arguments that matter when imagining what justice demands (Emon 2014).

Shari`a as Rule of Law?

When applied to shari`a talk, the analytic heft of rule of law rests on the long history of shari`a. From the premodern imperial world of Islam to the modern context of the Westphalian state system, changes in governing organization imply different and distinct boundary conditions for shari`a (Emon 2012a, 17–22, 60–68, 206–18). Accounting for such changes allows us to appreciate the extent to which premodern Islamic legal doctrines (for example, fiqh) were premodern answers to premodern questions whose intelligibility was premised on certain assumptions about the governing enterprise. But what does a change in governing enterprise imply about the questions that require legal response today? Drawing on the work of David Scott, I suggest that the challenge for those engaging in and analyzing shari`a talk in Muslim-majority states is to determine what questions premodern Islamic fiqh once answered, as well as whether the fiqh answers remain apropos to today's questions of law and governance (Scott 2004).

No account can likely offer a coherent image of the premodern claim space of shari`a as rule of law. At most, it can offer glimpses of different features that in aggregation inductively sketch the boundary conditions of intelligibility to premodern legal doctrines. Those features might include a conception of what counts as legal knowledge and education (a curricular component; see Berkey 1992; Emon 2012a, 189–95; Makdisi 1981), the relationship between judicial and enforcement institutions (an institutional component; see Emon 2012a, 183–88; Stilt 2012),[18] theories of interpretation and epistemic authority (an adjudicative component; see Emon 2009; 2012a, 195–206), the relationship between the sovereign and the law (Emon 2012a, 177–83; 2012b), and the role of law in regulating the relationship between the sovereign and the sovereign's other (Emon 2012b, 287–302).

The historical distance between the premodern context of empire (whether imagined or real) that informed the development of premodern legal doctrines begs important questions about whether those premodern doctrines are still good answers to more contemporary questions of governance when the predominant unit of governance today is the Westphalian state. Today's state, whether in the Muslim world or elsewhere, operates in a global context in which domestic law (constitutional and statutory) comes into contact with different forms of international law (whether customary or negotiated by the community of states), transnational corporations that manage global financial investment, and migrant labor flows, among other such things. In the context of transitional states in the MENA where shari`a discourses are increasingly prevalent, the presence of shari`a-based doctrines in the domestic legal arena complicates an already complex legal landscape. Put differently, increased resort to shari`a in countries such as Egypt and Tunisia showcases the high stakes of legal pluralism as different features of the contemporary rule of law claim space vie for priority amid what many worry is legal incommensurability.

In this context of considerable legal pluralism and a fear of incommensurability, opting for one legal tradition over another can be tempting—in short, legal monism. That temptation is not merely an option of political convenience. Rather, as I have argued, the tendency toward legal monism in a context of potential pluralism is inherent to legal systems, whether premodern or modern, Islamic, or constitutional democratic (Emon 2012a, 145–64, 260–313). This tendency is evident in the current debate among legislators in the United States about shari`a and international law, it is implicit in the concurring opinion in *Baker v. Canada*, and it was certainly part of the Islamic legal tradition, in which the presence of non-Muslims challenged the integrity of an avowedly Islamic public sphere. Drawing on the dhimmi rules as examples, I will suggest that the way *through* the Islamic legal tradition is to examine whether the incommensurability is facial or more substantive, investigating the possibilities that follow therefrom.

Legal Pluralism and Incommensurability: The Case of the Dhimmi Rules

The dhimmi rules were doctrines that applied to non-Muslim permanent residents in Islamic lands; examples include the following:

- Non-Muslims must pay a poll tax (*jizya*) to reside in Muslim lands while preserving their different faith commitments and traditions (Emon 2012a, 97–106).
- Non-Muslims must wear distinctive clothing so as to differentiate them from Muslims (Emon 2012a, 131–36).
- Non-Muslims cannot be witnesses in court (Emon 2012a, 136–41).

Facially, these rules discriminate against non-Muslims; there is little doubt that the dhimmi rules are fundamentally incommensurable with other boundary components of a modern Muslim state's rule of law claim space. But facial incommensurability does not actually get at the underlying conditions that made these rules intelligible historically but that render them suspect in a contemporary state legal system. Viewing shari'a as rule of law permits an appreciation of those conditions by inquiring about the premodern questions of governance to which the dhimmi rules were premodern answers. Accounting for the intelligibility of these rules as past answers to past questions allows us to work *through* the rules to reflect on whether the questions they once answered are still being asked and—if they are being asked—whether the dhimmi rules remain coherent answers to those questions today.

The analytic effect of shari'a as rule of law, when applied to the dhimmi rules, shows their intelligibility when tied to an imperial mode of governance premised on a universalist claim of the Islamic message. That mode of governance gave shape to the premodern rule of law claim space. Consider Karen Barkey's reflection on empire:

> An empire is a large composite and differentiated polity linked to a central power by a variety of direct and indirect relations, where the center exercises political control through hierarchical and quasi-monopolistic relations over groups ethnically different from itself. These relations are, however, regularly subject to negotiations over the degree of autonomy of intermediaries in return for military and fiscal compliance. (Barkey 2008, 9)

Empire presumes, at least initially, some mode of conquest and domination by which new subjects are brought under the aegis of the expanding regime. Empire also presumes both a center and a periphery, an assumption that has undeniable implications for the nature of authority and its delegation outward from the center. The negotiation between centralization and decentralization of law and governance across the empire can take, and has often taken, into account the empire's fiscal needs, as well as how to pass those costs to the empire's subjects through various taxation measures.

Empire as a mode of governing had distinct implications for the intelligibility of the dhimmi rules. Indeed, the premodern juristic assumptions of empire fundamentally informed the intelligibility of the dhimmi rules. For the purposes of this chapter, a few examples will suffice.[19] The first example concerns the well-known *jizya*, or poll tax, that dhimmis paid to reside within the Muslim polity while retaining their faith. The *jizya* is intelligible as a tax in an imperial context. As Muslim armies expanded the frontiers of the Muslim empire, they encountered local populations whose lands they sought to conquer. According to the rules of warfare in Islamic law, the Muslim army was to give these local populations three choices: The first was to convert to Islam and become full members of the Muslim empire. The second was to decline conversion but pay a poll tax, the *jizya*, to retain their religious tradition but reside within the Muslim polity. The third was to fight the Muslim army and, if defeated, become subject both in their person and property to the rules of law governing the spoils of war.

The *jizya* as a tax on non-Muslims had a two-pronged function. First, in a context of conquest and imperial expansion, it was a legal device to include new people under the aegis of the ruling regime without having to expend finances and personnel in expensive military battles. Second, as a tax specifically on non-Muslims as opposed to Muslims, it distinguished dhimmis from Muslims, only the latter of whom enjoyed full membership in the Muslim enterprise of governance. Dhimmis would be subject to the law and enjoy its protections but would not have the same scope of legal benefits or burdens as their Muslim coresidents: Their membership was partial, not full.

To both include and exclude the dhimmi was the fundamental function of the dhimmi rules. For example, dhimmis endured legal restraints on building and refurbishing their churches and synagogues in Muslim-governed lands. A review of those legal restraints illustrates that whether dhimmis could build or repair places of workshop depended on both how their land had come under Muslim suzerainty and the taxation regime that applied to the land they occupied.

For some jurists, what mattered most was how the land came under Muslim suzerainty. If the Muslim polity annexed the land through conquest, the dhimmis could not build new religious sites of worship, and some jurists precluded them from refurbishing old ones. Moreover, Malik b. Anas, al-Shafi`i, and Ahmad b. Hanbal required that religious buildings on such lands be destroyed. The Hanafis disagreed about what should happen to existing religious sites. Some Hanafis did not permit destruction; they converted the buildings to residential units. Others, such as Badr al-Din al-`Ayni, allowed dhimmis to refurbish old religious sites so long as they were not made larger than their original size (Emon 2012a, 120).

If the Muslim polity annexed the land through treaty negotiations, then whether the dhimmis could build new religious sites or refurbish old ones depended on how the treaty allocated governing authority and tax liability. Muslim jurists imagined three scenarios:

- If the Muslim governing authorities assumed authority over the land and responsibility for the land tax, the dhimmis could keep their existing religious sites but could not build new ones.
- If the Muslim governing authorities assumed authority over the land but the dhimmis were collectively liable for the land tax (not per capita but as a community having fixed tax liability), existing religious buildings could remain, and whether dhimmis could build new ones depended on the terms of the treaty.
- If the dhimmis retained authority over the land and were also responsible for the land tax, they could keep old religious buildings and build new ones (Emon 2012a, 121).

These regulations, in aggregate, find their intelligibility in an assumed imperial political reality. Conquest, treaty, and grants of regional autonomy informed the ways in which premodern Muslim jurists imagined the dhimmi in the shari`a rule of law claim space. The different allocations of authority and tax liability reveal distinct imperial strategies of expansion, centralization and decentralization, and fiscal management.

These imperial conditions must be appreciated if we are to appreciate the questions of governance to which the dhimmi rules were answers. All too often, these rules are read out of context, whether in the original Arabic or in translation, as if their meaningfulness and intelligibility are philologically self-evident to the modern reader. But the modern reader is himself or herself embedded in a context in which the prevailing enterprise of governance conditions the intelligibility of law on considerably different bases. To ignore the distance between the past and the present is to indulge a presentist reading of these rules that shari`a as rule of law is designed to correct.

Conclusion: Working It Through

As a corrective, shari`a as rule of law recasts legal doctrines as answers to questions that are premised on a set of governing conditions. On this approach, understanding legal doctrines such as the dhimmi rules requires that we examine the questions of governance the dhimmi rules were meant to answer. Consequently, suggesting that the rules were meant to answer whether Islam was, from its beginnings in the seventh century, tolerant or intolerant of the non-Muslim other seems simplistic. Such an argument would perpetuate an anachronism in the form of critique. The dhimmi rules were legal doctrines designed to manage demographic diversity in an Islamic imperial context. To the extent that these premodern answers are invoked in the present to justify certain governance outcomes, they pose real conflicts with other legal regimes to which modern states ascribe and that, in aggregate, constitute the modern state's rule of law claim space. Indeed, the modern nation-state, whether in the MENA or elsewhere, participates in an international context in which customary international law, treaty law, human rights conventions, and other multilateral, bilateral, and regional endeavors constitute and delimit its rule of law claim space. In the case of MENA countries that seek to apply Islamic law, the result is legal pluralism in a unitary, centralizing state. In short, whereas in the premodern period the dhimmi rules were responses to questions about how to govern a demographically diverse, decentralized, and imperial domain, in today's MENA, the dhimmi rules reflect a different question—namely, how to govern a modern state in a context of demographic diversity, a unified centralizing state, *and* legal pluralism.[20]

But legal pluralism in fact does not mean, however, legal pluralism as a normative commitment by which different and distinct legal traditions recognize their legal other, give space to their legal other, and ultimately even yield their own legal sovereignty in favor of their legal other. In the legally pluralist Middle East and North Africa, managing conflicts between competing legal traditions in unitary, centralized (or centralizing) states requires either a harmonization between legal traditions or a choice between them. But if we imagine rule of law as a claim space, then choosing one over the other might do violence to the very conditions that define the claim space at the outset. The more one chooses one legal tradition over another, the more the latter might be understood as having been fundamentally excised from the claim space. Though some might applaud the excision of Islamic law from the MENA region entirely, the discussion in part 1 shows not only why such excision is impractical but also why such an excision might incur serious social, cultural, and political costs. That is not to say, however, that activists, scholars, and political leaders ought not levy critiques as they work through the implications of Islamic law. For instance, when Islamic parties and activists invoke the dhimmi rules today, whether as political polemic or even as possible bases for constitutional organization, they fail to see that the intelligibility of those rules relied on certain political formations that no longer exist. This is no mere theoretical problem. At the time of writing, the Islamic State of Iraq and al-Sham (ISIS) has not only declared an imperial caliphate in Iraq but has invoked the dhimmi rules in regions of Syria under its control.[21] ISIS's invocation of the dhimmi rules, coupled with its quest for the redemptive caliphal empire, arguably reflects its utter disregard for the borders that demarcate nation-states. Ironically, though, its disregard is more form than substance; its promotion of an Islam that sanctions violent spectacle has certainly created sufficient compliance for purposes of (per)forming its state (Emon, 2011).

Returning, then, to the dhimmi rules, the question that remains is how to work *through* these doctrines in a context of legal pluralism. In modern MENA states, Islamist parties want to participate in the state even while inheriting legal systems that are highly integrated with the international community of states and transnational actors. In the context of this chapter, the way of working through will depend on the specifics of the particular legal issue and so will require an issue-by-issue engagement with the particular legal context. However, one way of thinking through the dhimmi rules in the context of the modern state is to recognize what the dhimmi rules were trying to do. First, they represent the messy business of governing a diverse polity—a challenge incumbent on any country that has a diverse demographic. Second, they represent a regime of both inclusion and exclusion. On the one hand, dhimmis were included within the Muslim polity as permanent residents, subject to the law of the Muslim sovereign and entitled to its protection. On the other hand, the dhimmi rules served as a constant reminder that though dhimmis were permanent residents, they were not full members of the polity. No less than premodern empires, modern states invoke laws on citizenship, immigration, and refugees to negotiate the different degrees to which those who are subject to their laws are rendered full or partial members of the state. Third, and most pressing in the Muslim-majority context, the dhimmi rules raised important questions of trust and belonging: Could those who are not full members of the polity be entrusted with leadership, military service, or any other task that upholds the interests of the sovereign? The dhimmi rules reflected this uncertainty by limiting the roles that dhimmis could play in the Muslim empire. For instance, dhimmis could not hold leadership positions or serve in the military, but they could serve in other capacities. In a modern state that measures inclusion and exclusion by means of citizenship and immigration laws, to what extent can—or should—the premodern dhimmi rules contribute additional content about who can be entrusted with leadership of the modern state?

These questions can merely be posed, no more, in this chapter—the answers must come from the polities whence these questions resound. But these questions showcase a way of thinking through Islamic legal doctrines such as the dhimmi rules. To think through the Islamic legal tradition in this way not only reflects the already existing repository of ideas and values in the region but also puts them into dialogue with other ideas and values that new regimes in the region have inherited as constituent of their state's rule of law claim space.

References

Ahdar, Rex, and Nicholas Aroney, eds. 2010. *Shari`a in the West*. Oxford: Oxford University Press.

Asad, Talal. 2003. *Formations of the Secular: Christianity, Islam, Modernity*. Palo Alto, CA: Stanford University Press.

Barkey, Karen. 2008. *Empire of Difference: The Ottomans in Comparative Perspective.* Cambridge, UK: Cambridge University Press.

BBC News. 2012. "Maldives MP Stabbed to Death Outside His Home." *BBC News*, October 2. http://www.bbc.co.uk/news/world-asia-19797538

Berkey, Jonathan. 1992. *Transmission of Knowledge in Medieval Cairo: A Social History of Islamic Education.* Princeton, NJ: Princeton University Press.

Brown, Nathan J., and Amr Hamzawy. 2008. *The Draft Party Platform of the Egyptian Muslim Brotherhood: Foray into Political Integration or Retreat into Old Positions?* Washington, DC: Carnegie Endowment for International Peace. http://www.carnegieendowment.org/files /cp89_muslim_brothers_final.pdf.

Center for Security Policy (CSP). 2010. *Shariah: The Threat to America.* Washington, DC: Center for Security Policy.

Central Intelligence Agency. 2013. *The World Factbook 2013–14.* Washington, DC. https://www.cia .gov/library/publications/the-world-factbook/geos/mv.html.

Doumato, Eleonore. Spring 2003. "Manning the Barricades: Islam According to Saudi Arabia's School Texts." *Middle East Journal* 57 (2): 230–47.

Dworkin, Ronald. 2004. "Hart's Postscript and the Character of Political Philosophy." *Oxford Journal of Legal Studies* 24 (1): 1–37.

Dyzenhaus, David. 1993. "Law and Public Reason." *McGill Law Review* 38:367–93.

Dyzenhaus, David, ed. 1999. *Recrafting the Rule of Law: The Limits of Legal Order.* Oxford: Hart Publishing.

Emon, Anver M. 2008. "The Limits of Constitutionalism in the Muslim World: History and Identity in Islamic Law." In *Constitutional Design for Divided Societies*, edited by Sujit Choudhry, 258–86. Oxford: Oxford University Press.

———. 2009. "To Most Likely Know the Law: Objectivity, Authority and Interpretation in Islamic Law." *Hebraic Political Studies* 4 (4): 415–40.

———. 2011. "Banning Shari`a." *The Immanent Frame*, September 6. http://blogs.ssrc.org /tif/2011/09/06/banning-shari.

———. 2012a. *Religious Pluralism and Islamic Law: Dhimmis and Others in the Empire of Law*, vol. of *Oxford Islamic Legal Studies.* Oxford: Oxford University Press.

———. 2012b. "On Sovereignties in Islamic Legal History." *Middle East Law and Governance* 4 (2/3): 265–305.

———. 2014. "On Statutory Interpretation and the (Canadian) Rule of Law: Interpretive Presumptions as Boundary Setting." *Theory and Practice of Legislation* 3 (1): 45–89.

Emon, Anver M., Ellen Lust, and Audrey Macklin. 2011. "Interview with Rabab al-Mahdi." *Middle East Law and Governance* 3 (1/2): 225–29.

Fuller, Lon. 1973. *The Morality of Law*, rev. ed. New Haven, CT: Yale University Press.

Hamid, Shadi. May/June 2011. "The Rise of the Islamists: How Islamists Will Change Politics, and Vice Versa." *Foreign Affairs* 90 (3): 40–47.

Helios Life Association. 2012. *Maldives: Sudden Reversals in the Implementation of ICCPR Commitments.* Etzgen, Switzerland: Helios Life Association. http://www2.ohchr.org /english/bodies/hrc/docs/ngos/HLA_Maldives_HRC105.pdf.

Henderson, Joan C. 2008. "The Politics of Tourism: A Perspective from the Maldives." *Tourismos: An International Multidisciplinary Journal of Tourism* 3 (1): 99–115.

Humphreys, Stephen. 2010. *Theatre of the Rule of Law: Transnational Legal Intervention in Theory and Practice, Cambridge Studies in International and Comparative Law.* Cambridge, UK: Cambridge University Press.

Kahn, Paul W. 2011. *Political Theology: Four New Chapters on the Concept of Sovereignty.* New York: Columbia University Press.

Kaplan, Robert D. 2010. *Monsoon: The Indian Ocean and the Future of American Power.* New York: Random House.

Kolig, Erich. 2010. "To Shari`aticize or Not to Shari`aticize: Islamic and Secular Law in Liberal Democratic Society." In *Sharia in the West,* edited by Nicholas Aroney and Rex Ahdar, 255–78. Oxford: Oxford University Press.

Makdisi, George. 1981. *The Rise of Colleges: Institutions of Learning in Islam and the West.* Edinburgh: Edinburgh University Press.

Milbank, John. 2010. "Shari`a and the True Basis of Group Rights: Islam, the West, and Liberalism." In *Sharia in the West,* edited by Nicholas Aroney and Rex Ahdar, 135–57. Oxford: Oxford University Press.

Mir-Hosseini, Ziba. 2003. "The Construction of Gender in Islamic Legal Thought and Strategies for Reform." *Hawwa* 1 (1): 1–28.

———. 2012. "Women in Search of Common Ground: Between Islamic and International Human Rights Law." In *Islamic Law and International Human Rights Law: Searching for Common Ground?,* edited by Anver M. Emon, Mark Ellis, and Benjamin Glahn, 291–303. Oxford: Oxford University Press.

Nasheed, Mohammad. 2013. "The Guesthouse Enterprise." *Minivan News,* March 23. http://minivannews.com/travelandarts/comment-the-guesthouse-enterprise-54979.

Nazeer, Ahmed. 2012. "Custom Seize Two Men Carrying Books about Christianity." *Minivan News,* September 30. http://minivannews.com/society/custom-seize-two-men-carrying-books-about-christianity-44580.

Nazir-Ali, Michael. 2010. "Islamic Law, Fundamental Freedoms, and Social Cohesion: Retrospect and Prospect." In *Sharia in the West,* edited by Nicholas Aroney and Rex Ahdar, 71–89. Oxford: Oxford University Press.

Niyaz, Ahmed. October 2010. "Terrorism and Extremism: A Threat to Maldives Tourism Industry." *UNISCI Discussion Papers* 24:221–31.

Philp, Catherine. 2014. "Pay Taxes in Gold or Die, Christians in Syria Told." *The Times* [London], March 4, 31.

Picard, Michel. 2008. "Balinese Identity as Tourist Attraction: From 'Cultural Tourism' (*Pariwisatabudaya*) to 'Bali Erect' (*Ajeg Bali*)." *Tourist Studies* 8:155–73.

Raz, Joseph. 1994. "The Rule of Law and Its Virtue." In *The Authority of Law: Essays on Law and Morality,* 210–29. Oxford: Clarendon Press. Originally published in *The Authority of Law* (Oxford: Clarendon Press, 1979).

Robinson, J. J. 2012. "Police Arrest Four in Connection with Murder of MP Afrasheem." *Minivan News,* October 3. http://minivannews.com/politics/police-arrest-four-in-connection-with-murder-of-mp-afrasheem-44832.

Scheyvens, Regina. August 2011. "The Challenge of Sustainable Tourism Development in the Maldives: Understanding the Social and Political Dimensions of Sustainability." *Asia Pacific Viewpoint* 52 (2): 148–64.

Scott, James. 1998. *Seeing Like a State.* New Haven, CT: Yale University Press.

Scott, David. 2004. *Conscripts of Modernity: The Tragedy of Colonial Enlightenment.* Durham, NC: Duke University Press.

Shakeela, Aishath, and David Weaver. 2012. "Resident Reactions to a Tourism Incident: Mapping a Maldivian Emoscape." *Annals of Tourism Research* 39 (3): 1337–58.

Skillen, James W. 2010. "Shari`a and Pluralism." In *Sharia in the West*, edited by Nicholas Aroney and Rex Ahdar, 91–102. Oxford: Oxford University Press.

Sruthijith, K. K. 2012. "GMR Maldives Spat: Maldives' Decision against GMR Part of Political Strategy That Pits Orthodoxy against India." *The Economic Times*, December 12. http:// articles.economictimes.indiatimes.com/2012-12-09/news/35689598_1_maldivian-people -s-majlis-gmr-infrastructure/2.

Stilt, Kristen. Fall 2010. "'Islam Is the Solution': Constitutional Visions of the Egyptian Muslim Brotherhood." *Texas International Law Journal* 46 (1): 73–108.

——. 2012. *Islamic Law in Action: Authority, Discretion, and Everyday Experiences in Mamluk Egypt.* Oxford: Oxford University Press.

Sunstein, Cass R., and Adrian Vermeule. 2003. "Interpretation and Institutions." *Michigan Law Review* 101 (4): 885–951.

Tamanaha, Brian Z. 2004. *On the Rule of Law: History, Politics, Theory.* New York: Cambridge University Press.

Taylor, Charles. 2003. *Modern Social Imaginaries.* Durham, NC: Duke University Press.

Toobin, Jeffrey. 2005. "Swing Shift; Annals of the Law." *The New Yorker* 81 (September 12): 42–51.

United States Agency for International Development (USAID). June 2005. *Afghanistan Rule of Law Project.* http://www.usip.org/sites/default/files/file/usaid_afghanistan.pdf.

Vermeule, Adrian. 2006. *Judging under Uncertainty: An Institutional Theory of Legal Interpretation.* Cambridge, MA: Harvard University Press.

Wickham, Carrie R. 2011. "The Muslim Brotherhood and Democratic Transition in Egypt." *Middle East Law and Governance* 3 (1/2): 204–23.

Williams, Archbishop of Canterbury the Rt. Rev. Dr. Rowan. 2010. "Civil and Religious Law in England: A Religious Perspective." In *Sharia in the West*, edited by Nicholas Aroney and Rex Ahdar, 293–308. Oxford: Oxford University Press.

Wright, Tom. 2012. "Diplomacy Falters in Maldives." *Wall Street Journal*, February 13. http://www .wsj.com/articles/SB10001424052970204795304577218790340193040.

Cases, Legislation, Government Documents

Baker v. Canada (Minister of Citizenship and Immigration), [1999] 2 SCR 817.

Code of Conduct for Judges (Maldives). http://en.jsc.gov.mv/docs/JudgesCodeFinal.pdf.

Fourth Tourism Master Plan, 2013–2017. http://www.tourism.gov.mv/downloads/news/2012/4TMP _DRAFT_Vol_2_BACKGROUND_ANALYSIS.pdf.

The Judges Act of the Maldives. Law No. 13/2010.

Judicial Services Commission Act (Maldives). http://en.jsc.gov.mv/docs/JSCAct.pdf.

Report on International Religious Freedom. 2012. Washington, DC: US State Department. http:// www.state.gov/j/drl/rls/irf/2012/sca/208434.htm.

Notes

1. See, for instance, the USAID 2005 report on the Afghan Rule of Law Project, available at http://www.usip.org/sites/default/files/file/usaid_afghanistan.pdf.

2. On rule of law debates generally, and on Islam specifically, see Dyzenhaus (1999) as well as Emon (2012a), especially chapter 5.

3. Available at http://www.capitol.tn.gov/Bills/107/Bill/SB1028.pdf.

4. Available at https://www.sos.ok.gov/documents/questions/755.pdf.

5. Anver M. Emon, "Banning Shari'a," *The Immanent Frame*, September 6, 2011, http://blogs.ssrc.org/tif/2011/09/06/banning-shari'a/.

6. On the other versions of this bill, see Emon, "Banning Shari'a."

7. For a critique of the secular as it relates to religion, see Asad (2003).

8. On the political context underlying Mir-Hosseini's analysis, see Mir-Hosseini (2012, 293–98).

9. Kaplan, Robert D. 2010. *Monsoon: The Indian Ocean and the Future of American Power.* New York: Random House.

10. On tourism and its implications for local cultural politics, see Picard (2008).

11. For the video, see http://www.youtube.com/watch?v=i5H64OOkeXA.

12. *Fourth Tourism Master Plan, 2013–2017* (Male: Maldives Ministry of Tourism, 2012), 19, http://www.tourism.gov.mv/downloads/news/2012/4TMP_DRAFT_Vol_2_BACKGROUND _ANALYSIS.pdf. For more on the ongoing political debates around guest houses, as well as former President Nasheed's characterization of the issue, see his speech (2013) on the guest house enterprise.

13. Moreover, in 2006, the Maldives issued a reservation to article 18 (freedom of religion and conscience) of the International Covenant on Civil and Political Rights (ICCPR). See http://www.geneva-academy.ch/RULAC/international_treaties.php?id_state=136.

14. Indeed, this is evident in the US State Department's *2012 Report on Religious Freedom*, available at http://www.state.gov/j/drl/rls/irf/2012/sca/208434.htm.

15. In a limited fashion, Christian missionaries continue to contest the Maldives' prohibitions against proselytizing faiths other than Islam. See, for example, Nazeer (2012).

16. One exception is Saudi Arabia's use of these rules to inform wrongful death compensation claims. See Emon (2012a, 232–45).

17. See, for example, Doumato (2003).

18. On the "institutional turn" in law, see Sunstein and Vermeule (2003).

19. For greater detail, see Emon (2012a, ch. 3).

20. On the state, see James Scott (1998).

21. On ISIS's invocation of the dhimmi rules, see Philp (2014).

3 Moral Contestations and Patriarchal Ethics: Women Challenging the Justice of Muslim Family Laws

Ziba Mir-Hosseini

ARTICULATION OF THE ethical values and norms of Islam's sacred texts has been, at least until recently, the business of Muslim scholars. The classical jurists—through fiqh, the science of Islamic jurisprudence—endeavored to translate these values and norms into legal rulings to govern various aspects of personal and public life in Muslim societies (see also this volume, chapters 1 and 2). These rulings (*ahkam*), which still constitute the established interpretations of shari'a, reflect premodern conceptions of justice that entitle individuals to different rights on the basis of their faith, status, and gender. During the twentieth century, however, these rulings were confronted by the ideals of universal human rights, equality, and personal freedom. In this encounter, some Muslims came to see the classical rulings as unjust and discriminatory and the interpretations of the textual sources on which they were based as hypocritical, or at best contradictory. The plethora of literature published by religious houses on relations between Islam and human rights, democracy, and women's rights, as well as the intensity of the debates among Muslims over what "true" Islam is and what shari'a stands for, speak of a collective anxiety that comes when old dogmas and constructs lose their theological validity.

This debate is nowhere more intense than in the area of gender relations, where the gap between contemporary notions of justice and rights and those that inform established interpretations of shari'a is most evident. These interpretations, as embodied in fiqh rulings, uphold a patriarchal model of family, treating women as second-class citizens and placing them under male authority. The religious legitimization of patriarchy raises a host of questions: The sacred texts speak of justice, but what do they mean by this? Does it include the notion of equality for women before the law? If so, how are we to understand those passages in the texts that appear not to treat men and women as equals? Can gender equality and shari'a-based laws go together?

Such key questions have been the subject of heated debate among Muslims for more than a century, a debate that continues to be tainted by the legacy and politics of the colonial occupation of Muslim lands. Broadly speaking, we can say that Muslim participants in this debate fall into three broad camps: The first are traditional Muslims and those Islamists who claim that the established interpretations of shari'a, as embodied in fiqh rulings, are divine, open neither to change nor to reinterpretation. The second camp consists of those feminists who consider religion to be inherently patriarchal and thus see any engagement with it to be a futile and incorrect strategy. The third camp comprises Muslim feminist scholars and activists who challenge the patriarchal ethics of Muslim family laws from within, demanding that law and practice reflect the egalitarian principles and values of Islam.

This difference of approach speaks of different reactions to the confrontation between two systems of values: one shaped by the ideals of universal human rights, equality, and personal freedom as found and advocated in international human rights documents such as CEDAW (the Convention on the Elimination of All Forms of Discrimination Against Women) and the other rooted in earlier conceptions of justice, gender, and rights as found in the classical fiqh rulings that continue as the source of family law, to legitimize and sustain gender inequality in contemporary Muslim contexts.

In this chapter, I explore this confrontation, which unfolded in the course of the twentieth century, giving birth to a new gender discourse that has changed the terms of several debates among Muslims—most of all the debate over gender rights. I refer to Musawah (www.musawah.org), which defines itself as a global movement for equality and justice in the Muslim family. Attracting partners from across the globe, the movement was launched in February 2009 at a gathering in Kuala Lumpur, hosted by the pioneering Malaysian women's group Sisters in Islam. Musawah links scholarship with activism to bring fresh perspectives on Islamic teachings, with the aim of contributing constructively to the reform of family laws and practices.

In 2011 Musawah initiated a long-term and multifaceted project on rethinking the notion of authority in Muslim family laws. As a founding member of Musawah and convener of this project, I describe the formation of the movement, conveying some of our thinking and our internal debates. I also write as an anthropologist, a participant-observer in these debates.

I begin by outlining the twentieth-century shifts in the politics of religion, law, and gender that in the present century have led to the emergence of new forms of research and activism of which Musawah is a part. I then discuss the foundation of Musawah as a knowledge-building movement, outlining Musawah's conceptual framework, the project on rethinking the construction of authority in Muslim family laws, and the challenges that Musawah confronts in bringing about an egalitarian construction of family law from within Muslim legal tradition. I end by considering the potential of this new research and of these emerging Muslim feminist voices for changing the patriarchal ethics of established interpretations of shari'a.

Two themes run through the chapter and link its different parts. First, gender equality is a modern ideal that has only recently, with the expansion of human rights and feminist discourses, become inherent to generally accepted conceptions of justice. In Islam, as in other religious traditions, the idea of equality between men and women was neither relevant to notions of justice nor part of the juristic landscape. To use an idiom from Muslim juristic tradition, gender equality is among the "newly created issues" (*masa'il mustahdatha*)—that is, an issue for which there are no previous rulings. Simply put, gender equality is an issue that Muslim jurists did not have to address until the twentieth century.

Second, the idea of gender equality has created an "epistemological crisis" in Muslim legal tradition that Muslims have been trying to resolve, with varying degrees of success, since the late nineteenth century. I borrow this concept from the philosopher Alasdair MacIntyre, who argues that every rational inquiry is embedded in a tradition of learning and that that tradition reaches an epistemological crisis when, by its own standards of rational justification, disagreements can no longer be resolved rationally (see also this volume, chapter 1). According to MacIntyre, this gives rise to an internal critique that will eventually transform the tradition if it is to survive (MacIntyre 1988, 350–52; 2000). In Muslim legal tradition, I contend, the internal critique and epistemological breakthrough came about only recently, with the rise of new reformist and feminist voices and scholarship (Mir-Hosseini 2013).

Twentieth-Century Shifts

In much of the Muslim world, the first part of the twentieth century saw the expansion of secular education, the retreat of religion from politics, and the secularization of laws and legal systems. With the end of colonial occupation, many of the new nation-states founded in Muslim-majority countries put aside Islamic jurisprudence (fiqh) in most areas of law. But in the area of family law, they selectively reformed classical fiqh rulings, codifying and grafting them onto new and unified legal systems inspired by Western models (Anderson 1976; Mahmood 1972; see also this volume, chapters 1 and 2). The best-known exceptions were Saudi Arabia, which preserved classical fiqh as fundamental law and attempted to apply it in all jurisdictional spheres; Turkey, which abandoned fiqh in all areas of law; and Muslim populations that came under communist rule. In other countries where classical fiqh remained the main source of family law, the impetus and extent of reform varied. However, with the exception of Tunisia (which banned polygamy), the classical fiqh construction of the marital relationship was retained more or less intact.

Reforms were introduced from within the framework of Muslim legal tradition by mixing principles and rulings from different fiqh schools and by established procedural devices such as eclectic choice (*takhayyur*) and mixing (*talfiq*); the exercise of *ijtihad* remained limited. Reforms focused on increasing the age of marriage, expanding women's access to judicial divorce, and restricting men's right to polygamy (Rahman 1980). This involved requiring the state registration of marriage and divorce or the creation of new courts to deal with marital disputes. The state now had the power to deny legal support to marriages and divorces that did not comply with official state-sanctioned procedures. Classical fiqh conceptions of marriage and family remained unchallenged (Mir-Hosseini 2009; Welchman 2004).

These developments transformed the interaction between fiqh and social practice and had two consequences that continue to haunt the Muslim politics of gender and law reform. First, the partial reform and codification of fiqh provisions led to the creation of a hybrid family law that was neither classical fiqh nor Western. As codes and statute books took the place of classical fiqh manuals, family law was no longer solely a matter for Muslim scholars operating within particular fiqh schools but also became the concern of legislative assemblies of a particular nation-state; these had neither the legitimacy nor the inclination to challenge premodern interpretations of shari`a. Deprived of the power to define and administer family law, the custodians and practitioners of traditional fiqh were no longer accountable to the community but were confined to the ivory tower of the *madrasa* or seminary. They lost touch with changing political realities and were unable to meet the epistemological challenges of modernity, including the idea of gender equality. These developments in practice worked against women, limited their ability to bargain with religious law and their access to legal justice, and gave fiqh rulings a new lease on life: They could now be applied through the machinery of modern nation-states. By contrast, recent studies of medieval and Ottoman court archive materials and judgments show that not only did judges generally take a liberal and protective attitude toward women, but also women could choose between legal schools and judges (Rapoport 2005; Sonbol 1996; Tucker 2000).

The second consequence of these changes was that putting aside fiqh as the source of other areas of law reinforced the religious tone of those provisions that related to gender rights, turning them into the last bastion of traditionalist Islamic authority. Thus, fiqh became a closed book, removed from public debate and critical examination. It was in these circumstances, then, that we witnessed the emergence of a new gender discourse and a genre of literature, which elsewhere I have termed *neotraditionalist* (Mir-Hosseini 1999; 2003), although perhaps *neofiqh* is a better term. Published by religious houses in both Muslim and Western countries, this literature is available (much of it on the internet) in a variety of languages, English among them. Largely written by men—at least until very recently—these texts range from sound scholarship to outright polemic. Not being strictly legal in their language or arguments, the texts are also accessible to the general public. Aware of and sensitive to criticisms of the patriarchal bias of Muslim family laws, these texts are punctuated by general and abstract statements such as "Islam affirms the basic equality between men and women," "Islamic law grants women all their rights," and "Islamic law honors and protects women." The authors' stated aim is to "clarify misunderstandings" about the "status of women in Islam." They quote Qur'anic verses and *ahadith* that affirm the essential equality of the sexes in marriage, which they define using the terms "equity" and "complementarity." They reread the sacred texts in search of new solutions to what they perceive to be a new and worrying challenge: women's demand for legal equality (Mir-Hosseini 2012).

Despite their variety and diverse cultural origins, what these rereadings have in common is an oppositional stance and a defensive or apologetic tone: oppositional because their concern is to resist the advance of what they see as alien "Western" values and lifestyles; apologetic because they attempt, by going back to classical fiqh texts, to explain and justify the gender biases that they inadvertently reveal. They see gender equality as an imported Western concept that must be rejected. In its place they put forward the notions of "complementarity" and "balance" in gender rights and duties. They formulate these notions, premised on a theory of the "naturalness" of shari'a law, as follows: Although men and women are created equal and are equal in the eyes of God, the roles assigned to men and women in creation are different, and classical fiqh rules reflect this difference. Differences in rights and duties, these authors maintain, do not mean *in*equality or *in*justice. On the contrary, if correctly understood, they are in line with human nature, hence the very essence of justice (Mir-Hosseini 2009).

In the second part of the twentieth century, with the rise of various new forms of political Islam, the neofiqh texts and their gender discourse became closely identified with Islamist political movements whose rallying cry was "return to shari'a." The new political Islam had its biggest triumph in 1979 with the popular revolution in Iran that brought Islamic clerics to power. The same year saw the dismantling of reforms introduced earlier in the century by modernist governments in Iran and Egypt, as well as the introduction of the Hudud Ordinances in Pakistan. Yet this was also the year when the UN General Assembly adopted the Convention on the Elimination of All Forms of Discrimination Against Women (CEDAW), giving gender equality a clear international legal mandate (Mir-Hosseini 2012).

The decades that followed saw the concomitant development, globally and locally, of two powerful but seemingly opposed trends. On the one hand, with the encouragement of CEDAW, in the 1980s, the international women's movement expanded and NGOs emerged, with international funding and transnational links, to give women a voice in policymaking and public debate over the law. On the other hand, Islamist political movements—whether in power or in opposition—started to invoke shari'a in order to dismantle earlier efforts at reforming or secularizing laws and legal systems. Tapping into popular demands for social justice, the Islamists presented this dismantling as "Islamization," the first step in bringing about their vision of a moral and just society.

Political Islam's drive for Islamization, however, had some unintended consequences. Most important, in several countries, the Islamists brought classical fiqh texts out of the closet, exposing them to unprecedented critical scrutiny and public debate. Muslim women now found ways to sustain a critique, from within, of patriarchal readings of shari'a and of the gender biases of fiqh texts. At the same time, a new wave of Muslim reform thinkers started to respond to the Islamist challenge and to take Islamic legal thought onto new ground. Using the conceptual tools and theories of other branches of knowledge, these thinkers expanded on the work of previous reformers and developed further interpretive-epistemological theories. In this respect, the works of Mohammad Arkoun (Gunther 2004), Khaled Abou El Fadl (2001), Nasr Hamid Abu Zayd (Kermani 2004), Mohammad Mojtahed Shabestari (Vahdat 2004), and Abdolkarim Soroush (Sadri and Sadri 2000) are among the most important and relevant. Unlike earlier twentieth-century reformist thinkers, these new thinkers no longer seek an Islamic fiqh genealogy for modern concepts such as equality, human rights, and democracy. Instead, they emphasize the ways in which religion is understood, religious knowledge is produced, and rights are constructed in Islamic legal tradition.

By the early 1990s, there were clear signs of the emergence of a new consciousness, a new way of thinking about gender that was feminist in its aspiration and demands, yet Islamic in its language and sources of legitimacy (Badran 2002; Mir-Hosseini 1996; 2006; Najmabadi 1998). Some versions of this new discourse came to be labeled "Islamic feminism"—a conjunction that was unsettling to many Islamists and some secular feminists. This new discourse is nurtured by Muslim feminist scholars, who are uncovering a hidden history and rereading textual sources to contribute to an egalitarian construction of Muslim family laws.

In short, twentieth-century shifts in the politics of religion, law, and gender brought Muslim women onto center stage. Rather than merely being the subjects of family law reforms, they became active participants in the production of religious knowledge and in the process of lawmaking. At the same time, gender equality became inherent in global conceptions of justice, acquiring a clear legal mandate through CEDAW, which all Muslim states (except Iran, Somalia, and Sudan) have ratified—though in most cases subject to "Islamic reservations" (Krivenko 2009; Musawah 2012).

The Making of Musawah

The new century opened with the politics of the "war on terror" in the aftermath of the September 11 attacks on the United States. This added another layer of complexity to the politics of gender and Islam, with the illegal invasions of Afghanistan and Iraq being justified, in part, as campaigns to promote "freedom" and "women's rights." In conjunction with the double standards employed in promoting UN sanctions, these initiatives showed that—as is also the case with shari'a and fiqh ideals—international human rights and feminist ideals are vulnerable to gross political manipulation, suffering a wide gap between ideal and practice. Many scholars and activists found themselves in the crossfire. On the one hand, Islamists were denying equality in the name of shari'a; on the other, hegemonic global powers were pursuing a neocolonial agenda in the name of feminism and human rights. For those of us who found ourselves in this position, the only way out of our predicament was to bring Islamic and feminist frameworks together lest our century-old quest for legal equality remain hostage to the fortunes of domestic political groups and global agendas (Mir-Hosseini 2012). Because the vast majority of women whose rights we championed were believers and wanted to live according to the teachings of Islam, effective change could come only through meaningful and constructive engagement with those teachings.

To pursue our ends, we needed to reclaim the egalitarian ethics of Islam, creating a public voice for our vision of Islam. We faced two different forms of resistance. The first came from religious establishments, leaders, and groups who claim to know and speak for "authentic" Islam. They view both international human rights and feminism with suspicion and refuse to engage meaningfully with their advocates. Their vision of Islam is the one that reaches most Muslim women, who consequently do not share our quest for legal equality. The other form of resistance is from women's rights nongovernmental organizations (NGOs) and activists, a large majority of whom are reluctant to address religious perspectives on women's issues. For many of them, Islam itself is the main obstacle in their struggle for equality; they work solely within the terms and discourse of human rights frameworks.

One of the very few women's NGOs that are happy to identify as both Islamic and feminist is the Malaysia-based Sisters in Islam (SIS). Since its inception in 1988, SIS has argued for women's rights and equality from within an Islamic framework, engaging scholars and the media in a public debate on religion. Zainah Anwar, founder and director of SIS, has written about her own journey from the local politics of Islam and women in Malaysia to the creation of SIS—and the launch of Musawah (Anwar 2009). In February 2007, she organized a workshop in Istanbul that brought together a diverse group of women's activists and scholars from different countries. The meeting led to the formation of a planning committee charged to set out the vision, principles, and conceptual framework of the movement that we called Musawah (Equality) with the aim of forging a new strategy for reform. Inspired by the activism of Moroccan women and their success at bringing radical reforms in Moroccan family law in 2004, we adopted their slogan: "Change is necessary and change is possible" (see Collectif 95 Maghreb-Egalité 2005). We sought to link research with activism to develop a holistic framework integrating Islamic teachings, universal human rights law, national constitutional guarantees of equality, and the lived realities of women and men.

We commissioned a number of concept papers by reformist thinkers such as Amina Wadud, Khaled Abou El Fadl, and Muhammad Khalid Masud, as a way of opening new horizons for thinking and to show how the wealth of resources within Islamic tradition, as well as in the Qur'anic verses on justice, compassion, and equality, can support the promotion of human rights and a process of reform toward more egalitarian family relations. These papers were published as the book *Wanted: Equality and Justice in the Muslim Family* (Anwar 2009); we made them available in Arabic, English, and French and used them as the basis for a wider discussion with a larger group of Muslim scholars and human rights and women's rights activists. Our discussions continued for two years and included two further workshops in Cairo and London, as well as regular electronic communications among the members of the committee. Our efforts culminated in the *Musawah Framework for Action* (Anwar 2009, 11–21).[1]

Drawing on the latest Muslim reformist thought and feminist research, our *Framework for Action* grounds our claim to equality and arguments for reform simultaneously in Islamic and human rights frameworks. Taking a critical feminist perspective, but working within the tradition of Islamic legal thought, we invoke two of the latter's main distinctions. The first distinction is between shari'a and fiqh. In Muslim belief, shari'a (lit. "the way"; see also this volume, chapters 1 and 2) is God's will as revealed to the Prophet Muhammad. Fiqh ("understanding") is Islamic jurisprudence, the process and the methodology for discerning shari'a and extracting legal rules from the sacred sources of Islam: the Qur'an and the *Sunna* (the practice of the Prophet as recorded in *ahadith* traditions). Like any other system of jurisprudence, fiqh is mundane, temporal, and local.

The second distinction is between the two main categories of legal rulings (*ahkam*): *'ibadat* (ritual/spiritual acts) and *mu'amalat* (social/contractual acts). Rulings in the first category, *'ibadat*, regulate relations between God and the believer, where jurists contend there is limited scope for rationalization, explanation, and change, since they pertain to the spiritual realm and divine mysteries. This fixity is not the case with *mu'amalat*, which regulate relations among humans and remain open to rational considerations and social forces. Most rulings concerning women and gender relations belong to the category of *mu'amalat*.

These analytic distinctions gave us the language and conceptual tools with which to challenge patriarchy from within Muslim legal tradition. The genesis of gender inequality in fiqh, we argued, lies in a contradiction between the ideals of shari`a and the patriarchal structures in which these ideals unfolded and were translated into legal norms. Islam's call for freedom, justice, and equality was submerged in the norms and practices of Arab society and culture in the seventh century and the formative years of Islamic law. As the fiqh schools emerged, patriarchal norms began to be assimilated into their rulings through a set of theological, legal, and social theories and assumptions that were part of the fabric of society and that reflected the state of knowledge of the time. Existing marriage practices and gender ideologies were sanctified, and women were gradually excluded from the production of religious knowledge (Mir-Hosseini 2003). Women had once been among the main transmitters of the *hadith* traditions, but by the time the fiqh schools were consolidated, more than a century after the Prophet's death, they had reduced women to sexual beings and placed them under men's authority. The farther we move from the era of the Prophet, we argued, the more we find women marginalized and deprived of political clout. Their voice in the production of religious knowledge is silenced, their presence in public space curtailed—their critical faculties so far denigrated as to make their concerns irrelevant to lawmaking processes. An extensive debate is ongoing in the literature on just this subject. Some argue that the advent of Islam weakened the patriarchal structures of Arabian society, others that it reinforced them. The latter also maintain that, before the advent of Islam, society was undergoing a transition from matrilineal to patrilineal descent and that Islam facilitated this by giving patriarchy the seal of approval— and, moreover, that Qur'anic injunctions on marriage, divorce, inheritance, and whatever relates to women both reflect and affirm such a transition (Ahmed 1992; Mernissi 1991; Smith 1985; Spellberg 1991).

Engaging with International Human Rights Law

Musawah actively pursues international advocacy and engagement with international human rights treaties and instruments, with a particular focus on CEDAW. Our aim is to break down the perceived dichotomy between Islam and human rights and promote perspectives derived from the Musawah framework. We share the framework with the CEDAW committee and other relevant actors as an alternative approach that demystifies religious-based objections and constructs arguments based on Islamic teachings, human rights, constitutional guarantees of equality, and social realities. We also submit thematic reports on article 16 of CEDAW, on which many Muslim states have placed reservations on the grounds of its incompatibility with "Islamic shari`a."[2] This article requires "state parties to take all appropriate measures to eliminate discrimination against women in all matters relating to marriage and family relations."

To understand the dynamics of interaction between Muslim countries and the CEDAW committee, and to offer our egalitarian vision of shari`a, we conducted a study in which we reviewed the documents of forty-two countries that are home to a Muslim majority or significant Muslim minority populations and that reported to the committee between 2005 and 2010. The report, published as *CEDAW and Muslim Family Laws: In Search of Common Ground* (Musawah 2011), comprises three parts: The first examines the justifications by Muslim states that failed to reform discriminatory elements of family laws in their countries. The second examines the CEDAW committee's responses to such justifications. In the third part, we show how the Musawah *Framework for Action* can be used to respond to Muslim states' justifications for noncompliance as well as to open possibilities for more just and equal Muslim family laws.

Our report reveals that Muslim states and the CEDAW committee are talking at cross purposes and how the language and rhetoric used by each side hinder meaningful dialogue. The justifications offered by states for their failure to introduce legal equality are either that the laws and practices in their respective countries are based on "shari`a" and are therefore immutable or that customs, traditions, and culture prevent them from implementing the CEDAW committee's recommendations. Not being in a position to challenge the state's version of the shari`a, the CEDAW committee has responded by reiterating its obligation to reform discriminatory laws and to comply with the committee's recommendation. We aim to break into this dialogue of the deaf by introducing the Musawah approach, and particularly by highlighting the crucial distinction between shari`a and fiqh. Through training sessions and seminars, we present the Musawah approach to those women's human rights NGOs and activists who are involved in preparing CEDAW shadow reports and are engaging with CEDAW committee members on key issues related to Islam and women's rights in their countries. (Shadow reports, which are submitted by NGOs, provide activists with an opportunity to present their own narrative of the status of women's rights in their respective countries as distinct from that presented by their government.)

Rethinking the Patriarchal Family

In 2010, as part of its knowledge-building area of work, Musawah initiated a long-term, multifaceted project to rethink the notion of authority in Muslim family laws. It has two interconnected elements.[3] The first is the production of new feminist knowledge that critically engages with those concepts that continue to legitimate and institutionalize a patriarchal model of family and gender relations. Here the focus is on the two legal concepts of *qiwama* and *wilaya*. As constructed in classical fiqh and as embodied in contemporary laws and practices in Muslim contexts, both concepts place women under male guardianship. *Qiwama* is understood as a husband's authority over and responsibility to provide for his wife. *Wilaya* denotes the guardianship rights of a father (or, in his absence, another male member of the family) over his sons until they are adults and his daughters until they are married. The second element of the project involves documenting the life stories of Muslim women and men in different countries with the aim of revealing how they experience, understand, and contest these two legal concepts in their lived realities.[4]

Our aim is to insert women's concerns and voices into the processes of production of religious knowledge and legal reform. In this sense, what we are doing is part of the larger struggle for the democratization of knowledge in Islam and for the authority to interpret its sacred texts. For the project, we commissioned eight background papers that expound and interrogate the construction of these two concepts in classical fiqh texts and their underlying religious and legal rationales. The papers focus on the theological, jurisprudential, ethical, historical, sociological, and legal aspects of *qiwama* and *wilaya*. They focus especially on Qur'an 4:34, which provides the main textual evidence in support of men's authority over women. Indeed, it is often the only verse that ordinary Muslims know that pertains to family law:

> Men are *qawwamun* (protectors/maintainers) in relation to women,
> according to what God has favored some over
> others and according to what they spend from
> their wealth. Righteous women are *qanitat* (obedient)
> guarding the unseen according to what God
> has guarded. Those [Women] whose *nushuz* (rebellion)
> you fear, admonish them, and abandon them in
> bed, and *adribuhunna* (strike them). If they obey you, do not
> pursue a strategy against them. Indeed, God is
> Exalted, Great.

This translation is by Kecia Ali (2003), who points out that any rendering of the highlighted words amounts to an interpretation—and indeed they are now the focus of debate among Muslims. The translations I have given approximate the consensus of classical jurists, as reflected in the rulings (*ahkam*) that they devised to define marriage and gender relations. Marriage is a contract that in legal structure was patterned after the contract of sale (*bay'*), which served as model for most contracts in Islamic jurisprudence. The contract establishes a set of default rights and obligations for each party, some supported by legal force, others by moral sanction. Those with legal force revolve around the themes of sexual access and compensation, as expressed in two legal concepts: *tamkin* and *nafaqa*. *Tamkin*, obedience or submission—specifically sexual access—was the husband's right and thus the wife's duty, whereas *nafaqa*, or maintenance—specifically, shelter, food, and clothing—was the wife's right and the husband's duty. A wife's refusal to fulfill her marital duties put her in a state of *nushuz* (disobedience), which could free the husband from the duty to maintain her (Mir-Hosseini 2003).

Such a conception of marriage, in modified form, continues to be the backbone of Muslim family laws. It reflects, we argue, the patriarchal culture and ethics of the world in which the classical jurists lived. It is premised on a single postulate: that God made men *qawwamun* of women and placed them under male authority. This postulate, we show, is derived from a reading of Qur'an 4:34 that is no longer in line with either contemporary notions of justice or the lived realities of the vast majority of Muslims.

In one of our studies, Omaima Abou-Bakr shows how and through what processes the first sentence—*al-rijal qawwamun 'ala al-nisa' bi-ma faddal Allah ba'dahum 'ala ba'd wa-bi-ma anfaqu min amwalihim* (men are *qawwamun* in relation to women according to what God has favored some over others and according to what they spend from their wealth)—was continually reinterpreted (Abu Bakr 2015). She identifies four stages in the evolution of interpretations. In the first, the sentence was isolated from the rest of the Qur'an and turned into "an independent and separate (trans-contextual) patriarchal construct." This, she shows, was done by taking the term *qawwamun* out of its immediate context and transforming it into a grammatical *masdar* (a verbal noun or infinitive) of *qiwama*. In the second stage, when the concept was consolidated, rational arguments and justifications were provided for hierarchal relations between men and women. In the third stage, *qiwama* was expanded by linking it to the idea that men have an advantage over women, from the last phrase in Qur'an 2:228—"But men have a *daraja* (degree) over them (women)." This phrase, part of a long passage on the theme of divorce, was again taken out of its immediate context and interpreted as further support for male superiority; moreover, selected *ahadith* were also invoked to establish women's duty of obedience. The final stage came in the twentieth century with the modernist thinkers, who linked *qiwama* with the theory of the naturalness of "Islamic law" and the ideology of domesticity, using pseudopsychological knowledge to argue for men's and women's different natures (*fitra*).

Our other studies show that male authority over women, being a juristic construct without Qur'anic basis, cannot be defended on religious grounds. The term *qawwamun*, from which the jurists derived the concept of *qiwama*, only appears once in the Qur'an in reference to marital relations. Many other verses speak of the essential equality of men and women in the eyes of God and the world. In relation to marriage, two other terms appear more than twenty times: *ma'ruf* (good practice) and *rahmah wa muwadah* (compassion and love).

The closely related term *wilaya* does occur in the Qur'an, in the sense of friendship and mutual support, but never as endorsing male authority over women—the interpretation of the term that is enshrined, alongside *qiwama*, in juristic rulings on marriage (Lamrabet 2015).

One of main objectives of the project is to bring insights from feminist theory and gender studies into the debates around Muslim family law, and to ask new questions. Why and how did verse 4:34, and not other verses in the Qur'an, become the foundation for the legal construction of marriage? Why is *qiwama* still the basis of gender relations in the imagination of modern-day jurists and Muslims who resist and denounce the idea of equality in marriage as alien to Islam? How, and through what juristic processes, was men's authority over women legitimated and translated into laws? What does male guardianship, derived from the concepts *qiwama* and *wilaya*, entail in practice? How can we Muslim women rethink and reconstruct these concepts in ways that reflect our own notions of justice? What kind of family do shari`a-based laws aim to protect? What do equality and justice mean for women and the family? Do they entail identical rights and duties in marriage?

Life Stories and Lived Realities

The second element of our project involves case studies from different countries, which show the actual working of these gendered concepts. The cases enable us to counter apologetic arguments based on ideology and hypothetical cases rather than on empirical evidence regarding women's experience and the lived realities of Muslim families. Islamist and traditionalist discourses present *qiwama* and *wilaya* as enjoining "protection," not discrimination. They argue that ensuring the "protection" of women guarantees a happy and stable family in which men are providers and women are maintained and protected.

These studies show that such arguments ignore the situation of most Muslim families today and conceal the domination and discrimination that men's authority over women entails in practice. The fiqh model of family rests on a series of assumptions: that in all classes, in all families, at all times, men are the sole providers and women do not contribute to household income; that a harmonious and stable family depends on men's rights to own, to decide, and to command; and that if women were given equal rights, the entire order would be threatened. If these assumptions were once valid (which is open to question), they are so no longer. Few families today—and generally only the better off—can exist with men as sole providers able to exert their legal authority, yet men's identity and sense of worth depends on the appearance, if not the fact, that they are the primary breadwinners and that their wives depend on them. When men fail to live up to an ideal that has little basis in reality, the result is often marital discord—and violence. The structure of authority by which men are, at least in legal theory, the owners of family resources and the sole decision makers often forces women to make unfair compromises in marriage and to give up the few rights they have. Polygamy and unequal access to divorce and child custody do not create harmony and happiness but only pain and suffering for women and children, and often for men too. Empirical studies, including those of marital disputes in courts, reveal a real disjuncture between the fiqh model of the family as defined in classical fiqh and practices (see, for instance, Al-Sharmani 2013; Mir-Hosseini 1993; Welchman 1999). Happy and stable families, we contend, are those in which there is equality, mutuality in rights and responsibilities, and resources shared by the spouses.

In 2015, the first outcome of the project appeared as a collected volume, *Men in Charge? Rethinking Authority in Muslim Legal Tradition* (Mir-Hosseini et al. 2015). Its main thesis is that male authority over women cannot be supported on religious grounds and that *qiwama* and *wilaya*, in the sense of placing women under male guardianship, are not Qur'anic concepts but juristic constructs that in time became the building blocks of patriarchy in Muslim legal tradition. The concepts rest on the assumption that God gave men authority over women, a theological fiction that became a legal postulate whose main function now is to sustain gender inequality. The contributors to the volume are scholars from different disciplines and backgrounds who use their expertise to demystify these terms and reinterpret them from within the Islamic tradition and its core theological and ethical principles. Above all, they ground these understandings in lived realities and women's experiences, which form the core of the life stories element of the project (Al-Sharmani and Rumminger 2015).[5]

Musawah is still in its formative phase, and the project I have outlined is still unfinished. The movement has, however, already been studied in several master's and doctoral theses, as well as in academic publications, and it has been recognized as an attempt to bridge the gulf between Islamic and human rights discourses, and also as a new and important social movement (for example Derich 2010; Sunder 2009). Musawah has also been the subject of academic criticism. For example, Margot Badran sees Musawah as promoting "communalism" and imposing a global agenda on women's local struggles for equality (Badran 2011, 83–85). Anthropologist Lila Abu-Lughod, on the other hand, criticizes Musawah and its advocacy of egalitarian Muslim family laws as an elitist project that is "incommensurable" with the lived realities of the Muslim women she studied in an Egyptian village. By opting for a rights framework, Abu-Lughod claims, Musawah's researchers fail to recognize the entanglement of their work with global governance and structures of inequality; thus, wittingly or unwittingly, they are conforming to "imperialist" and "neo-liberal" policies (Abu-Lughod 2013, 177–200). This is not the place for a detailed response to these criticisms.[6] Suffice it to say that, although Badran and Abu Lughod differ in their perspectives, their comments ignore or misunderstand the origins and objectives of the feminist project in Islam. They do not appreciate the personal, ethical, and spiritual side of the project, whose proponents seek to promote the values of equality, justice, and human dignity that they believe are inherent in their religion. Speaking for Musawah, I deny that we are naively idealistic; we are quite familiar with global politics and the shortcomings of the rights framework. Indeed, we are seeking to do something about both. We come from and operate in different local, national, regional, and institutional contexts, and we know our constraints. However, we are determined to be constructive—to aspire for and work toward bringing about egalitarian interpretations of shariʿa.

Concluding Remarks

Let me summarize my argument and consider the potential of Muslim feminist voices in transforming the patriarchal ethics in Muslim legal tradition. One of the key obstacles that Muslim women have confronted in their struggle for equality is the linkage between the religious and political dimensions of identity in Muslim contexts. This linkage is not new—it has its roots in the colonial era—but it took on a new and distinct expression in the 1970s with the resurgence of Islam as a political and spiritual force. With the end of the colonial era, the rise of secular and despotic regimes in Muslim countries and their suppression of progressive forces left a vacuum that was filled by Islamist movements. Strengthened dramatically by the success of the Iranian Revolution of 1979, Islamist movements gained momentum with the subsequent perceived defeat of communism. With the US response to the events of September 11—in particular its invasions of Afghanistan in 2001 and Iraq in 2003—Muslim women found themselves in the crossfire.

A second strand of my argument is that the rise of political Islam had certain unintended—yet, in my view, positive—consequences: notably, the demystification of power games conducted in a religious language. This, in turn, led to the emergence by the 1990s of new reformist and feminist voices and scholarship in Islam that began to offer an internal critique of premodern interpretations of shariʿa. Musawah is only one among many Muslim groups and voices that are now active in meetings as well as through lively online and social media, challenging patriarchy from within. In doing so, they are changing the terms of debates among Muslims and, above all, paving the way for the democratization of religious knowledge and for an egalitarian interpretation of shariʿa. Their very existence is clear proof that a paradigm shift in the politics of Islam and gender is well under way—the old rationale and logic for patriarchal laws, previously undisputed, have lost their power to convince and cannot be defended on ethical grounds.

Finally, in Muslim contexts, the struggle for gender equality is as much political as it is theological, and we find it difficult, and at times futile, to decide when theology ends and politics begins. A growing popular understanding of the nature of this struggle has been one of many unintended consequences of the rise of political Islam and the politics of the War on Terror. These developments revealed the extent to which the fate of women's rights in Muslim contexts is vulnerable to local and global power struggles between forces with other priorities. Groups such as Musawah articulate a public voice that can break down ideological polarizations such as those between "secular" and "religious" feminism, and between "Islam" and "human rights," to which women's quest for equality and, in turn, the transition to democracy have remained hostage since the early twentieth century. They point us to the main site of battle, which is between patriarchal and authoritarian structures on the one hand and egalitarian, pluralist, and democratic aspirations and forces on the other.

References

Abou El Fadl, Khaled. 2001. *Speaking in God's Name: Islamic Law, Authority and Women*. Oxford: Oneworld.

Abu Bakr, Omaima. 2015. "Interpretive Legacy of *Qiwamah* as Exegetical Construct." In *Men in Charge? Rethinking Authority in Muslim Legal Tradition*, edited by Ziba Mir-Hosseini, Mulki Al-Sharmani, and Jana Rumminger, 44–64. London: Oneworld.

Abu-Lughod, Lila. 2013. *Do Muslim Women Need Saving?* Cambridge, MA: Harvard University Press.

Ahmed, Leila. 1992. *Women and Gender in Islam: Historical Roots of a Modern Debate*. New Haven, CT: Yale University Press.

Ali, Kecia. 2003. "Muslim Sexual Ethics: Understanding a Difficult Verse, Qur'an 4:34," February 11. http://www.brandeis.edu/projects/fse/muslim/diff-verse.html.

Anderson, James Norman. 1976. *Law Reforms in the Muslim World*. London: Athlone.

Anwar, Zainah. 2009. *Wanted: Equality and Justice in the Muslim Family*. Kuala Lumpur: Musawah, an Initiative of Sisters of Islam. http://www.musawah.org/wanted-equality-and-justice-muslim-family-english.

Badran, Margot. 2002. "Islamic Feminism: What's in a Name?" *Al-Ahram Weekly Online* 569, January 17–23. http://weekly.ahram.org.eg/2002/569/cu1.htm.

———. 2011. "From Islamic Feminism to a Muslim Holistic Feminism." *Institute of Development Studies Bulletin* 42 (1): 78–87.

Collectif 95 Maghreb-Egalité. 2005. *Guide to Equality in the Family in the Maghreb*. Women's Learning Partnership for Rights, Development and Peace. http://learningpartnership.org/guide-to-equality.

Derich, Claudia. 2010. "Transnational Women's Movements and Networking: The Case of Musawah for Equality in the Family." *Gender, Technology and Development* 14 (3): 405–21.

Gunther, Ursula. 2004. "Mohammad Arkoun: Towards a Radical Rethinking of Islamic Thought." In *Modern Muslim Intellectuals and the Qur'an*, edited by Suha Taji-Farouki, 125–67. Oxford: Oxford University Press.

Kermani, Navid. 2004. "From Revelation to Interpretation: Nasr Hamid Abu Zayd and the Literary Study of the Qur'an." In *Modern Muslim Intellectuals and the Qur'an*, edited by Suha Taji-Farouki, 169–92. Oxford: Oxford University Press.

Krivenko, Ekaterina Yahyaoui. 2009. *Women, Islam and International Law: Within the Context of the Convention on the Elimination of All Forms of Discrimination against Women*. Leiden, Netherlands, and Boston: Martinus Nijhoff.

Lamrabet, Asma. 2015. "An Egalitarian Reading of the Concepts of 'Khilafah,' 'Wilayah' and 'Qiwamah.'" In *Men in Charge? Rethinking Authority in Muslim Legal Tradition*, edited by Ziba Mir-Hosseini, Mulki Al-Sharmani, and Jana Rumminger, 65–87. London: Oneworld.

MacIntyre, Alasdair. 1988. *Whose Justice? Which Rationality?* Notre Dame, IN: University of Notre Dame Press.

———. 2000. "The Rationality of Traditions." In *Moral Disagreements: Classic and Contemporary Readings*, edited by Christopher W. Gowans, 204–16. London: Routledge.

Mahmood, Tahir. 1972. *Family Law Reforms in the Muslim World*. Bombay: N.M. Tripathi.

Mernissi, Fatima. 1991. *Women and Islam: An Historical and Theological Enquiry*. Oxford: Blackwell.

Mir-Hosseini, Ziba. 1993. *Marriage on Trial: Comparative Study of Islamic Family Laws in Iran and Morocco*. London: I.B. Tauris.

———. 1996. "Stretching the Limits: a Feminist Reading of the Shari`a in Post-Khomeini Iran." In *Islam and Feminism: Legal and Literary Perspectives*, edited by Mai Yamani, 285–319. London: Ithaca Press.

———. 1999. *Islam and Gender: The Religious Debate in Contemporary Iran*. Princeton, NJ: Princeton University Press.

———. 2003. "The Construction of Gender in Islamic Legal Thought: Strategies for Reform." *Hawwa: Journal of Women in the Middle East and the Islamic World* 1 (1): 1–28.

———. 2006. "Muslim Women's Quest for Equality: Between Islamic Law and Feminism." *Critical Inquiry* 32:629–45.

———. 2009. "Towards Gender Equality: Muslim Family Laws and the Shari`a." In *Wanted: Equality and Justice in the Muslim Family*, edited by Zainah Anwar, 23–63. Kuala Lumpur: Musawah, an Initiative of Sisters of Islam. http://www.musawah.org/wanted-equality-and -justice-muslim-family-english.

———. 2011. "Beyond 'Islam' vs 'Feminism.'" *Institute of Development Studies Bulletin* 42 (1): 67–77.

———. 2012. "Women in Search of Common Ground: Between Islamic and International Human Rights Law." In *Islamic Law and International Human Rights Law: Searching for Common Ground?*, edited by Anver M. Emon, Mark S. Ellis, and Benjamin Glahn, 291–303. Oxford: Oxford University Press.

———. 2013. "Justice, Equality and Muslim Family Laws: New Idea, New Perspectives." In *Gender and Equality in Muslim Family Law: Justice and Ethics in Islamic Legal Tradition*, edited by Ziba Mir-Hosseini, Kari Vogt, Lena Larsen, and Christian Moe, 7–34. London: I.B. Tauris.

Mir-Hosseini, Ziba, Mulki Al-Sharmani, and Jana Rumminger, eds. 2015. *Men in Charge? Rethinking Authority in Muslim Legal Tradition*. London: Oneworld.

Musawah. 2011. *CEDAW and Muslim Family Laws: In Search of Common Ground*. Kuala Lumpur: Sisters in Islam. http://www.musawah.org/cedaw-and-muslim-family-laws-search-common -ground.

Najmabadi, Afsaneh. 1998. "Feminism in an Islamic Republic: Years of Hardship, Years of Growth." In *Islam, Gender, and Social Change*, edited by Yvonne Yazbeck Haddad and John Esposito, 59–84. New York and Oxford: Oxford University Press.

Rahman, Fazlur. 1980. "A Survey of Modernization of Muslim Family Law." *International Journal of Middle East Studies* 11:451–65.

Rapoport, Yossef. 2005. *Marriage, Money and Divorce in Medieval Islamic Society.* Cambridge, UK: Cambridge University Press.

Sadri, Mahmoud, and Ahmed Sadri. 2000. *Reason, Freedom, and Democracy in Islam: Essential Writings of `Abdolkarim Sorush,* translated and edited with a critical introduction. Oxford: Oxford University Press.

Al-Sharmani, Mulki. 2013. "*Qiwama* in Egyptian Family Laws: 'Wifely Obedience' between Legal Texts, Courtroom Practices and Realities of Marriages." In *Gender and Equality in Muslim Family Law: Justice and Ethics in Islamic Legal Tradition,* edited by Ziba Mir-Hosseini, Kari Vogt, Lena Larsen, and Christian Moe, 37–55. London: I.B. Tauris.

Al-Sharmani, Mulki, and Jana Rumminger. 2015. "Understanding *Qiwamah* and *Wilayah* through Life Stories." In *Men in Charge? Rethinking Authority in Muslim Legal Tradition,* edited by Ziba Mir-Hosseini, Mulki Al-Sharmani, and Jana Rumminger, 219–55. London: Oneworld.

Smith, Jane. 1985. "Women, Religion and Social Change in Early Islam." In *Women and Social Change,* edited by Yvonne Yazbeck Haddad and Ellison Banks Findly, 19–36. Albany, NY: SUNY Press.

Sonbol, Amira El Azhary. 1996. *Women, Family and Divorce Laws in Islamic History.* Syracuse, NY: Syracuse University Press.

Spellberg, Denise. 1991. "Political Action and Public Example: `Aisha and the Battle of the Camel." In *Women in Middle Eastern History: Shifting Boundaries of Sex and Gender,* edited by Beth Baron and Nikki Keddie, 45–57. New Haven, CT: Yale University Press.

Sunder, Mahdavi. 2009. "Reading Qur'an in Kuala Lumpur." *The Faculty Blog, University of Chicago Law School,* February 16. http://uchicagolaw.typepad.com/faculty/2009/02/reading-the-quran-in-kuala-lumpur.html.

Terman, Rochelle. 2016. "Islamophobia, Feminism and the Politics of Critique." *Theory, Culture and Society* 33, 2: 77–102.

Tucker, Judith. 2000. *In the House of Law: Gender and Islamic Law in Ottoman Syria and Palestine.* Berkeley: University of California Press.

Vahdat, Farzin. 2004. "Post-Revolutionary Modernity in Iran: The Subjective Hermeneutics of Mohammad Mojtahed Shabestari." In *Modern Muslim Intellectuals,* edited by Suha Taji-Farouki, 193–224. Oxford: Oxford University Press.

Welchman, Lynn. 1999. *Islamic Family Law: Text and Practice in Palestine.* Jerusalem: Women's Centre for Legal Aid and Counselling.

———. 2004. *Women's Rights and Islamic Family Law: Perspectives on Reform.* London: Zed Press.

Notes

1. Available in five languages; see http://www.musawah.org/about-musawah/framework-action.
2. See http://www.musawah.org/international-advocacy/thematic-reports.
3. See http://www.musawah.org/what-we-do/knowledge-building.
4. See http://www.musawah.org/what-we-do/qiwamah-and-wilayah.
5. The planned outcomes are videos and a book of women's narratives.
6. I have engaged with Badran's criticisms elsewhere (Mir-Hosseini 2011); see also Terman (2015) for an incisive analysis of why Abu Lughod's line of criticism is problematic.

4 Gender, Legality, and Public Ethics in Morocco

Zakia Salime

#RIPAmina/We Are All Amina Filali

The suicide of sixteen-year-old Amina Filali sparked a public outcry and heated controversies about unethical law in Moroccan society. Amina's case started with an alleged rape when she was fifteen years old; continued with her marriage to the alleged rapist, Mustafa, a twenty-four-year-old man; and ended with her death on March 10, 2012. Amina was a student and, according to some accounts, a factory worker; her husband works as a driver and lives with his parents. After spending a year in what some have described as a very abusive marriage, Amina ingested rat poison, readily available in subaltern neighborhoods, to end her life. But the heart of the controversy was not about this individualized economy of death, nor the "indirect" "structural violence" behind it (Skidmore 2004, 160), but rather its legalization.

At stake was article 20 of the Moroccan Family Code, which authorizes a judge to legalize the marriage of a minor (someone younger than eighteen years old), and article 475 of the penal code, which authorizes a judge to authorize the marriage of a rapist to his victim. Underlying this legal rationale are questions of family honor and a girl's disgrace in relation to a broken hymen. Article 475 states:

> Whoever, without violence, threats, or fraud, abducts or attempts to remove or divert a minor under eighteen years, is punished by imprisonment of one to five years and a fine of 200 to 500 dirhams. When a nubile minor is removed or diverted and marries her captor, the latter may only be prosecuted when a complaint is filed by a person(s) entitled to apply for annulment of marriage and cannot be sentenced until after the annulment of marriage been pronounced.

The news of Amina's suicide went viral on the internet as human rights and cyberactivists began to spread the word through Twitter and Facebook, gathering support and calling for action. Over the following week, the hashtag #RIPAmina choked Twitter feeds while activists formed online groups that soon materialized as street protests. The local press, even in its mainstream form, expressed the same outrage. Soon, too, the international press jumped on the news to reiterate its conviction that Islam and women's rights cannot coexist. According to *yabiladi*, an online Moroccan independent newspaper, "Morocco" was the fourth most popular search on Google on March 10, 2012 (Jaabouk 2012). To Amina's supporters, women's rights activists, and cyberactivists, Amina was a "child" forced to marry her rapist so that he could escape legal accountability and a prison sentence. But conflicting accounts about Amina's involvement in a "romantic" relationship with Mustafa, as described by Islamist ministers, cast doubts on her claims of rape. Widely shared media discussions of the "archaic" nature of Moroccan rape and marriage laws became further complicated through bloggers' emphasis on the postcolonial construction of the Moroccan penal code as a remnant of the legal French *Ancien Régime*.

I mapped these debates as they took place online and offline, in movie production, during international campaigns, on individual blogs, on Facebook pages, and in the feminist press. This map required hours of analysis of online traffic, including comments, blog posts, Facebook posts, satirist representations, and artistic expression. It also required scrutiny of the streams of reactions and responses posted online by individuals who entered the debate to understand, discuss, or share information about the case.

I ask the following questions: What does this plurality of voices say about the varied "ethical imaginaries" (Hefner 2013) that circulate in the cultural landscape of interconnected "revolutionary" subjectivities? How is religion positioned in this debate? What do these debates say about the plural normative orders through which women's lives are understood and regulated?

Amina and the "Arab Spring"

Morocco entered its Arab Spring on February 20, 2011, through mass protests spearheaded by the movement February 20 for Change (Feb20). If the protests pushed aside doubts about Morocco's alleged "exceptionalism" (Maghraoui 2011, 1), the royal address of March 10, 2011, restated this "exceptionalism" through constitutional reform, early elections, and promises for further consolidation of the rule of law. The November 2012 elections brought the Islamists of the Justice and Development Party to power after they won a majority vote, but the weekly agitations and street protests led by Feb20 did not fade. Extending the Arab Spring to Morocco, the movement opposed a "gifted constitution" and the king's continuing hold on the political institutions and the economic resources of the country (Maghraoui 2011; Salime 2012). The Feb20 protests were no different in their demands from those we have witnessed throughout the region. Not only have we seen the emergence of "new subjects" of "rights and dignity," but we have also heard claims about the necessary secularization of the everyday, including the rights to eat in public during Ramadan, to enjoy sexual freedom, to abort, to enjoy equal access to inheritance rights, and to enjoy cultural and religious pluralism.

Amina's suicide would have had little effect on public sentiment and collective affect had it not occurred at the peak of these protests. Instead, her suicide fueled an already tense political climate in streets marked by weekly protests organized by the Feb20 movement. New groups, including Woman-Choufouch, Alternative Movement for Individual Freedoms (MALI?), and Femen Maroc, became the expression of a "normative pluralism" (see this volume, introduction) that was mediated and contested through events such as the Slut Walk held in Rabat on August 13, 2011, or the calls for a public lunch during Ramadan by MALI? Amina's suicide served as a catalyst for this new wave of body and sexual politics.

We should also keep in mind that the North African uprisings were not the outcome of an organized movement having a centralized leadership or institutionalized structures. Instead, they were a multicentered, diffuse, and spontaneous response by a plurality of publics that came together around an individual act of self-immolation by a street vendor, Tunisian Mohamed al-Bouazizi (see Bamyeh 2011; Dabashi 2012). It is not surprising then, to see Amina's individual act transformed into a public uproar that transgressed the geographical boundaries of the nation state and the organizational frontiers of old feminist groups.

Amina's suicide brought to the surface the intensity of frustrations that social media activists, secularists, "new feminists" (Salime 2012; 2014), and established feminist organizations have had with the state's hold on public morality. More important, this is the first time that women's bodies and body parts, notably the hymen, have been the focus of a wide range of public debates, visual representations, documentaries, international petitions, and television shows. Amina became the icon of these modern subjects of rights or modern legal subjects whose formation is mediated through an urban middle-class sense of ethical legality.

Furthermore, Amina's case stirred the unsettled frustrations about the unfinished project of reforming family law that had been initiated and championed by Moroccan feminist groups since the 1990s. The case injected a new dynamic into feminist activism by enabling liberal feminists to force their entry into the gated and well-guarded article 20 of the Family Code. For instance, the Democratic Association for Moroccan Women, the Union for Women's Action, the Moroccan Democratic League for Women's Rights, all with a long history of activism on behalf of women's rights, adopted Amina's case by joining street protests and sit-ins and by providing a platform for voicing Amina's parents' version of the story, hiring lawyers, and helping then perform and recraft the narrative of rape before the media.

As was the case during the "agonistic" (Mouffe 2000; 2007) debates about the form of women's status in family law during the 1990s, the press played a central role in representing Amina's case within two clashing temporalities of the secular–modern–liberal and the "archaic" Islamists now heading the government. The controversial discourse of the Islamist ministers, some of whom dismissed talk of rape and others of whom defended Amina's marriage, only increased feminist fears about further Islamization of state laws.

Pluralist Sites and Publics

The protest over Amina's death did not emanate from well-established feminist organizations. Rather, scattered individuals occupying virtual locations raised the issue and led the mobilization. Thousands of tweets were dedicated to Amina through which a young generation of men and women, not necessarily having been active in previously organized movements, expressed their outrage. For instance, opening an account dedicated to Amina's memory @RipAmina, "Rest in Peace Amina" on March 17, a Twitter user wrote: "I am a 16 year-old cute girl who is looking for a gentle pervert, preferably a rapist for marriage and more if affinity develops" (Amar 2012).

Only three days after Amina's death, Woman-Choufouch created the Facebook page, "We are all Amina Filali," attracting thousands of members. Woman-Shoufouch, which started as an anti–sexual harassment group inspired by the Feb20 mobilization, championed Amina's case by mobilizing online and offline, bringing old feminist organizations, human rights activists, and international audiences to the virtual platform and the public square.

Unlike the heated debates that shaped the 2004 reform of women's status in family law and that crystallized around shari`a as a "hegemonic episteme" (see this volume, introduction) in both Islamist and feminist narratives, in Amina's case the shari`a appeared only sporadically in the public debate. A minor trend articulated by individuals in online magazines and newspapers blamed women for their relaxed sense of morality. The marginalization of religious discourse also meant that the core of the debate shifted from the usual opposed publics, Islamists and feminists, to more marginal actors, especially young social media activists, who became central to the debate on their keyboards.

Amina's spreading story resonated in a cyberspace already saturated with visual images of women's injured bodies and scrutinized body parts in the context of the hypermasculine, sexualized, and moralizing public space of "revolution" (see Al-Ali 2012; Amar 2011). For instance, the blogger Zeinobia wrote, after renarrating Amina's story in *Egyptian Chronicles*, "This is in nutshell the story behind that famous #RIPAmina hashtag suddenly appeared among all the political hashtags in the Arab region." Zeinobia continues: "Marrying the rapist is actually a punishment to the girl and to the woman and yet in our Arab world some families think that it is better than scandal!!!" (Zeinobia 2012). In addition, a new Facebook page, "The Uprising of Women in the Arab World," became an open platform for women's stories of sexual harassment, gendered violence, and patriarchal oppression across the Arab world.

Amina was not a part of an organized movement, however. Neither was her rape part of a state-sponsored physical assault of the kind experienced by Imane el-Oubeidi in the wake of the Libyan uprising, nor by Samira Ibrahim under military rule in "post-Mubarak" Egypt. Amina was not the first case of suicide after rape in Morocco, either. As her father testified before cameras, in her village alone, hers was the fourth case of rape that had been followed by a suicide attempt. Hence, we can only understand the intensity of the debates and the public outcry that her case instigated if we situate them in the contingencies of the North African uprisings and the traveling referents of dignity, justice, and rights carried by protestors throughout the region.

The case first made its way to the public through the independent newspaper *Al-Masa'e*, which did not simply provide information but also organized round-tables and meetings enabling the various stakeholders to argue their positions. But soon after the case went public, Feb20, the Moroccan Association for Human Rights, and several feminist organizations, joined Woman-Choufouch in street protests, including a first-of-its-kind sit-in in front of parliament, on March 17, organized by Woman-Choufouch. Online petitions were already on their way to an international audience, including on iPetitions and Avaaz.org. These attracted 812,137 signatures against article 475.

These heated debates were reminiscent of the old controversies around reforming family law in which the feminist and the Islamist movements had played a central role several years earlier. They also illustrated several significant paradigmatic shifts in the episteme of rights, and the centrality of the shari`a, as we will see from this genealogy of feminist activism.

Genealogy of the Debate: Paradigmatic Shifts

Moroccan feminism marked the turn of the twenty-first century with a radical reform of women's legal status as redefined in the newly codified family law of 2004. This reform was the outcome of contestations and negotiations that opened the gender field (Salime 2011, 2) to multiple actors. I have used the term *gender* in the sense of a field of struggle in which various actors—`ulama (religious scholars), Islamist groups, political parties, feminist groups—negotiate their access to a highly centralized political system. Thus gender is not only an organizing principle for states and societies but is also the field in which new subject actors of rights, feminists, and Islamists, in this context, negotiate the symbolic order and create new meanings that materialize in new bodies of laws. The recent history of the feminist and Islamist movements in Morocco shows how these changes have been taking place not only in the legal system but also in the movements themselves during particular "time events" or "movement moments" (Salime 2011, xvii).

The gradual incorporation of a religious argumentation by feminist groups to make the case for gender equality was one of the outcomes of an agonistic process in which state actors, Islamist activists, the 'ulama, liberal feminist groups, and Islamist feminists were involved. Liberal feminists' effort to carve out space for gender talk in most state institutions culminated in the 1997 National Plan of Action for Integrating Women in Development, which also included a project for reforming the women's status in the *mudawana* family law code. This project of reform prompted an unprecedented level of public debate, as well as contestations by the Islamists and conservatives alike, and culminated in the mass street rallies of March 2000 in Casablanca (Salime 2011). The rallies postponed the reform of family law for a few years while paving the way for an engineered "deliberative" process, mediated by the appointed Royal Council for the Revision of the *Mudawana*.

The council brought together conservative members from the judiciary, Islamists opposed to reform, conservative theologians, and three women more sensitive to the feminist plea: Judge Zhor El Hor, sociologist Rahma Bourquia, and medical doctor Nezha Guessous. The mission of the council was to listen to all parties, then engage in a Habermasian-type deliberation before arriving at a putatively consensual reform, which, painfully, did not arrive until four years later. The overwhelming number of conservatives and Islamists sitting on the council compelled feminist groups to build the equality narrative within the notion of *ijtihad*. Well-known scholar of Islamic law Wael Hallaq defines *ijtihad* as "the process of creative reasoning that the accomplished jurist employed in order to arrive at the best guess of what he thought the law pertaining to a particular case might be" (Hallaq 2013, 58). Thus *ijtihad* is tied to *maslaha* or "public interest" (Zubaida 2005, 15). While using his creative reasoning, the Muslim jurist must use his legal judgment to engage the changing historical context and needs of Muslims.

To feminist groups, activating *ijtihad* meant drawing on various Islamic historical narratives, varied legal Islamic practices, and opinions of Muslim jurists to engage in selective reading from varied schools of fiqh jurisprudence. In addition, feminist groups reached out to theologians from outside the council, as well as from within, who were thought to be more sensitive to gender equality and sympathetic to feminist proposals. These included Ahmed El-Khamlishi, a council member, as well as Driss Hamadi and Abdelhadi

Boutaleb, who inspired feminist groups and published books (El-Khamlishi 2004; Hamadi 2001) or essays in edited volumes supervised by feminist groups (see Joussour 2000).

These persons' ability to work with *"ulama al-ijtihad,"* or "interpretive `ulama," as feminist groups like to call them, gave legitimacy to the feminist claim that the problem lies not in the shari`a, understood here as both "a moral resource" (Hallaq 2013, 13) and a path for justice, but rather in the failure of the mainstream `ulama to practice *ijtihad.* This rhetorical shift is what marked the feminist discourse after the Casablanca rally.

Elsewhere I have analyzed this co-imbrication of Islamist and feminist politics and their construction of a "discursivized" (see this volume, introduction) shari`a (Salime 2011). In this chapter, however, I explore how these entangled genealogies opened the discursive field about women's rights to new actors who are now leading the debate about Amina's case. Whether through expert or nonexpert knowledge, we see in the Amina controversy the emergence of a justice-based discourse that has shifted the lens from the *immoral* woman who engages in premarital sex—the thesis defended by some Islamists—to the *unethical* law that punishes the victim and protects her rapist. What better testimony to this ethicodiscursive shift than this editorial, published in the *Assabah* daily newspaper?

> It's the law, an absurd and grotesque rule, which aims to remedy evil, the rape, with something even more repugnant: the marriage with the rapist . . . Who are we punishing in the end, the victim or her rapist? (Amar 2012)

These reactions were, in part, instigated by the ambivalence of the Islamist ministers and their response to the Amina rape story.

The Islamist Response

In sharp contrast to the media representation of the Islamist response as monolithic, I discovered the latter to be much more nuanced, less legalistic, and more grounded in the plurality of real and existing marriage practices than described. Commenting on the rape case, Mustapha Khalfi, the minister of communication, stated, "This girl was raped twice. The last time was when she got married." He also added, "We must embark on a profound study of this situation in order to consider the possibility of increasing punishments in the reform of the penal code" (Amar 2012). Bassima Hakkaoui, the minister of solidarity, women, family, and social development, started by admitting that article 475 was "a real problem" and that there was a need for debate in order to reform it. In both of these statements there was call for debate, an appeal that remained consistent throughout the Islamists' interventions.

Very soon the Islamist government's take on the issue changed. The minister of justice, lawyer Mustafa Ramid, was among the first to recast the debate as "an abduction of minor" that is punishable by law if it did not end up in "a consensual marriage." Ramid has a reputation of being a hard-liner in the Islamist Justice and Development Party. As a guest in the news hour on *Al-Oula* television station,[1] he detailed, from a strictly legal point of view, the process that led to the conclusion of the marriage and reminded the public that the "marriage of minors does not violate the Islamic shari`a." And, he added, similar to the "Spanish, French, and Belgian laws, the Moroccan legislature endorses the marriage of minors." By doing this, Ramid intended not necessarily to protect article 475 of the penal code but to protect article 20, which authorizes the marriage of minors in family law. Hinting at the controversies that had preceded the revision of the *mudawana* in 2004, Ramid restated that any revisions to article 20 must be the outcome of a process of deliberation and national consensus formation. He concluded on a moralizing note by claiming that this is "unfortunately what happens to girls who accept to enter these kinds of relationships."

Mustafa Ramid's several interventions before the press underscored the tensions inherent in the hybridity of the Moroccan legal system and the plurality of legal orders at work. In the same interview with *Al-Oula*, Ramid expressed doubts that the marriage of minors will end by a revision of the law. The practice, he believed, "will continue through the use and recitation of al-Fatiha" (the first chapter of the Qur'an) as an informal but perfectly legitimate way to enter into a marriage. Ramid claimed that the practice would continue as long as families wanted to see their daughters married at an early age. Ramid feared that the state would then face the issue of retroactive registration of marriages after the female minor reaches the age of majority. In addition, he asked, "What will happen in the case of a pregnancy?" He continued, "How are we going to deal with a divorce in this kind of union?"

These questions are a legitimate place to look at the co-imbrication of legal pluralism, fluid social practices, and public ethics. However, this is not the only juncture at which the Maliki School of jurisprudence followed in Morocco (which inspires some of these practices) and postcolonial positive law are not moving in tandem. The status of the child conceived in a marriage under al-Fatiha, though legitimate under the shari`a, remains problematic under positive law that would only recognize a child conceived in a formally registered marriage.

Hence, Ramid is right to think that abolishing article 20 would be detrimental to the child even before it was detrimental to the mother. Equally important are the tensions between the legal age of marriage at age eighteen—which feminist groups pushed for in the 2004 revised family code—and the age of majority at puberty in the regime of obligations and observances, regulated by Islamic jurisprudence for Muslims. Hence, Ramid argued, the practice of early-age marriages, notably in rural areas and among the lower social classes, justified his reservations.

Ramid's interview received several responses on YouTube. Barbie271 contested the minister's use of a shari`a talk: "Mr Minister, please do not justify this by Islam. Islam has nothing to do with this aberration." Similarly, bylyfresh1 said, "to this religious bigot: if a 54 year old man asked to marry your 16 year old daughter, will you give them your blessing?"

Another prominent Islamist figure involved in the Amina debate was Bassima Hakkaoui, who became the focus of social media and feminist campaigns when she invited the alleged rapist to a conference alongside the press and feminist groups. During this conference, she called for a public debate and a national consensus about abrogating the law, adding that the law "will not be abrogated, either today or tomorrow, just because of pressure from international campaigns." Nothing gave Amina's supporters more reasons to worry than when Hakkaoui claimed that "the marriage of a victim to her rapist is not always harmful to the victim." After this statement, the conference room became a protest scene as feminists and some members of the audience, already irritated by the presence of Amina's husband in the room, poured their outrage at the minister and walked out.[2]

In another television show, a spokesperson for the ministry of women claimed that rape could also have a happy ending when both families are supportive of the victim.[3] What these players were calling for is a regime of social support in which the community takes care of the raped woman, rather than a disciplinary legal regime that punishes the rapist. My point here is not to support this perspective but to highlight the varied ethical orders articulated during these debates.

Hakkaoui's reputation as a virulent antifeminist activist did not help (see Guessous 2012). Her appointment as minister of women was perceived as a major setback for the Arab Spring's electoral politics in Morocco. During the debates about Amina's rape, Hakkaoui became the target of campaigns of denunciations in the press and the social media, not only because of her ambivalent position on rape but also because of her past prominent role in mobilizing against the reform of family law.

Many months after Amina's case was discussed in the European Parliament (Jaabouk 2012), the Moroccan Parliament finally addressed the issue in the person of Prime Minister Abdelilah Benkirane. In a live broadcast of the December 24, 2012, session, the people's representatives listened to Prime Minister Benkirane as he argued that the Filalicase "did not involve any rape" but was "a consensual relationship between two young people that ended in a consensual marriage" (Amar 2012). Mobilization was already hitting a peak.

Rape with the Complicity of the State

"We are all Amina Filali," #RIPAmina, "Bassima Stop It!," and "Resignation" are but a few e-activist platforms through which the Amina case made its way to an international audience. Other calls were directed at the state: "No to rape with the complicity of the state," "Article 475 killed me," and "I am a Moroccan woman, I don't matter" were very popular slogans in the performative scene of street protests. But few postings better represented this focus on the state than a caricature posted on #RIPAmina's Facebook page. Written in English to grant it wider diffusion, it thanked the government and the courts for allowing a "mess" of a man to marry a beautiful and intelligent woman simply by raping her.

Feminist groups did not wait for the suicide to take place to organize against the penal code. Already by 2005 the feminist organization Democratic League for Women's Rights had proposed a memorandum for "dignity and protection of women's individual rights."[4] In March 2010 an umbrella organization, *Rabi' al-Karama* (the Springtime of Dignity), was born. It comprised twenty-two women's rights organizations, including the Union of Women's Action. The latter responded to the alarming numbers of women victims of domestic violence and the persistence of laws that discriminate against women. Echoing *Rabie al-Mousawat* (Springtime of Equality), through which feminist groups organized their response to the Islamist rally of 2000, Rabie al-Karama focuses on "dignity" rather than "equality," marking a semantic shift from an abstract notion of equality to the embodied and affective notion of dignity that resonates broadly well beyond middle-class circles.

The notion of dignity has long been common in the everyday speech practices of the average Moroccan, Algerian, and Tunisian, all of whom express their longing for a better life by using the term *l'hogra* (see also Hannoum 2013). The term literally means the feeling of being "nobody"—"crushed." But *l'hogra* is not helplessness. It is a call for a bodily disposition to revolt, as the lyrics of rap music bear witness. Hence the appearance of dignity as a master narrative and a main trope in the Arab revolts has been informed by the everyday politics of subalternity, whether in the form of organized movements or of spontaneous collective acts of dissent, or "nonmovements," as Asef Bayat has called them (Bayat 2010). It is within this interplay of *l'hogra* as bodily disposition, affective economy, and class positions that we can begin to understand this new appeal for ethical legality.

It worth noting that Amina's suicide took place after the adoption of the amended constitution in July 2012. One can see the effects of feminism on the drafting of the constitution in the language of full equality of men and women before the law, as well as the use of the term "parity" in the new constitution. While recognizing African, Mediterranean, Arabic, and Amazigh sources of national identity, the constitution still stipulates that Islam is the religion of the state and defines Morocco as a Muslim country. Hence although the constitution recognizes all international treaties and conventions on human rights, it does so only so long as these laws do not contradict the cultural specificities of Morocco (Maghraoui 2011).

This legal and ethical pluralism, with its contradictions and varied sources of inspiration, has also shaped the varied gendered orders through which women's lives have been regulated and their resistance organized (see Salime 2015). During several talk shows that brought together feminist leaders, social media activists, and state representatives before an attentive invited audience, heated debates broke out about the discrepancies between the entrenched sexism of the legal system and the equalitarian aspirations of the new constitution. Without making reference to the shari'a, feminists and social media activists discussed the meaning of constitutional legality and the importance of the integration between the Moroccan legal system and international law.

Morocco is a signatory member of the International Convention on the Elimination of all Kinds of Discrimination Against Women (CEDAW), the Universal Declaration of Human Rights (UDHR), and the United Nations Convention on the Right of the Child (NCRC), among other such agreements (see this volume, Mir-Hosseini, chapter 3). Morocco retracted its reservations from CEDAW in 2008 and thereby became obligated to act according to the convention's stipulations. This is the hegemonic legal background against which most of the debates about Amina took place.

This focus on the state machinery and international law was not exclusive, however. The debate also amounted to a trial of Moroccan society and the "archaic mentalities" that sustained practices such as early-age marriages. For instance, in the interactive show *Mubasharatan Ma'akum*, aired by the television station 2M, Fouzia Assouli, the president of the Democratic League of Women's Rights, contested the fact that "rape is considered an assault on the family, society, and the collectivity, rather than an assault on the woman herself, her dignity, and physical integrity." In the same roundtable, psychologist Nadia Kadiri presented the case of Amina's suicide as a wakeup call "for a society that continues to define women by their hymen." To her, Amina's suicide must make society rethink the "adequacy of constructing a moral regime of honor around a woman's virginity." She asked a question: If "an intact hymen defines a woman, what would be the bodily equivalent for a man?"

But it was Ahmed Assid, an activist for the cultural rights of Moroccan Amazigh population, who pointed his finger directly at religion when he referred to the assumed "supremacy of the text over the individual and her rights." To him, "no text, whether religious or other, should be sanctified and more important than the person and her rights." Assid blamed "conservative discourse" and its "culture talk" about "our traditions" for the persistence of early-age marriages and the cultural valuation of virginity as a code of honor. "We need to undermine the three priorities upon which the conservative discourse stands," he argued: "first, the priority of a text, whether it is law or religion, over the individual and his dignity; second the priority of the collectivity over the individual; third, the supremacy of men over women."[5] According to Assid, the judiciary's concern about "saving the rapist, rather than protecting the woman" can only be understood within "this matrix of a patriarchal tradition, a sanctified text, and a sexist law."

Through Twitter, Facebook, and electronic messages, then, men and women from all over Morocco participated in a great interactive program. Their opinions on the issue were no different from those of the show's guests. For instance, Zakariya asked for the "abrogation of the law that permits the marriage of minors to their rapists." Asmae asked, "How can anyone accept the marriage of a minor to her rapist. Are we living in the dark ages?" Mbarak stated that "what happened to Amina is a warning that the Moroccan society needs to move forward to preserve women's dignity." Rachid called "the marriage of minors a crime against humanity." And Ahmed denounced Moroccan society for "always putting the blame on women whether they are minors or adults."

Amina and French Law

Amina's case did not leave the blogosphere indifferent. Personal blogs debated article 475 by tracing its genealogy to the French colonial legal system. A Moroccan jurist writing under the pseudonym of Ibnkafka[6] stressed the postcolonial legacy of the Moroccan Penal Code. Ibnkafka's intervention disturbed the stability of the master narrative about an intrinsically Moroccan or Islamic origin of the code. Under the title "Amina, Article 475, and the French Jurisprudence," Ibnkafka subjected the code to a new scrutiny, tracing its origins to the pre-revolutionary French *Ancien Régime* that preceded the Napoleonic Code. Ibnkafka stated that neither in the French patriarchal regime nor in the Moroccan code is this legislation concerned with rape or the sexual integrity of the young girl. Rather, article 475 is aimed at the "preservation of parental authority, re-established through marriage." Under French law, the abduction of the nubile minor was considered an assault on the authority of the parents, not on that of the woman. The Moroccan code borrows its terms directly from the French law, speaking about "Abduction and Non-Representation of Minors, not rape or sexual violence." Hence, article 475 does not necessarily define rape, though it might imply it:

> When a nubile minor is removed or diverted and then marries her captor, the latter may only be prosecuted when a complaint is filed by a person(s) entitled to apply for annulment of marriage and cannot be sentenced until after the annulment of marriage been pronounced. (Article 457, Moroccan Penal Code)

Ibnkafka shows that rape is regulated not under article 475 but under article 486 of the Penal Code. The code defines rape as a "man forcing a woman into a sexual encounter," an act "punishable by 5 to 10 years in prison." Ibnkafka blames individual judges for failing to seriously investigate rape, using article 475 to avoid any difficulty.

Ibnkafka's detailed account of the postcolonial Moroccan reproduction of the laws of France's *Ancien Régime* prompted diverse responses from the readers of his blog. For instance, Souleyma wrote:

> Excellent article Ibn Kafka! a blow of fresh air in this climate of craziness that took over those who believed in their civilizing mission, and who were ready to point figures on us, accusing and blaming, as usual. We continue to suffer from the legacy of the French colonialism and yet we still continue to believe they have solutions to our problems, as if we were incapable to stand on our own feet.

Souleyma shared her own findings about the status of rape in Islam after announcing that the problem exists in all monotheist religions. She shared two verses from Exodus:

> If a man seduces a virgin who is not engaged and has a sexual encounter with her he will pay her a monetary compensation (dowry) and take her for a wife. If the father does not agree on the marriage, the man will pay the monetary compensation of a virgin." (Exodus 22:16–17)

She also researched scholarly publications and concluded:

> I have done a research in the encyclopedia of women in Islam and other texts related to *hudud*, the system of punishments in the shari'a. One case of rape was reported to the prophet, and he decided that the man should receive the capital punishment. He never blamed it on the woman . . . [N]ow the so-called Islamists are conflating adultery, fornication, and rape . . . The problem is not Islam but Patriarchy. . . . it is clear that in all cultures, all religions, the woman is denigrated, her body is a good traded first by her father, then possessed by her husband. Nothing belongs to her . . . [B]ut rights are never given they are taken, and this is what Moroccans should do, helped by our friends and sympathizers. (Souleyma, March 16, 2012)

Aisha, another reader, acknowledged that Ibnkafka's article pushed her to do more research about the origin of the Moroccan penal code, notably the articles related to women and their rights. In her post she followed Ibnkfka's pedagogical style by putting the articles side by side and showing that the aberrations of the Moroccan penal code—notably the gendered systems of punishment of adultery and the crimes of "honor" that sentence women to harsh punishments while excusing men—all derive from the French penal code.

Ibnkafka's blog was also discussed on one of *Al-Jazeera*'s numerous talk shows about the case. In the interactive program *The Stream*, several guests from Morocco and elsewhere joined viewers from all over the world that tweeted their contributions to the story.[7] One important line of thought that emerged from the thirty-five-minute conversation was a general sense that a postcolonial logic, such as the one implied in Ibnkafka's blog, might be historically accurate but not necessarily ethically useful. As Moroccan-based activist Zineb Benlla stated,

> All I want is to see this legislation revoked, I do not care where it has originated . . . I am not looking for whom to blame . . . [T]he law must change . . . Morocco ratified the CEDAW, and this case offers an additional opportunity for the state to move forward and bring about real changes to its laws.

Personal blogs became a vibrant site for knowledge production: for sharing arguments, information, and resources as well as news about Morocco's adherence to international conventions on women's rights. But, as we shall see, the blogs are only one site where contestations were taking place about gender, legality, and the state's responsibilities toward its citizens, notably women. More individual actors entered the debate by intervening directly into Amina's life and by reconstructing the narrative, putting the disparate pieces together in "homemade" documentaries. The films *475 When Marriage Becomes Punishment* and *Trêve de Silence (Break the Silence)* deepened the narrative about child marriage, extending its scope to a debate on the sexual oppression of women and the unethical legal regime in place.

475, When Marriage Becomes Punishment

In this thirty-minute documentary about Amina Filali, director Nadir Bouhmouch, a film studies undergraduate at San Diego State University, investigated the case camera in hand. He was joined by Layla Belmahi, one of the cofounders of Woman-Choufouch, and by cinematographer Riley Dufurrena. After producing the film, Nadir and his team showed it in two geographically disparate sites: first, during his own university's commemoration of the Amnesty International's Human Rights Festival, on February 18, 2013, and then in Rabat, at the Moroccan Association for Human Rights, on March 21, 2013.

For many months, the film was publicized on its Facebook page, "475 When Marriage Becomes Punishment," as well as on the Woman-Choufouch Facebook page and the Facebook page of the "pan-Arab" feminist network, "The Uprising of Women in the Arab World." After the film was translated into Chinese, its Facebook page read, "Amina's story is now accessible to another billion people."

In an interview for the on-line news magazine, Jadaliyya, Bouhmouch observed, "To show the extent to which a film has an impact on me, before *475*, I did not consider myself a feminist and actually refuted the term as a label that could be applied to me. Now I am proud to say that I am a feminist. It is really hard for me to explain to what extent these films have had an impact on me." (Bouhmouch 2013)

Bouhmouch's film was a personal investigation of Amina's case. The film crew interviewed human rights activists, feminist leaders, and members of Amina's community as well as lawyers, Amina's parents, and her husband. One of the most powerful moments of the movie was the heartbreaking testimony of the cowife and second spouse of Amina's father. Interviewed by Houda Lamkaddem, and to the surprise of the public, the second wife shared her own story of having been raped by Amina's own father. Her story also resulted in her marriage with the rapist and a domestic life marked by domestic violence and hardship living with the rapist, now her husband.

The movie testifies also to Bouhmouch's heightened feminist sensibility, as does his choice of Houda Lamkaddem as a coproducer, assistant director, and narrator. Houda, a victim of rape when she was seventeen years old, was one of the few women who reported her rape story to her parents and the police, then put it in writing in a blog, which she headed, "It is not your fault" (Lamqaddam 2012a).

Adding to the complexity of these interwoven stories of rape, and using her particular standpoint as a survivor, Houda transgressed the spatial and emotional distance that separates the filmmaker from her characters. Moved by the second spouse's tears and narrative of physical, moral, and psychological hardship, Houda gave the woman a human touch and shifted her positionality from producer to a survivor by acknowledging: "I understand you, I feel your pain. I was raped too . . . but you should not stay with him." In June 2013, Houda's contribution to the movie earned her the *Deutshe Welle Social Activism Award*.

In Bouhammouch's film, Amina's story was almost displaced by her stepmother's daily struggle for survival and her powerful testimony against Amina's father. The stepmother did not hesitate to state that she was now ready to end the cycle of violence and leave Amina's father. All she was waiting for was the end of Ramadan and a few addresses of feminist groups who could help her begin a new life. This was all taking place in the course of an interaction between the two survivors of rape. Amina's suicide has certainly liberated speech while highlighting the struggle of women's rights organizations over the past two decades to open shelters and grant legal, psychological, and financial assistance to victims and survivors. Bouhamouch's two films point also to the rise of a new generation of "social entrepreneurs" who want to contribute to social and political change through the production of a situated knowledge that becomes formative of their own subjectivities.

The second individual endeavor to highlight the plight of women victims and survivors of sexual violence was Hind Bensari's film *475: Trêve de Silence*, or *475: Break the Silence*. The film recounts Malika Slimani's rape and struggle with the court in her case against Hassan Arif, a current member of parliament and former president of town hall of Ein Aouda. Hind Bensari is a Moroccan female graduate of the University of Edinburgh in economics and Middle Eastern studies. She lived in England and had never touched a camera before but was compelled by the repeated stories of rape in the Moroccan cyberspace to act. Hind decided to undertake her own investigation into Malika Slimani's story of rape, denial of paternity by Arif, and dismissal by the court despite evidence of rape and a DNA test proving paternity. Hind worked in the same manner as social media activists: She created a Facebook page to publicize her project, used crowdfunding through Indiegogo to support her project, and posted news on the film to cultivate her audience (Saddiqi 2013). Her investigation into Malika Slimani's case gave Malika the face and voice she had been denied by the court system for more than two years.

This film not only reveals the changing subjectivities of young people and the importance of feminist imaginaries in the "e-governance" (see Peletz 2013a, 613) of everyday manifestations of gender oppression but also shows the possibilities opened by the new media and the growth of individualized forms of e-funding and new modes of cultural entrepreneurship, as well as individualized forms of cultural consumption and political action, enabled by the internet. The rise of the rights-bearing subject is interwoven with the right of that subject to be an entrepreneur in the neoliberal era.

As this confluence of events illustrates, as a result of the multisited nature of knowledge production and the dispersed-yet-connected linkages of audience and funding, the struggle to end rape and sexual violence against women has extended well beyond specific feminist organizations or state-based groups.

New Feminist Sites: *I Was Raped*

New feminist websites also contributed to this expansion of knowledge production by offering a more individualized platform which men and women could join. A call made by the feminist magazine *Qandisha* under the heading "I was raped"[8] attracted a stream of responses, testimonies, and reactions. *Qandisha* is a "collaborative feminine magazine" (*magazine collaboratif feminin*), as its founder, young physicist Fedwa Misk, defines it. According to the magazine,

> The aim was to demonstrate that no woman who underwent this physical and psychological injury could find comfort in the legal union to the abuser. It will seem absurd to some of you, because it is so obvious. However, the absurd is Moroccan and section 475 proves it. (Misk 2012)

Published first in French, the magazine soon made English and Spanish translations of the women's stories. The striking—or perhaps not so striking—similarity between all the women who decided to testify under anonymous names was their earlier silence. None of them thought of filing a complaint, reporting the case to the police, or speaking to family and friends. Most of them did not share their experience before putting it in writing on the web page. Though only nine women narrated their story, the long thread of responses brought more stories of sexual assault. It also brought more outrage among the readers who reacted to rape from the vantage point of their male or female subjectivities, national belonging, and religious or secular sensibilities. Most readers expressed sadness; some said they had been unable to continue reading all the stories. Some even asked for forgiveness. Such was the case with Mourad, a male reader:

> We have to come together and ask for forgiveness for failing to protect you, for failing to hold your aggressors accountable before the law, and for not having protected you from this obscene, bestial violence that haunts you, because HE is still running free. I could not read all the stories ... I can't find words ... too many stories ... what to say? What to do? ... [S]ociety is waking up, in dis-belief, in solidarity but groggy with the weight of traditions, and sometimes a system of beliefs that betray us. We have to live our time, the present time, that of modernity, of scientific knowledge and justice ... Maybe we need to remind each other [that we live in the present time], and maybe we should just state it. May women be emancipated! Let's abrogate the Penal Code and stand for the honor of all women.

Atika asked Mourad a question:

> Mourad, do you think that we stand a chance to be free with this minister (Bassima Hakkaoui)? This is a woman who is telling us loudly that we are looking for it? I don't think we stand a chance, and shame on us that she is part of our government!!!

Nour-eddine expressed his outrage:

> As a man I am feeling embarrassed to be related to this violent, schizophrenic, and unhealthy society. As a father, I am conscious that my daughter is lucky to be living outside of this jungle that is Morocco. All my sympathy and support to all the women of my country who fall under the daily tyranny that our men inflict upon them.

This thread of ninety-six comments and stories brought together psychologists, the Moroccan diaspora, European women victims of sexual violence living in Morocco, and foreign journalists asking for more information for their projected books or films in Europe. "The pain was intense," said some. Other women just said, "Society is punishing us because we are women." There is also a similar rejection of "blaming it on others" of the kind we have seen with regard to Ibnkafka's post. For instance, responding to a post in which a participant contested the use of the description of Morocco as a "shitty" country (*pays de merde*) by another poster, Samar wrote:

> We should overcome our chauvinism and face the facts. Think about the young woman before thinking about the reputation of this country. This country is nothing without its men and women.

Najib, another male respondent, acknowledged:

> These stories make me deeply sad. Our leaders, from top to bottom, are criminal because they do not punish crimes. They are criminals because they have not worked hard to educate the society and get people out of ignorance . . . We definitely need a regime change. Too much is too much!

What do these widely disseminated debates about Amina say about public ethics, state authority, and gender politics? The disputes about rape and marriage laws, the visual landscape developed around her story, the proliferation of women's micronarratives of rape, and the individuated sentiments shared on the cyberspace by varied audiences were all constituent of an emergent discursive field through which public affect, the "ordinary ethical" (see this volume, introduction), and new and contested forms of state legality were engaged, contested, and re-articulated. Each group or individuals contributed to this discursive field through varied systems of knowledge, both expert and "common-sensical" (Peletz 2013b, 14), as well as through modes of affect: shame and embarrassment, revolt and outrage, belief and disbelief, victimhood and strength, among others. By presenting the case as a legal aberration and focusing on legal reform, each of these interlinked individuals contributed to the legitimization of the state as a groundwork for legal rationality, but at the same time, they enabled what Peletz calls "the business of government" to be reinvented (Peletz 2013b, 15). But how can we understand the marginal place accorded the shari'a in these disputes about reforming article 475, in contrast to co-imbrication of shari'a and human rights talk during earlier public debates, such as those surrounding the campaign to reform family law? To what kind of rupture does this marginalization of "shari'a talk" bear witness?

Ruptures

I suggest that the sporadic reference to shari'a in these disputes does not necessarily indicate that the social imaginaries of a "just" legal order are not already embedded in ethical modalities that are formed and informed by an "Islamic register" (Osanloo 2006, 193). As we have seen, several responses in blogs and chat rooms used shari'a in the sense of a "moral resource" (Hallaq 2013, 12) with which to condemn rape and protest the law. As one of the inspirational sources of public ethics that "is always already available" (Emon 2013, 2, and this volume, chapter 2), shari'a has informed the debate about law, justice, and equality for several decades. Negotiations of both secular and religious sensibilities had to articulate shari'a imaginaries, of right and wrong, just and unjust, corrupt and fair. Gender has always been central to these negotiations.

As has been argued elsewhere (Osanloo 2006; Salime 2011), feminist activism took issues of women's rights from the privacy of marriage laws and domestic space to the public sphere where these laws have been debated, scrutinized, and, in some cases, reformed. In the contestations about gender equality in Morocco, we have seen not an expulsion of the shari'a from the public debate but rather its co-imbrication of rights talk and shari'a talk.

At the same time, the encounter of feminism and Islamism has led to the expansion of notions of equality and gender justice beyond the control of religious groups and the learned community of 'ulama. Amina's case points to both a crisis in the Islamist discourse and a rupture in a moral order that cannot legitimize rape through a shari'a talk, nor legislate it through the legal regimes in place. The ways in which multiple actors and audiences reacted to the Islamist ministers' positionings on the case indexes the presence of a crisis of "Islamism" as a "moral movement" (Hallaq 2013, 12) and moralizing discourse.

One powerful moment in that rupture came from a highly respected figure in Islamist circles, Muslim thinker and legal scholar, Tariq Ramadan. In a policed conference room, packed beyond capacity, Ramadan clearly and loudly condemned the law, declaring that there should be a second thought about the criminal nature of the case, and therefore the legal nature of rape. "The place of a rapist is prison," said Ramadan. YouTube clips of the talk received more than 70,000 hits. We can watch Ramadan loudly condemning any attempt to contain rape within marriage or within a shari'a talk: There is "no room or possibility for justifying rape in Islam, or for repairing it through marriage,'" he repeated. Ramadan's intervention in this debate delinked shari'a talk from the Islamist discourse of the government.

Third, in these controversies, the focus on childhood by feminists and social media activists, rather than adolescence, and on rape rather than romance, enabled old and new publics—women's rights organizations, cyberactivists, human rights groups, and individuals—to convert the religiously tinted debate about sexuality outside of marriage into a broader debate in which liberal and secular claims could be made about women's sexual freedom, bodily integrity, and individual rights, as well as about the need for laws to protect them. The message? By committing suicide, Amina interrupted this patriarchal encoding of her hymen as a "public good" to be secured through a "forced marriage," with the complicity of the state and its laws. The cry for legal reform has legitimized the everyday reproduction of the state as a legal rationality.

Amina's case was also indicative of the ways in which the subaltern "patriar-chy" displayed in most documentaries about Amina's parents mediates the possi-bilities of such transactions in the court system while also becoming the object of multidisciplinary discourses of victimization and empowerment by middle-class cyberactivists. Though no one directly condemned the parents for the marriage, the various intrusions into their modest home, the narratives about their precari-ous lives, and their visual representation became the object of multidisciplinary discourses of victimization. Most narratives displaced Amina as an agent embed-ded in the structures of subaltern modernity—schooling and labor, romance and rape, marriage, and suicide—for a focus on law and its reform. The focus on law kept intact the socioeconomic context of deprivation in which her romance and rape, marriage, and suicide took place (see Salime 2015, 536).

References

Al-Ali, Nadje. 2012. "Gendering the Arab Spring." *Middle East Journal of Culture and Communication* 5:26–31.

Amar, Paul. 2011. "Turning the Gendered Politics of the Security State Inside Out? Charging the Police with Sexual Harassment in Egypt." *International Feminist Journal of Politics* 13 (3): 299–328.

Amar, Ali. 2012. "Les Islamistes veulent enterrer l'affaire Amina Filali." *Slate Afrique*, March 23. http://www.slateafrique.com/84527/maroc-islamistes-affaire-amina-el-filali-femmes-viol -mariage.

Bamyeh, Mohamed. 2011. "The Arab Revolutions and the Making of a New Patriotism." *Orient: German Journal for Politics, Economics and Culture of the Middle East* 52:3.

Bayat, Asef. 2010. *Life as Politics: How Ordinary People Change the Middle East.* Stanford, CA: Stanford University Press.

Bouhmouch, Nadir. 2013. "Exposing Sexual Violence in Morocco: An Interview with Nadir Bouhmouch." *Jadaliyya*, February 27. http://www.jadaliyya.com/pages/index/10234 /exposing-sexual-violence-in-morocco_an-interview-w.

Dabashi, Hamid. 2012. *The Arab Spring: The End of Postcolonialism.* London and New York: Zed Books.

Emon, M. Anver. 2013. "Shari`a and the Rule of Law." Presentation at "Shari`a and Islamic Ethics in Transitions," Boston University, March 7–8.

Guessous, Nadia. 2012. "Having a Conversation on Other Terms: Gender and the Politics of Representation in the New Moroccan Government." *Jadaliyya*, January 9. http://www .jadaliyya.com/pages/index/3983/having-a-conversation-on-other-terms_gender-and-th.

Hallaq, Wael. 2013. *The Impossible State: Islam, Politics and Modernity's Moral Predicament.* New York: Columbia University Press.

Hamadi, Driss. 2001. *Afaq tahrir al-Mar'a fi al-Shari`a al-Islamiya.* Rabat, Morocco: Dar abi Raqraq.

Hannoum, Abdelmajid. 2013. "Tangier in the Time of Arab Revolutions: An Ethnopolitical Diary." *Journal of North African Studies* 18 (2): 272–90.

Hefner W. Robert. 2013. "The Co-Imbrication of Islamic Law and New Public Ethics in Contemporary Muslim Politics and Culture." Presentation at "Shari`a and Islamic Ethics in Transitions," Boston University, March 7–8.

Jaabouk, Mohammed. 2012. *"Le suicide d'Amina Filali examiné au Parlement européen."* *Yabiladi*, March 20. http://www.yabiladi.com/articles/details/9518/suicide-d-amina-filali-examine -parlement.html.

Joussour. 2000. *Question féminine et rôle de l'ijtihad en Islam*. Colloque International. Tifak Press.

El-Khamlishi, Ahmed. 2004. *Limatha la narbit baina al-Tanthir w-al-Mumarassa? Manshuratal-Zaman*. Casablanca, Morocco: Matba't al-Najah al-Jadida.

Maghraoui, Driss. 2011. "Constitutional Reforms in Morocco: Between Consensus and Subaltern Politics." *The Journal of North African Studies* 16 (4): 679–99.

Misk, Fadwa. 2012. "I Was Raped." *Qandisha.ma*, March 26. http://www.qandisha.ma/2012/03/26 /i-was-raped/.

Mouffe, Chantal. 2000. "Deliberative Democracy and Agonistic Pluralism." Vienna: Institute for Advanced Studies. http://www.ihs.ac.at/publications/pol/pw_72.pdf.

———. 2007. "Artistic Activism and Agonistic Spaces." *Journal of Ideas, Contexts and Methods* 1 (2).

Osanloo, Arzoo. 2006. "Islamico–Civil 'Rights Talk': Women, Subjectivity, and Law in Iranian Family Courts." *American Ethnologist* 33 (2): 191–209.

Peletz, Michael G. 2013a. "Malaysia's Shari`ah Judiciary as Global Assemblage: Islamization, Corporatization, and Other Transformations in Context." *Comparative Studies in Society and History* 55 (3): 603–33.

———. 2013b. "Continuities and Transformations, and Cultural Politics in Malaysia's Islamic Judiciary." Presentation at "Shari`a and Islamic Ethics in Transitions," Boston University, March 7–8, 2013.

Saddiqi, Dalal. 2013. *"Hind Bensari brise le tabou du viol en donnant la parole à la société marocaine."* May 21. https://web.archive.org/web/20130808005911/http://www.medias24 .com/121021052013Hind-Bensari-brise-le-tabou-du-viol-en-donnant-la-parole-a-la-societe -marocaine.html.

Salime, Zakia. 2012. "A New Feminism? Gender Dynamics in Morocco February 20th movement." *Journal of International Women's Studies* 13 (5): 101–14.

———. 2011. *Between Feminism and Islam: Human Rights and Shari`a Law in Morocco*. Minneapolis: University of Minnesota Press.

———. 2014. "New Feminism as 'Personal Revolutions': Micro-Rebellious Bodies." *Signs: The Journal for Women in Culture and Society* 40 (1): 14–20.

———. 2015. "Arab Revolutions, Legible Illegible Bodies." *Comparative Studies of South Asia Africa and the Middle East* 35(3): 525–538.

Skidmore, Monique. 2004. *Karaoke Fascism: Burma and the Politics of Fear*. Philadelphia: University of Pennsylvania Press.

Zeinobia. 2012. "#RIP Amina: You Are Not the First nor the Last." *Egyptian Chronicles*, March 14. http://egyptianchronicles.blogspot.fr/2012/03/rip-amina-you-are-not-first-nor-last.html.

Zubaida, Sami. 2005. *Law and Power in the Islamic World*. London and New York: I.B. Tauris.

Notes

1. *Al-Oula* news hour interview with Mustapha Ramid, available at http://www.youtube .com/watch?v=nLCnkwfm9Ik.

2. The meeting can be viewed in a documentary aired by the French television station 7&8, available at http://www.youtube.com/watch?v=8rcxSU16Wcc.

3. 2M Television interactive show, "Mubacharatan maakom," Wednesday, March 21, 2012, http://www.youtube.com/watch?v=lBxu9Pruhyg.

4. Ibid.

5. Ibid.

6. Amina, "L'Article 475 et le Droit Français," http://ibnkafkasobiterdicta.wordpress
.com/2012/03/15/amina-larticle-475-et-lancien-droit-français/.

7. The show can be found at http://stream.aljazeera.com/story/morocco-legal-loophole
-questioned-after-girls-death-0022130. The programs also aired some of the Moroccan protests of the case, as well as a long stream of responses from viewers.

8. Fadwa Misk, "I Was Raped," *Qandisha.ma*, March 26, 2012, http://www.qandisha
.ma/2012/03/26/i-was-raped/.

9. Tariq Ramadan, http://www.youtube.com/watch?v=ndoMvekGncA.

ISLAMIC LAW AND THE STATE

5 Constitutionalizing a Democratic Muslim State without Shari`a: The Religious Establishment in the Tunisian 2014 Constitution

Malika Zeghal*

RELIGIOUS ESTABLISHMENTS AND authoritarianism are quasi-universal in the Arab Middle East. In most of the Middle East, state authorities proclaim themselves the main religious authorities, and the state is the custodian of Islam, constitutionally and otherwise. In particular, Middle Eastern states financially and administratively sustain their Islamic institutions (for example, places of worship, religious education, and Islamic law), which they also strive to control and regulate. In this sense, most Middle Eastern states are "Muslim states." In Egypt and Tunisia, two countries where democratic transitions were put in motion after the 2011 uprisings, the religious establishments remained as strong as ever. Their persistence is not the result of the Islamist electoral victories that occurred after the fall of Ben Ali and Mubarak but rather the consequence of a broad and long-held agreement between Islamists and non-Islamists on the necessity of the state's being "Muslim."

In this chapter, I discuss the debates that took place in the 2012–14 National Constituent Assembly (NCA) that drafted Tunisia's 2014 constitution.[1] Many of these debates focused on what it meant for the state to be Muslim and democratic, revealing broad agreement among constituents on maintaining a religious establishment. Constituents all agreed on ascribing the custodianship of Islam to the state, as well as on the state's having to sustain religious institutions to protect Islamic values and ways of life. However, these debates also revealed a

* I thank the Radcliffe Institute for Advanced Study at Harvard University, where I was the Rita E. Hauser Fellow during 2013–14, for the support it provided me as I conducted this research. I also thank Fa'iq Habash and Nisreen Shiban, my research partners at the Radcliffe Institute, for their transcriptions of most of the debates I have used for this chapter. I am heavily indebted to Adel Allouche, Owen Fiss, Robert Hefner, Baber Johansen, Hédi Kallal, Anthony Kronman, Mary Lewis, Kristen Stilt, and Muhammad Qasim Zaman for their invaluable comments on an earlier draft of this chapter. Any errors are mine alone.

disagreement on the nature, strength, and extent of the religious establishment, a disagreement arising from three seemingly irreconcilable understandings of the religious establishment, forming an ideological cleavage that did not strictly follow the divide between Islamists and their political adversaries: a strong establishment that would operate as a tool for the management and control of Islam and that would restrict the influence of Islamist ideologies on society, a strong establishment that would aim at expanding the presence of Islam in public life and at restricting non-Islamic ways of life, and a light, nonlegislative and merely identity-related establishment that would not interfere with individual ways of life. Amid extreme tensions, a compromise was reached that recognized that the state could very well be Muslim without the constitutionalization of shari'a. Such a state of affairs would allow citizens to be Muslim in different ways, albeit within limits. On the one hand, Islamists, who viewed Islam as an essential counter-power constraining the state in democratic governance renounced making shari'a law the (or even a) source of legislation so long as the constitution guaranteed Muslim ways of life through the state's custodianship of Islam. On the other hand, their political adversaries, while agreeing with the state's custodianship of Islam, desired that freedom *from* religion be guaranteed by the introduction of the notion of "freedom of conscience" in the constitution, a rarity in the Middle East. These two opposite guarantees limited each other and reflected an original compromise, albeit one that contained significant contradictions, foreshadowing potential future problems and conflicts.

The analysis of the 2012–14 Tunisian constitutional experiment is of particular interest because it took place in a democratic context in which Tunisians could, for the first time, freely express their vision of an ideal Muslim state, describing its implementation and its concrete consequences. This provides us with an invaluable entry into the intricate process of shaping what they saw as a democratic and Muslim state. Although some have hypothesized the impossibility of a modern Muslim state (Hallaq 2013), one thing is certain: After 2011, Tunisians actively debated how they could ensure that their modern and newly democratic state would remain a Muslim state. This democratic transition made these debates the most introspective such moment in Tunisia's modern history. Wael Hallaq has argued that the modern state cannot be Muslim, because it is necessarily devoid of the moral content essential to Islamic governance. Even so, in 2012–14, Tunisian constituents drafted a constitution that established what they viewed as a modern and Muslim state and that, although it did not include any mention of shari'a, made Tunisians part of what they saw as a Muslim community—from a moral as well as a political point of view.

Whether they succeeded in establishing a "true" and "authentic" Muslim state is not the topic of this chapter, even supposing that such a thing could be ascertained. Rather, I examine the debates that took place from February 3, 2012, when the NCA started its deliberations, until the NCA's adoption of the constitution on January 26, 2014.[2] In the first section, I describe the main political actors, and I analyze the Islamist al-Nahdha Party's renunciation of shariʻa in the constitution as well as the persistence, after 2011, of the 1950s authoritarian constitutional compromise about Islam and the state. In the second section, I analyze the main points of agreement in the NCA (a democracy, a Muslim identity, a "modern Islam," and a religious establishment) and the main points of disagreement on nonreligious issues. In the third section, I delineate three competing understandings of the religious establishment put forward by the constituents, as well as the divide within al-Nahdha on this issue. In the fourth section, I analyze how the constituents reached an innovative but perilous compromise in which the state was at the same time the main custodian of Islam and the protector of freedom of conscience.

The Issue of Shariʻa as "Source of Legislation": Implementing a Muslim State without Shariʻa

Authoritarian postcolonial Tunisia, although often hastily considered one of the most "secular" Middle Eastern states, explicitly defined itself as "Muslim" early after independence. The 1959 constitution included an ambiguous clause that made Islam the religion "of the state" or "of Tunisia," depending on how one interpreted article 1, which read: "Tunisia is a free, independent, and sovereign state. Its language is Arabic, its religion is Islam and its regime is the Republic."[3] It also guaranteed freedom of creed (*hurriyat al-muʻtaqad*) and of religious worship (*hurriyat al-qiyam bi'l-shaʻir al-diniyya*) within the limits of "public order" (article 5), and it never mentioned shariʻa law. After the uprisings of 2011, Tunisia began a political transition that led to the first free and fair elections of its history.[4] The 1959 constitution was abrogated, and Tunisians freely elected a National Constituent Assembly (NCA) that reexamined the place of Islam in the constitution.

The Constituents: Islamists and Non-Islamists

October 23, 2011, saw the election of a 217-member NCA comprising 61 women and 156 men. Islamist party al-Nahdha won 89 seats (41 percent of the total), of which 41 were won by women.[5] The electoral law enforced gender parity by requiring electoral lists in each district to alternate between men and women, but the vast majority of the lists (93 percent) placed a male candidate in first position. Because al-Nahdha was the only party to win multiple seats in more than two districts (thirty of thirty-three districts), no other party actually came close to gender parity. Center-left party Congress for the Republic (CPR) won 29 seats (13 percent of the total), and 26 seats (12 percent of the total) went to Al-Aridha al-Chaabiya (The Popular Petition), a populist coalition of electoral lists whose leader had been a member of al-Nahdha until he left the movement in 1992.

Social-democratic party Democratic Forum for Labor and Liberties (Ettakattol) obtained 20 seats (9 percent of the total). Other parties included the Progressive Democratic Party (PDP), a leftist party with old Baathist roots (16 seats, for 7 percent of the total) and *al-Moubadara* (The Initiative), a vestige of the former ruling single-party RCD (5 seats, for 2 percent of the total). In addition, the Modernist Democratic Pole (PDM), a coalition of leftist parties such as al-Tajdid, a remnant of the Communist Party, explicitly campaigned against Islamism on a "modernist" platform but won only 5 seats (2 percent of the total). Overall, these electoral results reflected a clear rejection of the previous authoritarian regime as well as an endorsement of Islamism and, to a lesser extent, of political opposition parties that had not been previously coopted by Ben Ali's regime.

Al-Nahdha and the Popular Petition can both be classified as "Islamist": Unlike other parties, they claimed this label for themselves and were broadly recognized as such. Yet labeling other parties as "secularists" would be misleading, for very few members of these parties would call themselves "'*ilmaniyyin*," although some of them were so labeled by their Islamist political adversaries. Non-Islamist parties often called themselves "modernists" (*hadithiyyin*), a label also claimed for themselves by some Islamists. Even the leftist PDM coalition, after having campaigned on an anti-*Nahdha* theme, toned down its anti-Islamist rhetoric, perhaps in light of its meager electoral results. The views of a minority of sympathetic intellectuals notwithstanding, these non-Islamist political parties shared with their Islamist political opponents the assumption that Islam must be established in the state. They did not argue for separation of religion and state. For lack of a better word, I will therefore call them "non-Islamists" rather than "secularists."

After the elections of October 23, 2011, the "Troika," an alliance between al-Nahdha, CPR, and Ettakattol, governed the country from December 14, 2011, to January 9, 2014. In a context of unprecedented freedom of expression, of renewal of political elites, and of economic crisis and social unrest, the issues of the relationship between Islam and the state, as well as of the role of shari'a in legislation, came to the fore in public discussions and in the media. Tunisian society, as well as the NCA, was split into two seemingly irreconcilable camps: On the one hand, Islamists wanted to recover a Muslim identity that, they argued, had been muted by more than fifty years of authoritarianism and that must be reasserted as the foundation of the state and of legislation. On the other hand, non-Islamists saw signs of progress and modernity in the policies adopted by the postcolonial state in the religious domain. This deep and ancient cleavage crystallized around a number of key questions, including references to Islam and shari'a law in the constitution, women's rights, and freedom of conscience and expression. Even the governing coalition reflected this divide, with Islamists (al-Nahdha) and non-Islamists (CPR and Ettakattol) opposed in the Troika—although, as we will see, some CPR MPs leaned toward an understanding of the state close to that espoused by al-Nahdha.

The Issue of Shari`a as "Source of Legislation"

As the NCA drafting committees began drafting the new constitution in early 2012, a public debate that had started a year earlier about shari`a law in the constitution gained traction. The Salafi currents born after January 14, 2011, but excluded from the 2011 elections, as well as the right wing of al-Nahdha, demanded the inclusion of shari`a as "a" or "the" source of legislation in the constitution, demonstrating in front of the NCA in spring 2012.

At the time, and in convergence with most other Arab countries, several opinion polls showed that the overwhelming majority (almost 80 percent) of Tunisian men and women alike wanted legislation to be partially or wholly founded on shari`a.[6]

On February 28, 2012, political parties, coalitions, and independent MPs presented their conceptions of the future constitution of Tunisia, providing a valuable window into the main parties' ideal representations of state–religion relations. MP Sahbi Atiq spoke for al-Nahdha. This graduate of the Zaytuna University, born in 1959, presented al-Nahdha's ideal state as an "Islamic state" that was also a "civil state" and in which shari`a would play a central role. He did not specify, however, what the institutional workings of such a state would be. In a style reminiscent of the Muslim Brothers' ideology, he invoked Islam as "a doctrine [`aqida], a worship [`ibada], a morality [khuluq], an integral shari`a [shari`a mutakamila], and a way of life [manhaj li al-hayat]." He added: "Politics, as we conceive of it, is an activity situated at the most elevated level of worship, and religion cannot be a private affair in the internal conscience of the individual person [sha'nan khassan fi al-dhamir al-dakhili li al-insan]." Overall, he presented a more comprehensive conception of Islam than could be found in al-Nahdha's October 2011 electoral platform, which did not include references to shari`a (perhaps to keep from frightening parts of the electorate and derailing the transition). For Sahbi Atiq, Islam needed to be present "in the structures of the state, and not be a mere slogan." He added, "Islam relates to the life of the individual, to the affairs of the family, to society's rules, to the foundations of the state, and to the relations with the world."[7] He also made a reference to the seventh-century Charter of Madina as the first "constitution" of Islam. Although he did not explicitly argue in favor of mentioning shari`a as source of legislation in the future constitution, his argument could easily be interpreted in such a way.

During the same session, representatives from the (Islamist) Popular Petition articulated the same type of pronouncements and envisioned a state and a legal system founded on "Islam." One of its MPs, Mohamed Hamdi, proposed to make "Islam the main source of legislation" and presented an understanding of the political system in the Islamist vein, but with a more pronounced focus on social justice and economic redistribution than al-Nahdha. He argued for the use of "Islam" rather than of shari`a, "because Islam's meaning is broader than . . . the meaning commonly given to the term shari`a."[8]

In contrast with Islamists, non-Islamist parties either rejected mentioning shari`a in the constitution explicitly or avoided speaking about this issue. Social–Democratic Ettakattol MP Mouldi Riahi explicitly rejected including shari`a in the constitution as "the" source or "a" source of legislation because for him, the content, sources, and limits of shari`a were subject to too many different interpretations, which could threaten the unity of the nation and its religious integrity. In his view, it was sufficient to use article 1 of the 1959 constitution and to know that Tunisian legislation had been founded in part on shari`a, the Personal Status Code's having been inspired by Islamic law. On the other hand, leftist PDM MP Fadhel Moussa did not address the issue of shari`a and only spoke of the Islamic and Arab identity of the country. Rather than invoking a constitutional Islamic genealogy, as al-Nahdha did, he anchored the constitutional history of Tunisia in the precolonial legal reforms—the 1857 Security Pact (`ahd al-aman) and the 1861 constitution. In contrast, CPR MP Abdelraouf Ayadi criticized the 1857 Security Pact as having been drafted "under foreign pressures" and insisted on the Islamic and Arab identity of the nation without invoking shari`a law.[9] He also underlined that the constitution had to be founded on general principles rather than on overly specific ones, perhaps with an eye to justifying his refusal to invoke shari`a law.

In sum, the expositions of each party's understanding of the future constitution revealed a broad agreement on the Muslimness of the state and on the Muslim identity of Tunisia but showed a clear divide between Islamists and non-Islamists on the role of shari`a (or of Islam) in legislation.

Al-Nahdha's Renunciation of Shari`a in the New Constitution: The Role of the Electoral Law in the Engineering of a Compromise

At the end of March 2012, contradicting the pronouncements of al-Nahdha MP Sahbi Atiq, al-Nahdha's president, Rached Ghannouchi, announced that his party would not ask for a reference to shari`a in the new constitution. This decision came after a vote in the Founding Committee of the party: According to Rached Ghannouchi, thirteen committee members voted against and fifty-three for.[10] Before this vote, a preamble draft that originated from al-Nahdha and that included shari`a as "one of the main sources of legislation" had been circulated.[11] Al-Nahdha's renunciation of shari`a in the constitution was openly opposed by some of its prominent members. On social networks such as Facebook, and in street demonstrations, Islamist activists also insisted that shari`a be the source of legislation and that the constitution inscribe this principle as a perennial rule (as in most other Arab countries).

What drove al-Nahdha leaders' renunciation of shari`a in the constitution after their party had been consecrated the primary political force in the country? And how can we explain al-Nahdha's having gone against a public opinion so clearly in favor of inscribing shari`a in the constitution?

We must note, first, that although al-Nahdha gave a strong electoral performance, it did not win an outright majority of the NCA seats, and its two center-left coalition partners were not in favor of shari`a in the constitution. This electoral outcome, and the necessity for the eventual winner to compromise as part of a coalition, had been engineered *ex ante* through the new electoral law crafted after the fall of Ben Ali. The NCA was elected pursuant to a system of proportional representation with closed lists in one round, using the largest remainder method (also called Hare's method) and no formal vote threshold. This specific electoral system was deliberately chosen by the transitional elites to accomplish a particular aim: Aware of the potential electoral strength of al-Nahdha, and afraid of a winner-takes-all situation, they sought to constrain the likely winner into a coalition and a compromise.[12]

Al-Nahdha also faced resistance from a great number of adversaries, not only in the political arena but also in civil society, such as from organizations for the defense of women's and human rights and, particularly, from the UGTT labor union (Union Générale Tunisienne du Travail). The UGTT converged ideologically with the center-left and was staunchly opposed to al-Nahdha's ideology. It often organized strikes and demonstrations against the Troika government. Al-Nahdha's decision was thus pragmatic, aimed at minimizing tensions in a period of political transition in which social instability was omnipresent, especially considering the high rate of unemployment.[13] There were repeated episodes of violent conflicts in the street between rival political constituencies.[14] Al-Nahdha's decision made it possible to defuse conflicts, albeit at the cost of producing divisions between the party's liberal and pragmatic current on the one hand and its more conservative and radical wing on the other.

Implementing a Muslim State without Shari`a: The Postcolonial Authoritarian Compromise and the Quasiconstitutional Status of the 1956 Personal Status Code

Al-Nahdha leadership's renunciation of shari`a may also have had a deeper rationale: the recognition that the institutions of the modern state made the implementation of a Muslim state conceivable without recourse to shari`a in the constitution. This recognition fell in line with the postcolonial authoritarian compromise embodied in the 1956 Personal Status Code (PSC) and in article 1 of the 1959 constitution. However, the 2014 constitution gave more flesh to the meaning of this compromise.

After independence, Bourguiba's regime chose to eliminate shari`a courts and to unify the judicial system, in line with his broader project of economic and social development. Shari`a was absent from the 1959 constitution, although the preamble proclaimed the people's representatives' "faithfulness to the teachings of Islam." Islam was also mentioned in article 1 in an ambiguous formulation that left open whether Islam was the religion "of the state" or "of Tunisia." Article 5 guaranteed freedom of belief and of religious practice within the limits of "public order." A Personal Status Code (PSC) proclaimed in August 1956—even before the new constitution was drafted—antagonized conservatives by prohibiting unilateral repudiation and polygamy. Yet, because inheritance regulations still conformed to Islamic law, others argued for a further modernization of the code. For the regime, especially when it began confronting its Islamist opposition in the 1970s, the PSC became a law endowed with a quasi-constitutional status. For the elites in power, it could not be amended—neither to accommodate conservatives' demands to make it conform more strictly to shari`a law, nor to satisfy those who wanted to make it more progressive and to further gender equality.

The 1956 PSC was described by some, and by state official voices in particular, as conforming to "shari`a" and even as deriving from it. According to the official interpretation, the PSC was the result of an *ijtihad* based on Islamic texts and was thus in conformity with shari`a. In an effort to underline the Islamic foundations of the PSC, the first editions of the code included many footnotes that made reference to Hanafi and Maliki interpretations of shari`a, highlighting the work that had been carried out to codify shari`a law (Zeghal 2013a). For those opposed to it, however, the PSC did not adhere to shari`a, and the references to shari`a were purely symbolic.

The 1956 Constituent Assembly did not discuss the PSC other than indirectly, and Bourguiba imposed it authoritatively, even before the constitution was drafted, without submitting it to any real public debate. Several `ulama criticized the PSC but did not succeed in substantially influencing its content.[15] It was not the process of codification as such that irked the `ulama at the time—they did not seem to be opposed to the principle of *talfiq*, which allowed drawing on various schools of law to legislate. Rather, they were opposed to the new contents of the law that were in blatant contradiction with Islamic law. They also resented not having been called on to contribute to the codification project.

The regimes of Bourguiba and Ben Ali promoted the PSC as a distinctive symbol of Tunisian modernity and also kept insisting on its conformity with shari`a. Consequently, progressive and conservative Tunisian jurists continued to argue about interpretations of the PSC as it applied to specific legal cases that came before the tribunals. Describing the PSC as being "modern" because it sustained women's rights while being in conformity with shari`a by being based on an interpretation of Islamic law allowed the regime to maintain a balance between liberal and conservative interpretations of the code with no regard for those who, rejecting all compromise, either wanted to modernize it completely or wanted to return to the prescriptions of Islamic law that had been eliminated from it. No real public and open debate took place on this question, and the authorities kept a lid on it until the uprisings of 2010–11.

The Postcolonial Authoritarian Compromise Persists after 2011

After Ben Ali's fall in 2011, the debates between Islamists and their opponents on the issue of shari`a produced little clarity about its precise legal content. This might be explained by the absence—under Bourguiba's and Ben Ali's authoritarian regimes—of any public and free reflection on the content of shari`a, whose meaning remained elusive. Another reason might be that shari`a as a practiced legal institution (the teaching of fiqh and *usul al-fiqh* and its practice in the shari`a courts) had essentially disappeared after the judicial system unification, although some judgments still referred to it.[16]

On the PSC issue, the post-2011 public debates quickly resulted in a compromise: Immediately after his return from exile, al-Nahdha's leader Rached Ghannouchi declared that his party would not call for any modifications to the PSC. In this sense, he was in Bourguiba's regime continuity, although he remained very critical of Bourguiba's policies regarding Islam. Also for this reason, NCA discussions about gender were not as prominent as were debates about shari`a or about freedom of conscience. As a result, they seemed less contentious. The PSC remained unchanged after 2011, although several Islamist MPs explicitly disagreed with their non-Islamist counterparts, and also with past state elites, on the ideal content of the law, as we will now see.

Agreements and Disagreements in the 2012–14 NCA Debates

The discussions that took place in the NCA from 2012 to 2014 were public, being transmitted on live television and accessible in video format on the NCA website.[17] In addition, the constituents chose not to resort to an experts' draft but broadly consulted with civil society and with Tunisian and international legal and political experts, giving MPs and civil society ownership of the process and thus of its outcome. As al-Nahdha MP Nabiha Torjmane pointed out with satisfaction, the new constitution was "not written in the corridors of foreign embassies."[18] This made compromises more acceptable to all parties, as Mustapha Ben Jaafar, the president of the NCA and the leader of Ettakattol, publicly declared.[19] However, it had the disadvantage of lengthening the drafting process.

NCA committees were set up to draft specific chapters of the constitution. Their composition mirrored the NCA's, featuring an Islamist majority in each committee. This produced tensions and delays. Recognizing that the constitution could only be drafted by finding sufficient common ground, a consensus committee was formed in 2013 that represented all NCA political sensibilities equally, paving the way for a compromise.

The NCA drafting committees held their meetings behind closed doors, and the content of their deliberations largely remained unknown to the public. Although some compromises were reached before any public discussion actually took place in the NCA, the public debates nonetheless clearly reflected the lines separating the different parties. In fact, as some MPs told me, the NCA public debates were less conciliatory than the drafting committees discussions, precisely because political parties exploited the publicity of the debates to showcase their specificities.[20]

The political events taking place in Tunisia and elsewhere in the Middle East at that time weighed on the debates, particularly the assassination of two leftist members of the Tunisian political opposition in 2013 and the emergence of Salafi groups that demanded more Islamization.[21] The news of the summer 2013 Egyptian military coup also undoubtedly pressured the constituents to reach a compromise and hasten the drafting process. The fear of an "Egyptian scenario," which was reminiscent of the January 1992 Algerian military coup, was palpable in the NCA and led its members to find a consensus on the most contentious issues, particularly those involving Islam.

Although a compromise was eventually reached, divisions ran deep in the NCA. It was widely recognized that a compromise was reached in spite of profound disagreements about the role of Islam. Al-Nahdha MP Nabiha Torjman acknowledged the high polarization among MPs, saying, "Each camp fears for its identity."[22] There were numerous violent disputes, and many sessions were interrupted and adjourned. For instance, leftist Mouvement des Patriotes Démocrates MP Mongi Rahoui accused al-Nahdha of monopolizing Islam and reproached the president of the NCA for giving preference to Islamists during the debates: "Islam is common to all of us and does not belong to any party."[23] Al-Nahdha MP Mounira Omri addressed the opposition harshly before the president of the NCA interrupted her for being too polemical: "Say it honestly! You refuse Islam! Say it with courage! Say that you want to uproot Islam from society and that you want to remove it from all laws to build a secular state (*dawla la'ikiyya*)! I do not like this allergy to Islam. Aren't the MPs ashamed?"[24] At the end of July 2013, tensions reached their apex. After the assassination of leftist MP Mohamed Brahmi and while the repression against the Muslim Brothers was raging in Egypt, a group of about seventy opposition MPs suspended their participation in the NCA and demanded the removal of the Troika government. There were also tense moments during which MPs traded insults, and in at least one instance the national hymn was sung by non-Islamists while Islamists countered by reciting Al-Fatiha.[25] These theatrics were surely encouraged by the NCA debates' transmission on live public television, making the NCA sessions perfect opportunities for MPs to stage political spectacles and publicize their political stances.

Some MPs eventually expressed a sense of "fatigue" about the religious discussions, which they thought had become sterile if not downright absurd. Center-left CPR MP Hasna Marsit argued that there was too much debate on religion: "If we accept that in Islam there is no religious state [a statement made many times by both Islamist and non-Islamist MPs], then the Islamists versus secularists conflict is sterile. This is a struggle that threatens to divide our society."[26] In the same vein, leftist PDP MP Mohamed Gahbich argued that when the Tunisian people rose for its revolution, they did not ask themselves, "Who are we?" In his view, "too much effort [had] been wasted in sterile discussions about identity. Since the Tunisian people [were] attached to their Islamic identity and history, these discussions [were] irrelevant."[27]

The Main Points of Agreement: A Democracy, a Muslim Identity, A "Modern" Islam, and a Religious Establishment

The NCA debates revealed a number of important points of agreement: breaking with the authoritarian past, building an electoral democracy based on the separation of powers and on the independence of justice, having political alternation, and putting in place a constitutional court. For the constituents, the new democratic regime should guarantee individual rights and freedoms—although, as we will see, the issues of freedom *of* religion and freedom *from* religion proved highly contentious.[28]

When it came to Islam in the constitution, the constituents all spoke of Islam as shaping "the identity [*huwiyya*] of Tunisia" and the "personality" (*shakhsiyya*) of its people. They all associated—or equated—the values of Islam (*qiyam al-islam*) with "universal values" (*qiyam kawniya*) and human rights (*huquq al-insan*). There was an agreement that the kind of Islam envisioned was a "modern Islam"—or, phrased differently, that Islam was compatible with "modernity." The notion of modernity (*hadatha*) had been invoked by postcolonial regimes to legitimize their repression of Islamists. However, during that time, it was also rehearsed by the non-Islamist political opposition, which advocated for a reformist and democratic agenda. After the fall of Ben Ali, Islamists rehearsed that same concept, refusing description as "antimodern." Thus almost all MPs agreed that Islam had to be "modern" in one sense or another.

For instance, Ahmed Nejib Chebbi, leader of the leftist PDP, spoke of Islam as a religion "of this age," consciously avoiding the notion of *hadatha* (modernity) and replacing it with the notion of 'asri (of the age): "If we are realistic and look at ourselves, we, Tunisians, in our national identity are Muslims of this age [*muslimin 'asriyyin*] . . . . When we say that we belong to this age, we mean that various cultures, arts, sciences, and ideas belong to us, that we interact with them in our lives. . . . Therefore, we are Muslims of this age. As for the one who says I am of this age ['*asri*] and I am not a Muslim from a civilizational point of view [*hadhariyyan*] . . . he is guaranteed freedom of conscience. This is an individual issue. However, we belong to a history. We have roots, we have a civilization, and we have values."[29] For Ahmed Nejib Chebbi, Islam was to be present in the constitution as a civilization that interacted with others and as an identity, but also as a set of values. He also argued, in line with the postcolonial compromise on the PSC, that women's legal rights could not be altered—although some might think that they contradicted "our sacred heritage" (*mawruth muqaddas*).

Al-Nahdha's MPs also insisted that the constitution speak of a "modern Islam." For instance, Ahmed Mechergui stated, "These battles about the constitution are imaginary [*wahmiyya*]. We heard those who spoke about their fear for Islam, and we heard those who fear for modernity [*hadatha*]. I say that there are no contradictions between the spirit of Islam and the spirit of modernity."[30] Sadok Chourou, a prominent member of al-Nahdha who had initially advocated for shari'a as a "source for the codification of the law,"[31] underlined, a year later, the convergence of Islam and "modernity" when he accepted article 1 in its 1959 formulation without shari'a. However, he made it explicit that he interpreted article 1 as meaning that the state "derived its principles from Islam."[32]

That said, there were a few critiques of the notion of "modernity" by those who had long rejected its instrumentalization by Bourguiba's and Ben Ali's regimes against the Islamist opposition. For instance, center-left CPR MP Abd al-Raouf Ayadi spoke of the 1959 constitution as having built "a decor of modernity." In contrast with leftist PDP leader Chebbi, he disagreed with the image of a Tunisia situated "at the crossroad of civilizations," a formula he described as having been "imposed by the tyranny [of the previous regime]." He added, "Our constitution must start with our identity, our Arab and Islamic identity."[33]

Regarding the issue of the religious establishment, Islamists and non-Islamists agreed that the state should not be theocratic—that is, not be administered by religious specialists—and thus should be explicitly defined as a civil state. However, no NCA member clearly argued for the separation of state and Islam.[34] The necessity of a religious establishment was recognized by all MPs but was most clearly expressed by al-Nahdha. "The civil character of the state [*madaniyyat al-dawla*] does not mean that religion is separate from the state," said al-Nahdha MP Soulaf Ksantini when explaining why she agreed with the notion of a "civil state" (*dawla madaniyya*).[35]

The Main Points of Disagreement on Nonreligious Issues

The main divisions (on nonreligious issues) between the NCA's various blocs and parties revolved around whether the regime should be presidential or parliamentary, with al-Nahdha leaning toward a parliamentary system as a shield against a presidential takeover and as a way to preserve the Islamist Party's presence and weight in future legislatures. Some of the non-Islamists leaned toward a mixed system or a strong presidential system. There were also divisions on the extent of state welfare provisions. Although no MP argued against the state's involvement in the economy or against state welfare, the Islamist Popular Petition and the parties on the far left argued in favor of more generous welfare. The NCA was also divided on Tunisia's stance toward the state of Israel. Arab nationalists and Islamists were particularly vocal in their demands to inscribe a prohibition of the normalization of Tunisia's relations with Israel in the new constitution.

The Competing Meanings of the Religious Establishment

Although there was no disagreement on the principle of a religious establishment, the most significant and visible contentions in the NCA revolved around the nature and extent of this establishment and on the limits it set on religious freedom and on freedom of conscience. The June 1, 2013, constitutional draft crystallized some of these contentions, with various articles in this draft invoking Islam explicitly or implicitly. Article 1 was left identical to its 1959 version. Article 2 was new ("Tunisia is a civil state founded on citizenship, on the people's will and on the supremacy of the law"), and so was article 6 ("The state is the custodian of the religion [ra`iyat al-din], guarantees freedom of belief and conscience [hurriyat al-mu`taqad wa al-dhamir], and freedom of religious practice [al-sha`a'ir al-diniyya]. It protects sacred things [muqaddasat] and guarantees the neutrality of mosques and places of worship with respect to partisan instrumentalization [al-tawdhif al-hizbi]"). Finally, to clarify the 1959 formulation of article 1—which could be interpreted as stating "Islam is the religion of the state" or "Islam is the religion of Tunisia"—al-Nahdha's MPs introduced article 141, which stated, in particular, "No constitutional amendment can harm [nala min] Islam as religion of the state." All these articles remained in the final draft of the 2014 constitution, with some modifications, except for article 141, which was removed in the face of strong opposition. Although there was a broad agreement on the principle of a religious establishment, non-Islamists did not accept such a clear rejection of article 1 and rejected article 141. The discussions that led to this outcome and to the final constitutional draft in 2014 reveal three competing versions of the religious establishment. In so doing, they provide an invaluable window into the existing political cleavages on the issue of Islam and the state.

The Light Nonlegislative Establishment Envisioned by the Social–Democratic Ettakol Party

The Social–Democratic Ettakattol Party advocated for a light, bureaucratic, identity-related and nonlegislative establishment. In such an establishment, the state would provide a religious infrastructure to its citizens and manage religious institutions without imposing its own interpretation of Islam and while also ensuring religious freedom. Also, for Ettakattol, political activism and religion had to be kept as separate as possible in public life. A young member of Ettakattol's leadership told me, "Article 1 does not mean much more than what it says. Whoever invented it was a genius. But it is out of the question that there be any article on shari`a being a source of legislation."[36] In other words, the very idea of shari`a was frightening for Ettakattol's leadership, whereas the broader notion of "Islam" was not, referring to a collective identity rather than to specific legal prescriptions. In line with past official interpretations, Social–Democratic Ettakattol interpreted the PSC as conforming to Islam but wanted to keep the very idea of shari`a at bay.

During the February 28, 2012, NCA session during which each party presented its conception of the future constitution, Ettakattol's general position was voiced by MP Mouldi Riahi, a high school teacher who held a master's degree in Islamic Philosophy from the University of Tunis. For him, Islam was "the source of [Tunisians'] unity" and represented "the identity of the people. . . . This identity interacts with the universal values [*qiyam kawniya*] described in the Universal Declaration of Human Rights." He also added that Islam needed to be kept away from "doctrinal contentions and from all political instrumentalizations." Mouldi Riahi underlined that the Tunisian Republic needed to be defined as civil, that it should not bear any resemblance to "republics that call themselves 'Islamic republics,' and that it should not be a military republic, either. However, in his view, the state needed to protect the people's identity. He did not question the state's management of religious institutions, but he outlined specific domains in which religion and politics should not interact. For him, the state needed to enforce the political neutrality of places of worship and needed to prohibit the use of religion in political activities. He also described himself as being against a state monopoly on religion and religious interpretations. For him, there was a risk that this monopoly might take the form of a "rigid and extremist reading of our religion," with the state "meddling with coercive methods in the private lives of citizens" and thereby threatening to "harm their rights and freedoms." With this description, he seemed to refer to an "Islamic republic." On the other hand, Mouldi Riahi also stated that this monopoly might take the shape of an authoritarian "interpretation of modernity, which could lead to the elimination [*ilgha'*] of religion from public life in coercive ways," a description that seemed to refer to Ben Ali's regime, and perhaps to the Bourguiba era as well. This would, in his view, lead again to "a confrontation between the state and religion." Mouldi Riahi also categorically opposed the introduction of shari`a in article 1, arguing that shari`a had many interpretations and that Tunisians would be divided on its legal implementation, "all the more so [seeing] that we have based all our legislation on article 1 since independence, in particular our Personal Status Code and our Penal Code. We based this legislation on article 1 in accordance with the values of our tolerant religion [*dinuna al-samha'*] and by deriving [these values] from the great Koran and the sayings of its noble prophet."[37] Everything considered, Ettakatol argued for leaving article 1 unchanged from its 1959 formulation, reflecting a light version of religious establishment.

The Contrasting Strong Religious Establishments Envisioned by Leftist PDM and Islamist al-Nahdha

Within the opposition to the Troika, some non-Islamist parties advocated for a strong religious establishment that would be bureaucratic and identity-related and that would operate as a tool for the management and control of Islam. For instance, for MP Samir Taïeb, a member of the Political Bureau of the Tajdid Party (formerly the Communist Party) in the PDM coalition, the state had to manage and regulate religious institutions in a way that would explicitly restrict the influence of Islamist ideologies. When I met with him in summer 2012 in the NCA, he told me, "We are against secularism defined in the French way. We are against separation between religion and state. The state cannot abandon the regulation of mosques. These mosques would fall into the hands of Islamists. If we did the same with education, we would have the Taliban. However, we want to separate religion and politics. . . . One can refer to religion in a political platform, but should not say that this or that verse of the Koran prescribe this or that behavior. We are against the instrumentalization of religion by the state. We need an independent administrative authority to watch over religion."[38] Like the Islamists, PDM MP Samir Taïeb argued for a strong bureaucratic establishment restricting freedoms, although it was the Islamists' freedom of expression that they explicitly aimed at restricting in order to protect society from Islamism. Note that although he firmly argued against separation of state and Islam, he advocated for keeping Islam out of politics, a pervasive trope of authoritarian Middle Eastern regimes, including Bourguiba's and Ben Ali's.

On the other hand, the Islamist version of the religious establishment aimed at expanding the presence of religion in public life. Although some Islamists did argue for restricting their political opponents' individual freedoms, Islamists did not want to circumscribe Islam and put it under state surveillance as envisioned by PDM MP Samir Taïeb. They advocated for the expansion of Islam to be implemented through the channels of education and legislation. Al-Nahdha MP Sadok Chourou provided a precise interpretation of article 1: "Islam legislates for all aspects of life and guarantees justice and dignity."[39] He added that Islam limited freedoms in order to prevent obscenity (*fahisha*) and apostasy (*khuruj 'an al-din*). He argued that the sovereignty of the people derived from the sovereignty of God and stated, "Our highest constitution is the Koran and the highest sovereignty is to God before it is to the people . . . Since we are writing the constitution of a Muslim people, our article 1 should state that the highest sovereignty belongs to Allah." To further justify his demand, he added, "We would not be the first ones to do that." He cited the example of Canada's constitution that mentions "the sovereignty of God,"[40] and asked, "Are we less Muslim than they are?"

We have seen earlier how al-Nahdha MP Sahbi Atiq argued for Islam's playing an integral role in the state. He also stated that legislation should not contradict the certainties contained in the Qur'an and the *Sunna*. He invoked freedom of religion, in particular freedom to choose one's way of life, and argued, "a democratic state does not have the right to meddle in people's lives, impose ways of life, doctrines, or tastes [*anmat al-hayat, 'aqa'id, wa adhwaq*]." His conception of a state that should remain neutral with regard to religious doctrines converged with Social–Democratic Ettakattol's position described in the previous section. However, it was strikingly at odds with his own argument in favor of shari'a law. Sahbi Atiq did not seem to be aware of this contradiction, perhaps because by "the meddling of the state" in individual beliefs he referred to Bourguiba and Ben Ali regimes' repressive strategies toward al-Nahdha and Islamists' religiosity rather than to a state's religious establishment that would impose religious norms on society at large.

The Divide among Islamists

Al-Nahdha MP Sahbi Atiq had participated in the 18 October movement under Ben Ali's regime, as part of which, starting in 2005, prodemocracy activists from the center-left and al-Nahdha attempted to work on a broad agreement about a number of issues such as gender equality and freedom of conscience. Although this group found a modicum of commonality on the subjects of gender equality, freedom of conscience, and religion and state, even publishing common position papers on these issues, Sahbi Atiq published a dissenting position on the question of religion and state. The common position rejected the coerciveness of the existing religious establishment and the use of religion by the authoritarian regime but also advocated for a relation between Islam and the state in the following terms: "A democratic state must award a special place to Islam, because it is the religion of the majority of the people, without monopolizing or instrumentalizing Islam. In addition, [this state must] guarantee the rights of all beliefs and convictions and the freedom of religious practice" (*Al-Mawqif* 2009, 5). Beyond the "special place" granted to Islam by the state, the common position did not offer more specifics on the exact structure it envisioned for the relation between Islam and the state, but in light of the 2012–14 NCA debates, it is likely that it imagined a light, nonlegislative establishment (as advocated by Social–Democratic Ettakattol). In his 2005 dissenting argument, Sahbi Atiq defended a stronger role for Islam as "the religion of the state."

Sahbi Atiq was representative of a conservative current within al-Nahdha that elicited strong reactions from non-Islamists. For instance, in reference to al-Nahdha MP Sadok Chourou, who called for the implementation of Islamic *hudud* against street demonstrators, Social–Democratic Ettakattol MP Ali Bechrifa argued during the January 23, 2012, session, "It is not acceptable that under the roof of this assembly there be calls to cut hands and legs. Tunisia must not be the country of the Taliban!"[41] In order to defuse this tension, some of al-Nahdha MPs often used the terms "*maqasid al-shari`a*" to underline that they were not intent on implementing the specific legal rules of shari`a, particularly the *hudud* penalties, but rather on implementing shari`a's "purposes." They claimed that shari`a represented the spirit of Islamic law, rather than its letter, as a way of reassuring their political opponents who were frightened by the idea of *hudud*. However, al-Nahdha MP Abd al-Majid Najjar vocally condemned his party's decision to renounce shari`a in the constitution and to focus on the spirit rather than on the letter of shari`a law. He argued that shari`a law was not a set of "purposes" but rather "a set of rules" and criticized his own party for contradicting one of the central tenets of its ideology.[42]

The Islamist Popular Petition MP Iskander Bouallag, on the other hand, argued for including "Islam as source of the law" in the constitution without invoking shari`a law.[43] Some sessions later, he stated that in his view, Islam was already the source of "99% of the laws" in Tunisia.[44] A year later, during the January 4, 2014, session, when article 1 was discussed for the final vote, the Islamist Popular Petition continued to defend this position, whereas al-Nahdha had already agreed to a compromise. In the end, out of the 74 MPs in attendance (of a total 217), only 3, all from the Popular Petition, refused to vote for article 1 in its 1959 formulation.[45]

Al-Nahdha's Compromise: Implementing a Muslim State without Shari`a, with Islam as a Counter-Power in Democratic Governance

Even the most conservative al-Nahdha MPs who had explicitly argued in favor of shari`a as the source of legislation in the constitution, such as Habib Ellouze and Sadok Chourou, voted for article 1 in its 1959 formulation.[46] This was the result of a political compromise—not only between Islamists and their political opponents but also within al-Nahdha itself. Indeed, the view that Islam was an integral set of values to be implemented in all domains of life was not shared by all members of al-Nahdha's leadership. Even more important, it became clear within al-Nahdha that implementing a Muslim state did not require constitutionalizing shari`a law.

It is particularly noteworthy that al-Nahdha's female MPs played a crucial role in building compromises with al-Nahdha's political adversaries, as well as within al-Nahdha itself, when it came to religious issues. About half of al-Nahdha's female MPs were new members of the party in 2011, although they had affinities with al-Nahdha's movement prior to their political careers in the NCA (Ben Ismail 2014). As a result, and in contrast with most al-Nahdha male MPs, who had been molded, often for decades, in the movement's doctrine, as newcomers to political life, al-Nahdha female MPs had broader margins of maneuver and displayed more flexibility in their ideological orientations.

On July 6, 2013, al-Nahdha female MP and member of the Preamble Committee Sanaa Haddad, also a lawyer with her own practice and a PhD student in private law, explained the compromise made by her party on shari`a law. She interpreted article 1 as meaning that Islam was the religion "of the state." This, she added, did not make the state a "religious state": "In our Committee, we have defined the civil nature of the state. It means the supremacy of the law and the sovereignty of the people. Never ever will it mean that the state is secular, i.e.[,] that religion and state are separate and that religion and law are separate!" She also put into perspective the preamble committee's renunciation of Islam as source of legislation: "I do not want to say that we have changed the principle that Islam is a source of legislation, but I say that the party of the majority [al-Nahdha] in the NCA has decided that *article 1 was enough by itself to compel the state, with its institutions and its three branches of government, to respect Islam.* This article guarantees by itself the Islamic reference of the state."[47] Sanaa Haddad reminded her audience that this Islamic reference was not "foreign to our country," pointing to the PSC and to the Real Estate Code, as well as to a statement by the court of cassation according to which in case of ambiguity or obscurity in the codes of law, shari`a law should be referred to. She insisted that article 1 should be interpreted as meaning that Islam "is the religion of the people and of the state, not just of the people. [If it were merely the religion of the people] it would mean that Islam does not constrain the state in any way."[48] She added that an independent justice system would protect "against extremism . . . would anchor society in its values, and would protect us from being imposed a specific way of life." In sum, in Sana Haddad's conception of government, Islam constituted an essential counter-power constraining the state *and* a necessary ingredient of democratic governance that guaranteed the preservation of Islamic values and ways of life. Obviously, this conception has its contradictions: The reference to Islam in the constitution is both democratic (it respects the desire of the majority of citizens to live as Muslims) and antidemocratic (it limits non-Muslim ways of life).

The Unresolved Disagreements about the Religious Establishment

The issue of whether to interpret article 1 as meaning that Islam was the religion "of the state" or "of the people" remained unresolved, and Islamists and non-Islamists insisted on rehearsing their own various interpretations until the very end of the drafting process. A few weeks before the final draft was passed, center-left CPR MP Rafik Tlili argued that article 1 was ambiguous: "Is it the religion of the people or of the state? Article 141 was proposed to lift this ambiguity by explaining that it is the religion of the state, but it almost caused the disintegration of the NCA and, with it, of the political experiment we are living right now."[49] For him, it was necessary to add to article 1—"Islam is the religion of its people"—because "it is the people who will have to face the last judgment day, not the state." Al-Nahdha MP Warda Turki disagreed with this suggestion, because for her, as for her fellow al-Nahdha MP Sanaa Haddad, Islam was the religion of all the institutions of the state, not merely the religion of the people, since the state must be "in unison with the aspirations of its people, and not be estranged from its people."[50] Earlier on, liberal Afek MP Rym Mahjoub had criticized this understanding of the state by describing it as a "doctrinal state" (*dawla `aqa'idiyya*) in response to al-Nahdha MP Sana Mirsni's argument that article 141 "represented the spirit and the philosophy of the constitution."[51]

Other al-Nahdha MPs, a few sessions before the final vote on the constitution's final draft, attempted to give more flesh to their party's interpretation of the relationship between Islam and the state. For instance, on January 4, 2014, al-Nahdha MP Sonia Toumia explained the phrase "the state is the custodian of Islam" in article 6 (which will be analyzed in more detail in the next section) by the role of the state in religious guidance (*irshad*) to "help citizens make choices." Al-Nahdha MP Mounia Gasri defined the term "sacred things" (*muqaddasat*) in article 6 as "the divine existence [*al-dhat al-ilahiya*], the heavenly books, the messengers and the prophets, and the places of worship."[52]

It is also worth noting that other political parties that were not markedly Islamist also shared al-Nahdha's conception of a state required to enforce Muslim norms in the public space. For instance, Moubadara (an offspring of the single-party RCD formerly in power) MP Mouna Ben Nasr argued that civil servants should conform to Islam by respecting the prayer schedule, stating that she was against freedom of conscience.[53]

An Innovative but Perilous Compromise: The State as "Custodian of Islam" and Defender of "Freedom of Conscience"

In the face of these strong disagreements about the meaning, nature and extent of the religious establishment, the Islamist and non-Islamist camps, each fearing manipulations of the constitutional language by the other in future legislatures, drafted mutually limiting clauses about Islam in a newly introduced article 6. This was an innovative compromise, albeit one that left the door open to potential future problems and conflicts.

Interpretative Ambiguities and the Fear of Future
Constitutional Language Manipulations

The constituents accepted article 1's ambiguity perhaps because they knew, from past experience, what to expect from it. Jawhara Tiss, a female al-Nahdha MP from a younger generation, recognized that it was impossible to define once and for all what "Islam" meant in article 1, and that the constituents had to live with this ambiguity. She argued, "The issue of religion remains, the issues of what Islam is, and of how Tunisian elites represent Islam today. *It is impossible to solve this issue in the constitution.* The NCA debates have revealed that there are those who see Islam as mere rituals [*tuqus*] and teachings that only matter for the relation between the individual and Allah. There is another view, however, that sees Islam as one of the sources of knowledge, and therefore, as one of the sources of the law."[54] She did not offer an answer to the issue of, in her own words, "what Islam is" and was willing to leave it at that. In that sense, she was at odds with an older generation within al-Nahdha that essentially equated Islam with "shari'a law."

When debating new constitutional language outside of article 1, each camp fearfully imagined how the other camp could use this language to impose its interpretation of the religious establishment and thus either rejected the new language or demanded more clarity.[55] For instance, reacting to the December 2012 preamble draft, which stated that the constitution was drafted on the basis of "the constants and the aims" of Islam (*thawabit wa maqasid al-islam*), center-left CPR MP and lawyer Samia Abbou argued that the term "constants" was difficult to interpret. She added, "The problem is, who will interpret these constants? The problem is that an extremist majority might have a wrong interpretation of Islam and might make the legislation it wants . . . For instance, today, an MP said that capital punishment [*qassas*] is part of the constants. This means that we might pass a law that will flog the [citizen] who drinks alcohol and will cut the hand of the thief. We might pass laws that violate freedoms and go against the constitution with the permission of the constitution."[56] For Samia Abbou, the notion of "constants" of Islam could be interpreted as meaning "the rules of shari'a law" and was therefore to be removed. Criticizing article 6 of the June 1, 2013, draft according to which the state "protects the sacred" (*muqaddasat*), center-left CPR MP Hasna Marsit criticized the absence of definition of the meaning of "sacred" and the lack of explanation about the intent of the article, adding that this "might lead to a wrong use [of article 6]."[57] For leftist PDP MP Mohamed Baroudi, nobody doubted that the Tunisian people belonged to the Islamic and Arab identity. "However," he added, "we interpret the religious text in different ways and we fear that a day will come when the interpretation of the text will be influenced by a reactionary interpretation that will destroy what we have accomplished with the 1959 constitution."[58] In sum, non-Islamists either rejected proposed constitutional clauses or wanted them to be more specific in hopes of preventing future Islamist interpretations of the constitution.

Similarly, Islamists feared future manipulations of the constitutional language by non-Islamists. For instance, al-Nahdha MP Adel Ben Attia argued against the principle of freedom of conscience in the following terms: "The meaning of this kind of freedom [freedom of conscience] is not clear, and each school of thought has its own definition . . . I request a precise explanation of its meaning, and the introduction of a word [in the draft] that will show that there is no contradiction between the individual's freedom of conscience and the people's freedom of conscience." By "the people's freedom of conscience," he meant the Muslim identity and values of the Tunisian people.[59]

Article 6: Freedom of Religion and Freedom from Religion

The NCA was deeply divided on the issue of delimiting individual freedoms related to Islam, and this cleavage did not strictly follow the Islamist/non-Islamist divide. One camp wanted to inscribe limits to freedom *of* religion in the constitution—for example, by banning *takfir* (accusations of apostasy)—while their opponents wanted to limit freedom *from* religion—for example, by rejecting the right to freedom of conscience. Rather than leave the issue unresolved (as had happened with article 1), each camp crafted explicit limits on the other camp's conception of freedoms in article 6. The final version of article 6 complemented article 1, and provided more specifics about the state's relation with Islam. It stated: "The state is the custodian of the religion [*ra`iyat al-din*]. It guarantees freedom of belief, freedom of conscience and of religious worship [*hurriyat al-mu`taqad wa al-dhamir, wa mumarasat al-sha`a'ir al-diniyya*]. It ensures the neutrality of mosques and places of worship and protects them from partisan instrumentalization. The state shall commit to spreading the values of moderation and tolerance, to protecting sacred [things] [*muqaddasat*] and to preventing attacks on them. It shall also commit to prohibiting *takfir* [accusations of apostasy] and incitements to hatred and violence, and to confronting them." This article was augmented from its June 1, 2013, version by prohibiting *takfir* (accusations of apostasy, presumably against those making use of their freedom of conscience) but also by making the state the protector of sacred things (presumably allowing the state to limit freedom of conscience and expression). It continued to designate the state as the main agent of regulation and protection of Islam—"the" religion it clearly referred to using the words *"ra`iyat al-din."* The word *ra`i* refers to the shepherd and, in the tradition of classical Islam, to the ruler who watches over and leads his flock. Also related to the idea of "custodianship," article 39 stated that Islamic values should be disseminated to the youth in public education ("the state ensures that the Arab and Muslim identity is rooted in the youth") in combination with "nationalism" and with "the values of human rights."[60]

The notions of freedom "of belief" and freedom of religious worship were already present in the earlier constitutional vocabulary of Tunisia. In contrast, freedom of conscience was an innovation. Harking back to eighteenth-century Europe, the modern formulation of freedom of conscience means "the person's freedom to choose their religious convictions for themselves" (Sandel 1998) and is part of the conception of a secular state that adopts a theoretical position of neutrality toward all religions.[61] In that sense, the innovation brought by the NCA with article 6 added a radically new element to Tunisia's constitutional tradition: In addition to the freedom to exercise one's own religion, article 6 gave Tunisians the freedom to choose their religious convictions (as well as the freedoms not to believe and not to worship). However, article 6 also limited this freedom, for in its formulation, the state, as custodian of Islam and protector of sacred things, was not a neutral power vis-à-vis the religion of Islam. In addition, article 39 made explicit the pedagogical role of the state in inculcating Islamic values in its citizens. Freedom of conscience became a contentious issue for Islamists as well as for some non-Islamists, being understood as freedom *from* Islam and thus in blatant contradiction with article 1 and with the principle of the state's custodianship of Islam inscribed in article 6 itself.

Discussing the June 1, 2013, constitutional draft, Fidélité (an independent electoral list from Kasserine) MP Mabrouk Hrizi, who later joined center-left CPR, argued that article 1 (Islam as religion of the state and/or Tunisia), article 2 (defining the state as civil), article 6 (making the state the custodian of Islam and guaranteeing freedom of conscience), and article 141 (Islam as the religion of the state) should be interpreted as a whole and that they guaranteed necessary limits to freedom of conscience: "The question is: can freedom be absolute, without limits and without responsibility? Can freedom of conscience be without a conscience? Can workers go on strike without limits? Can freedom of expression be left without a watchdog [*raqib*]?"[62]

In the same vein, other non-Islamist MPs argued against freedom of conscience. Center-left CPR MP Rabii Abdi said, "We have reservations about freedom of conscience. Some will understand that we have reservations about freedom. There is no dispute about freedom. The problem is not freedom of conscience but its consequences."[63] He then listed a series of eclectic—and, in his view, problematic—examples of such consequences: objectors of conscience, doctors refusing to perform abortions, gay marriage, magistrates refusing to apply a law in which interest rates are involved, and legalization of radical Islamist group Ansar al-Shari`a.[64] In his view, freedom of conscience was problematic not merely because the state was Muslim or because Islam was the religion of the Tunisian people but also because "freedom of conscience will contradict our legal structure."[65]

Azed Badi, another CPR MP, also argued against freedom of conscience, although his reasons were more explicitly religious. He refused to accept the expression of atheism in public and argued that freedom of conscience was "imposed by foreign agendas."[66] Leftist PDP MP Iyad Dahmani, as well as liberal Afek MP Rym Mahjoub, opposed Azed Badi on this issue, with Rym Mahjoub arguing against any limits to human rights.[67] In the same vein, Afek Party MP Chokri Beaich underlined the contradiction between a state that protects freedom of conscience and that is at the same time the "custodian of the religion." "Here," he added, "minorities are ignored, even though they are very few."[68]

The statements of some CPR MPs against freedom of conscience were consistent with those made by al-Nahdha MPs. For instance, al-Nahdha MP Kamel Ben Amara argued, "When we speak of the civil nature of the state, we speak about it in the framework of civil human and universal values, but not in the framework of the global universal values founded on absolute liberalism and on the principles of secularism and *laïcité*."[69] For him, a notion of freedom of conscience that would allow an individual to renounce his religion or chose any religion was unacceptable. In his view, article 1 served to limit this type of freedom. Al-Nahdha MP Khalil Belhaj also argued for limiting the extent of freedoms by invoking moral norms, which he considered absent from secular constitutions: "Secular constitutions assert the absolute freedom of the individual without relating it to morality [*akhlaq*]. The freedom we want is a freedom constrained by our culture and our morals."[70]

Freedom of conscience was eventually introduced in the 2014 constitution and counterbalanced the conception of a state that was the custodian of Islam and the protector of "sacred things." This way, freedom *of* religion and freedom *from* religion were inscribed in the constitution, although each with strong limitations. The final version of article 6 was a compromise that kept in check the "extremists" of each camp—those who might accuse fellow Muslims of apostasy or restrict the freedoms of religious minorities on the one hand and those who might publicize anti-Islamic statements and practices on the other. This was a way for the state to guarantee that both camps could coexist in the new democratic polity, albeit with strong constraints on their respective freedoms. Article

6 could seem incoherent because of the contradictory functions it attributed to the state—guardian of the communal order defined as "Muslim" on the one hand and protector of individual freedoms on the other. However, it was coherent by reflecting the existence of a real and important cleavage in Tunisian society while attempting to mitigate the most dangerous manifestations of that cleavage.

The solutions provided by the NCA in the drafting of article 1 and article 6 were each of a different nature. Article 1 rehearsed an old and ambiguous constitutional clause that had been crafted under authoritarianism. In contrast, article 6 expressed an innovative but perilous compromise that had been reached in a democratic context. In this compromise, the state was the main caretaker of Islam and religious institutions, and freedom *of* religion and freedom *from* religion explicitly limited each other. However, article 6 did not specify the exact limits of these freedoms. Both articles deferred interpretative issues for future adjudication in courts of law and in future legislative and public arena debates. They undoubtedly foreshadowed future problems and conflicts.

Conclusion

The 2014 constitution contained all the elements of a democratic polity—for example, the sovereignty of the people, free elections, separation of powers, judicial independence, and a constitutional court. Article 1 ("its religion is Islam") remained ambiguous and unchanged from the 1959 constitution, with the addition that it could not be changed. In addition, as in 1959, shari`a was never explicitly mentioned—in large part because shari`a was neither deemed necessary by al-Nahdha nor desirable by its political adversaries for implementing a Muslim state. Behind article 1 were three competing and seemingly irreconcilable conceptions of the religious establishment, forming an ideological cleavage that did not strictly follow the divide between Islamists and non-Islamists: a nonlegislative identity-related light establishment (Ettakattol), a strong establishment limiting and controlling Islam (PDM), and another strong establishment urging that Islam be expanded in public life and constitute a necessary counter-power in democratic governance (al-Nahdha). In spite of these differences, broad agreement held, among Islamists and non-Islamists alike, that Islam and the state not be separated. A compromise was reached in article 6, which took a middle path and allowed citizens to be Muslim in different ways so long as certain mutually constraining red lines—*takfir*, as well as, on the flip side, offenses against the sacred—were not crossed. It thus made the state the arbitrator of religious conflicts as well as the authority setting the lines differentiating between acceptable and unacceptable ways of life of its citizens.[71] It also carried with it obvious contradictions, as well as future potential problems and conflicts. Echoing numerous polls that demonstrated that most Tunisians wanted "Islam and democracy," the

2014 constitution illustrated the desire for a democratic state whose custodianship of Islam set limits on freedom *from* religion.

References

Ben Ismail, Youssef. 2014. "The Political Rise of Ennahdha's Women: Changing the Markers of Legitimacy." MA thesis, Center for Middle Eastern Studies, Harvard University.

Cammett, Melani, and Edmund Malesky. December 2012. "Power Sharing in Postconflict Societies: Implications for Peace and Governance." *Journal of Conflict Resolution* 56:982–1016.

Hallaq, Wael B. 2013. *The Impossible State. Islam, Politics, and Modernity's Moral Predicament.* New York: Columbia University Press.

Al-Jumhuriyya al-Tunisiyya, al-Ma`had al-watani li al-ihsa. August 2012. *Al-Tashghil wa al-bitala, al-thulathi al-awwal 2012.* Tunis.

Latiri, Kawther, and Malika Zeghal, with Tawfik Hermassi. July 2012. "Socio-economic/Religious Cleavages and Electoral Choices after the Arab Spring: The Case of the Tunisian Elections of October 23, 2011." Working Paper.

Lerner, Hanna. 2011. *Making Constitutions in Deeply Divided Societies.* Cambridge, UK: Cambridge University Press.

Al-Mawqif. 2009. "Fi al-`alaqa bayna al-dawla wa al-din." December 18.

Sandel, Michael. 1998. "Religious Liberty: Freedom of Choice of Freedom of Conscience." In *Secularism and Its Critics,* edited by Rajeev Bhargava, 73–93. New Delhi: Oxford University Press.

Zeghal, Malika. 2013a. "The Implicit Shari`a. Established Religion and Family Law Codification in Tunisia." In *Varieties of Religious Establishments,* edited by Lori Beaman and Winnifred Sullivan, 107–30. London: Ashgate.

———. June 2013b. "Competing Ways of Life: Islamism, Secularism, and Public Order in the Tunisian Transition," *Constellations* 20 (2): 254–74.

———. Forthcoming. *Sacred Politics: Islam and the State in the Middle East.* Princeton, NJ: Princeton University Press.

Notes

1. To my knowledge, there are no available records of the debates that took place in the Egyptian Constituent Assembly that drafted the 2012 constitution that was later abrogated.

2. These debates are available in video format on the NCA website at http://www.anc.tn /site/main/AR/docs/vid_debat.jsp?id=03022012&t=t and are published in the Republic of Tunisia's *Official Gazette.* At the time of writing, only a small number of debates were published, and most of the debates I used were available only in video form.

3. Article 37 required that the president of the republic be a Muslim.

4. For further analysis of the 2011 Tunisian elections, see Latiri and Zeghal (2012). In spite of some *ex post* irregularities, the results of these elections were widely accepted by Tunisians and by international observers. Moreover, unlike in previous Tunisian elections, the results were not predetermined *ex ante.*

5. Born out of the Islamic Tendency Movement, the al-Nahdha movement (*ḥarakat al-nahdha*) was created in the early 1980s and until 2011 was relegated to illegal status by the

authoritarian regimes of Bourguiba (1956–87) and Ben Ali (1987–2011). During that time, only sham elections took place, and legalized parties were either co-opted by the regime, being assigned a few seats in the legislature—as well as financial and other resources—or were repressed and lived on the margins of political life.

6. Sigma Conseil, "Les Tunisiens, la politique et la religion," poll of May 3–4, 2012. Dalia Mogahed, "Arab Women and Men See Eye to Eye on Religion's Role in Law," June 25, 2012, http://www.gallup.com/poll/155324/Arab-Women-Men-Eye-Eye-Religion-Role-Law.aspx.

7. NCA Morning Session of February 28, 2012.

8. NCA Afternoon Session of February 28, 2012.

9. NCA Morning Session of February 28, 2012. This is a common trope among anti-Western political actors, including some Islamists. The 1857–61 legal reforms were in fact both the product of foreign pressures and of indigenous projects. Moreover, both foreigners and Tunisians were ambivalent about these reforms. See Zeghal (forthcoming).

10. *Al-sharq al-awsat*, March 29, 2012, no. 12175.

11. Al-Nahdha Party, "Draft of a Constitution," Tunis, n.d. In this draft, article 1 remained the same as in the 1959 constitution. Article 10 read: "The Islamic shari`a is one of the main sources of legislation" (*al-shari`a al-islamiyya masdar asasi min masadir al-tashri`*).

12. For further analysis of the deliberate choices made by the transitional elites during the crafting of the electoral law after the fall of Ben Ali, see Latiri and Zeghal (2012). For an empirical analysis of the benefits of closed list proportional representation systems, see Cammett and Malesky (2012).

13. In the first quarter of 2012, official unemployment reached 18.1 percent nationally and was as high as 28.4 percent in the interior regions, according to the National Institute of Statistics of Tunisia (Al-Jumhuriyya al-Tunisiyya 2012, 2–4). For much higher estimates, see Latiri and Zeghal (2012).

14. This was the case, for instance, with the mob attack against the Nessma Television offices on October 9, 2011, and with the violent street conflict between UGTT Trade Union members and the Leagues of Protection of the Revolution on December 4, 2012.

15. For example, in August 1956, *al-Istiqlal*, the mouthpiece of the Old Destour, published an open letter to the government, carrying 137 signatures, asking whether the PSC were up for discussion and requesting that the `ulama participate in its drafting. See also *al-Istiqlal* 1, no. 47 (September 14, 1956): 1 for Shaykh `Abd al-`Aziz J`ayyit's response to a request for a legal opinion (*fatwa*) on the PSC calling for the removal of several articles.

16. I thank Robert Hefner for suggesting this important argument.

17. The Tunisian NGO Albawsala also tweeted the debates and collected and published on its website important information about the activities of the NCA; see http://www.marsad.tn/.

18. NCA Session of July 11, 2013.

19. NCA Session of July 1, 2013. Recognizing the existence of deep tensions around the question of Islam, he also argued that these anxieties were exaggerated, for the NCA eventually reached a compromise.

20. Fieldwork notes, Tunis, June 2012.

21. Chokri Belaid, leader of the Democratic Patriot Movement (left, 1 NCA seat) was assassinated on February 6, 2013. Mohamed Brahmi, member of the NCA and leader of the People's Movement (Arab nationalist left, 2 NCA seats) was assassinated on July 25, 2013. The Ministry of the Interior blamed radical Salafi groups for both assassinations.

22. NCA Session of July 11, 2013.

23. NCA Session of January 3, 2014. Mongi Rahoui was the only MP elected on the list of the Movement of the Democrats Patriots, which was led by Chokri Belaid, who was assassinated on February 6, 2013.

24. NCA Session of July 8, 2013.

25. NCA Session of July 1, 2013.

26. NCA Session of July 6, 2013.

27. NCA Session of July 11, 2013. Center-left CPR MP Bechir Nafsi made a similar statement during the same session.

28. Mohamed Fadhel Moussa, referred to "rights of conscience" (*haqq al-dhamir*). NCA Morning Session, February 28, 2012.

29. NCA Session of July 11, 2013.

30. NCA Session of July 11, 2013.

31. NCA Session of October 24, 2012.

32. NCA Session of January 4, 2014.

33. NCA Morning Session of February 28, 2013.

34. The argument for separation of Islam and state was made by MP Salaheddine Zahaf (*Voix de l'Indépendant*, 1 seat) who argued in the July 2, 2013, session that Tunisians had revolted for temporal and not for ideological or religious aims and that this required a "clear separation (*fasl*) between religion and state." However, he contradicted himself in the same session of the NCA when, criticizing article 6 of the draft under examination, he refused the principle of a state "custodian of Islam" and argued that the state should be the custodian of "all religions."

35. NCA Session of July 6, 2013.

36. Interview with a member of Ettakattol, Tunis, June 18, 2011.

37. NCA Morning Session of February 28, 2012. http://www.anc.tn/site/main/AR/docs/vid_debat.jsp?id=28022012m&t=m.

38. Interview with Samir Taïeb, June 15, 2012, NCA, le Bardo.

39. NCA Session of July 6, 2013.

40. The Canadian Charter of Rights and Freedoms begins, "Whereas Canada is founded upon principles that recognize the supremacy of God and the rule of law . . ."

41. NCA Session of July 8, 2013.

42. NCA Session of January 3, 2014.

43. NCA Session of February 28, 2012. In the same session, another group argued in favor of "the Koran and the *Sunna*" as a main source of law.

44. NCA Session of July 11, 2013.

45. One voted against article 1, and two abstained. The only change from 1959 was the addition of the words "This article cannot be amended."

46. http://www.marsad.tn/fr/vote/52c9ba0712bdaa7f9b90f436.

47. NCA Session of July 6, 2013, emphasis mine.

48. NCA Session of July 6, 2013.

49. NCA Session of January 4, 2014.

50. NCA Session of January 4, 2014.

51. NCA Session of July 8, 2013. Salma Mabrouk (Ettakattol) also argued in the same session that article 141 threatened women's rights.

52. NCA Session of January 4, 2014.

53. NCA Session of January 4, 2014.

54. NCA Session of July 8, 2013, emphasis mine. Jawhara Tiss, born in 1985, was one of the youngest members of the NCA.

55. Hana Lerner similarly found in the cases of Israel, India, and Ireland that "ambivalent legal language and the inclusion of contrasting provisions in the constitution . . . allow the deferral of controversial choices" (Lerner 2011).

56. NCA Session of January 18, 2013.

57. NCA Session of July 6, 2013.

58. NCA Session of January 4, 2014.

59. NCA Session of July 8, 2013.

60. Also, in continuity with the 1959 constitution, only Muslims voters can be candidates for president of the republic.

61. Michael Sandel distinguishes between different definitions of freedom of conscience (as free exercise and as the autonomous individual's free choice) in the case of the US legal history (Sandel 1998). In the case of the Tunisian constitutional discussions, freedom of religion meant freedom to exercise one's religion (as previously understood in the 1959 constitution), whereas "freedom of conscience" meant freedom *from* religion.

62. NCA Session July 11, 2013. Mabrouk Hrizi and nineteen other MPs from al-Nahdha and CPR also proposed the amendment of article 6 to suppress freedom of conscience.

63. NCA Session of July 6, 2013.

64. In Tunisia, abortion has been legal and subsidized by the state, up to the third month of pregnancy, since 1973.

65. NCA Session of July 6, 2013.

66. NCA Session of January 4, 2014.

67. NCA Session of January 3, 2014.

68. NCA Session of July 8, 2013.

69. NCA Session of July 11, 2013. See also the July 8, 2013, remarks of Adel Ben Attia (Nahdha) against freedom of conscience.

70. NCA Session of July 11, 2013.

71. See Zeghal (2013b).

6 Transformations in Muslim Views about "Forbidding Wrong": The Rise and Fall of Islamist Litigation in Egypt

Clark B. Lombardi and Connie J. Cannon

THE QUR'AN SUGGESTS in several places that the Muslim community is obligated to "command right and forbid wrong." Exploring what this command might mean, classical Islamic jurists identified certain circumstances in which Muslims should interfere to stop their fellow Muslims from engaging in sinful activities, and they explained what types of interference were appropriate. The classical legal literature on "forbidding wrong," or hisba, appears to have focused very little on the possibility that Muslims might try to forbid wrong by filing a lawsuit seeking to enjoin unrighteous behavior or to have a wrongdoer punished. Indeed, some modern scholars suggest that classical scholars would not have conceptualized such an act as "forbidding wrong" at all. Changes in Egyptian government and society, however, helped provoke transformations in Egyptian thinking about how and when Muslims should forbid wrong. A number of Egyptians concluded that in a modern state, this duty could—and often should—be satisfied through the filing of a lawsuit. This change in thinking led to changes in behavior that provoked yet more transformations in Egyptian Islamic thought and action.

At the end of the twentieth century, legal reforms in Egypt led to the formation of powerful courts and to the rise of a robust judiciary and bar, many of whose members were deeply interested in European political theory and in the idea of the liberal rule of law. A confluence of interests between Egyptian liberals and the judiciary allowed legal activists to influence both state policy and private behavior through litigation. Increasingly, some legally trained Islamists became inspired by the success of liberals and began to bring their own suits in state-run courts. They began by trying to strike down un-Islamic laws but eventually expanded their activities to include filing lawsuits against private individuals, seeking to publicize their belief that those individuals were engaging in sinful behavior and, if possible, to create unpleasant consequences for the malefactors.

As Islamist litigation expanded, Islamic intellectuals began to theorize so-called "hisba" litigation as a uniquely valuable method of forbidding wrong in a modern state whose constitution declared it to be simultaneously Islamic, democratic, and liberal.

The experience of litigating led some Islamists to reexamine traditional doctrines. In the years leading up to the fall of Hosni Mubarak, there were hints of convergence among Islamists and liberals with respect to governmental structure. Islamists came to share liberals' commitment to the goal of establishing a government in which the executive was checked by an independent and powerful judiciary. Furthermore, one found a new willingness to explore potentially overlap between Islamic and liberal principles. Some optimistic observers suggested that Egypt might be on the cusp of a new era in which the judiciary could use Islamist lawsuits as an opportunity to mediate a broadly acceptable solution to fraught debates about the respective roles of Islam and liberalism in modern Egypt.

This vision proved overly optimistic. After the ouster of President Mubarak in 2011, fierce political contest erupted between secularists and a variety of mutually antagonistic Islamist factions. In the chaotic and increasingly violent transition away from the Mubarak regime, an Islamist government was elected and then removed in a military coup that was apparently approved by the courts. In the process, the judiciary came to be viewed by many, both among Islamists and some diehard liberals, as untrustworthy. At the time of writing, Egypt is deeply divided; some Islamists have turned to violent resistance, and it seems unlikely in the foreseeable future that Islamists will turn to the courts to help them forbid wrong and, in the process, to mediate their contest with non-Islamist factions.

Although it has not had a fairy-tale ending, the rise and fall of hisba litigation in Egypt tells us important things about the process by which shari`a transitions unfold in the contemporary Muslim world. It reminds us how dynamic modern Islamic thought has become and illustrates how cycles of Islamic transformations can, under the right conditions, emerge and feed on themselves: Social and political developments in a majority Muslim society can inspire creative rethinkings of Islamic law, influencing people to change their behavior and transforming society in ways that themselves provide fuel for new experiments in Islamic thought. The story illustrates, too, how political and social developments can interfere with transitional cycles of that are well underway or even, at times, stop them altogether.

Forbidding Wrong: Hisba in the Premodern Sunni Tradition

The Qur'an suggests in several places that the Muslim community is obligated to "command right and forbid wrong." Qur'an 3:104 says, "Let there be one community (*umma*) among you, commanding right and forbidding wrong."

The obligation to command right and forbid wrong, in Arabic *al-amr bi'l ma'rūf wa'l nahy'an al-munkar,* is mentioned again in 3:110 and 9:71 as well as in several *hadith.* The most widely reported of these states, "Whoever sees a wrong and is able to change it with his hand, let him do so; if he can't then with his tongue, if he can't then in his heart. That is the bare minimum of faith" (Cook 2006, 32–35).[1] The act of intervening in wrongdoing was occasionally referred to as "hisba" (Cook 2006, 447–49).

During the classical era, leading Islamic legal scholars organized themselves into self-regulating private scholarly guilds called *madhhabs.* Often referred to as "the Sunni schools of law," these *maddhabs* established the parameters of legitimate interpretation and accredited scholars to elaborate God's law for society. The credentialed jurists, the so-called *fuqaha,* came generally to be recognized as the only authoritative interpreters of God's law, the shari'a (Lombardi 2006, 13–18). In monumental recent works, Michael Cook has catalogued exhaustively the ways in which these classical jurists interpreted the individual's obligation to forbid wrong (Cook 2003; 2006). As Cook shows, premodern Sunni legal thinkers agreed that rulers had the primary obligation to ensure that wrongs were forbidden in his realm. Recognizing the consensus on this point, some rulers delegated this duty to an appointed official, called a *muḥtasib,* who had authority to both identify and punish wrongdoing (Cook 2003, 68–69; cf. Cahen and Talbi 1960–2007; Stilt 2012). The question for scholars was not whether the obligation existed for the community but rather whether individual Muslims had some obligation to forbid wrong when a ruler failed to fulfill his duty or, worse, when the ruler or his lieutenants engaged in wrongdoing. Most scholars argued that individuals did, but disagreed about the scope of this obligation.

The *hadith* already described suggests three modes of forbidding wrong: by force (by the hand), by public rebuke (by the tongue), or by affirming in one's own mind that a wrong has been perpetrated (by the heart). Premodern Islamic scholars tended to be skeptical about the idea that people who had neither an official position nor training in Islamic law had any obligation to forbid wrong "by the hand." Some scholars suggested that such individuals might be able to forbid wrong by reporting wrongdoers to the state, but not all agreed (Cook 2003, 70–71; 2006, 81, 136, 367, 380–81, 465, 474–75). Indeed, many scholars concluded that a ruler's lay subjects were permitted to rebuke wrongdoers at most, and some discouraged them from engaging even in this more mild form of forbidding wrong (Cook 2003, 33–34; 2006, 326–27, 343, 367, 414–15). Most scholars thus placed significant barriers in the way of anyone from outside the scholarly elite who wished to forbid wrong by the tongue or hand.

There appears to have been very little discussion of the possibility that individuals should forbid wrong by filing a court action against the wrongdoer.[2] Some historians working in court records have recently identified private lawsuits that they speculate were brought by plaintiffs who were primarily driven by a desire to criticize behavior that they considered to violate God's law (for example, Marcus 1989, 177; Peirce 2006, 71–93; cf. Cook 2006, 522).[3] Even assuming that some litigants tried to forbid wrong through the filing of court cases, this practice does not seem to have been broadly encouraged in the premodern scholarly literature, and it appears to have been rare.

Early Modern Transformation of the Egyptian Political System and Its Impact on Thinking about Forbidding Wrong

In the nineteenth and early twentieth centuries, the Muslim world experienced massive technological developments and social changes that led to a breakdown of consensus on questions of Islamic religious authority (Lombardi 2006, 59–80). As more Muslims began to write publicly on questions of Islamic law, an explosion of creative thinking and vibrant debate took place. In this period, Muslims began to reinterpret many principles of Islamic law, including the processes by which Muslims should "forbid wrong."

As modern Islamic thinkers were reexamining old orthodoxies, the Muslim world was being reorganized into nation states, and Muslims were experiencing novel forms of political structure and legal organization (Brown 1997, 2–7). Modern states were highly intrusive, and their coercive apparatus was far more powerful than anything that Muslims had seen before (ibid.; Hallaq 2009, 549). However, these states also offered individuals previously unheard of opportunities to publicize morally questionable behavior and to shape state responses to it. Some states experimented with electoral democracy, giving Muslim citizens a role in selecting the nation's executive—the modern analogue of the classical ruler who had the primary duty to forbid wrong. Furthermore, citizens of many states had access to judiciaries that were, at least on paper, more independent from the executive and more powerful than the judiciaries of premodern Muslim governments. Judges in some countries, including Egypt, asserted that they should be given the power to identify and correct governmental violations of the law. In particular, they claimed authority to strike down any law and enjoin any government action that either had failed to follow the procedures of administrative law or had violated constitutional rights and values. In this rapidly changing political and legal environment, a number of Egyptian Islamic thinkers, both classically trained 'ulama and modern "Islamic intellectuals," began to question the traditional rules about performing hisba. Some suggested that premodern scholars might have misunderstood the principle behind the obligation to forbid wrong. Others proposed that the classical rules had been correct at the time they were developed but that rapidly changing circumstances required that the traditional principles be applied in new ways.

As Cook illustrates, a first wave of rethinking focused on the idea that Muslims living in modern states should see political participation as an obligatory form of forbidding wrong in the modern world. In countries that held elections, all citizens could, in theory, share in the power to make state laws and to ensure that those laws were enforced. By engaging politically, therefore, individuals in democratic states could collectively take on the communal function of forbidding wrong. Building from this insight, a number of nineteenth-century scholars in the Ottoman heartland, as well as the Tunisian statesman Khayr al-Din Pasha, argued for the adoption of parliamentary government precisely on the ground that it would allow citizens to forbid wrong in a novel but highly effective way. In Egypt, Rashīd Riḍā cited Muhammad ʿAbduh for the proposition that Qurʾan 3:104 be interpreted to require modern Muslims to establish limited constitutional government. Riḍā concluded, therefore, that Muslim governments in the modern age should include representative assemblies (Cook 2003, 112–14).

Presented with these arguments, many Egyptians came to agree that Muslims living in parliamentary states were obliged to forbid wrong by using their newfound political power to appoint officials who understood God's law and would try to enforce it. They disagreed, however, about whether political activity was sufficient to satisfy the obligation. What should a citizen do if, notwithstanding his or her best efforts to influence the executive and legislature, the government permitted public and private wrongdoing? Controversially, some important voices argued that if citizens of a modern state had tried in good faith to change government policy, they had no more obligation to forbid wrong. Indeed, around the middle of the twentieth century, important Egyptian Islamic thinkers, including the influential radical Muslim Brother Sayyid Quṭb, took this position (Cook 2003, 121; 2006, 528–29). Not all agreed. Indeed, some thought that engaging politically could never absolve someone of the duty to act when political participation failed to produce a moral society.[4]

Even if one did not go this far, there was reason to question whether political participation in a country such as Egypt could ever be effectual enough as to satisfy the obligation to forbid wrong. Like many other Muslim countries, Egypt held formal elections, but the elections were rarely free and fair. Particularly in a sham democracy where election results were tainted by corruption, some believed that civilian Muslims should act to forbid wrongs that the government was committing or failing to prevent. For example, Roel Meijer has described how in the 1970s members of the Islamic revivalist group *al-Jamāʿa al-Islamiyya* came to reject the idea that one should perform hisba by influencing state policy and instead engaged in vigilante action to suppress immoral behavior by government officials and private citizens alike (Meijer 2009).

Furthermore, when Islamist radicals found that they were no more effective at changing state behavior than Islamist politicians, a new idea began to emerge—an idea that seemed to compromise between the views of those who thought that political participation satisfied the obligation to forbid wrong and those who believed that citizens had an individual duty to forcibly forbid wrongs that the government permitted to occur. From the 1980s onward, a growing group of Islamist legal activists began to use litigation as a means of forbidding wrong either on the part of the government or fellow Muslim citizens. In doing so, they both adopted and modified a tactic that influential liberals in the Egyptian bar and judiciary had pioneered. This eventually led to some convergence between Islamists and liberals on ideas about the role of the judiciary in a modern democratic state even as it incited bitter controversy.

Transformation of the Egyptian Legal System and Further Evolution in Thinking about Forbidding Wrong

As late-twentieth-century Egyptian Islamic thinkers explored new approaches to forbidding wrong, the Egyptian legal system was continuing to develop in dramatic ways. As it evolved, liberals in the bar and judiciary began to take advantage of opportunities that the system created for people who wanted to check government abuses of liberal rights or influence government policies more broadly. Liberal activism inspired some Islamists to reevaluate court action as a possible supplement to their attempts to forbid wrong through violence or politics. Exploring the implications of a government with divided powers, some Islamist activists began to argue that if Muslims found themselves unable to elect officials who would voluntarily forbid wrong, Muslims could and should ask the judicial branch to intervene.

Transformation of the Egyptian Legal System

In the late nineteenth and early twentieth centuries, Egypt adopted a Western-style legal system. During this period, the Egyptian judiciary and bar had embraced the core idea of "the rule of law." They pushed for judicial independence and power and established a strong bar dominated, for the most part, by figures espousing a liberal philosophy (Brown 1997; Ziadeh 1968). During the second half of the twentieth century Egypt's liberal judiciary found itself increasingly in contest with the nation's military-led government. In the two decades after Gamal Abdel-Nasser took power in a 1952 coup, Nasser and his regime systematically built up an authoritarian political structure and tried to control all of Egypt's economic, political, and social institutions. After violently suppressing Egypt's most powerful independent political parties, Nasser tried to undercut the independence of the bar and judiciary (Lombardi 2013a, 406–7; Rutherford 2008, 42–43, 141). He failed to achieve his goals, however, and his successor moderated the regime's policies toward the opposition.

Although it was initially able to suppress opposition from both powerful Islamist organizations such as the Muslim Brotherhood and the traditionally liberal legal cadre, Nasser's regime faltered in the late 1960s as it faced a series of economic setbacks and military defeats. By the time of Nasser's death in 1970, Egypt's middle classes in particular had begun to turn toward the suppressed opponents of the regime, with some inclining to the liberal opposition and others to a range of Islamist groups. In response, Nasser's successor Anwar Sadat was compelled to rebuild support for the regime among the disaffected middle classes. Shortly after ascending to the presidency, Sadat drafted a new constitution and reformed laws in ways that made subtle but significant concessions to both liberals and Islamists (Lombardi 2013a, 407–13). Over time, these reforms led to the reempowerment of the judiciary and the rise, first, of liberal legal activism and then, later, of Islamic legal activism.

The Rise of Liberal Legal Activism

For liberals, Sadat opened the political sphere slightly. However, because the government refused to run free and fair elections, Egyptian liberals in the 1970s enjoyed little success in electoral politics. Yet Sadat had also included in his 1971 constitution a number of liberal rights guarantees and declared that the government would pledge to respect "the rule of law." This latter term was generally understood to mean the "liberal rule of law" and was accompanied by a series of measures that reestablished the judiciary's independence from the executive branch. It explicitly granted the judiciary new powers, including the power of judicial review, which was vested in a new Supreme Constitutional Court (SCC; see Moustafa 2007, 78–79; Rutherford 20008, 45).

These overtures induced liberals to adopt a new strategy for influencing government behavior. Having failed to achieve significant representation in the legislature or influence within the executive branch, liberals turned to the courts, including the new SCC, and asked them to enjoin violations of liberal rights and to strike down illiberal laws. By the 1980s plaintiffs were winning some of these cases, successfully forcing incremental changes in law and policy (Moustafa 2007; Rutherford 20008, 32–76). Worried about its still fragile legitimacy, the government generally obeyed these judgments, which encouraged liberals in civil society and the judiciary. In the second half of the 1980s, the increasingly confident courts took another daring step: They increased the scope of judicial review by holding that the government must respect not only those limited rights explicitly placed in the constitution but also a host of unenumerated rights that were implicitly protected (Brown 1997, 188–189). As a result, Egypt began to undergo further economic and political liberalization.

In the second half of the 1990s, the government began to wake up to the threat posed by a liberal bar and emboldened judiciary and, as Tamir Moustafa described, began again trying to weaken the courts (Moustafa 2007, 118–218). Hoping to forestall even more serious attacks, the courts made a concerted effort to reach out to Egyptians outside the ranks of the liberals who had traditionally formed their core base of support. The judiciary at this time made particular efforts to reach out to Islamists and to encourage them to try using litigation as a tool for changing government behavior (Lombardi 2008). Although the courts were able to broaden considerably their base of support, increasing government pressure finally forced the courts to temper their activism (ibid.). The courts ceased to compel government compliance with human rights principles, but legal activists nonetheless found that filing court cases was still one way to embarrass the government, exerting indirect pressure that sometimes still shaped state behavior.

Hence by the 1990s, liberal lawyers and judges had demonstrated the power of litigation as a tool for publicizing their dissatisfaction with government behavior and, in some cases, changing government action. Their success using courts as a platform for dissent encouraged Islamists to try their hand at litigation as well—both against private actors whom they believed were engaging in wrongdoing and against the government. Indeed, as Islamists began theorizing litigation initiated by private citizens as a mode of forbidding wrong, they began to use courts to push their own agenda.

The Rise of Islamist Legal Activism

Islamists were slower than liberals to make use of the judiciary's willingness to strike down unconstitutional laws. As was the case with liberal legal activism, however, transformations in Egyptian law allowed the judiciary to create a new forum in which Islamic law could be discussed, eventually driving Islamists to the courts in their attempt to create change where political participation and social action had failed. As Islamists brought more cases to court, they also began to theorize legal activity as an important new way of forbidding wrong in a modern state.

In the 1970s and 1980s Islamists devoted most of their energy to the task of building social and political organizations that could theoretically serve as the base for powerful political parties in a more open political environment. Unfortunately for them, the electoral system was rigged to favor the ruling party, and—notwithstanding their organization and growing popularity—Islamists were unable to win significant representation in parliament. Other than making concessions in the area of cultural politics, the ruling party rarely considered Islamist concerns when it set policy (Kepel 1985, 236–40).

After the government expanded opportunities for legal education in the 1970s and 1980s, a growing number of Islamists began to get law degrees. These new Islamist lawyers sometimes came into conflict with the long-established liberal factions within the bar (Rutherford 2008, 46–47). Before Islamists could systematically turn to courts in their attempts to influence society, however, they had to overcome several hurdles. For one thing, Islamists did not fully trust the bona fides of the judiciary. Historically, there had been some overlap between the community of legal liberals and Islamists.[5] However, that overlap declined over the course of the twentieth century and was not significant by the 1970s. There was also a growing gap between the positions of mainstream Islamists and legal liberals with respect to many hot-button topics. Since the 1960s Islamists had grown increasingly conservative on social issues, unlike the legal liberals who dominated the judiciary and bar, and Islamists thus feared that the liberal commitments of elite judges would prevent the courts from engaging in open-minded ways with Islamist arguments. During the 1980s, however, Islamists overcame these obstacles, gaining ground in the courts and imagining new ways of forbidding wrong in a modern state.

To reach out to Islamists, Sadat had included in article 2 of the 1971 constitution a statement that the principles of the Islamic shari'a are "a" chief source for Egyptian legislation. In short order, he strengthened and clarified this ambiguous provision by amending article 2 again in 1980 to say that Islamic legal principles were to be "the" chief source of legislation. This change was widely understood to make article 2 a "shari'a guarantee clause"—a clause barring the government from enacting laws or policies inconsistent with Islamic principles (Lombardi 2013b, 754–58). In the 1970s and 1980s, Islamists occasionally filed litigation in the SCC asking it to enforce the new shari'a guarantee clause.

Elite liberal judges on courts such as the Supreme Constitutional Court did not share the leading Islamists' socially conservative interpretation of Islamic law, and they had no desire to constitutionalize it. Nevertheless, they believed that the government should keep its constitutional promises, including the promise to respect Islam. Seeing themselves as good Muslims, albeit liberal ones, most judges were happy to enforce this promise so long as Islam could be interpreted liberally.[6] As noted already, power struggles between courts and other government branches gave judges a strong incentive to bring as many Islamists as possible into court and to demonstrate that they would treat their claims respectfully (Brown 1997, 93–128; Lombardi 2008, 249–50; Moustafa 2007, 118–218). If the large and powerful Islamist opposition came to see the courts as allies, they might support them in any future battle with the executive. Against this backdrop, the courts began to issue decisions that cautiously encouraged Islamists to file lawsuits seeking to compel government respect for Islamic law—but suggested that Islamic law itself could, and indeed should, be interpreted in a manner that was also consistent with liberal values.

In a momentous decision in 1985, the Supreme Constitutional Court held that article 2 required the government to respect shari'a principles and that courts were permitted to strike down any new laws or policies that were inconsistent with those principles. With this decision, the court established itself as a forum in which Egyptians could argue not only about whether the government was acting in a way that violated fundamental individual rights but also about whether the government was acting in a manner that was inconsistent with Islamic law. Courts thus became a place in which Islamists could publicly press claims that they were unable to present either through the political process or the government-controlled media. Intrigued, a number of conservative Islamist activists and thinkers set aside their traditional skepticism about the judiciary and began to test the constitutional court's willingness to engage seriously with questions about the role of Islam in state law.

From the late 1980s, the court began to hear challenges to a number of Egyptian laws on the claim that they violated the Egyptian constitution's shari`a guarantee clause (Brown 1997; Moustafa 2007; Rutherford 2008). To resolve these article 2 cases, the SCC articulated a method of legal interpretation that was broadly consistent with theories promoted by a number of Islamist intellectuals, including many associated with the Brotherhood. Both emphasized Islam as a religion occasionally requiring obedience to a narrow set of literal scriptural rules but more often concerned with demanding that people (and governments) act in a manner consistent with broad and somewhat malleable ethical principles such as "justice" and "public interest" (Lombardi 2006).

The court used this method, however, in a different way than conservative Islamists anticipated. The court's method of interpretation allowed the SCC to plausibly interpret Islam in a way that enforced liberal values while rejecting Islamists' more socially conservative—and contentious—claims (Lombardi 2006). Thus in the late 1980s, the SCC struck down as un-Islamic restrictions in a number of laws that limited the rights of private property. However, it decided to uphold numerous controversial amendments to Egyptian family laws—including amendments that gave women rights that they had not enjoyed under classical Islamic law. More controversial still, the SCC also upheld a ban on *niqāb* veils in public schools (Brown and Lombardi 2006). Islamists won a handful of cases, but not as many as they had hoped.

Although conservative Islamists were disappointed by the constitutional court's rulings, they were delighted by the publicity that these suits generated and were heartened by language in court opinions that suggested that the court might be willing to consider adopting a more conservative interpretation of Islamic law at some unspecified point. In addition, the SCC was not the only court signaling its willingness to adjudicate cases of Islamic interest. Islamists were further encouraged in the 1990s when the Supreme Administrative Court (SAC) also began to hear article 2 challenges.

Generally, the Supreme Administrative Court applied the same method of reasoning as the SCC and tended to reach similarly liberal results. However, in opinions we will discuss henceforth, the SAC also implicitly suggested that it recognized a central claim of Islamists—that liberal principles might have to be applied slightly differently in an explicitly Islamic state than in an explicitly secular one (Egyptian Supreme Administrative Court 1997; 2007). This left open the possibility that Egyptian judges might be convinced to strike down some laws that protected liberal rights at the expense of traditional Islamic values in the future.

Conceptualizing Litigation as Forbidding Wrong

During this period, some Islamists began to theorize litigation as an important method of expressing dissent and exerting pressure for social and political change—at least in states having an independent judiciary. Some evidence suggests that early pioneers of Egypt's Islamist litigation understood their own actions as attempts to "forbid wrong."[7] However, as far as we have been able to tell, none of these early activists attempted to develop a systematic theory that would explain why Muslims would forbid wrong through litigation or why Egyptian society should encourage their activities.[8] At some point during the 1980s or early 1990s, however, some thinkers must have begun developing such a theory, for this emerging theory came to be publicly articulated during the early 1990s during an infamous suit against Muslim intellectual Nasr Hāmid Abū Zayd (Agrama 2012; Bälz 1997; Berger 2003; Dupret and Berger 1998; Egyptian Court of Cassation 1996; Najjar 2000; Olsson 2008; Sullivan 2004).

Abū Zayd was a liberal Muslim scholar whose writings about Qur'anic interpretation riled some conservatives. In 1993, a group of conservative Islamist attorneys filed an explosive case in a personal status court criticizing Abū Zayd's descriptions of the prophet as blasphemous and asking the court to punish him. Egyptian law holds that a Muslim woman can be married only to a Muslim man. The Islamist attorneys argued that blasphemy was evidence of apostasy, making his marriage to a Muslim woman invalid. This case represented a new and quite startling type of suit; rather than citizens asking courts to use their power of constitutional review to stop wrongful *government* action, the attorneys here were asking courts to enforce private laws with the goal of stopping the activities of *private citizens.*

Private laws permit a citizen to seek redress against a fellow citizen whose violation of the law has caused him or her harm. Thus a person who is harmed by a neighbor may sue in tort. A person whose spouse's violation of marriage law harms that person may seek dissolution of their marriage. Egyptian procedural law describes the situation by saying that private lawsuits may be brought when (and only when) a violation of private law affects a citizen to the point that he is considered to have a "personal and direct interest" in ensuring that the law was enforced. Conversely, if a plaintiff is not personally and directly harmed by an illegal activity, he has no right to seek punishment for the malefactor. In this case,

Abū Zayd's activities caused the Islamist plaintiffs harm only insofar as he had publicly engaged in activities alleged to violate God's law.

Abū Zayd's supporters urged that the Islamist plaintiffs had no personal and direct interest in the case, arguing that the courts were not permitted even to hear their claim. (However, supposing that the courts *did* hear the case, they disputed not only that Abū Zayd's writings were blasphemy but also that blasphemy alone voided a Muslim man's marriage to a Muslim woman.) The trial court agreed that the plaintiffs had no standing, dismissing the suit without addressing the question of whether Abū Zayd had committed blasphemies that made him apostate.

Islamists appealed the dismissal, arguing that if their suit was recognized as an attempt to engage in hisba, they did indeed have a personal and direct interest (Agrama 2012, 48–52). As they saw it, article 2 of the Egyptian constitution makes the principles of the Islamic law "the chief source of Egyptian legislation," which requires courts to interpret every statute, as far as possible, to respect Islamic principles. Since Islamic law requires every Muslim individual to forbid wrongs that the government has wittingly or unwittingly permitted to occur, this implies two things: first, that each Muslim is personally and directly harmed by the open practice of sin in their society; second, if the state prevents Muslims from criticizing the sin and petitioning the courts to stop it, then the state has compounded this harm. To ensure that the statute is consistent with Islamic principles, they argued, it had to be interpreted to permit litigation by individuals who are trying to forbid flagrant public wrong. Those individuals, in turn, must accept the court's judgment on the question of whether the contested action is, in fact, harmful (Agrama 2012, 52).

An intermediate appeals court cautiously agreed with the Islamists, and on further appeal, Egypt's highest appeals court, the Court of Cassation, upheld the intermediate court ruling in their favor (Dupret and Berger 1998; Egyptian Court of Cassation 1996). The decision was highly controversial. In its opinion, the Court of Cassation concluded that article 2 of the Egyptian Constitution not only prohibited the executive and legislative branches from enacting statutes inconsistent with Islamic legal principles but also required judges to construe ambiguous statutes in a way that comports with Islamic principles. Because the concept of "personal and direct harm" was an ambiguous one, it had to be interpreted in light of the classical Islamic principle that every Muslim has an obligation to forbid wrongs that the state has failed to prevent. It followed, therefore, that Muslims should be construed to have standing to bring "hisba suits"—even if their only interest lay in a desire to publicize and punish behavior that they believe violates Islamic law (Egyptian Court of Cassation 1996). Having interpreted the statute as granting Islamists standing to sue, the judges, moving on to the merits of their claim, concluded that Abū Zayd's behavior did indeed constitute an act of apostasy, rendering his marriage void (Rutherford 2008, 69). Abū Zayd and his wife fled to the Netherlands, which recognized their marriage and allowed them to remain together.

As Hussein Ali Agrama's recent book *Questioning Secularism* describes, the courts' reasoning in Abū Zayd's case fused civil law and Islamic law concepts in a way that demonstrated an evolution in Egyptian thinking about the concept of hisba. Agrama perceptively notes that the moral criticism inherent in the principle of forbidding wrong had been transformed and expanded as it became subject to the institutions and frameworks of the modern legal system. As Islamists conceptualized litigation as a tool that they could use to command the right and forbid the wrong, the principle of hisba also began to incorporate some precepts that resonate with "liberal" ideas about the state (Agrama 2012, 59–67). Nevertheless, the results in this case were decidedly illiberal. In the face of an uproar both at home and abroad, the government decided to amend its laws of procedure and specifically bar plaintiffs from bringing similar suits. It enacted new regulations to prevent private citizens from filing suits for marital dissolution unless they had an interest beyond that of ensuring that God's law is not openly flouted. Under the new regulations, only the public prosecutor was granted the power to "forbid wrong" through the filing of civil suits and had total discretion about when to use that power.

The new statute had less effect than one might have expected. After the legal reforms inspired by the Abū Zayd cases, Islamists were statutorily barred from bringing private suits in cases in which they had suffered no harm other than moral outrage. The legal reform did not, however, stop Islamists from filing suits. They continued to bring court actions not only against the government but against private citizens who had acted in ways that were allegedly contrary to Islam. In many cases, Islamists could find an Islamist plaintiff who could make a colorable argument that a fellow citizen's morally offensive action had caused her some concrete harm, however inconsequential. For some time, in fact, courts appeared to encourage litigation by Muslims concerned about the proper interpretation and enforcement of Islamic law, particularly when the litigation was aimed against the government.

In some cases, courts also appear to have facilitated Islamist attempts to get around the statute barring them from bringing hisba suits against private citizens. Many courts appear to have winked at Islamists's filing of cases that were, in essence, hisba suits. In 1997, while the Abū Zayd case was still much on the minds of the Egyptian public, the SAC resolved an Islamist challenge to a government ban on the practice of female genital mutilation (FGM). In that case, some of the Islamist plaintiffs appeared to have suffered no direct and personal harm other than the harm of seeing their government act in ways that they believed violated the principles of the Islamic shariʻa. The SAC admitted that Egyptian law prohibited people from filing cases unless they had a direct personal interest in the case, as well as that the government had enacted statutes saying explicitly that in suits between private citizens, the harm of seeing God's law violated was not sufficiently "direct and personal" to support a plaintiff's standing. This being a case between a private citizen and the government, however, the statute did not on its face apply to these cases, and the court was not inclined to extend the limit on suits any farther than it had to. In a revealing passage, the judges seemed implicitly to question whether one could take seriously the statute's basic premise—namely, that a Muslim was not personally, directly entitled to sue when he witnessed violations of God's law.

> There is no doubt, that the desire of the respondents, who adhere to Islam, to settle on the correct legal ruling on female circumcision, due to their belief that it is encouraged by the shari'a . . . [gives them] a direct personal interest that is affected immediately and personally, by the [government action] that it has been requested be nullified. (Egyptian Supreme Administrative Court of Egypt 1997)

Egypt's courts thus granted Islamists broad leeway to bring article 2 suits against almost any law that they considered inconsistent with Islamic principles. The leeway that courts gave individuals to file cases of this sort was wide enough that some Egyptian Islamists became notorious for regularly filing suits against the government or against private citizens that were, for all practical purposes, hisba suits. Yūsuf al-Badrī was one of Egypt's most litigious Islamists and a serial plaintiff in suits challenging both official and private activity. Al-Badrī himself has also characterized his activities as attempts to forbid wrong, stating in one interview that, "I am executing the command of God . . . . God is the one that commanded me [to do this]. I am obligated to take the initiative to change the wrong" (Al-Wasat 2009). Plaintiffs such as al-Badrī did not always win their suits. But even when a lawsuit failed to stop sinful activity outright, it served as public criticism of the offensive behavior and exerted indirect pressure on individuals who were perceived as engaged in wrongdoing.

The media reported widely on the activities of these Islamists and often characterized lawsuits filed by them as hisba cases. It is hard to quantify the number of civil cases that were filed in the 2000s primarily out of a desire to publicize and punish immoral actions. Liberal Egyptians, however, were convinced that the number grew throughout the decade. One human rights activist noted that despite post–Abū Zayd legislation meant to bar individuals from bringing personal status suits without a direct interest in the case, "the rest of the doors of hisba remained completely legal and completely open before whoever wants to enter" (Al-Namnam 2012, 175). Another was quoted in several media reports as saying that hisba suits continued to rise in the decade after the Abū Zayd decision and that the number of suits peaked in the year 2008 (Al-Namnam 2012, 175).

Tamir Moustafa has sensitively observed that Islamists continued to be largely unsuccessful at winning judgments, but the discursive shift mentioned above led them to continue mobilizing through judicial avenues, which had "radiating" effects throughout Egyptian society (Moustafa 2010, 24–25). One of these effects was that Islamists, like liberals, came to see an active judicial branch and wide access to courts as important features of an ideal state.

Further Transformations: Effects of Hisba Litigation on Islamists and on Egypt

Broad social and political changes throughout the twentieth century had inspired Islamists to rethink traditional approaches to forbidding wrong, whereas transformations in Egypt's judicial system encouraged Islamists to seek redress from the courts. The experience of litigating provoked further rethinking of the religious and legal doctrines surrounding the duty to command right and forbid wrong. As Islamist litigation became a feature of the Egyptian legal landscape, Islamists who had legal training began to engage more consistently and thoughtfully with the liberal lawyers who dominated the legal academy and higher judiciary. In the process, some important Islamist thinkers began to explore and highlight possible overlaps between Islamist and liberal theories about the desirability of a government that would be limited by judicially enforced constitutional commitments and a respect for individual rights.

In some cases, discussions about how and whether individual Muslims should use lawsuits to forbid wrong sparked discussion about specific individual rights. For example, in 1998, the influential Islamist intellectual (and trained lawyer) Muḥammad Salīm al-'Awwā, published a group of essays on the Abū Zayd case, republished in 2003 (al-'Awwā 1998). His essays argued strongly that Islam requires Muslims to forbid wrong and that litigation is an appropriate way of fulfilling that duty. Accordingly, a state such as Egypt, which purports to respect Islamic law, must allow citizens broad room to file suits designed to ensure both that the state does not enact legislation that contravenes Islamic law and that individuals who violate Islamic law are subjected to criticism and all possible legal penalties. Nevertheless, he argued that Islam prohibits far less than many Islamists believe. In particular, he cautioned against the use of hisba suits to stifle those who hold different views on contested issues of Islamic interpretation, and he specifically criticized the decision of religious conservatives to bring suit against Abū Zayd (id.).

Classical Islamic law traditionally recognized the principle that individuals have a degree of autonomy. This gave individuals the right to be free from anyone prying into their nonpublic activities. It also gave them a right to act in accordance with any plausible interpretation that they chose on disputed questions of Islamic law without fear that their neighbors would attack or rebuke them for doing so. Modern, legally trained Islamists such as al-`Awwā highlighted this history to support the proposition that although a person's right to forbid wrong could not be denied, it had to be balanced against the right not to have one's actions wantonly forbidden. This point was also implicitly echoed by other important Islamist theorists of hisba, including the cleric Yūsuf al-Qaradāwī, who was influential among many members of the Muslim Brotherhood.[9]

Of course, Islamists and liberals often did not agree about which individual rights should be protected. But concern for individual rights also led to convergence between Islamists and liberals with respect to another idea: However cautious one had to be when forbidding the wrongs of private citizens, individuals should aggressively forbid wrongs committed by the government, including government violations of some rights that were revered by both liberals and Islamists alike. In its article 2 jurisprudence, Egypt's Supreme Constitutional Court had early suggested the existence of areas of overlap between their goals in enforcing article 2 and the goals of liberals, proposing that many government acts that could be characterized as violations of "human rights" were simultaneously violations of the shari`a (Lombardi 2006). Liberal Islamist thinkers began to pursue this line of thinking and to explore its ramifications. As they saw it, Muslims living in a state that aspired to be Islamic and liberal had the right (indeed the duty) to file hisba suits to criticize or end violations of human rights. This type of thinking brought the priorities of at least some important Islamists at least partly in line with the work of activists who wished to promote the liberal rule of law. Put differently, these thinkers believed Islamists should be more cautious about forbidding private citizens' wrongs but, at the same time, more aggressive about forbidding government violations of fundamental rights.

The rise of quasiliberal Islamism did not go unnoticed. Some liberals noted with approval the appearance of Islamists who were reimagining hisba as a duty that could be fulfilled in a way that recognized and reinforced liberal values. Thus the liberal author of a 2012 publication discussing the rise of hisba litigation and the right to free expression decried the ongoing use of litigation as a method used by conservatives to exert moral pressure on private citizens and restrict their free speech rights. Nevertheless, the author opined that there had been some positive developments in the use and conceptualization of litigation as a method of forbidding wrong. Specifically, he appeared to condone the modern ability to use hisba litigation to correct wrongdoing by authoritarian rulers. He also highlighted the potential for discussion of a concept that he called "civil hisba." "Civil hisba," according to his definition, encompasses those cases that "express a beneficial desire to defend the values of public society, and the rights of citizens. They transform hisba from a merely religious, belief-based, or political judgment . . . into civil judgment that defends both the citizen's right and his humanity" (Al-Namnam 2012, 185). He gave two examples, both revolving around issues that both conservatives and liberals at that time agreed involved a legitimate public interest rather than mere attempts to censure individuals or limit un-Islamic speech. In one, an Egyptian Muslim had filed an administrative suit over a decision by the Egyptian Doctors' Syndicate that would prohibit organ transplantation between citizens of different religions.[10] The plaintiff argued that this decision was contrary to Islamic law, the principles of other religions around the world, and Egyptian civil law. In another, plaintiffs claimed that government officials failed to protect the health of citizens when it continued to allow a local cement factory to emit harmful air pollutants (Al-Namnam 2012, 186–90).

The rise of a semiliberal faction within the community of Islamist lawyers forbidding wrong obviously did not guarantee the total convergence of Islamist and liberal thought. That Islamists might come to recognize a zone of protectable private interests merely begged the question how far that zone of privacy extended. And the recommitment of Islamist resources to combating state violations of human rights forced a new discussion about precisely which human rights violations were also violations of Islamic law. Nonetheless, it was significant that important Islamists and important liberals were beginning to focus on these questions and were beginning to engage in a discussion that the judiciary seemed eager to encourage and to mediate.

As Islamists considered the ways that litigation could be used to forbid wrongs perpetrated by the government, their ideas also began to converge with liberals in one final, crucial area—that of constitutional design. As some leading Islamists and liberals began cautiously to explore possible reframings and compromises of their philosophies, they seemed increasingly to appreciate the potential role of the courts as mediators in their discussion. Liberals had long pushed for the strengthening of the courts, confident that the courts would represent their interests against the executive. During the 1980s and 1990s, some Islamists came also to see the courts as allies in their struggle against the authoritarian, secular ruler and increasingly believed that the courts were institutions that could midwife an acceptable compromise between their views and those of secular liberals. Liberals conceptualized litigation before such courts as enforcing the rule of law. Islamists conceptualized it as forbidding wrong and performing hisba. But the different nomenclature should not blind us to the growing faith in litigation as a means for effecting change—nor that this led to the same demand for strong legal institutions and the assurance that citizens would have broad access to them.

Indeed, it is striking that during the last years of the Mubarak regime, Egyptian Islamist discourse shifted significantly on the governmental structure of the ideal Islamic state, and their preferences overlapped in significant ways with those of legal liberals. Leading Islamists continued to emphasize the importance of having a democratically elected legislature and executive committed to promoting God's law and the public interest. In a world in which there was reasonable disagreement about what God's law required, however, a growing number seemed to recognize that the ability of a majority to unilaterally impose their preferred order had to be constrained. A strong and independent judiciary, it was believed, could be empowered to correct any manifest governmental errors, including government violations of those human rights that were protected by both God's command *and* international law. More controversially, the judiciary would also act as a backstop if the government underenforced generally agreed-on rules of morality. Generous rules of standing would permit all citizens to call out public violations of God's law and demand the imposition of any punishments that the law established for such violations (`Abd al-Khāliq 2011; Badr 2011).

The desire for judicial empowerment was not confined to intellectual circles. Across the board, Egyptians seem to have become ever more committed to the ideal of a democracy in which the behavior of a democratically elected government would be policed by an independent and powerful judiciary. That Egypt's Islamists as well as its secularists embraced this ideal is reflected in the extraordinarily broad support that Egyptians expressed for the reempowerment of the judiciary. A Pew poll taken shortly after the fall of President Mubarak showed that support for a strong and independent judiciary was one of the few priorities shared by all Egyptians. Although only 41 percent and 38 percent of poll respondents said that equal rights for men and women and for minorities, respectively, were "very important" in the post-Mubarak state, an overwhelming 81 percent of those polled identified a fair judiciary as "very important" (Wike 2013).

The growing commitment to judicial empowerment also appeared in the platforms of the many political parties that formed during the window of free political participation following the overthrow of 2011. During the first parliamentary and presidential elections after the fall of Mubarak, both secular and Islamist parties called for strong guarantees of judicial independence and power. The Muslim Brotherhood's Freedom and Justice Party not only included in its platform a long provision on the independence of the judiciary but also called for generous rules of standing that would allow citizens to carry out public litigation designed to ensure that the state respects its obligations (Hizb al-Hurriyah wa'l-`Adalah 2013).[11] The platform of the Nūr Party, representing Salafī interests, also contained a provision calling for the protection of judicial independence (Hizb al-Nūr 2013).

Liberal Islamists surely wanted the judiciary to define the zone of personal privacy differently than traditional liberals and, in the public sphere, to uphold different substantive values. Nevertheless, significantly, the two sides were agreeing on the nature of the questions that had to be resolved and suggesting that they shared views about what sorts of institutions should be used to broker a broadly acceptable compromise on these questions. Having taken these first steps, competing political factions stood to actually build up a sustainable practice of inclusive, peaceful judicially managed political dialogue about the issues that divided them.

Epilogue

Sadly, the hopes of Egyptians were not realized. After the ouster of President Mubarak in 2011, a fierce political contest erupted between secularists and a variety of mutually antagonistic Islamist factions. In the chaotic transition away from the Mubarak regime, new tensions emerged between Islamist and liberal political factions, and the courts were drawn into the increasingly bitter contest between them. Ultimately, the courts issued a series of rulings that were widely perceived by Islamists as biased in favor of secularist groups. Islamists also accused judges of tacitly supporting the 2013 military coup that removed a freely elected Islamist government and led to the violent suppression of Islamists. Whatever the truth of these accusations, the judiciary lost its reputation as a neutral, reasonable arbiter of disputes involving Islamists. It seems unlikely that Islamists will turn to the courts in the foreseeable future to help them forbid wrong and in the process mediate their contest with non-Islamist factions.

Although this story has not had a fairy-tale ending, the rise and fall of hisba litigation in Egypt tells us important things about the dynamics of transition in the contemporary Muslim world. Transformations in modern Muslim societies encouraged movements to revisit important classical Islamic legal and political doctrines, including the classical doctrine that both the state and individuals have a duty to aggressively "forbid wrong." Rethinking this idea in light of changes in the political and legal system of Egypt, some thinkers began to imagine and then to realize a world in which Muslims tried broadly to shape government policy and private behavior not only through mechanisms such as vigilantism but also through mechanisms that were unavailable to subjects of premodern Islamic rulers—journalism and political participation. During the 1970s and 1980s, a resurgent judiciary had begun cautiously to police government violations of liberal values and could, in theory, be invoked occasionally to prevent un-Islamic private behavior that the government was willfully permitting to occur. This led Islamists to embrace a new mode of forbidding wrong—litigation.

Islamists who support the idea that citizens can and should forbid wrong through litigation share some, though clearly not all, the commitments of legal liberals. Most important, they have embraced the ideal of an electoral democracy coupled with a judiciary that is empowered to enforce laws that are consistent with national values and to strike down those that are not. Indeed, these Islamists have repackaged, in a manner compelling to a wide cross section of pious Muslims, a commitment to the basic structures that are necessary for the liberal democratic rule of law. In so doing, they have helped establish a remarkable public consensus in favor of a strong, independent judiciary that is widely accessible to the people and that will play a significant role in ensuring that the government respects all its constitutional obligations and impartially enforces statutory laws.

As Islamist lawyers and intellectuals began arguing in the judicial settings that had long been dominated by liberals, they began to identify areas in which the theory of forbidding wrong could integrate liberal ideas and the practice of forbidding wrong could reinforce the work of liberal legal activists. Although Islamists and liberals still diverged in significant areas, during the first decade of the twenty-first century, a growing number in each camp seemed to believe that courts could play a valuable role in determining whether their differences were irreconcilable and—if not—in producing an acceptable solution. We will never know whether this belief would have been vindicated. One of the many tragedies of Egypt's experience in the wake of Hosni Mubarak's fall in 2011 was that the courts felt compelled to intervene in the political process and that their actions unintentionally shattered many Islamists' newfound trust in the courts as a neutral arbiter of important disputes about liberalism and Islam in a democratizing Egyptian state.

Taken together, this reminds us of how dynamic modern Islamic thought has become, illustrating the ways in which cycles of Islamic transformations can, under the right conditions, emerge and feed on themselves: Indeed, social and political developments in a majority Muslim society can inspire creative rethinking of Islamic law. These reinterpretations can and do provoke changes in Muslim behavior, transforming society in ways that in turn feed new experiments in Islamic thought. The story illustrates, too, how political and social developments can interfere with Islamic transitions that are well under way, even preventing them from continuing.

References

`Abd al-Khāliq, Farīd. 2011. *Al-ḥisba fi-l-islam `ala dhu al-jahwa'l-sultān*. al-Qāhirah, Egypt: Dāral-Shurūq.

Agrama, Hussein Ali. 2012. *Questioning Secularism : Islam, Sovereignty, and the Rule of Law in Modern Egypt*. Chicago, IL, and London: The University of Chicago Press.

al-'Awwā, Muḥammad Salīm. 1998. *Al-ḥaqq fī al-ta'bīr*. al-Qāhira, Egypt: Dāral-Shurūq.

Badr, Muhammad. 2011. "Report of Panel Discussion" in the appendix to `Abd al-Khāliq, *Al-ḥisba fi-l-Islam*. al-Qāhirah, Egypt: Dāral-Shurūq.

Baker, Raymond William. 2003. *Islam without Fear: Egypt and the New Islamists*. Cambridge, MA: Harvard University Press.

Bälz, Kilian. 1997. "Submitting Faith to Judicial Scrutiny through the Family Trial: The `Abū Zayd Case.'" *Die Welt Des Islams* 37:135–55.

Berger, Maurits S. 2003. "Apostasy and Public Policy in Contemporary Egypt: An Evaluation of Recent Cases from Egypt's Highest Courts." *Human Rights Quarterly* 25:720–40.

Bernard-Maugiron, Nathalie. 2004. "Can Hisba Be Modernised? The Individual and the Protection for the General Interest before Egyptian Courts." In *Standing Trial: Law and Person in the Modern Middle East*, edited by Baudouin Dupret, 318–44. London: I.B. Tauris.

Brown, Nathan J. 1997. *The Rule of Law in the Arab World: Courts in Egypt and the Gulf.* Cambridge, UK: Cambridge University Press.

Brown, Nathan J. and Clark B. Lombardi. 2006. "The Supreme Constitutional Court of Egypt on Islamic Law, Veiling and Civil Rights: An Annotated Translation of Supreme Constitutional Court of Egypt Case No. 8 of Judicial Year 17 (May 18, 1996)." *American University International Law Review* 21: 437–60.

Cahen, Claude, and Mohammed Talbi. 1960–2007. "Hisba." In *Encyclopedia of Islam*, 2nd ed., edited by Peri Bearman et al. Leiden, Netherlands, and Boston, MA: Brill. http://referenceworks .brillonline.com/entries/encyclopedia-of-islam-2/h-isba-COM_0293

Cook, Michael. 2003. *Forbidding Wrong in Islam: An Introduction.* New York: Cambridge University Press.

——. 2006. *Commanding Right and Forbidding Wrong in Islamic Thought.* Cambridge, UK: Cambridge University Press.

Dupret, Baudouin, and Maruits Berger, trans. 1998. "Jurisprudence Abû Zayd." *Egypt Monde Arabe*, special issue *Droit d'Egypte: Histoire et Sociologie* 34: 169–201.

Egyptian Court of Cassation, Judgment in *Naṣr Ḥāmid Abū Zayd et al. v. Muhammad Ṣamīda 'Abd al-Ṣamd et al.*, Appeals 475, 478, 481 of Judicial Year 65 (1996).

Egyptian Supreme Administrative Court, Judgment in *Minister of Health v. Yūsuf al-Badrī et al.*, Appeal 5257 of Judicial Year 43 (1997).

Egyptian Supreme Administrative Court, *President of the American University in Cairo v. Aymān Taha Muḥammad al-Zayni et al.*, Appeal 3219 of Judicial Year 48 (2007).

Hallaq, Wael B. 2009. *Shari'a: Theory, Practice, Transformations.* Cambridge, UK: Cambridge University Press.

Hizb al-ḥurriyah wa'l-'Adālah ("Freedom and Justice Party"). 2011. *"Barnāmaj hizb al-ḥurriyah wa'l-'adālah"* ("Platform of the Freedom and Justice Party"). https://kurzman.unc.edu/ files/2011/06/FJP_20111.pdf.

Hizb al-Nūr ("Party of Light"). 2011. *"Barnāmaj Hizb al-Nūr"* ("Platform of the Party of Light") https://kurzman.unc.edu/files/2011/06/AlNour_2011_brnameg_alnoor.pdf.

Kepel, Gilles. 1985. *Muslim Extremism in Egypt: The Prophet and Pharaoh.* Berkeley: University of California Press.

Lombardi, Clark B. 2006. *State Law as Islamic Law in Modern Egypt: The Incorporation of the Shari'a into Egyptian Constitutional Law.* Leiden, Netherlands: Brill.

——. 2008. "The Supreme Constitutional Court of Egypt: Managing Constitutional Conflict in an Authoritarian, Aspirationally Islamic State." *The Journal of Comparative Law* 2: 234–53.

——. 2013a. "The Constitution as Agreement to Agree: The Social and Political Foundations (and Effects) of the 1971 Egyptian Constitution." In *Social and Political Foundations of Constitutions*, edited by Dannis J. Galligan and Mila Versteeg, 398–431. Cambridge, UK: Cambridge University Press.

——. 2013b. "Constitutional Provisions Making Sharia 'a' or 'the' Chief Source of Legislation: Where Do They Come From? What Do They Mean? Do They Matter?" *American University International Law Review* 28:733–74.

Lubaydī, Ḥasan. 1983. *Da'āwīal-ḥisbah*. Assiut, Egypt: Jāmi'at Asyūṭ, Kullīyatal-Ḥuqūq.

Marcus, Abraham. 1989. *The Middle East on the Eve of Modernity: Aleppo in the 18th Century*. New York: Columbia University Press.

Meijer, Roel. 2009. *Global Salafism: Islam's New Religious Movement*. New York: Columbia University Press.

Moustafa, Tamir. 2007. *The Struggle for Constitutional Power: Law, Politics, and Economic Development in Egypt*. Cambridge, UK: Cambridge University Press.

———. 2010. "The Islamist Trend in Egyptian Law." *Politics and Religion* 3:610–30.

Najjar, Fauzi. 2000. "Islamic Fundamentalism and the Intellectuals: The Case of Nasr Hamid Abū Zayd." *British Journal of Middle Eastern Studies* 27 (2): 177–200.

al-Namnam, Helmī. 2012. *Al-ḥisba wa ḥurriyat al-ta'bīr*. al-Qāhira, Egypt: al-shabaka al-`arabiyya l-ma'lūmāt ḥuqūq al-insān.

Olsson, Susanne. 2008. "Apostasy in Egypt: Contemporary Cases of ḥisbah." *The Muslim World* 98:95–115.

Peirce, Leslie. 2006. "A New Judge for *Aintab*: The Shifting Legal Environment of a Sixteenth-Century Ottoman Court." In *Dispensing Justice in Islam: Qadis and Their Judgments*, edited by Muhammad Masud Khalid, Brinkley Messick, and David Powers, 71–93. Leiden, Netherlands: Brill.

Qaradawi, Yusuf al. 1997. *Min Fiqh al-Dawlafi'l-Islām*. Cairo: Dar al-Shurūq.

Rutherford, Bruce K. 2008. *Egypt after Mubarak: Liberalism, Islam, and Democracy in the Arab World*. Princeton, NJ: Princeton University Press.

Stilt, Kristen. 2012. *Islamic Law in Action: Authority, Discretion, and Everyday Experiences in Mamluk Egypt*. Oxford: Oxford University Press.

Sullivan, D. 2004. "Ḥisba Law and Freedom of Expression in Islam: Two Case Studies of Prosecution in Contemporary Egypt." *Journal of Mediterranean Studies* 14 (1/2): 213–36.

Al-Wasat. 2009. "*Al-Shaykh Yūsuf al-Badrī: allah `amarni bi-taghyīr al-munkir*." *Al-Waṣaṭ*, September 15. http://www.el-wasat.com/portal/News-55566258.html.

Wike, Richard. 2013. "The Tahrir Square Legacy: Egyptians Want Democracy, a Better Economy, and a Major Role for Islam." *Pew Research Global Attitudes Project*, January 24. http://www.pewglobal.org/2013/01/24/the-tahrir-square-legacy-egyptians-want-democracy-a-better-economy-and-a-major-role-for-islam/

Ziadeh, Farhat Jacob. 1968. *Lawyers, the Rule of Law and Liberalism in Modern Egypt*. Stanford, CA: Hoover Institution on War, Revolution, and Peace, Stanford University.

Notes

1. In his discussion, Cook translates "*yughairuhu*" as "put it right" rather than "change."

2. As this chapter makes clear, modern Egyptian thinkers have started to encourage Muslims to file suits against actions that are contrary to widely accepted precepts of Islamic law—whether involving a "right of God" or a "right of men." Islamic activists who bring such suits understand themselves as acting to stop activity that is morally offensive and, if failing to stop it, as having criticized the wrong.

3. Cook argues that such cases should not, in fact, be considered attempts to forbid wrong (Cook 2006, 522). Cook cites secondary literature that discusses the practice in the premodern Muslim world of reporting wrongdoing to judges (Cook 2006, 522n23). But these wrongdoings are apparently cases in which a particular *type* of sinful behavior is taking place—one in

which the "rights of God" are implicated. Cook argues that such cases as involving something other than "forbidding wrong" (ibid.). It is not clear to us that the acts that Cook sees as falling within the acts categorized as "forbidding wrong" can easily be distinguished from this second type of act. Furthermore, even if classical jurists made a clear conceptual distinction, we think that the distinction has largely disappeared in modern Egyptian discourse.

4. To him, the Quṭbian position represents "a flagrant divergence from the classical tradition and an unmistakable assertion of political quietism" that "would not prove generally acceptable in a period of highly politicized Islamic resurgence" (Cook 2003, 120). This seems to be too strong.

5. We thank Nathan Brown for pointing this out and citing, as merely the most obvious example, the great Arab jurist and judge ʿAbd al-Razzaq al-Sanhūrī.

6. This was expressed during interviews one of the authors conducted with justices on the Supreme Constitutional Court during the early 2000s.

7. No one has yet conducted a systematic study of whether Egyptian litigants in the 1980s and early 1990s invoked the concept of hisba, or "forbidding wrong," when filing litigation. Nathalie Bernard-Maugiron discusses a case from 1981 in which a plaintiff invoked the concept of hisba in the administrative courts in an action to abrogate a presidential decree. This use of the concept was rejected by the court, although the case was allowed to proceed on other claims (Bernard-Maugiron 2004, 318–44; see also Baker 2003, 65–66). Although Bernard-Maugiron links this type of "hisba" back to civil law concepts rather than the Islamic obligation to "forbid wrong," it is unclear to us whether such a strong distinction can be made. We do not know the original intention of the plaintiff in that case, and we find no reason to consider the religious and civil legal concepts that have variously been called hisba mutually exclusive; in fact, we suggest that they are often linked.

8. Anticipating such a development, a law professor at a regional university suggested in 1983 that judicial review of legislation could be seen as a form of judicial hisba. This study, conducted by a member of the law faculty at the University of Asyut and entitled "Hisba Suits," explicitly described nullification cases, whether in the Supreme Constitutional Court or the administrative courts, as a type of hisba (Lubaydī 1983, 76, 99). It is not clear that this work was widely known among Islamist lawyers or the judges who were hearing Islamist lawsuits; we think it probably was not. In its numerous article 2 opinions up through the mid-1990s, the SCC gave no indication that Islamist litigants challenging immoral laws had claimed to be "forbidding wrong."

9. In 1997, al-Qaradāwī, a classically trained scholar influential with members of the Muslim Brotherhood, published a book arguing that the state and individuals each have an obligation to forbid wrong. The state should thus legislate against immoral activity and should also encourage a wide range of private activity, including lawsuits, that serve to forbid wrong. Like al-ʿAwwā, however, al-Qaradāwī believes that private actions such as lawsuits are only appropriate in unusual cases in which the moral principle involved is "widely shared within the community and supported by a consensus among jurists" (Rutherford 2008, 124, citing Qaradawi 1997, 94).

10. For a media report on this, see http://www.alraimedia.com/Alrai/ArticlePrint.aspx?id=74430.

11. The platform specifically stated that the party seeks "establishment of the right of every citizen to raise a general case without fulfilling the conditions of capacity and interest." The 2011 Arabic version of the Freedom and Justice Party platform explicitly called this type of case a "hisba" case. As of 2013, the provision was changed to call for the right of every citizen to raise "general" cases, though the explicit reference to hisba was omitted.

7 Shari`a, Islamic Ethics, and Democracy: The Crisis of the "Turkish Model"

Ahmet T. Kuru

Turkey was long regarded as the nation most likely to produce a harmonized combination of Islamic ethics and democratic principles. Several commentators noted that the Justice and Development Party (AKP) rule in Turkey could, at least in practice, provide such a combination even though the party lacked the intellectual depth to provide an ideational synthesis of Islamic political thought and democratic theory. I myself even presented the AKP as a model to Arab Islamists when defending the viability of a middle way between assertive secularism and Islamism (Kuru 2013a). However, recent developments in Turkish politics, from the Gezi events to the corruption scandal, have revealed that the AKP has failed to combine Islamic ethics and democratic institutions, let alone model them for other countries.

Since 2013, the AKP's leader, Turkey's prime minister, and then president Recep Tayyip Erdoğan have moved toward Islamism and away from passive secularism. The AKP has embraced a Machiavellian approach that justifies almost any means—including but not limited to demonizing the Hizmet ("service") movement led by Fethullah Gülen, turning the progovernment media into a propaganda machine, and establishing a *mukhabarat* (intelligence) state—to cover up corruption allegations and keep Erdoğan in power. In general, the AKP has shown that it has neither fully embraced Western democratic standards nor produced an Islamic alternative in terms of political, economic, and media ethics. The Hizmet movement has also made mistakes during recent controversies, particularly by being overly politicized throughout its power struggles against the assertive secularist generals and, more recently, against Erdoğan.

Whence came optimism about the idea of the "Turkish model," and why did it fade so quickly? This chapter begins with three main reasons for the optimistic expectations: (1) the historical and geopolitical importance of Turkey, (2) the ethics-based understanding of shari`a developed by Bediüzzaman Said Nursi (d. 1960) and Gülen, and (3) the transformation of the AKP from

Islamism to passive secularism. I then elaborate on recent political and ethical crises in Turkey, particularly the Gezi, corruption, and mining scandals, examining how Islamist support for Erdoğan has continued despite these scandals—which has prompted critics of Erdoğan to question the links between Islamism and public ethics.

Reasons for Optimism: History, Ideas, and Politics

The Ottoman Legacy, Assertive Secularism, and Islamism

The historical and geopolitical importance of Turkey as inheritor of the Ottoman Empire have prompted several observers to look to Turkey for a model combination of Islam and democracy. A third of current Muslim-majority countries in the world (seventeen of forty-nine) were once Ottoman territories. Even some Muslims in other parts of the world, such as those on the Indian subcontinent, regarded the Ottoman sultan as the caliph of Muslims. In addition to their religious status, Ottomans have also been pioneering reformists, embracing European institutions as early as 1839, if not earlier. Thus Turkey, which was founded by the Ottoman elite, became, to no one's surprise, not only the first secular republic among Muslim-majority countries (Özbudun 2012) but also a member of NATO.

Mustafa Kemal Atatürk's (d. 1938) assertive secularist policies, inaugurated in 1924, were followed by other leaders in the Muslim world, such as Reza Shah (d. 1944) in Iran, Amanullah Khan (d. 1960) in Afghanistan, Muhammad Ali Jinnah (d. 1948) in Pakistan, Sukarno (d. 1970) in Indonesia, Gamal Abdel Nasser (d. 1970) in Egypt, and Habib Bourguiba (d. 1987) in Tunisia. Their idea of keeping Islamic groups and institutions under state control, however, was bound up in authoritarianism, and these secular autocrats largely failed to satisfy their people's expectations of political and socioeconomic development.

The Iranian Revolution of 1979 created a new wave of Islamist republicanism. Although Islamists came to direct power in only a few countries, such as Sudan and Afghanistan, they became a major opposition force in many others. Their formalistic understanding of shari'a has not, however, done any better than secular autocrats' ideologies at providing solutions to political and socioeconomic problems. Islamists have displayed an obsession with issues of criminal law (Bacık 2013) and with restricting women's public lives, all while undermining the importance of Islam's moral principles and ethical goals (for various interpretations and implementations of shari'a, see El Fadl 2014; Grote and Röder 2012; Hallaq 2009; Hefner 2011; and Kadri 2012). In the so-called Islamic states, rulers have used religious legitimacy as an instrument to consolidate their authoritarian regimes and to avoid accountability. Putting God's name on some state flags did not honor Islam but rather sacralized the state (Kuru 2013a, 4). The so-called

Islamic state has appeared to be not merely unnecessary but in fact an obstacle to the pursuit of the general principles and goals of shari`a.

In short, neither assertive secularism nor Islamism has successfully addressed sociopolitical problems in Muslim-majority countries. Under these circumstances, Turkey was regarded as a major case in which a new relationship between Islam, democracy, and secularism could emerge.

Ethical Understanding of Shari`a: Nursi and Gülen

An effective challenge to Islamists' literal and formal understanding of shari`a necessitates an alternative Islamic approach. In Turkey, Nursi proposed such an alternative, emphasizing the role of reason in interpreting Islam. In his words, "[W]hen reason and religious text [the Qur'an and the *hadith*] conflict, reason is referred to and the text is interpreted. Yet reason should be 'reason'" (1911b, 1996). He stressed that the spread of Islam in the modern age could be achieved through persuasion and economic development of Muslims rather than through military power (1909, 1930). He also emphasized that teaching students only religious sciences, thereby excluding modern sciences, would produce "bigotry" (1911a, 1956).

Nursi was politically active in Istanbul and his native Eastern Anatolia during the late Ottoman era. He supported the second constitutional process started in 1908, as well as the Young Turks policy that allowed Armenians and other non-Muslims to hold high-level bureaucratic positions such as governorships (1911a, 1945). In 1909, there was an uprising in Istanbul in which a major slogan was "We Want Shari`a!" The Young Turks repressed the uprising and brought many into courts martial. During his trial, Nursi was asked, "You also wanted shari`a?" He responded: "Ninety-nine percent of shari`a is about ethics, worship, the hereafter, and virtue. Only 1 percent of it is about politics; the rulers are supposed to think about that part" (1909, 1922).

Following the foundation of the Republic, Kemalists pursued authoritarian reforms, including the abolition of the caliphate, replacement of Arabic script with Latin, Turkification of the *ezan* (call to prayer), and the obligation of wearing a European top hat. Although Nursi was exiled, imprisoned, and tortured, he encouraged peaceful resistance and stressed that violence could only be used against foreign enemies in interstate military conflicts. To explain his peaceful stance, Nursi repeatedly referred to a verse in the Qur'an: "No bearer of burdens can bear the burden of another" (17:15). For him, this verse emphasized that individuals cannot be held responsible for the misdeeds of their relatives or societies, whereas in a political struggle, one generally attacks a whole group of people as if they were a single entity (1949–60, 1850). Nursi did not even directly challenge the secular state. In one of his trials, Nursi was asked whether he was against secularism. He answered: "I understand the secular government as neutral, in a sense that it does not intervene in pious and religiously-devoted people, as it does not intervene in non-religious and dissolute people, regarding the principle of the freedom of conscience" (1936–49, 1030).

During the republican era, Nursi rejected his political activism in the late Ottoman period and embraced an ascetic life. He defined politics as contradictory to spiritual development because it generally led to arrogance, conflict, and corruption. Nursi also noted that politicization would undermine Islamic services by creating doubts about their sincerity and by making political rivals oppose them (Kuru and Kuru 2008, 102–3). Instead of (party) politics, Nursi promoted "positive action" (*müspet hareket*) and tried to disseminate Islamic messages through his network of followers, delivering moral education while rarely criticizing Kemalist policies.

Nursi wrote more than a hundred pamphlets about Islamic faith and worship, entitled *Risale-i Nur* (Epistles of Light). These pamphlets were mostly copied and distributed by villagers at a time when most Islamic publications were banned. His works aimed to convince even rationalist readers to believe in the pillars of the Islamic faith, as well as to practice daily prayers and fasting, by bringing explanations and analogies from the universe, the human body, and society. They generally responded to questions that modern perspectives put to Islam: What are the reasonable proofs about the existence of God and the hereafter? Why does God create evil? Why are there repetitions in the Qur'an? Why did the Prophet get married to multiple wives?

An anecdote reveals how Nursi focused on the individual inner experience of Islam rather than top-down "Islamization" of public institutions. While he was in exile in northern Anatolia, some high school students visited Nursi and said, "Make us know about our Creator; our teachers do not mention God." Nursi neither complained about the secular curriculum nor mentioned a future Islamization of schools as a solution. Instead, he recommended that the students interpret the sciences using their faith rather than submitting to the interpretation of the teachers: "Each and every scientific discipline you study constantly mentions God and makes you know about the Creator with its own particular language; listen to the sciences, not the teachers" (1936–49, 954–55).

Nevertheless, Nursi did not completely disregard party politics. After the end of the Republican People's Party (CHP)'s single-party rule, which lasted from 1923 to 1950, Turkey became a multiparty democracy. Nursi recommended that his disciples support the center-right Democrat Party (DP), hoping that it would expand religious freedom and end the CHP's oppression. Nursi wrote a letter noting that the DP would be better than an Islamist party because if Islamists came to power, they would have to use religion for political purposes (1949–60, 1878). Paradoxically, the government persecution of Nursi continued during the DP rule until he died in 1960. Two month after his death, the military staged a coup d'état. The junta opened Nursi's tomb and moved his body to a still unknown place (Güsten 2012).

Nursi's ideas have affected a broad range of actors in Turkey, including members of the influential Hizmet movement. The movement's main areas of activism have been education, the media, and intercultural dialogue (see Marty 2015; Shinn 2015). Its public face is the Journalists and Writers Foundation, which has organized the Abant Meetings to bring together intellectuals from various ideological backgrounds (White 2004, 91–92). Currently, Hizmet has about 20 universities and more than 1,000 schools in more than 100 countries (see Yükleyen 2012). It is also affiliated with a media network that includes the *Zaman* daily, the *Aksiyon* weekly, *Today's Zaman* (in English), Dünya TV (in Kurdish), and two journals on Islamic sciences—*Yeni Ümit* (in Turkish) and *Hira* (in Arabic).

Like Nursi, Gülen is an ascetic who has never married and who does not own personal property. In his four-volume series on Sufism, *Kalbin Zümrüt Tepeleri* (Emerald Hills of the Heart), Gülen emphasizes the importance of deepening individual faith, spreading ethical values, and better representing Islam in practice. He has become an internationally known promoter of interfaith dialogue (Emon 2012, 4). Gülen has taken a stance against the idea of an "Islamic state." In his words, "Islam does not propose a certain unchangeable form of government or attempt to shape it. Instead, Islam establishes fundamental principles that orient a government's general character, leaving it to the people to choose the type and form of government according to time and circumstances" (2001, 134).

Assertive secularists in Turkey accused Gülen of planning to create a shari'a-based Islamic state. He gave several interviews to refute these allegations. In one television interview, Gülen criticized the secularist slogan "Damn shari'a!" used in some rallies in Turkey, calling it insulting to all Muslims. Following Nursi, Gülen also stresses that 95 percent of shari'a is about personal and social piety, including worship, contemplation (*tefekkür*), and family life. Thus individuals, not the state, must make shari'a part of life. Only 5 percent of shari'a is about issues related to the state, which may concern state rulers. When he was asked, "There are those who want shari'a; what do they really want?" Gülen responded, "Most of them probably do not know what they want. They may not be aware that 95 percent of it is already practiced" (1997).

Gülen's understanding of shari'a is largely based on general principles (Yılmaz 2003). While discussing issues related to Islamic law, an important source of reference for him is Imam Shatibi and his formulation of *maqasid* (higher objectives; see this volume, chapter 1). As an example, Gülen explains why suicide bombing is anti-Islamic by referring to Shatibi: "One of the five main things that a person has a duty to protect is life . . . As Shatibi systematizes in *Al-Muwafaqaat*, the entire legal system is based on the 'five methods'—the protection of life, religion, property, intellect, and posterity. The protection of life is at the top of this list" (2012).

Unlike Yusuf al-Qaradawi, Gülen emphasizes that suicide bombings cannot be justified under any circumstances. Referring to Ibn Abbas's interpretation of particular Qur'anic verses on murder, Gülen notes that there is a strong possibility of eternal hellfire for a murderous terrorist even if he or she is a Muslim (2004; see also 2015b).

Gülen's views on women's rights also differ from those of some orthodox scholars. He stresses that the Hanafi school recognizes women's ability to hold leadership positions, including by being judges and rulers (his interview in Sevindi 2008, 92). He defines polygamy as a "special dispensation" under certain circumstances, such as wars that left many widows: "The Prophet began having more than one wife after the age of fifty-five . . . [T]he rule is marriage with one woman" (Sevindi 2008, 112–13). Gülen also strongly opposes domestic violence: "[The Prophet] helped with housework[,] . . . never used force against any woman, and never used harsh words" (Sevindi 2008, 67). He recommends that women beaten by their husbands, in contexts where there is no sufficient police protection, either get divorced (if they have no children), or learn martial arts for protection: "[I]f her husband gave her one slap, she could return two. . . . Beating is an unjustifiable physical attack and is a crime. Defending yourself against this attack is legitimate" (quoted in Kurucan 2008).

According to Gülen, classical Islamic jurisprudence on gender equality should be reinterpreted. He gives the example of slavery, for which the entire body of legal opinions has been abolished despite references to it in some Qur'anic verses and *hadith*: "[Women] lag behind men in terms of education and cultural achievements. Slavery has disappeared, and, today, no one argues that it should be reintroduced on the basis of the debates about slavery in classical Islamic jurisprudence. Why don't we employ the same progressive approach to the status of women, without contradicting the essence and basic tenets of Islam?" (2014b).

Nursi and Gülen's ethical understanding of shari`a is not confined to Turkey's peculiar conditions; instead, it is similar to the perspectives of some non-Turkish Muslims scholars. One influential example is Tariq Ramadan, who is knowledgeable about both Islamic and Western thought. Ramadan was one of the earliest commentators who stressed the importance of the "Turkish model" for Egypt and other countries experiencing the recent Arab uprisings (Ramadan 2011; see also this volume, chapter 1).

Ramadan's book *Radical Reform* (2009) encourages an ethical understanding of shari`a in which he calls on Muslims to stress substance rather than form. Ramadan criticizes the literalist understanding of Islam; instead, he proposes a holistic and dynamic perspective that emphasizes higher objectives. The higher goals include "promoting and protecting Dignity (of humankind, living species, and nature), Welfare, Knowledge, Creativity, Autonomy, Development, Equality, Freedom, Justice, Fraternity, Love, Solidarity, and Diversity" (2009, 139). While referring to the higher objectives of shari`a, as Gülen does, Ramadan makes frequent references to Shatibi (2009, 65–76). At the Center for the Study of Islam and Democracy Conference in Tunis (March 29, 2013), I asked Ramadan whether the higher objectives of shari`a à la Shatibi—protection of life, religion, property, intellect, and posterity—are similar to John Locke's emphasis on God-given rights of life, liberty, and property. He replied that any such similarity should not be surprising, for Western and Islamic thought share several overlapping concepts.

For Ramadan, shari`a refers mainly to the divine origin of higher, revealed principles instead of legal details. Thus particular laws are not sacred; they are human productions "associated with the open and relative activity of human intelligence" at "a given moment in human history" (2009, 122–23). This contextual human production should not be taken as divine, because "no scholar has ever approached the texts without being, in one way or another, influenced by the culture in which she or he lived" (2009, 191). The formalistic understanding of Islamic law, according to Ramadan, misses the substance. The formal, literalist approach to *halal* meat, for instance, is obsessed with slaughtering techniques while ignoring "outrageous treatment of animals . . . marked by overconsumption and excessive productivity" (2009, 243).

Ramadan also challenges the authority of the `ulama. He argues that the `ulama are not well equipped to respond to contemporary challenges Muslims face. Thus the process of producing Islamic theory should include experts from several fields, "even non-Muslim experts." Ramadan simply calls the `ulama "text specialists" who have no superiority over experts in other fields. The role of the `ulama in producing knowledge should be limited: "We can no longer leave it to scholarly circles and text specialists to determine norms (about scientific, social, economic, or cultural issues) while they only have relative or superficial, second-hand knowledge of complex, profound, and often interconnected issues" (2009, 124). Ramadan also rejects classification of fields of science as "Islamic" or not, which wrongly provides a sacred position to the former: "[E]xtracting rules for interpretation and understanding from a 'body of texts' is no more 'Islamic' or 'sacred' than identifying a principle in the functioning of the human body" (2009, 110). At this point, Ramadan seems to agree with Nursi's famous depiction of the universe as a "book" (*kitab-ı kebiri kâinat*) to be read as one reads a religious text.

Ramadan's call to respect expertise and division of labor is crucial for modern times. The `ulama could have claimed an all-encompassing knowledge in the past—similar to classical philosophers whose expertise covered almost everything from politics to health, from music to ethics. Yet today, vast amounts of information require specialization and division of labor, leaving even geniuses unable to claim expertise on all issues. Thus despite the misleading claim that there is no separation between religion and the state in Islam, a clear division exists between expertise on religious issues and proficiency at solving political problems in the modern world.

Ramadan's emphasis on higher principles is in line with Nursi's and Gülen's understandings of shari'a as a set of higher goals rather than a collection of legal codes. These goals depend on revelation, which is sacred for Muslims, whereas state-imposed shari'a laws are a subjective human production. In this regard, Nursi and Gülen's ethical interpretation of Islam affected the transformation of Islam and politics in Turkey—until the recent crisis.

The AKP: From Islamism to Passive Secularism

The main Islamist movement in Turkey, the Milli Görüş (National Outlook), was founded by Necmettin Erbakan (d. 2011) in 1969. The Milli Görüş was much more moderate than its counterparts in Arab countries for three reasons: (1) the Turkish military played a guardianship role, imposing assertive secularism, (2) multiparty democracy encouraged avoiding radicalism by those who seriously hoped to win elections, and (3) mainstream Muslim scholars, especially Nursi and Gülen, promoted a more ethical and less formal understanding of shari'a. The Milli Görüş adopted Islamist discourses on foreign policy, economics, and various other policy areas, but its views about the Islamization of the legal system remained unclear. Erbakan's parties were closed down four times in three decades; each time, he founded a new party without even organizing street protests against the closures. In 1974–78, the Milli Görüş party took part in coalitions, and Erbakan became vice-premier minister in three different governments. Erbakan also served as the prime minister in 1996–97.

After the "soft coup d'état" on February 28, 1997, the military reminded the country, again, that it would not let Islamists rule the nation. Erdoğan founded the AKP with Abdullah Gül and Bülent Arınç, dropping Islamism and declaring that they had removed "the shirt of the Milli Görüş." Erdoğan became the prime minister in 2003. Cornered by both Erbakan and the assertive secularists, he allied with Hizmet movement and liberal intellectuals. The alliance composed by the AKP, Hizmet, and liberals defended Turkey's integration into the European Union, democratization, and demilitarization (Kuru 2007). The allies also resisted the Kemalist elite's assertive secularism and tried to replace it with a more liberal version of secularism—what I call passive secularism—that allows public visibility of religion (Kuru 2009, 171–72). This alliance ended the tutelage of the Kemalist military and judiciary over Turkish democracy (Kuru 2012; Kuru and Stepan 2012, 9–10). A reflection of this transformation is a recent decision by the Turkish Constitutional Court, which previously had been the bastion of assertive secularism. In April 2013, in a 15-2 decision, the court criticized strict (that is, assertive) secularism and endorsed liberal (that is, passive) secularism (decision # 2012/128).

The AKP's evolution from Islamism to passive secularism, together with the Turkish state's transformation from assertive to passive secularism, made several observers optimistic about Turkey's possible role in the Muslim world as a model of democracy and moderate state–Islam relations. During its third term (2011–15), however, the AKP ended its cooperation with liberal intellectuals and the Hizmet movement. Erdoğan embraced Islamism and authoritarianism, ruining Turkey's international image as a model Muslim democracy. The following section will explain how this happened.

The Crisis of the "Turkish Model"

Gezi, Corruption, and Mining Scandals

The fall of the Kemalist hegemony had created a substantial power vacuum in Turkish politics, and that vacuum was fully filled by Erdoğan's personality. After its 2011 electoral victory, the AKP became an extremely leader-centric party as Erdoğan even marginalized President Gül and Deputy-Prime Minister Arınç. He also brought state institutions, especially the National Intelligence Organization (MİT), under his personal control. Loyalty to Erdoğan became the criterion for promotion in the AKP as well as the bureaucracy. Erdoğan's favored businessmen bought media outlets and turned them into a propaganda machine. As a father figure, Erdoğan began to intervene in everything from abortion to beverages, from mining to education, from urban planning to the arts. The project of drafting a new constitution was blocked by Erdoğan's ambition to design an ultra-powerful presidency for himself.

With no checks or balances mitigating his authority, Erdoğan also leaned toward Islamism. His policy toward the Arab Spring shifted from supporting democratization to backing Muslim Brothers regionwide. He adopted the "R4BI4" sign, symbolizing the Muslim Brothers' resistance to the military coup in Egypt, as his main populist gesture, raising his four fingers in political rallies (see Kuru 2015). In domestic politics, Erdoğan declared a new vision of educating a "pious generation," in which the public (Islamic) Imam–Hatip schools gained a pivotal role. He used a discriminatory discourse against the Alevis and secular segments of society. Erdoğan asked those who drink alcohol to drink it at home and called them alcoholics, then announced a plan to legally prevent male and female students from renting apartments and residing together. He also employed the Directorate of Religious Affairs (Diyanet) as an instrument of his increasingly Islamist political agenda.

The Gezi events began in May 2013 as a popular reaction to Erdoğan's authoritarianism, his desire to rule until 2024, and his ambition for favoring the construction industry over the environment. A physical representation of these three elements in Ankara was the construction of a massive 1,150-room presidential palace for Erdoğan in the middle of the Atatürk Forestry Farm. Despite court orders to halt the construction, Erdoğan ordered its continuation. In April 2013, Erdoğan pronounced that a rebuilt historic barracks, for use as either a mall or a residence, would replace the similarly important Gezi Park, in Istanbul's Taksim Square. A month later, the police and municipal officers began bulldozing the park, evicting protesters using tear gas, then burning their tents. This led to nationwide demonstrations, which, though widely covered by the Western media, were mostly disregarded by the Turkish media, which feared Erdoğan. Meanwhile, Erdoğan further provoked the protestors by using insulting language, insisting on building the barracks despite a court decision prohibiting its construction. To motivate his religiously conservative followers against the protestors, Erdoğan claimed that protestors had attacked a headscarved woman and drunk alcohol in a mosque, accusations later discovered to be false and manipulative. Erdoğan and his followers also accused several "conspirators," including Western media outlets, Western airways, "the Jewish lobby," and "the interest lobby" of interference, portraying the Gezi events as a Western conspiracy that had nothing to do with genuine environmental or political sensitivities. The Gezi events abundantly showed that the AKP had not developed an "Islamic ethics of environmentalism" during its twelve-year rule.

A corruption and bribery probe that began seven months later further degraded Erdoğan's and the AKP's democratic images. Prosecutors accused three cabinet ministers of receiving bribes from an Iranian businessman, Reza Zarrab, who had also become a Turkish citizen, and several others, including a fourth minister, of corruption connected with government tenders and construction projects. After the resignation of these ministers, the accusations reached to Erdoğan and his son. The CHP documented that Bilal Erdoğan's foundation had received $100 million from an unidentified donor. Similar to their tactics during the Gezi events, Erdoğan and his followers employed Islamic symbols to refute the corruption allegations. The police discovered $6 million hidden in shoeboxes in the house of the Halkbank CEO, who was accused of receiving the money as a bribe from Zarrab. The CEO claimed that the money was a donation for construction of an (Islamic) Imam–Hatip school—a narrative strenuously defended by Erdoğan and his supporters in the media, who depicted the CEO and Zarrab as philanthropists (Munyar 2013).

Erdoğan defined the probe as a coup d'état staged by the "parallel state"—his name for the Hizmet movement. Erdoğan and the media under his control attacked several individuals and organizations as parts of the conspiracy against the AKP government, including the president of Germany, the US ambassador, Freedom House, the BBC, the CNN, the president of the Turkish Constitutional

Court, the president of Turkey's bar associations union, the CHP, the Doğan media group, the Koç Holding, and the Turkish Industrialists' and Businessmen's Association. But Erdoğan's primary target was Gülen, whom Erdoğan implicitly called "a false prophet" while naming Hizmet followers as spies, viruses, blood-seeking vampires, assassins, and lovers of Israel. Erdoğan also questioned Gülen's religious credentials, criticizing his remarks on headscarves in the late 1990s, when Gülen had defined wearing a headscarf as a "secondary issue" in Islam and encouraged students to continue their education even if they had to remove their headscarves on university campuses (for the headscarf ban, see Akbulut 2015a; Akbulut 2015b). Using this remark, Erdoğan depicted Gülen as being against headscarves, prompting boos at political rallies. Erdoğan unapologetically announced "a witch hunt" against Hizmet, as part of which the pro-Erdoğan media have pursued a smear campaign against Hizmet in hopes of criminalizing it. Members of the media have made such absurd claims as that Hizmet controls the Brookings Institute and has turned pro-Armenian US congresspersons against Turkey.

In response, Hizmet's media outlets have extensively covered allegations against Erdoğan and other AKP members. Gülen has given interviews to and written opinion pieces for the international media, including the BBC, the *New York Times*, the *Wall Street Journal*, and *Asharq al-Awsat*, refuting Erdoğan's accusations and supporting the corruption probe (2014a; 2015a). He has noted that the prosecutors and policemen conducting the probe are a diverse group composed of nationalists, leftists, and others—not only Hizmet sympathizers.

To block the corruption investigations, Erdoğan reassigned and then fired dozens of prosecutors and thousands of senior police officers, including some who had prosecuted military generals on his behalf, allowing him to dominate Turkish politics. Meanwhile, Erdoğan had several laws passed with which to control the judiciary, censor the internet, and close down college preparation schools—about a quarter of which were run by Hizmet. Another very controversial law expanded the authority of MİT and granted it far-reaching immunities similar to those in Arab *mukhabarat* (intelligence) states. President Gül immediately signed all these bills into law, upsetting many observers in Turkey and abroad, who had considered him to be more democratic than Erdoğan (NYT Editorial Board 2014). But Erdoğan's attempts to cover up the investigations could not stifle the social media. After legal evidence, including wiretapped phone conversations and full texts of original indictments, were leaked to the internet, Erdoğan blocked access to Twitter and YouTube within Turkey until the Constitutional Court lifted the blockage.

The wiretapped phone conversations include dozens of shocking subjects. Some of them allegedly revealed how Zarrab was distributing bribes to cabinet ministers and other figures, how crony businessmen were buying media outlets on Erdoğan's orders, and how Erdoğan secretly owned several villas. Erdoğan confirmed some conversations, unapologetically acknowledging having called media executives to censor the coverage of an opposition leader, intervened in a governmental tender to cancel a project of the Koç group, and interfered with a court case against the Doğan group. However, he denied the authenticity of several more politically risky conversations, such as the one in which Minister Egemen Bağış allegedly ridiculed the Qur'an. The most sensational recording included five phone calls allegedly made between Erdoğan and his son Bilal on the day the corruption probe started. In the recording, Erdoğan asked his son to relocate a large sum of money hidden in houses of the family members. Toward the end of the day, Bilal called his father back, reporting that he had handled most of the money but still had €30 million to turn into "zero" (see the *Economist* 2014; Lowen 2014). This recording, which was heard on YouTube about 5 million times in five days, Erdoğan immediately rejected as a "montage." Yet he also added that his encrypted phone had been tapped, perceived as an unintentional authentication of the recording. The leader of CHP, Kemal Kılıçdaroğlu, called the recording "as authentic as Mount Ararat" and played it at his party's group meeting in Parliament. Thus the corruption scandal disclosed how the AKP had failed to produce an "Islamic ethics to prevent corruption" and an "Islamic media ethics."

Five months later, another scandal erupted in Soma, Manisa, when 301 miners died in a coal mine disaster. Their insufficient safety measures, equipment, training, and other working conditions revealed the lack of sufficient governmental regulation and inspections. Because Erdoğan had recently put all mining activities under his office's control, he was held particularly responsible. Erdoğan quickly visited the town, but instead of apologizing and sharing in the grief, he called such incidents "ordinary," describing them as parts of "the nature of [the mining industry]." He also gave examples from other mining accidents, such as those suffered by Britain in the nineteenth century, to normalize the disaster (Scott 2014). This speech outraged the townspeople, who began to boo him and shout "resignation!" Erdoğan lost his temper and slapped one miner as his advisor kicked another. Again, this incident shows that behind the façade of economic success, Turkey remained far below the standards of developed countries in terms of providing workers with fair conditions. Thus the AKP failed to infuse an "Islamic ethics of protecting labor rights" into capitalism.

During these three crises, the unquestioned loyalty of many religiously conservative politicians, journalists, bureaucrats, and businesspersons, as well as of Islamic scholars, *tariqas*, and communities, disappointed those in other segments of Turkish society who were critical of Erdoğan. When these critics began to regard religious conservatives as people who uncritically followed their leaders instead of ethical principles, Turkey's political controversy became an ethical crisis.

Years earlier, when Erdoğan had been struggling against the Kemalist generals, he had received substantial support from liberal intellectuals in Turkey and abroad. Today, however, most liberals, including Ergun Özbudun, Şahin Alpay, Nazlı Ilıcak, and Orhan Pamuk, criticize his authoritarianism, and Erdoğan receives his primary ideational support from Islamist ideologues.

Islamist Support for Erdoğan

In January 2014, Erdoğan presented the Diyanet foundation's "centennial awards" to several scholars for their services to Islamic culture. One of the awardees, Hayrettin Karaman, had a central place in the ceremonial protocol standing next to Erdoğan. Karaman, a professor of Islamic law, has been a columnist in the daily *Yeni Şafak*, which is owned by the family of Erdoğan's son-in law. Karaman's ideas have recently become more influential, together with Erdoğan's increasingly Islamist rhetoric. Regardless of whether his ideas influence Erdoğan or are used to justify Erdoğan's already-decided policies, Karaman has moved to the center of political controversies in Turkey.

In his *Yeni Şafak* column, Karaman has supported various remarks and policies of Erdoğan, such as prohibiting the residence of mixed-sex students: "If there is an unmarried couple or mixed-sex students who are living together in a house . . . the state inspects and raids such houses in order to hinder illegitimate behaviors, and punishes these perpetrators" ("Hangi Eve Girilemez," November 10, 2013). Karaman has also sided with Erdoğan in his recent campaign against the Hizmet movement. When Hizmet cooperated with an Alevi foundation to build a complex in which a mosque and an Alevi *cemevi* (house of worship) coexisted, Karaman took exception, arguing, "One religion cannot have two temples" ("Bir Dinin İki Mabedi Olmaz," September 13, 2013).

During the corruption scandal, Karaman was accused of issuing a *fatwa* that has been used by AKP members to receive commissions in governmental tenders. In his reply, Karaman wrote that he would permit public authorities to encourage, channel, and even require businesspersons to donate money to particular institutions in exchange for giving them governmental tenders. Moreover, he expressed satisfaction at the thought of businesspersons' making donations under pressure of losing tender or with the expectation of receiving future tender ("Rüşvete ve Yolsuzluğa Fetva Verilmez," December 27, 2013). In responding to allegations of corruption, Karaman has encouraged Muslims to regard politicians and other suspects as innocent until appeal courts uphold their convictions. Until then, he writes, it is "immoral" and "cruel" to circulate the details of corruption allegations in the media. He has also added that judges can be "ignorant, traitorous, and wrongful." For him, "in democracies the nation has the last word"—as if the ballot box will decide whether allegations are right. Muslims, he has said, sometimes should choose "the lesser of two evils." What then was his implicit message? Corruption is bad—but losing the AKP government would be worse ("Hakimler ve Savcılar Masum mu?" January 9, 2014).

According to Karaman, Turkey has emerged as the only country that can play a leading role in unifying and empowering Muslims in the Middle East. He argues that Western countries, which focus on protecting Israel and their oil interests, might well pursue various conspiracies against the AKP government. After making sure the readers understand the importance of keeping the AKP in power, Karaman refers to article 26 in the general principles list of the Mecelle— the civil code compiled in the late Ottoman era: "In order to eliminate a public [larger] damage, a private [smaller] damage would be preferable." Then he translates this principle into contemporary Turkish politics: "In order to prevent a damage to the public and the ummah, a damage to a person, a region, or a group is tolerable, justifiable" ("Türkiye'nin Dostları ve Düşmanları," December 19, 2013). This article created strong reactions, with critics arguing that it amounted to justifying Erdoğan's oppressive policies against Hizmet.

Karaman unapologetically defends "neighborhood pressure," arguing that conservative Muslims comprise a majority in society and saying that the majority has the right to impose moral rules in the public sphere. In his words, "individuals should 'voluntarily' not perform some of their freedoms for the respect of the majority . . . If they insist on performing, then 'neighborhood pressure' becomes the right of the majority, whose values are violated" ("Mahalle Baskısının Hak Olması," November 17, 2013). Nonetheless, even the members of the majority should know their limits: "In an Islamic democracy . . . Muslims cannot conduct immoral and sinful behaviors in the public sphere; in private sphere their acts would not be investigated—as long as they are not harmful to society" ("Islam, Demokrasi ve Laiklik," September 23, 2011).

Karaman asserts that "each and every Muslim should be an Islamist; even if he/she does not use this term, he/she should accept the meaning and content of this concept ("Müslüman Sıfatı Yetmemiş," August 30, 2012). For him, Islam is incompatible with all forms of secularism; Islam and secularism "cannot come together." Karaman also regards democracy and Islam as definitely incompatible, because "according to philosophical basis of democracy, human being is equal to, superior to, or independent of the Creator." Western democracy is based on "equality of values, positions, and rights"—further proof that it is irreconcilable with Islam ("İslam, Demokrasi ve Medine Vesikası," May 29, 2014). Muslims, he adds, should question the Western origins of democracy, the multiparty system, and pluralism. They ought to ask "do they have a divine origin?" or "are they productions of human reason and ego?" Yet Karaman justifies the AKP's usage of secularism, democracy, and pluralism as temporary instruments: "If our conditions require the usage of some means while we are

172 | Shari'a Law and Modern Muslim Ethics

marching toward Islam step-by-step, we would use such means . . . Necessity justifies the means" ("Demokrasi Çoğulculuk Laiklik ve İslam," May 25, 2014).

Karaman is just one example—though probably the most influential—of religious scholars who have supported Erdoğan throughout the recent crisis. Some have even argued that listening to and spreading evidence of corruption, such as wiretapped conversations, is a "sin" from an Islamic point of view. The president of the Diyanet, Mehmet Görmez, has also pursued a blatantly progovernment course, disregarding any concern for religious or (as a civil servant) bureaucratic neutrality. A day after the YouTube ban and two days before the crucial March 30, 2013, elections, the Diyanet's centrally drafted Friday sermon, recited in all mosques in Turkey, reminded Muslims that "freedom does not mean being irresponsible" and warned them that "the number of those who want to pierce the ship [implying political stability in Turkey] has increased via the mass communication technologies (Alp 2014).

Through these and other measures, the corruption scandal became a moral controversy that has polarized and divided Turkish society, going well beyond a mere political crisis for Erdoğan (Gültekin 2014a; 2014b). Secular and even some religious segments of society are now questioning the relationship between religion and ethics. The idea that Islamic ethics may be a positive force in Turkish public life has never been as controversial—nor, arguably, as unconvincing—as it is today.

Conclusion

In *The Gulf War Did Not Take Place* (1995), Jean Baudrillard showed how the media's representation of social reality might become more influential than that reality itself, as well as how concepts such as war and freedom might lose their conventional meanings. In Turkish politics, the pro-AKP media have worked hard to represent the Gezi, corruption, and mining scandals differently than the empirical reality of each of these situations. In this propaganda war, several concepts, such as coup d'état, people's sovereignty, and Islamic ethics, have lost their once familiar meanings. At the same time, however, the pro-AKP media have had very limited influence over international public opinion; from Western to Arab countries, the scandals were extensively reported. When BBC World News broadcast the video of Erdoğan slapping a miner, the pro-AKP media's claim that such an incident did not take place became meaningless. In the face of such negative international coverage, Turkey can no longer convincingly claim to represent a model of Islamic ethics interacting with and strengthening democratic institutions.

The recent scandals revealed that the AKP has failed to provide a public ethics capable of combating corruption, respecting principles of journalism, protecting the environment, and defending workers' rights. The Turkish case has also revealed the glaring gap between the Islamists' promise of bringing ethics into public life and the practical realities of their exercise of power. The slogan "Islam is the solution" does not automatically solve anything. The clear lesson is that Muslim-majority countries must fulfill the universal criteria of democracy and civic governance before they can claim to have brought about a synergistic synthesis of democracy and Islamic ethics.

The recent scandals also triggered a major public debate about the problem of political ethics in Turkey. Despite the scandals, Erdoğan never considered resigning, nor apologizing for any of his deeds. Critics in social media stressed that smaller crises in Western and East Asian countries have led to resignations. They also asked just why the political ethics of accepting responsibility has been so much weaker in Muslim-majority countries. The Turkish experience has indicated that political ethics must be developed in conjunction with, and within, political institutions, not through formal religious discourses alone. Training ethical individuals and society requires effective institutions. A student is likely to avoid plagiarism or cheating if he or she habitually learns in an institutional setting that these behaviors are wrong. Without institutional training and effective and continuing ethical socialization, Islamist slogans and even personal piety will never be sufficient to guarantee an ethical public life.

In order to resolve its ongoing sociopolitical crisis, Turkey needs to learn more from Western and other democracies' institutional practices and principles. The lessons to learn include the importance of government checks and balances, differentiation, and meritocracy (Kuru 2013b). Erdoğan has shown himself deficient with regard to each of these three principles. His leadership refused to abide by political checks and balances (in the AKP as well as in Turkey as a whole), he intervened in and reduced the autonomy of all spheres of life (religion, arts, the media, science, sports, urban planning, and so forth), and he packed the bureaucracy with loyalists regardless of their merits. Although Erdoğan is an extreme case, these three shortcomings are shared by almost all political parties and religious groups in Turkey. Hizmet, for example, is leader-centric, dealing with various spheres of life without putting clear limits on its areas of experience, and it favors its followers, sometimes by violating principles of meritocracy. The AKP, Hizmet affiliates, Kemalists, Kurdish nationalists, and others in Turkey have all been plagued by these same social and ethical problems. Leader-centrism has impeded creativity and diversity, the mixture of spheres of life has hindered expertise and competition, and crony favoritism has prevented fairness and efficiency. Only if sociopolitical and religious groups in Turkey solve the problems of leader-centrism (by promoting participation and checks and balances), mixture of spheres (by encouraging specialization and differentiation), and favoritism (by strengthening meritocratic institutions), will they be able to infuse democratic principles with Islamic ethics and thereby become a source of inspiration for other Muslim-majority countries.

References

Akbulut, Zeynep. 2015a. "Veiling as Self-disciplining: Muslim Women, Islamic Discourses, and the Headscarf Ban in Turkey," *Contemporary Islam* 9 (3): 433–53.

———. 2015b. "The Headscarf Ban and Muslim Women's Rights Discourse in Turkey." In *Contesting Feminisms: Gender and Islam in Asia*, edited by Huma Ahmed-Ghosh, 115- 34. Albany: SUNY Press.

Alp, Aysel. 2014. "Diyanet'ten 'Geminin Dibini Deldirmeyin' Hutbesi," *Hürriyet*, March 28.

Bacık, Gökhan. 2013. "The Unwanted Truth: Muslim Enemies of Islam." *Today's Zaman*, February 3.

Baudrillard, Jean. 1995. *The Gulf War Did Not Take Place.* Bloomington: Indiana University Press.

Economist. 2014. "Turkish Politics: Everything Is Possible," *Economist*, March 1.

Emon, Anver M. 2012. *Religious Pluralism and Islamic Law: Dhimmis and Others in the Empire of Law.* Oxford: Oxford University Press.

El Fadl, Khaled Abou. 2014. *Reasoning with God: Reclaiming Shari`ah in the Modern Age.* New York: Rowman & Littlefield.

Grote, Rainer, and Tilmann Röder, eds. 2012. *Constitutionalism in Islamic Countries: Between Upheaval and Continuity.* Oxford: Oxford University Press.

Gülen, M. Fethullah. 1997. "*Devlet ve Şeriat*," Gülen interview with Yalçın Doğan. Kanal D TV, April 16. http://tr.fgulen.com/content/view/227/141/.

———. 2001. "A Comparative Approach to Islam and Democracy," translated by Elvan Ceylan. *SAIS Review* 21 (2): 133–38.

———. 2004. "*Teröre Girmiş İnsan Müslüman Kalamaz*," Gülen interview with Nuriye Akman. *Zaman*, March 23.

———. 2012. "*Intihar*," Gülen talk, June 18. http://tr.fgulen.com/content/view/20980/9/.

———. 2014a. "From His Refuge in the Poconos, Reclusive Imam Fethullah Gulen Roils Turkey." *Wall Street Journal*, January 20.

———. 2014b. "Disbelief May Prevail, but Tyranny Will Not." Interview with Manuel Almeida. *Asharq al-Awsat*, March 25. http://www.aawsat.net/2014/03/article55330430.

———. 2015a "Turkey's Eroding Democracy." *New York Times*, February 3.

———. 2015b "Muslims Must Combat the Extremist Cancer." *Wall Street Journal*, August 27.

Gültekin, Levent. 2014a. "*17 Aralık ve 30 Mart'ın Asıl Kazananı ve Kaybedeni.*" May 8. http://www .internethaber.com/-17-aralik-ve-30-martin-asil-kazanani-ve-kaybedeni-15992y.htm.

———. 2014b. "What about My Hostility toward Erdoğan?" *Today's Zaman*, May 25.

Güsten, Susanne. 2012. "Shadow of Military Removed, Turkey Seeks a Spiritual Leader's Remains." *New York Times*, December 19.

Hallaq, Wael B. 2009. *Shari`a: Theory, Practice, Transformations.* New York: Cambridge University Press.

Hefner, Robert W., ed. 2011. *Shari`a Politics: Islamic Law and Society in the Modern World.* Bloomington: Indiana University Press.

Kadri, Sadakat. 2012. *Heaven on Earth: A Journey through Shari`a Law from the Deserts of Ancient Arabia to the Streets of the Modern Muslim World*. New York: Farrar, Straus & Giroux.

Kuru, Ahmet T. 2007. "Changing Perspectives on Islamism and Secularism in Turkey: The Gülen Movement and the AK Party." In *Muslim World in Transition: Contributions of the Gülen Movement*, edited by Ihsan Yilmaz, 140–51. London: Leeds Metropolitan University Press.

———. 2009. *Secularism and State Policies toward Religion: The United States, France, and Turkey*. New York: Cambridge University Press.

———. 2012. "The Rise and Fall of Military Tutelage in Turkey: Fears of Islamism, Kurdism, and Communism." *Insight Turkey* 14 (2): 37–57.

———. 2013a. "Muslim Politics Without an 'Islamic' State: Can Turkey's Justice and Development Party Be a Model for Arab Islamists?" Policy Briefing, Brookings Doha Center, February 2013.

———. 2013b. "Constitution, Presidentialism, and Checks and Balances: Comparing Democracy in Turkey and the United States." *Turkish Review* 3 (6): 572–79.

———. 2015. "Turkey's Failed Policy toward the Arab Spring: Three Levels of Analysis," *Mediterranean Quarterly* 26 (3): 94–116.

Kuru, Ahmet T., and Alfred Stepan, eds. 2012. *Democracy, Islam, and Secularism in Turkey*. New York: Columbia University Press.

Kuru, Zeynep Akbulut, and Ahmet T. Kuru. 2008. "Apolitical Interpretation of Islam: Said Nursi's Faith-Based Activism in Comparison with Political Islamism and Sufism." *Islam and Christian–Muslim Relations* 19 (1): 99–111.

Kurucan, Ahmet. 2008. "Intra-Family Violence and Islam," *Today's Zaman*, October 28.

Lowen, Mark. 2014. "Turkey's Erdogan Battles 'Parallel State'," December 17, BBC, http://www.bbc.com/news/world-europe-30492348.

Marty, Martin E., ed. 2015. *Hizmet Means Service: Perspectives on an Alternative Path within Islam*. Oakland: University of California Press.

Munyar, Vahap. 2013. "Zarrab Hayırsever, Aslan Saf ve Dürüst," *Hürriyet*, December 26.

Nursi, Bediüzzaman Said. 1996 [1909]. *"Divan-ı Harbi Örfi."* In *Risale-i Nur Külliyatı*. İstanbul: Nesil.

———. 1996 [1911a]. *"Münâzarat."* In *Risale-i Nur Külliyatı*. İstanbul: Nesil.

———. 1996 [1911b]. *"Muhakemat."* In *Risale-i Nur Külliyatı*. İstanbul: Nesil.

———. 1996 [1936–49]. *"Şualar."* In *Risale-i Nur Külliyatı*. İstanbul: Nesil.

———. 1996 [1949–60]. *"Emirdağ Lahikası II."* In *Risale-i Nur Külliyatı*. İstanbul: Nesil.

NYT Editorial Board. 2014. "Turkey's Internet Crackdown," *New York Times*, February 21.

Özbudun, Ergun. 2012. "Secularism in Islamic Countries: Turkey as a Model." In *Constitutionalism in Islamic Countries: Between Upheaval and Continuity*, edited by Rainer Grote and Tilmann Röder, 135–45. Oxford: Oxford University Press.

Ramadan, Tariq. 2009. *Radical Reform: Islamic Ethics and Liberation*. New York: Oxford University Press.

———. 2011. "Democratic Turkey Is the Template for Egypt's Muslim Brotherhood." *Huffington Post*, February 8. http://www.huffingtonpost.com/tariq-ramadan/post_1690_b_820366.html.

Scott, Alev. 2014. "Erdoğan's Self-Defence over Soma's Mining Disaster Was Badly Misjudged," *Guardian*, May 15.

Sevindi, Nevval, ed. 2008. *Contemporary Islamic Conversations: M. Fethullah Gülen on Turkey, Islam, and the West*, with an introduction by Ibrahim M. Abu-Rabi` and translated by Abdullah T. Antepli. Albany, NY: SUNY Press.

Shinn, David H. 2015. *Hizmet in Africa: The Activities and Significance of the Gülen Movement*. Los Angeles: Tsehai Publishers.

White, Jenny B. 2004. "The End of Islamism? Turkey's Muslimhood Model." In *Remaking Muslim Politics: Pluralism, Contestation, Democratization*, edited by Robert W. Hefner, 87–111. Princeton, NJ: Princeton University Press.

Yılmaz, İhsan. 2003. "*Ijtihad* and *Tajdid* by Conduct: The Gülen Movement." In *Turkish Islam and the Secular State: The Gülen Movement*, edited by M. Hakan Yavuz and John L. Esposito, 208–37. Syracuse, NY: Syracuse University Press.

Yükleyen, Ahmet. 2012. *Localizing Islam in Europe: Turkish Islamic Communities in Germany and the Netherlands*. Syracuse, NY: Syracuse University Press.

8 Islamic Modernism, Ethics, and Shari`a in Pakistan

Muhammad Qasim Zaman

THIS CHAPTER SEEKS to provide an overview of Islamic modernism in Pakistan—a major intellectual, religious, and political current whose history can shed much light on the course of Islam and politics in the country. I understand modernism as the aspiration and the effort to rethink Islamic norms, reinterpret foundational Islamic texts, and reform particular Muslim institutions in ways that simultaneously align them with the "spirit" of Islam and bring them in accord with what are taken to be "modern" needs and sensibilities. The underlying assumption of much modernist discourse in Pakistan, as with modernist initiatives in colonial India and in other colonial and postcolonial Muslim societies, is that true Islam is eminently suited to changing times—that not Islam itself, but rather centuries of wayward beliefs and practices carrying its name, have caused the Muslim world to decline. Properly understood, Islam contains powerful ethical ideals that once served as the panacea for peoples' ills and that could do so again provided these ideals are rescued from an excessively formalistic understanding and application of the shari`a in which they have long been entombed.

The modernists who spearheaded the movement for a separate Muslim homeland in the Indian subcontinent aspired to see Islamic ethical ideals embodied in their new state. There were enormous problems that Pakistan faced at its birth. It was, nonetheless, as Mohammad Ali Jinnah (d. 1948), Pakistan's founding father, noted in a broadcast to the American people in February 1948, the largest Muslim state and the world's fifth largest (Zaidi et al. 1993–2009, 7:114).[1] Pakistan had come into existence—in what was the first time for a state in modern Muslim history—on an explicitly religious basis rather than on an ethnic, linguistic, or geographic one. And it sought to serve as the center of gravity for Islam not only in South Asia but in the Muslim world at large.

In hindsight, blurred as memories are by the state's chronic political instability and eventual dismemberment in 1971, it is easy to miss the excitement that the creation of Pakistan had brought to many of its citizens. This excitement did nothing to alleviate the severe problems that the country faced in its early and subsequent years, but making sense of the grandiose rhetoric we will encounter requires an understanding of the euphoria that accompanied the birth of Pakistan.

My purpose in this chapter is to do more, however, than document some themes in Pakistani modernist discourse and the light they shed on modernist conceptions of the shari'a and political ethics—that is, conceptions of the good as they relate to the public and political spheres.[2] I also aim to highlight ambiguities and contradictions that have both accompanied and enervated modernist thought. Many of these ambiguities have had to do with the fact that, while modernist intellectuals have sought to foreground their ethical commitments and to shape the world around them in their terms, they have often found themselves mired in alliances with the country's authoritarian rulers. This is partly understandable as an outworking of the desire to bring about change in a hurry, from the top down, and partly as a function of the modernists' belief that traditionalist and Islamist authoritarianism cannot be combated in any other way. But quite apart from questions of strategy, modernist discourses themselves also exhibit an authoritarian streak whose implications have sometimes been clearer to their opponents than to modernists themselves.

Modernist Islam in Pakistan: The Early Years

In an uncomplimentary piece on the guerilla warfare then taking place in Kashmir, the influential American magazine *Life* observed in January 1948 that "Jinnah still had no real national program for Pakistan except the incitation of fanatic Moslem zeal" (reprinted in Zaidi et al. 1993–2009, 7:68). Despite the prominence of Islam in his prepartition discourse, "fanaticism" was far from Jinnah's temperament, however, and when necessary, he tried to reassure his audiences on that score. In the aforementioned broadcast to the American people in February 1948, he had noted: "Pakistan is not going to be a theocratic State, that is, rule of or by priests with divine mission. We have many non-Muslims such as Hindus, Christians, Parsis. But they are all Pakistanis and equal citizens with equal rights and privileges and every right to play their part in the affairs of Pakistan national state" (Zaidi et al. 1993–2009, 7:116). In his very first speech as the president of the constituent assembly of Pakistan, he had offered similar assurances, indeed in language that sits uncomfortably with the idiom he frequently used to make the case for Pakistan:

> If you will work in co-operation, forgetting the past, burying the hatchet, you are bound to succeed. If you change your past and work together in a spirit that every one of you, no matter to what community he belongs, no matter what relations he had with you in the past, no matter what is his colour, caste[,] or creed, is first, second and last a citizen of this State with equal rights, privileges and obligations, there will be no end to the progress you will make . . . We should begin to work in that spirit and in course of time all these angularities

of the majority and minority communities, the Hindu community and the Muslim community . . . will vanish . . . You are free; you are free to go to your temples, you are free to go to your mosques or to any other places of worship in this State of Pakistan. You may belong to any religion or caste or creed—that has nothing to do with the business of the State. (Constituent Assembly of Pakistan [hereafter CAP]), 1947–54, 1/2, August 11, 1947, 19–20)

At a moment of wild communal frenzy, these stirring words may have been Jinnah's way of urging calm and of underlining the state's commitment to the welfare of all its inhabitants, including religious minorities. On other occasions, however, he continued to affirm his Islamic commitments. "If we take our inspiration from the holy Qur'an, the final victory . . . will be ours," he said at a public rally in Lahore in October 1947 (Zaidi et al. 1993–2009, 6:220). A few months later, addressing the Karachi Bar Association, he castigated those "who deliberately wanted to create mischief and made propaganda that the Constitution of Pakistan would not be made on the basis of Shari`at" (Zaidi et al. 1993–2009, 7:57–58).

What Jinnah seems to have meant by shari`a (Urdu *shari`at*) was, however, what the British in India had meant by it—Muslim laws of personal status governing matters such as marriage, divorce, and inheritance. For all the political compromises Jinnah might have been willing to make in defining the scope of their application (Gilmartin 1988, 169–74), such laws were an expression of Muslim identity, and there was no question of setting them aside in the new state. There is little to suggest that he envisioned—as the Islamists and many among the `ulama did—any expansive corpus of Islamic law that the state was meant to implement.[3] Instead, Islam had a pronounced ethical dimension to it, and so, therefore, did the new state that was to be guided by its teachings.

Jinnah's modernist successors continued to articulate their Islamic sensibilities with much fervor but, again, with some very particular assumptions about what that entailed. One of the most striking expressions of such sensibilities was a resolution, passed in March 1949 by the constituent assembly under the stewardship of Liaquat Ali Khan (d. 1951), the country's first prime minister, outlining the objectives of the constitution then being framed. The Objectives Resolution began by declaring that "sovereignty over the entire universe belongs to God Almighty alone and the authority which He has delegated to the State of Pakistan through its people for being exercised within the limits prescribed by Him is a sacred trust." It then went on to affirm the "principles of democracy, freedom, equality, tolerance and social justice, as enunciated by Islam," and assured fundamental rights to all its citizens, including minority groups. At the same time, Muslims were to "be enabled to order their lives in the individual and collective spheres in accord with the teachings and requirements of Islam as set out in the Holy Quran and the *Sunna*."[4]

It is easy to identify elements of incoherence in the Objectives Resolution (cf. Binder 1961, 142–54; Jalal 1990, 284–85). God and the state of Pakistan are both sovereign, but precisely what that entails is not spelled out. There is a commitment to liberal values but how they are to be inflected by Islam and what that would mean for non-Muslims remains unstated. There is also some tension between the affirmation of freedom, tolerance, and fundamental rights for all on the one hand and the state's envisioned role of enabling people to lead good Muslim lives on the other.

Yet modernist supporters of this resolution were little troubled by such tensions. That God and the state were both sovereign was a way not of setting up dueling claims to ultimate authority but, from the modernist perspective, of affirming the state's democratic commitments—since this sovereignty was to be exercised by the people—and of underlining the view that even the people could not overturn certain fundamental commitments. And despite worries that appeals to Islam might be a means of curbing democratic institutions,[5] Liaquat Ali Khan was emphatic about his government's desire "to build up a truly liberal Government" (CAP 1947–54, 5/1, 5 [March 7, 1949]). To these modernist politicians, far from there being any conflict between Islam and liberal values, Islam was their very embodiment. For its part, the "enabling clause" of the Objectives Resolution, as it came to be known in Pakistan's constitutional history, was simply what one would expect of a state that had been created to allow Muslims to preserve their particular way of life and their religion. It had great promise for others, too. To quote from the prime minister's speech in support of the resolution, "this clause seeks to give the Muslims the opportunity . . . to set up a polity which may prove to be a laboratory for the purpose of demonstrating to the world that Islam is not only a progressive force in the world but it also provides remedies for many of the ills from which humanity has been suffering" (CAP 1947–54, 5/1, 5 March 7, 1949).

The experiments that were to be carried out in this laboratory created unease in many circles. The 'ulama did not want to see the modernists conduct their experiments unsupervised. Conversely, secular Muslim voices inside and outside the constituent assembly warned against a constitution based on religious ideas. Some of the most vocal opposition came, however, from representatives of the non-Muslim minority in the constituent assembly. According to the 1951 census, Hindus made up about 13 percent of the country's population, including 22 percent of the population of East Pakistan (*Census of Pakistan* 1951, 1). Muslim modernists inside and outside the house insisted that Islam could only promote the liberal and democratic orientation of the new state, but leaders of the Hindu minority could not shed the fear that they would be relegated to the status of second-class citizens in this polity. One leader of the Congress, the opposition party in the constituent assembly, discussed the matter with some 'ulama from the Punjab and was not reassured by their insistence that only a Muslim could head a Muslim state (CAP 1947–54, 5/1, 90–91 [speech by Sris Chandra Chatto-padhyaya], March 12, 1949). Indeed, so close was the association in people's minds between being Muslim and being a Pakistani that this Hindu member had been asked, when traveling in Europe, how he could consider himself a Pakistani at all (CAP 1947–54, 5/1, 93).

Muslim modernists have seldom spoken with a single voice. Yet, broadly speaking, theirs is an Islam that is democratic, though not necessarily according to Western specifications; it is pluralistic, though with a premium on unity; and rather than being legalistic, it is anchored in ethical norms that are best derived from the Islamic foundational texts. If it is not the Islam of the secularists, it is even less that of the `ulama. For all the barely concealed disagreements of their own, the `ulama had wanted to reserve a role for themselves in determining that no legislation was repugnant to the teachings of the Islamic foundational texts. The constitution that was finally put into force in March 1956 gave them no such role. It had significant Islamic content, but it was almost entirely in accord with modernist sensibilities.

The Objectives Resolution served as the preamble to the constitution. The "enabling clause" was part of the constitution, too, and so were provisions stipu-lating that no law would be "repugnant" to the Qur'an or the *Sunnah* and that laws already on the books would be brought in accord with the foundational texts. To this end, a commission was to be appointed to advise the government on matters of repugnancy to Islam (CAP 1947–54, article 198). This, incidentally, was the modernist answer to the `ulama's demand that they should be able to deter-mine whether the laws of the land conformed to Islamic norms. The constitution also envisioned a research institution "to assist in the reconstruction of Muslim society on a truly Islamic basis" (CAP 1947–54, article 197).

Pakistan's first constitution, however, had little time to put down roots. One unstable government followed another, and the country's bureaucracy and the military soon lost patience with the politicians. Martial law was declared in October 1958, and General Ayub Khan (d. 1974) became the de facto ruler, and soon the president, of the country.

Modernism in the Ayub Khan Era

In his view of Islam, Ayub Khan shared much with the modernist politicians he had replaced. As he told the `ulama in a speech in May 1959 at a prominent *madrasa* belonging to the Deobandi Sunni orientation, Islam was a "progressive religion," but a great distance had come to separate religion and life (Khan n.d., 110–11). In good modernist fashion, Ayub Khan chastised the `ulama for reducing Islam to a set of dogmatic beliefs and practices, presenting it as the enemy of progress for "impos[ing] on twentieth century man the condition that he must go back several centuries in order to prove his bona fides as a true Muslim" (Khan n.d., 111). Rather than being stuck in their sectarian squabbles, the 'ulama, he said, needed to help bring people together on the basis of shared beliefs while learning to speak to them across educational and occupational divides. He also alerted them to the threat of Communism then facing the world. This was best combated not through Western materialism but rather through Islam, which, he said, echoing Liaquat Ali Khan's speech on the Objectives Resolution, "alone provides a natural ideology that can save the soul of humanity from destruction" (Khan n.d., 112–14; quotation at 113).

Though he had called for the 'ulama's assistance in the task of national development, the 'ulama would have seen it more as harangue than as earnest appeal for cooperation. It is on military, bureaucratic, and judicial officers that he relied for ideas and governance, and even the functioning of the "basic democracy" that he envisioned for Pakistan depended on them. In 1962, the president provided the country with a new constitution to replace the one he had abrogated four years earlier. The new constitution had its share of Islamic provisions, several of them in line with the previous constitution. The president was required to be a Muslim, a version of the Objectives Resolution again formed the preamble to the constitution, and the "enabling" and "repugnancy" clauses were duly included (Constitution 1962, article 6; ibid., chapter 2, article 8). This constitution, too, provided for the Advisory Council of Islamic Ideology and the Islamic Research Institute (Constitution 1962, articles 199–207).

There also were significant contrasts with the previous constitution on matters Islamic. While the Objectives Resolution and the 1956 constitution had spoken of sovereignty as a sacred trust from God to be exercised by people "within the limits prescribed by Him" (Constitution 1956), the preamble to the 1962 constitution left out any reference to such limits. It had also failed to mention that the Islam that the government was to enable people to live by was the one "set out in the Holy Quran and *Sunnah*."[6] This, presumably, was a way of articulating the ethical spirit of Islam without being encumbered by how it may have been delineated in the foundational texts, let alone in the Islamic legal tradition. Even the official name of the state was the Republic—not the *Islamic* Republic—of Pakistan (Constitution 1962, article 1, clause 1).

These departures from the previous constitution were short-lived. Fewer than two years after the promulgation of the constitution, the Islamic provisions of the 1956 constitution were brought back in all their fullness. The country's name, too, became the Islamic Republic of Pakistan once again (*Dawn* 1963; Khursheed-ul-Hasan 1963). The president's retreat on the more expansive Islamic provisions was not merely a recognition of the influence of the 'ulama and the Islamists but also a nod to pragmatic politics. With the new constitution in effect, he had decided to enter the political arena, which meant that he needed to allow greater space to people's religious sensibilities than he would have liked. Yet for all that, modernism was still in its element. And no one represented it better during the 1960s than did the noted Western-educated scholar Fazlur Rahman.

The son of a Deoband-trained religious scholar, Rahman (1919–88) had earned a DPhil from Oxford in 1949, with a dissertation that provided a critical edition of a work on psychology by the great Muslim philosopher Avicenna (d. 1037). He taught for some years at the University of Durham in England, and then at the Institute of Islamic Studies at McGill University, before returning to Pakistan. Soon he was appointed director of the Institute of Islamic Research, founded "to define Islam in terms of its fundamentals in a rational and liberal manner and to emphasize, among others, the basic Islamic ideals of universal brotherhood, tolerance and social justice" (*Islamic Studies* 1962, 1). Rahman did not lose any time in helping realize this vision. The inaugural issue of the institute's journal contained the first installment of a series of articles by him, published soon afterward in a book that sought nothing less than to offer a new approach to Islamic legal hermeneutics (Rahman 1965b).[7]

In line with contemporary Western scholarship, Rahman argued that much of what is attributed to the Prophet in the form of *hadith* does not go back to him but reflects instead the evolving views of the early community. Unlike many Western scholars, however, he did not see *hadith* merely as pious forgery— statements attributed to the Prophet by subsequent generations of Muslims in pursuit of their particular ends. Instead, he argued that the early community had come to model itself on the practice of the Prophet while continuing to elaborate on and to develop its understanding of this practice in light of changing circumstances. *Hadith* gave expression to this "living *Sunnah*," which could be glimpsed through it (Rahman 1965a, 80). Yet the idea—one that became the defining feature of Sunni orthodoxy—that the *Sunna* could only be found in fixed statements attributed to the Prophet meant that it ceased to be a living and evolving tradition, henceforth to be found only in hallowed texts having their own gatekeepers, rather than in the community's dynamic practice. Reclaiming Islam's original dynamism required that modern Muslims liberate themselves from servitude to these texts and instead seek guidance in the principles discernible behind the Prophet's *Sunna* (cf. Rahman 1965a, 75, 188–90). Even the Qur'an, for all its preeminent authority, was not necessarily binding in all its particulars. Its teachings were meant to be interpreted by people in light of their changing circumstances, which required something other than a literalist submission to them.

Rahman was not squeamish about aligning his scholarly views with government policies. Some years into his tenure as the director of the Institute of Islamic Research, he was commissioned by Ayub Khan to write on "the ideology of Islam." He produced a number of articles on this subject, all published in the institute's journal.[8] Though the regime collapsed before he had had a chance to compile them in book form, the articles shed some light on his vision for Islam in Pakistan (Rahman 1967a; 1967b; 1967c). Much in them would have pleased Ayub Khan.

Rahman called in his articles for close regulation of the religious sphere—suggesting, for instance, that imams and preachers be recruited to provide "moral backing" to the local administration (Rahman 1967c, 117–18). A statist vision was on display in other respects as well: "Islam is a charter for interference in society," Rahman wrote bluntly, "and this charter gives to the collective institution of society, i.e. the Government, the right and duty to constantly watch, give direction to, and actually mould the social fabric" (Rahman 1967c, 107, adducing Qur'an [hereafter Q] 22:41 as well as 3:104, 110, 114 and 9:72 in support). A Qur'anic justification is offered even for press and media censorship: "The Qur'an . . . asks the Government to disallow the public broadcast of news which is not in the public interest, and denounced such practices as a mischievous license calculated to demoralise the people and disunite them" (Rahman 1967c, 112, adducing Q 4:82; cf. Rahman 1967a, 215). In 1960, General Ayub Khan had promulgated his notorious Press and Publications Ordinance, which had drastically curtailed the freedom of the press. If the government needed a belated endorsement of it from the Qur'an, Fazlur Rahman thought he could provide it.

In keeping with such statist views, it is no surprise that Rahman underlines the need for a strong man at the helm of state affairs. But some of his language is extraordinary—for instance, when elucidating how the Qur'an presents God: "God's concept is functional, i.e. God is needed not for what He is or may be but for what He does. It is exactly in this spirit that Aristotle compares God to a general of the army. For the general (in Aristotle's concept) is not a soldier among other soldiers—just as God is not an extra-fact among facts—but represents 'order,' i.e. the fundamental function of holding the army together" (Rahman 1967b, citing Aristotle 1947, 2:167).

But not everything in these articles fit the government's policies well. For instance, they strongly emphasized social justice, and though the constitution spoke of it as well, it would have been discordant in Ayub Khan's Pakistan. As the country's chief economist had observed in 1967, a mere twenty-two families had come to control 66 percent of the country's industrial resources and 80 percent of its banking industry (Afzal 2001, 323). On the other hand, common people had seen the price of basic food commodities skyrocket. This was a long way from the promises of social justice heard in the first years of Pakistan. In sum, however, Rahman's was a largely unflinching effort to provide an Islamic justification for the policies of the government and the "moral backing" it needed to reshape the religious sphere.

In 1966, Fazlur Rahman had published a new book, *Islam*, a broad-ranging survey of key facets of the religious tradition from a distinctly modernist perspective (Rahman 1966). Before long, the book became part of public debate in Pakistan, and the chapter on the Qur'an gave to the `ulama what they had been looking for. Here Rahman had argued for the agency of the Prophet in the making of the Qur'an, a view that went against orthodox insistence that Muhammad was simply the deliverer of a divine revelation that was altogether external to him. Rahman's critics saw it as an attack on the timeless universality of the Qur'an and the nonnegotiable authority of its norms. Soon Rahman's position as the director of the Institute of Islamic Research appeared no longer tenable, and he resigned from it in September 1968. The president, facing growing opposition across the country, noted helplessly in his diary that day, "[I]t is quite clear that any form of research on Islam which inevitably leads to new interpretations has no chance of acceptance in this priest ridden and ignorant society. What will be the future of such an Islam in the age of reason and science is not difficult to predict" (Khan 2007, 253 [entry for September 5, 1968]).

In tendering his resignation, Rahman had stated that he had not written this book at the bidding of the government, and that it was written *before* he had taken up his position at the Institute (*Imroz* 1968). Ironically, the book that he *was* then writing at the behest of the president, on the ideological underpinnings of Pakistan, might have made his views on Islam even more noxious to religious groups than they were already.

The Bhutto and Zia al-Haqq Years

Ayub Khan relinquished power in March 1969, handing the reins of the nation to the commander-in-chief of the Pakistani military, General Yahya Khan. The very first general elections in the country's history were held in 1970 under the new military administration. By that time, an active secessionist movement had taken hold in East Pakistan. The election results gave the Bengali secessionist party, the Awami League, all the seats from East Pakistan but none from the West Pakistan provinces. Zulfikar Ali Bhutto's Pakistan People's Party won a majority of seats from West Pakistan; it had not even bothered to put up candidates from East Pakistan. Though the Awami League had more seats overall in the National Assembly, the military government wavered in handing power to it and decided eventually to launch military operation against the secessionists. This led to a full-fledged civil war in 1971, a war with India, and the breakup of Pakistan. The erstwhile East Pakistan emerged as Bangladesh, and the provinces of West Pakistan were all that remained of Pakistan. Against this backdrop, Bhutto assumed the reins of power and proceeded to frame a new constitution—the country's third (Afzal 2001, 376–458).

A good deal of the extraordinary optimism that had characterized modernist circles in Pakistan's early years had dissipated by this point. It is remarkable how little public discussion has taken place in Pakistan about the events leading to the secession of East Pakistan—which, according to Bangladeshi claims, had resulted in the death of nearly 3 million people (cf. Memon 1983). Nonetheless, Bhutto's image was clearly tarnished by those events, and many people in Pakistan blamed him for preventing the transfer of power to the Awami League of East Pakistan, thereby holding him indirectly responsible for the country's breakup.

Bhutto had other vulnerabilities, too. He had come to power on a platform of "Islamic socialism," but many `ulama and Islamists, not to mention the powerful landowning elite, remained unreconciled to it. A much publicized *fatwa* issued in 1970, denouncing the idea of Islamic socialism, had carried more than 100 signatures by the `ulama, some of them influential figures in the religious sphere (Pirzada 1993). There was also the perception that the heterodox Ahmadis had contributed generously to Bhutto's election campaign, presumably in hopes of benefiting from his rise to power (cf. Rahman 1974, 3–4, enclosed with Rahman to Reuben Frodin, October 7, 1974; Ford Foundation, Grant #74–141 [hereafter FF 74–141]). The Ahmadis regard Mirza Ghulam Ahmad (d. 1908), the founder of their community, as a prophetic figure and are thus held by other Muslims to contravene the cardinal doctrine that Muhammad was the last of God's prophets. An `ulama-led campaign to have the Ahmadis declared a non-Muslim minority soon became too large for the government to ignore, leading to a constitutional amendment in September 1974 that defined "Muslim" in such a way as to exclude the Ahmadis.

Bhutto strove hard to bolster his Islamic credentials. The 1973 constitution was richly endowed with Islamic provisions, though these were largely in line with the provisions of the country's two previous constitutions. In March 1974, the summit meeting of the Organization of Islamic Conference, a pan-Islamic body with its headquarters in Jeddah, Saudi Arabia, was held with much fanfare in Lahore. In hosting this conference, Pakistan signaled that it still aspired to play a prominent role in the Muslim world, though it was surely also motivated by Bhutto's own desire to gain a measure of religious legitimacy within Pakistan. In addition to declaring Ahmadis a non-Muslim minority in Pakistan, Bhutto also came to distance himself from the more hardline leftist elements in his own party (Rahman 1974, 9, FF 74–141), again in an effort to reassure his religious critics. To similar effect, in October 1974, a new ministry of religious affairs was established. It has continued in existence ever since.

Significantly, Fazlur Rahman, by then professor of Islamic thought at the University of Chicago, was among the people whose advice the government again sought on Islamic matters. Rahman was keen to offer it, sometimes taking the initiative himself. For instance, in December 1974, he wrote to Bhutto, commenting on the prime minister's statement on the occasion of the parliament's declaring the Ahmadis to be non-Muslims. Bhutto had stated that this was "a secular decision because we live in modern times and we have a secular constitution and we believe in the citizens of the country to have their full rights" (National Assembly of Pakistan 1974, 567). "But surely," Rahman wrote to Bhutto,

> living in modern times and belief in the equal rights of all citizens are not *secular* for Muslims but Islamic; nor do we have a secular constitution but an Islamic one—and self-professedly so! And this Islamic Constitution has *Islamically* granted Fundamental Rights to all citizens ... It is commonly said that "Islam comprehends both religious and secular matters," or that "Islam is at the same time a religion, a polity, a law etc." Such clichés are always misleading since they insinuate the dichotomy of the religious and the secular all over again into Islam which is seen as something composite of the two. The truth seems to be rather that Islam, as such, is concerned with all moral values—whether these are in the social, economic or political fields.[9] (December 2, 1974, FF 74–141)

To this Bhutto responded by saying that the statement in question

> related not to the *content* of the decision of the National Assembly but to the *process* by which it was taken. What I wanted to convey was that this process was entirely democratic and, therefore, quite within the comprehension of people who have a secular orientation. A decision of this kind has to be understood not only by Muslims but also by others ... As you know, we cannot afford to let a misunderstanding arise that we are running a theocratic state." (January 5, 1975, FF 74–141; emphasis in the original)

Together with Leonard Binder, a political scientist also at the University of Chicago, Rahman was then directing an ambitious multicountry project called Islam and Social Change, funded by the Ford Foundation, and he was keen to have the assistance of the bureaucracy in facilitating research in Pakistan. Of more importance, however, he would have seen in his contacts with the new Pakistani government an opportunity to pursue some of the goals that had been interrupted with the fall of the Ayub Khan regime.

Despite his misgivings, already mentioned, about "the dichotomy of the secular and the religious," Rahman did not hesitate to offer specific suggestions about what goals the newly created ministry concerned with religious affairs ought to set for itself. In part, he said, it was necessary "to present Islam in socio-moral terms and to link these socio-moral principles positively with the broad ideals of rational, liberal and humanitarian progress." This had been done, he said, "for the first time" under Ayub Khan, but as he now saw things, it had been done to the neglect of "religious emotion": "[T]he regime had hoped that this religious emotion will, in course of time, be largely channeled towards the socio-moral side, which did not happen on any large scale" (Rahman 1975, annexure b, 1). The new ministry of religious affairs thus needed to systematically address this side of Pakistani religious life—for instance, by turning devotional practices such as those relating to the Prophet's birthday into "opportunities to effectively communicate to the masses the positive virtues of Islam like good neighbourliness, mutual help, sacrifice for others and for social progress, cleanliness, honesty, etc. The vast emotional fund must be turned towards *positive moral and social* virtues of nation building and national integration. Otherwise, this emotionalism will become riotous and end up as a negative and destructive force" (Rahman 1975, annexure b, 1–2; emphasis in the original). In line with his statist views of the Ayub Khan era, and in the hope of shaping the religious sensibilities of the people, he suggested that the ministry set up a "directorate of public preaching" to train and employ mosque imams. He also proposed the establishment of an Islamic university to educate the 'ulama and to help reduce some of the distance between traditional Islamic and the modern sciences, and he floated the idea of a *Dar al-ifta*, an official body that would issue juridical rulings on particular matters to do with Islam (Rahman 1975, annexure b, 2–4).

Rahman expressed some similar ideas in a note he wrote in 1975 at the request of the government, in which he made recommendations about what the People's Party should say on Islam in its manifesto for the next general elections. Leaving the specific recommendations aside, his introductory comment, which echoes his earlier letter to Bhutto, is worth quoting here:

> It is commonly believed that Islam is not just a "religion" in the narrow sense regulating an individual's relationship with God but "a comprehensive way of life" regulating mutual human relationships in the family and in the public life . . . The only sense in which this formula is tenable and practicable is that Islam be viewed as a set of *values* and social *objectives* to be gradually realized in a given society rather than any fixed system of law deduced at any given period of time, past and future. Any system of law and institutions that, in the public sector, will seek to realize these eternal values at a particular time will be the *Islamic system for that time*. (Rahman 1975, annexure a, 1–2; emphasis in the original)

These ideas were noticeably similar to what Rahman had said in his *Islamic Methodology in History*, published in 1965. He might have felt that a democratically elected government such as Bhutto's would have better success than an authoritarian regime in fostering an understanding of Islam that was based on "values and social objectives" rather than being wedded to an anachronistic religious law. If so, he was to be disappointed: The Bhutto regime was nervous about the challenge the religious parties posed to its legitimacy, and the manifesto that the People's Party unveiled in launching its election campaign showed little interest in any Islamic experimentation.[10] Instead, it was largely content to affirm its

Islamic credentials by designating Friday the weekly holiday rather than Sunday (*Pakistan People's Party Manifesto* n.d., 40).

Such measures did not do much, however, to assuage the religious parties, which formed a powerful electoral alliance against the government. The official results pointed to a victory for the People's Party, but the opposition alleged widespread rigging and launched a countrywide agitation to dislodge Bhutto and to install "the system of the Prophet" (*nizam-i Mustafa*). The unrest in the country led, in July 1977, to the imposition of martial law by General Muhammad Zia al-Haqq; Bhutto was hanged two years later. Zia al-Haqq stayed in power till 1988, overseeing the most extensive effort thus far to "Islamize" Pakistani society and economy.

It is tempting to see the Zia al-Haqq years (1977–88) as marking a sharp decline in the fortunes of Islamic modernism in Pakistan. In broad terms, that would not be an unfair assessment, but two caveats should be noted. First, though the `ulama and the Islamists received a good deal of state patronage in the Zia al-Haqq era, the civil and judicial bureaucracy continued to be staffed by many of the same Western-educated people who had manned these offices in earlier decades. Moreover, despite its rhetoric of Islamization, the regime itself took measures to carefully delimit its scope. Banks continued to deal in financial interest, though they now had "interest-free" sections as well. And Ayub Khan's Muslim Personal Laws Ordinance of 1961, another bête noire of the Islamists and the `ulama for what they saw as its contravention of Islamic laws relating to marriage, divorce, and inheritance, was protected against judicial review at the hands of the Federal Shari`at Court—whose mandate, ironically, was to see to it that new and existing laws were in conformity with the shari`a. But, second, it is important to recognize that modernism was in retreat already under Bhutto (cf. Hussain 1994). There was some mention of Islamic social justice and related themes in the pages of *Islamic Studies*, the journal of the Institute of Islamic Research, during the Bhutto years, but there was little, in that journal or anywhere else, to parallel such modernist discourse as had been witnessed in the Ayub Khan era. Instead, as we have observed, Bhutto was keen to bolster his Islamic credentials, and this meant not taking positions that could be controversial in Islamic terms. Furthermore, as Fazlur Rahman had observed in reporting on his trip to Pakistan in 1975, "the government [was] . . . anxious to keep on the right side of Saudi Arabia both for reasons of economics and of a political Islamic solidarity" (Rahman 1975, 5). This, too, served to discourage modernist experimentation in Pakistan.

Some of those who might have been important contributors to modernist discourse had left that camp well before Bhutto came to power. There is perhaps no better illustration of this than the career of Muhammad Hasan `Askari (d. 1978), a much respected Urdu literary critic. `Askari had acquired some prominence in literary circles already before the partition of the Indian subcontinent, and he consolidated this reputation in the years following the establishment of Pakistan. He was fiercely patriotic—a stance that led him, for instance, to castigate those associated with the left-leaning Progressive Writers Association for putting their class-based ideological commitments above their loyalty to the new state. Yet 'Askari himself had leftist leanings. Before partition, he had defended the demand for Pakistan on grounds that "it would be the first populist and socialist state in the Indian subcontinent. As such, it would serve the interests not just of the Muslims but also of the Hindu masses, since it would assist in uprooting capitalism ... and in the establishment of a permanent peace and security" (Ahmad 1994, 37, quoting from a May 1946 article by 'Askari). In the 1950s, he remained bitterly critical of Pakistan's alignment with the United States in the Cold War in ways that accorded well with left-leaning sensibilities.

Things changed during the Ayub Khan era. Newspaper columns and writings in literary magazines had been the main vehicles of 'Askari's expression, but the Ayub Khan regime imposed severe restrictions on the press. By the time of Ayub Khan's fall, as Aftab Ahmad, a close associate of 'Askari has recounted it, the literary critic was a different man. Some leftist leanings remained, making him a staunch Bhutto loyalist. But in other respects, 'Askari had gravitated irrevocably to the camp of the 'ulama. The late colonial Deobandi scholar and Sufi Ashraf 'Ali Thanawi (d. 1943) was for him the yardstick of the orthodox tradition now, and 'Askari spent his last years translating into English a major Urdu commentary on the Qur'an by Mufti Muhammad Shafi', a disciple of Thanawi and the founder of the largest Deobandi *madrasa* in Pakistan (Ahmad 1994, 17–55).[11]

'Askari's traditionalism was never quite that of Deoband. It was at least as indebted to the perennialist philosophy of René Guénon (Sedgwick 2004) as it was to Thanawi, and his critique of modernism had its roots in his dissatisfaction with literary modernism in Europe. It is significant nonetheless that his conflation of European antimodernist and Islamic trends took him all the way to *Deobandi* traditionalism in Pakistan. Around the time of the fall of the Ayub Khan regime, he had written a short book, *Jadidiyyat* (Modernism), specifically for the benefit of *madrasa* students ('Askari 1979; cf. Ahmad 1994, 43). In it he sought to introduce those who were training to become 'ulama to key moments in the history of Western thought, laying much of the blame for the deleterious effects of unrestrained individualism and the breakdown of religious authority on the rise of Protestantism ('Askari 1979, 41). His concern was not, of course, to defend Catholic structures of authority but rather to urge the 'ulama to be cautious in their criticism of Catholic Christianity, for what they said about Catholic priests was echoed in what Westernized Muslims had come to say about the 'ulama themselves ('Askari 1979, 28). His larger purpose in this treatise was to make

Western thought and its specialized terminology intelligible to his *madrasa* audience so that they could better defend themselves and others against the challenges this thought posed, as well as against its lure. By extension, he aimed to alert the `ulama to certain Muslim modernist proclivities, shaped by exposure to the West, in order to combat them effectively. For instance, `Askari argued that eighteenth- and nineteenth-century European thinkers had tended to separate morality from religion, basing the former not on revealed truth but rather on human nature and reason. Instead of thinking of morality and ethics as being facets of religion, European thinkers had reduced religion to them. This way of thinking had significantly affected the pioneering Indian modernist Sayyid Ahmad Khan (d. 1898) and his successors. Consequently, "the `ulama need to be on their guard when English-educated people praise the ethical principles of Islam. For these people tend to think of [all Islam,] even Sufism, as mere ethics" (`Askari 1979, 59–60, quotation at p. 60). In a similar vein, in a work written as a companion to his book on modernism, he enumerates some characteristic modernist errors for the benefit of the `ulama. Those especially relevant here are "seeing Sufism as *merely* a means towards moral training"; "considering social welfare and the serving of the nation as the goals of religion"; "taking the view that the purpose of religion is the building of character, with 'character' signifying practices that are beneficial to societal life"; and "understanding religion, and especially Sufism, as a form of solicitude for other human beings and of friendship towards them" (`Askari 1979, 101–2; emphasis added).[12]

Even as the `ulama have faced sharp polemic from the modernist camp, they have been able, as the case of Muhammad Hasan `Askari suggests, to make some prized inroads into that camp. What this example also shows is that the `ulama have received some unexpected help from the modernizing governing elite themselves in making such incursions. At the very time when Islamic modernism was practically a matter of state policy, Ayub Khan's harsh curbs on the freedom of expression might have done more than the `ulama themselves could to draw the likes of `Askari in their direction (cf. Ahmad 1994, 40–43). Yet the opposition to modernism, and to modernist ethics, has also inhibited the `ulama from venturing beyond their longstanding concern with the ethical formation of the individual toward any sustained engagement with social and political ethics (see, for instance, Uthmani 2010).[13] If anything, such engagement within the ranks of the `ulama has declined in recent decades.[14]

The rise to power of the Harvard- and Oxford-educated Benazir Bhutto after Zia al-Haqq's death in 1988 appeared to create new openings for Islamic modernism, but despite the popular mandate that she carried, she was ever vulnerable to charges of being overly westernized, too little committed to Islamic norms in the public sphere. During his last months in office, in an attempt to shore up any remaining legitimacy, Zia al-Haqq had promulgated the Implementation of

Shariah Ordinance. The lapse of this ordinance did not improve perceptions of Bhutto's weak religious commitments, and allegations of widespread corruption paved the way for the dismissal of her government in 1990. The next government, led by Nawaz Sharif (1990–93), was keen to flaunt its Islamic zeal, which it did with the prompt passage of the Enforcement of Shari`ah Act of 1991. During a second stint in office (1997–99), which followed a second government that Bhutto had headed (1993–96), Sharif took further steps toward implementation of shari`a. These measures seemed better suited to help the government withstand opposition challenges, however, than they did to have it "eradicate corruption at all levels and to provide substantial socio-economic justice, in accordance with the principles of Islam"—as the language of a proposed constitutional amendment had it (*Dawn* 1998). They did, however, show that the winds were not blowing in a direction conducive to modernism. Yet, considering that modernist initiatives have usually been sponsored from the top down, a change of government can create quick opportunities for a reversal of trends antithetical to them. A military coup in 1999 created such opportunities. There were to be concerted efforts to imbue Islamic modernism with new life in the years when General Pervez Musharraf was in power in Pakistan (1999–2008), and it is to a brief review of these, in the aftermath of the terrorist attacks of September 11, 2011, that I now turn.

The Years of "Enlightened Moderation"

The September 11 attacks and their aftermath have exacted an enormous price from Pakistan. In being forced to abruptly change course from being a sponsor and key supporter of Afghanistan's Taliban regime to an ally of the United States in the War on Terror, the Musharraf government faced the wrath of the country's Islamist and other religiopolitical groups. The years after the September 11 attacks saw the emergence of a neo-Taliban insurgency not just in Afghanistan but also in Khyber Pakhtunkhwa, the former North-West Frontier Province of Pakistan. The militant groups associated with this insurgency have continued to resist the military operations that have been periodically launched against them and have also carried out scores of suicide bombings and other terrorist acts that have put severe strains on the economy and society and imperiled the country's stability. Nearly 30,000 civilians and about 4,000 military personnel are believed to have died in terrorism-related violence in Pakistan between September 2001 and early 2013 (*Dawn* 2013).

However, the aftermath of the September 11 attacks also gave the military regime of General Pervez Musharraf some additional space to recharge a dormant modernism. As the new government tried, with uncertain vigor, to confront militant Islamists and allied groups, it also took it on itself to pursue a larger modernist program. Thus in 2002 the government was able to secure a new ruling on the vexing question of financial interest from a reconstituted Shari`at Appellate Bench of the Supreme Court—the highest judicial body established in the Zia al-Haqq era to rule on questions relating to Islamic law. In 1991, the Federal Shari`at Court, another highlight of Zia al-Haqq's Islamization, had determined that all forms of financial interest constituted the *riba* prohibited by the Qur'an, and the Shari`at Appellate Bench of the Supreme Court had upheld that judgment in 1999, requiring the government to end all interest-based transactions by June 2002. That year, the Shari`at Appellate Bench set those earlier rulings aside, however, sending the case back to languish with the Federal Shari`at Court and signaling a new willingness to chart a more confident modernist path (Zaman 2008). The Musharraf regime also took some steps toward regulating the affairs of the country's numerous *madrasas* as a way of reining in the influence of the `ulama in society and polity. In late 2006, moreover, it amended the Hudood (Ar. *hudud*) Ordinances that General Zia al-Haqq had promulgated in 1979 in an ostentatious effort to put the country's colonial-era criminal laws on an Islamic, and indeed specifically Qur'anic, footing. Passed by parliament as the Protection of Women Act 2006, this law narrowed the scope of the Hudood Ordinances and made them less likely to be implemented. It also made it more difficult for people to use them as instruments for the social control of women—for instance, by bringing accusations of sexual impropriety to court (Zaman 2011, 220–26).

The regime had coined a term for its modernist initiatives. Musharraf liked to speak of "enlightened moderation." "It is a two-pronged strategy," he wrote in a programmatic article in the *Washington Post* in June 2004: "The first part is for the Muslim world to shun militancy and extremism and adopt the path of socioeconomic uplift. The second is for the West, and the United States in particular, to seek to resolve all political disputes with justice and to aid in the socioeconomic betterment of the deprived Muslim world" (Musharraf 2004). Musharraf presented this vision to the Organization of Islamic Conference and received an endorsement from it (Akhlaque 2004). Not for the first time in the history of Pakistani modernism, Pakistan appeared to have a role to play both within the Muslim world and in facilitating better relations between the Muslim world and the West. There was some talk as well of making enlightened moderation a part of the social studies curriculum in Pakistani public schools (Ghumman 2006). But none of this would survive the fall of the Musharraf regime in 2008.

Some of the ambiguities of this phase in Pakistani modernism are worth bringing out with reference to Javed Ahmad Ghamidi (b. 1951), an ally of sorts that Musharraf had found during his years in power. Ghamidi, a Lahore-based commentator on the Qur'an, was once a member of the Islamist Jama`at-i Islami but had left that organization over disagreements with its founder, Sayyid Abu'l-A`la Mawdudi (d. 1979). He was an informal but lifelong student of Amin Ahsan Islahi (d. 1997), a prominent Qur'an exegete who in his early career had himself been a leading figure in the Jama`at-i Islami. Ghamidi had been writing well before the advent of General Musharraf, and some of his ideas came to be seen as well suited to the regime's interests (for an overview of Ghamidi's thought, see Masud 2007).

Ghamidi has argued, for instance, that Muslim religious scholars, the `ulama, should not meddle in politics but ought rather to concentrate on the religious guidance of the people as well as of the ruling elite (Masud 2007, 368). In marked contrast with Mawdudi, he holds that the establishment of an Islamic state should not be considered a religious obligation (Masud 2007, 370). Moreover, unlike the expansive view that Islamists tend to take of the powers of the state, Ghamidi believes that, in religious terms, the state cannot require its Muslim citizens to do anything more than believe in God and the Prophet, perform their ritual prayers, and pay the *zakat* (Ghamidi 2008, 490–92). It cannot, for instance, obligate them to perform the pilgrimage to Mecca nor to fast, and it does not have the authority, on Islamic grounds, to conscript them for jihad (Ghamidi 2008, 492). Nor does he believe that jihad can be prosecuted by any but an established government, thus ruling out jihad on the part of militant groups and other nonstate actors. Ghamidi has also spoken of the need to reform the country's draconian blasphemy laws, which have their origins in the colonial era but which were greatly expanded in scope and rigor by the Zia al-Haqq regime (Walsh 2011; on these laws, see Ahmed 2009). In arguing that the vigilante violence that has often accompanied accusations of blasphemy has no sanction in the Qur'an, he has helped bolster governmental efforts to amend the blasphemy laws—though not enough, thanks to conservative opposition, to effect any change in them. It is worth noting, finally, that Ghamidi has been highly critical of Zia al-Haqq's Hudood Ordinances, which he sees as contravening the shari`a on a number of grounds. Views such as these lent useful support to the Musharraf regime as it battled Islamist militants and worked, in particular, to revise the Hudood Ordinances. Ghamidi was appointed a member of the Council of Islamic Ideology. Since 2002, a significant number of new television channels have made their debut in Pakistan, helping give Ghamidi a new prominence in the country—and, by extension, greater usefulness from the viewpoint of the government (Aziz 2011, 598–99).

Yet the accord between Ghamidi's positions and the concerns of the government was far from perfect. For instance, to Ghamidi, all forms of financial interest are covered by the Qur'anic prohibition of *riba* (Ghamidi 2008, 511)—hardly a convenient view from the perspective of the Musharraf regime. The idea that a Muslim government can only impose a very small number of religious obligations on its citizens might have been welcomed by the government as an antidote to Islamist conceptions of the state, but it is opposed to the expansive powers *any* modern government claims for itself, not just an Islamist one. The narrow textualism on which Ghamidi bases such views represents, moreover, a very different approach from, say, that of Fazlur Rahman, whose work often exhibits a detailed engagement with the Islamic religious tradition in defending or critiquing particular positions. Another contrast between the two is also worth noting. Though on the question of hudud Ghamidi leaves the imposition of the penalties to the discretion of the state as a way of restricting the application of the severest punishments,[15] he does not question the *principle* of the continued applicability of *hudud* laws (Ghamidi 2001, 81–84; 2008, 615, 628–30). Rahman, for his part, had sought in the Ayub Khan era to offer an ethical reinterpretation of *hudud* by arguing that it is not the content or the authority of hudud laws that should be seen as invariant—as the traditionalist jurists have tended to see them—but rather their goal of deterring people from committing certain crimes and of reforming the criminals (Rahman 1965a).

Though Ghamidi's television appearances were presumably watched by many urban middle-class Pakistanis, he lacked any meaningful social base in the country. And even the government of General Pervez Musharraf had no compunctions about ignoring him when doing so seemed politic. In the days leading up to the tabling of the Protection of Women Bill in the parliament in 2006, for instance, the regime decided to rely on a team of `ulama rather than its own Council of Islamic Ideology, leading Ghamidi to briefly resign his membership of this body. On the other hand, Ghamidi's conservative views on many Islamic matters did little to shield him from the wrath of the militants. The editor of his monthly journal was injured in an attack, and one of Ghamidi's close associates was later assassinated. Ghamidi himself was forced to flee to Malaysia in 2010 (Walsh 2011).

Conclusion

Islam, as imagined by the Pakistani modernists, has strong ethical sensibilities. This fact, together with the modernists' reach into the corridors of power and how that has impacted their religious discourses, make them an especially illuminating subject of study so far as questions of ethics in relation to the shari`a and the state are concerned. Modernist conceptions of Islam and of shari`a are characterized, to recall the Objectives Resolution of 1949, by the "principles of democracy, freedom, equality, tolerance and social justice." This modernist foregrounding of ethics is alluring enough that literary critic Muhammad Hasan `Askari warned even the `ulama against its appeal. Such concerns have continued to guide the modernists even in exile. They lie, for example, at the heart of Fazlur Rahman's influential book, *Major Themes of the Qur'an*, first published in 1980 (Rahman 1980) and incorporating, incidentally, some of the ideas first adumbrated in the articles he had written on the ideology of Islam for Ayub Khan (cf. Rahman 1967b). Similarly, when Rahman was awarded the Giorgio Levi Della Vida Medal in 1983 by the Center for Near Eastern Studies at UCLA, in recognition of his contributions to the study of Islam, the theme of the conference was none other than "ethics in Islam" (Hovannisian 1985). Ghamidi, too, has continued to develop his ideas in exile—for instance, on the matter of Pakistan's blasphemy laws.

Although some of the decline of Pakistani modernism can surely be imputed to the Islamization policies of the late 1970s and the 1980s, which themselves were part of global Islamic "revivalist" trends of those decades, the story, as I have tried to suggest here, is considerably more complex (cf. Hussain 1994). The fact that modernist initiatives have emanated from the governing elite or from those seen as allied with them, and that such elites themselves have often enjoyed only tenuous political legitimacy, have also contributed much toward weakening, if not discrediting, such initiatives. Some of the vehemence with which Fazlur Rahman's religious views were opposed by the 'ulama surely had to do with his very visible association with an authoritarian regime. Nearly four decades later, similar misgivings presumably led Qazi Husain Ahmad, the leader of the Jama'at-i Islami, to characterize Musharraf's "so-called enlightened moderation as a threat to the identity of Pakistan and Islamic values" (Dawn 2005).

But it is not just the embrace of the governing elite that has threatened to undermine Pakistani modernism. Authoritarianism has also tended to narrow the space in which modernists may have been able to articulate their views, as the case of Muhammad Hasan 'Askari tellingly illustrates. Furthermore, the modernists themselves have often been less than eager to reassure those who are skeptical of their intentions. Their attitude toward the 'ulama has often been one of thinly disguised contempt. Considering the 'ulama's influence in society, this has not served the modernists well. Nor have modernist discourses been particularly comforting to non-Muslim minorities. The commission established by Ayub Khan to make recommendations for a new constitution for the country might have revealed more of its biases than it intended to when commenting on a former Hindu parliamentarian's complaints that young Pakistani Hindus were being forced to seek employment in neighboring India:

> As a matter of fact, it appears to us that these "brilliant young men" are not anxious to work for Pakistan. There have been, we understand, cases of persons, of the Hindu community, who had been abroad on scholarships earned in Pakistan, going away to India after being fully qualified. This indicates that these young men are not seen in employment in our country not because they are unable to secure it, but because they are not desirous of serving this country. They apparently do not feel happy here, which indicates that they are not reconciled to the idea of Pakistan. (*Report of the Constitution Commission* 1962, 75–76)

For a country that then had a substantial Hindu minority, this was an extraordinary statement to come from the highest echelons of government. The Islamists and the 'ulama could hardly have expressed their misgivings about minorities more bluntly.

For all the robustness of the modernists' ethical sensibilities, then, some of their blind spots have contributed no less to modernism's declining fortunes in Pakistan than has the determined opposition facing it from various fronts. Another point is also worth making in conclusion. With some exceptions, Muslim modernists have shown little serious interest in giving intellectual substance to their ethical concerns (cf. Smith 1957, 226, 236–37), further weakening modernism and its ethical commitments. There is, of course, a long history of ethical thought in Islam, both in the world of the scholars of Islamic law and outside it (notably in Sufism, philosophy, and political thought). The modernists, however, and especially the governing elite among them, have largely been content to equate their ethical concerns with all that they take to be good in the Western liberal tradition and to then go on to claim that it is in Islam that these ideals—of democracy, social justice, equality, and so forth—find their most complete expression. This approach has not satisfied the secularists any more than it has reassured religious minorities, and such rhetoric can hardly be expected to have much appeal for ordinary citizens if it does not address, as it seldom does, their daily problems. Moreover, it has done little to soften the `ulama's and the Islamists' longstanding opposition to the modernists. Instead, it has contributed to some suspicion of ethical concerns themselves vis-à-vis other facets of Islam in the public and political spheres. From the vantage of at least some among the `ulama and those allied with them, modernist ethics comes across as being an alternative to the shari`a rather than a part of it. Few modernists have made any sustained effort to show that this is not the case. And the authoritarianism that frequently buttresses modernist ethical sensibilities in Pakistan has not done much to broaden their appeal.

References

Afzal, M. Rafique. 2001. *Pakistan: History and Politics, 1947–1971*. Karachi, Pakistan: Oxford University Press.

Ahmad, Aftab. 1994. *Muhammad Hasan `Askari, aik mutala`a: Dhati khutut ki rawshani main*. Lahore, Pakistan: Sang-i mil Publications.

Ahmed, Asad Ali. 2009. "Specters of Macaulay: Blasphemy, the Indian Penal Code, and Pakistan's Postcolonial Predicament." In *Censorship in South Asia: Cultural Regulation from Sedition to Seduction*, edited by Raminder Kaur and William Mazzarella, 172–205. Bloomington: Indiana University Press.

Akhlaque, Qudssia. 2004. "OIC to Discuss Challenges Faced by Muslim World." *Dawn*, June 1.

Aristotle. 1947. *Metaphysics*. Translated by Hugh Tredennick for the Loeb Classical Library. Cambridge, MA: Harvard University Press.

`Askari, Muhammad Hasan. 1979. *Jadidiyyat*. Rawalpindi, Pakistan: `Iffat Hasan.

Aziz, Sadaf. 2011. "Making a Sovereign State: Javed Ghamidi and 'Enlightened Moderation.'" *Modern Asian Studies* 45:597–629.

Binder, Leonard. 1961. *Religion and Politics in Pakistan*. Berkeley: University of California Press.

Census of Pakistan, 1951: Population according to Religion (Table 6). 1951. Karachi, Pakistan: Office of Census Commissioner.

Constituent Assembly of Pakistan. 1947–1954. *Debates.* 16 vols. Karachi: Manager of Publications, Government of Pakistan.

The Constitution of the Islamic Republic of Pakistan. 1956. Karachi: Department of Advertising, Films and Publications, Government of Pakistan.

The Constitution of the Republic of Pakistan. 1962. Washington, DC: Embassy of Pakistan.

Dawn (Karachi). 1963. "Text of Fundamental Rights Bill." December 28–29.

———. 1998. "Text of Fifteenth Constitutional Amendment Bill." August 29.

———. 2005. "Enlightened Moderation Threat to Country: Qazi." March 23.

———. 2013. "While Govt Mulls Talks with TTP, Terror Victims' Voices Go Unheard." February 23.

Farooqi, Mehr Afshan. 2012. *Urdu Literary Culture: Vernacular Modernity in the Writing of Muhammad Hasan Askari.* New York: Palgrave Macmillan.

Ford Foundation. Grant # 74–141: Islam and Social Change (reel # 3087). Rockefeller Archive Center, Sleepy Hollow, New York. *See also* Rahman, Fazlur.

Ghamidi, Javed Ahmad. 2001. *Burhan,* 3rd ed. Lahore, Pakistan: Dar al-ishraq.

———. 2008. *Mizan,* 3rd ed. Lahore, Pakistan: al-Mawrid.

Ghumman, Khawar. 2006. "Oct 12 Takeover Made Part of SSC Curriculum." *Dawn,* December 30.

Gilmartin, David. 1988. *Empire and Islam: Punjab and the Making of Pakistan.* Berkeley: University of California Press.

Hovannisian, Richard G., ed. 1985. *Ethics in Islam.* Malibu, CA: Undena Publications.

Hussain, Mir Zohair. 1994. "Islam in Pakistan under Bhutto and Zia-ul-Haq." In *Islam, Muslims and the Modern State,* edited by Hussin Mutalib and Taj ul-Islam Hashmi, 47–79. New York: St. Martin's Press.

Imroz (Lahore). 1968. "Idara-i tahqiqat-i Islami ke director Fazlur Rahman musta`fi hogae." September 6.

Islamic Studies. 1962. "Introducing the Journal." 1 (1) (March): 1–4.

Jalal, Ayesha. 1990. *The State of Martial Rule.* Cambridge: Cambridge University Press.

Khan, Mohammad Ayub. 2007. *Diaries of Field Marshal Mohammad Ayub Khan, 1966–1972,* edited by Craig Baxter. Karachi, Pakistan: Oxford University Press.

———. n.d. "Islam—A Dynamic and Progressive Movement." In *Speeches and Statements by Field Marshal Mohammad Ayub Khan, President of Pakistan,* vol. 1. (October 1958–June 1959). Karachi: Pakistan Publications.

Khursheed-ul-Hasan. 1963. "Fundamental Rights Bill Passed by N.A." *Dawn,* December 25.

Masud, Muhammad Khalid. 2007. "Rethinking Shari`a: Javed Ahmad Ghamidi on Hudud." *Die Welt des Islams* 47:356–75.

Memon, Muhammad Umar. 1983. "Pakistani Urdu Creative Writing on National Disintegration: The Case of Bangladesh." *Journal of Asian Studies* 43 (1): 105–27.

Mufti, Aamir R. 2007. *Enlightenment in the Colony: The Jewish Question and the Crisis of Postcolonial Culture.* Princeton, NJ: Princeton University Press.

Musharraf, Pervez. 2004. "A Plea for Enlightened Moderation." *The Washington Post,* June 1.

National Assembly of Pakistan. 1974. *Debates,* September 7. Karachi, Pakistan: Manager of Publications.

Pakistan People's Party Manifesto, January 1977. n.d. Rawalpindi: Pakistan People's Party Central Secretariat.

Pirzada, Sayyid A. S. 1993. "Islam and Socialism in the 1970 General Elections: A Case Study of the Jam`iat `Ulama-i-Islam Pakistan." *Journal of the Pakistan Historical Society* 41:397–404.

Rahman, Fazlur. 1962. "Concepts *Sunnah, Ijtihad* and *Ijma'* in the Early Period." *Islamic Studies* 1 (1): 5–21.

———. 1965a. "The Concept of *Hadd* in Islamic Law." *Islamic Studies* 4:237–51.

———. 1965b. *Islamic Methodology in History*. Karachi, Pakistan: Central Institute of Islamic Research.

———. 1966. *Islam*. London: Weidenfeld and Nicolson.

———. 1967a. "The Implementation of the Islamic Concept of State in the Pakistani Milieu." *Islamic Studies* 6 (3): 205–23.

———. 1967b. "The Qur'anic Concept of God, the Universe and Man." *Islamic Studies* 6 (1): 1–19.

———. 1967c. "Some Reflections on the Reconstruction of Muslim Society in Pakistan." *Islamic Studies* 6 (2): 103–20.

———. 1974. "A Report on My Visit to Pakistan." Ford Foundation Grant # 74–141.

———. 1975. "Report of Professor Fazlur Rahman's Visit to Pakistan in Summer 1975 . . ." Annexure A: "Suggestions for the PPP Election Manifesto (1976) on the Subject of Islam"; Annexure B: "A Note on the Task before the Ministry of Religious Affairs." Ford Foundation Grant # 74–141.

———. 1980. *Major Themes of the Qur'an*. Minneapolis, MN: Bibliotheca Islamica.

Report of the Constitution Commission, Pakistan, 1961. 1962. Karachi, Pakistan: Manager of Publications.

Sedgwick, Mark. 2004. *Against the Modern World: Traditionalism and the Secret Intellectual History of the Twentieth Century*. New York: Oxford University Press.

Shafi`, Mufti Muhammad. 2005. *Ma'ariful Qur'an*, vol. 1. Translated by Muhammad Hasan Askari and Muhammad Shamim. Karachi, Pakistan: Maktaba-i Dar al-`Ulum.

Smith, Wilfred Cantwell. 1951. *Pakistan as an Islamic State: Preliminary Draft*. Lahore, Pakistan: Shaikh Muhammad Ashraf.

———. 1957. *Islam in Modern History*. Princeton, NJ: Princeton University Press.

`Uthmani, Muhammad Taqi. 2010. *Islam awr hamari zindagi*. 10 vols. Lahore, Pakistan: Idara-i Islamiyyat.

Walsh, Declan. 2011. "Islamic Scholar Attacks Pakistan's Blasphemy Laws." *The Guardian*, January 20.

Zaidi, Z. H., et al., ed. 1993–2009. *Quaid-i-Azam Mohammad Ali Jinnah Papers*. Islamabad, Pakistan: Quaid-i-Azam Papers Project.

Zaman, Muhammad Qasim. 2008. "Religious Discourse and the Public Sphere in Contemporary Pakistan." *Revue des mondes musulmans et de la Méditerranée* 123:55–73.

———. 2011. "Pakistan: Shari`a and the State." In *Shari`a Politics: Islamic Law and Society in the Modern World*, edited by Robert W. Hefner, 207–43. Bloomington: Indiana University Press.

———. 2012. *Modern Islamic Thought in a Radical Age: Religious Authority and Internal Criticism*. Cambridge, UK: Cambridge University Press.

Notes

1. Wherever possible, I have spelled proper names as the protagonists themselves spelled them—hence *Mohammad Ali Jinnah* rather than *Muhammad `Ali Jinnah*.

2. As Wilfred Cantwell Smith observed in 1951, drawing on his discussions with Pakistani intellectuals, the widespread "demand that Pakistan should be an Islamic state is a Muslim way of saying that Pakistan should build for itself a good society. Not merely an independent or a strong or a wealthy or a modern society; all those things, perhaps, but also a good society" (Smith 1951, 68; cf. Smith 1957, 239).

3. The term `ulama refers here to those educated in institutions of traditional Islamic learning and basing their claims to religious authority on a sustained engagement with the historically articulated Islamic scholarly tradition. The Islamists, by contrast, tend to be

200 | *Shari`a Law and Modern Muslim Ethics*

autodidacts, more often than not being the products of Westernized colleges and universities rather than of institutions of Islamic learning and breaking with the scholastic tradition that is the bedrock of the `ulama's understanding of Islam. The single-mindedness of the Islamists' concern with the public implementation of Islamic norms also sets them apart from the `ulama—which is not to say, however, that the `ulama lack political commitments or are necessarily averse to using political means to see Islamic norms implemented.

4. Emphasis mine. For the text of the resolution as moved by the prime minister, see CAP 1947–54, 5/1: 1–2 (March 7, 1949).

5. Cf. Charles W. Lewis Jr., to George Marshall, June 21, 1948, US National Archives, 845 F. 00/6-2148, reprinted in Zaidi et al. (1993–2009, 7:450).

6. Compare the respective preambles to the 1956 and the 1962 constitutions. Also compare the 1956 constitution, article 25, clause 1 with the 1962 constitution, "Principles of Policy," no. 1.

7. For the first of his articles in this series, see Rahman (1962).

8. Khan (2007, 90), diary entry for April 30, 1967. Ayub Khan does not mention here that he had commissioned this book, but this is noted by Rahman on his curriculum vitae submitted to the Ford Foundation in 1972 (see enclosures with L. Binder to R. Frodin, July 21, 1972), FF 74–141. I am grateful to Megan Brankley Abbas for drawing my attention to these archives and for sharing them with me.

9. The italicized words are emphasized in the original. The words I have underlined are added to the typed letter in pen.

10. The manifesto did, however, echo Fazlur Rahman's recommendation to the Ministry of Religious Affairs to set up an institution to train imams and preachers; see *Pakistan People's Party*, n.d., 40.

11. I base my account of `Askari's intellectual transformation on Aftab Ahmad's interpretation (Ahmad 1994). On `Askari, see also Farooqi (2012) and Mufti (2007, 14–21). `Askari had translated only the first 400 pages or so of Shafi`'s multivolume commentary by the time of his death: see the foreword by Muhammad Taqi `Uthmani to Shafi` (2005, xvii–xviii).

12. The second work, published together with the first, is titled "A List of Those Western Ideas Which Create Misunderstandings and Errors in Religion" (`Askari 1979, 95–129).

13. This ten-volume work, whose title may be rendered *Islam and Our Life*, is a collection of a number of Taqi `Uthmani's writings and sermons. The volumes deal with matters of belief, ritual, and other religious practices (vols. 1–2, 10), good and bad morals and etiquette (vols. 7–9), Sufi ethics (vol. 6), the family (vol. 5), the teachings of Islam on economic matters (vol. 3), and the norms of social comportment (vol. 4). Although this is a work on ethics, `Uthmani's interest is overwhelmingly in personal ethics rather than in the ethical dimensions of public and political life. Indeed, as he argues in commenting on Q 5:105, the best path to the reform of society is through reforming the self. See `Uthmani (2010, 6:45–62).

14. See Zaman (2012, 221–60) for a discussion of the `ulama's discourses on socioeconomic justice.

15. See Ghamidi (2008, 610–30, esp. 611, 614, 626). Following his mentor, Amin Ahsan Islahi, and the latter's teacher, Hamid al-din Farahi, Ghamidi also argues against stoning to death as the penalty for adultery; see Ghamidi (2001, 34–124, esp. 81–84) and Masud (2007, 371–74).

SECTION III

New Ethical Imbrications

9 "Shari`a" as a Moving Target? The Reconfiguration of Regional and National Fields of Muslim Debate in Mali

Dorothea E. Schulz

For the past twenty years—that is, since the introduction of multiparty democracy in 1991—Mali has been the darling of Western donor organizations that have intervened in sub-Saharan Africa.[1] The country also served policy advisors as the model of a successful transition to democratic politics. Accordingly, international media have tended to portray the March 2012 coup d'état and the resulting political turmoil in central Mali[2] and in its northern regions as an unforeseeable turn of events. They commonly blame international Islamist terrorist networks and the breakdown of the Gaddafi regime for the rise of several Muslim militant groups in Mali's north that frame their political aspirations as a project of establishing shari`a in an independent *Azawad*, or Tuareg cultural area. Only a few analyses point to the roots and historical antecedents of Islam's recent career as a "political religion" that seems to echo similar developments throughout Africa and beyond (Hall 2011a; 2011b; Klute 2013; Lecocq and Schrijver 2007; see Marshall 2009). Yet even these analyses portray the shari`a regulations implemented by Muslim militant groups in the course of 2012 as coercive impositions. They thereby fail to account for the favorable echo that some shari`a measures have generated among segments of the local population (see, for example, Lecocq et al. 2013, 11).

This chapter counters this portrayal by describing the longstanding historical genesis of the tensions and concerns that led to the recent turmoil in Mali's southern and northern regions, discussing the significance of Islamic ethics and shari`a politics for these developments. I trace the gradual invigoration of Muslim political and social activism in the national and regional arenas, focusing on developments since the late 1970s to illustrate how they reflect Malians' changing understandings of the relevance of Islamic ethics to the ordering of public and domestic life. The rise of Muslim militant groups in the north, and the favorable response they have received on the part of certain segments of the local

204 | *Shari`a Law and Modern Muslim Ethics*

population, should be seen as the culmination of a longstanding, steadily ger-
minating discourse of moral and political renewal that—though rooted in local
religious traditions and social institutions—presents Islam as a blueprint for a
just social and political order.

The Legacy of the Colonial State in Present-Day Shari`a Politics

Islamic culture has been rooted in the Sudanese societies of West Africa for
centuries, yet substantial differences existed between regions in the degree and
forms of integration of Islamic traditions into local everyday life. In the north of
present-day Mali, Islam made its presence felt in urban centers since the ninth
century. In subsequent centuries, religious affiliation acquired new political and
economic functions (McDougall 1986; Stewart 1973), and merchants and the rulers of the Songhai Empire transformed the northern cities of Timbuktu, Djenné,
and Gao into centers of Islamic erudition. Islamic culture further expanded
southward when the Songhai Empire of Gao brought under its control the area of
the "kingdom" of Segu located in the country's southeast.

In the south, Muslim communities constituted "pockets" in heterogeneous
religious fields, in which various local religious traditions coexisted with Islam.
The primary association of Islam with an urban identity of merchants and
religious scholars changed in the mid-nineteenth century with the theocratic
empire-building of reformers such as El Hajj Umar Tall. The subsequent Islamization of rural areas in the French colonial period followed a different logic and
relied on other categories of social actors (Mann 2003; Peterson 2011).[3]

For centuries, religious knowledge transmission was central to an Islamic
intellectual tradition that, based on Arabic as a lingua franca, was shared by
a scholarly elite across distances and connected this elite to the wider world.
In the slaveholding societies of the West African Sudan and Sahara, it enabled
a discourse of Muslim erudition and religious devotion that served as a shared
framework of reference within which masters and slaves worked out their
individual relationships (Hall 2011a, 23). But Islamic knowledge played differently
into existing social divisions and into how people in southern and northern Mali
have claimed an identity as proper Muslims since the late colonial period.

Throughout the southern triangle, claims to religious erudition were a cornerstone in a centuries-old "discourse of truth and ignorance" espoused by Muslim scholars in their struggles to impose religious orthodoxy (Brenner 1993a;
1993b). Islamic religious argument also served to justify existing sociopolitical
hierarchies—for instance, between slaves and their masters (see Hanretta 2009,
ch. 1, 7; Klein 1998). In the north, Islamic intellectual traditions rested on an intricate connection, centuries old, between social status, political hierarchy, Muslim
identity and erudition, and a discourse on *racial* difference (Hall 2011a). Starting

in the seventeenth century, Islamic legal arguments helped Muslim scholars justify political domination and shaped socioeconomic inequalities as well as a discourse of black racial and legal inferiority in terms of people's "stain of original disbelief" (Hall 2011a, 236; 2011b). In the early twentieth century, the idiom of religiously sanctioned social difference served the formerly privileged "white" Tuareg from clerical- and warrior-based confederations in confrontations with their former slaves over questions of land and livestock inheritance; it also allowed them to frame their resistance to the colonial order in terms simultaneously racial and religious. This discourse of religious and racial superiority was taken up again after independence during the first and second Tuareg uprisings (1963–63 and 1990–95), during which Tuareg and later Arab rebels framed their opposition against the government of "Mali" as a struggle for independence from the yoke of "blacks," ex-slaves, and unbelievers (Hall 2011a, ch. 7, 8).

Key elements of the discourse have reappeared in the political project of present-day Muslim militant groups in Mali's north. Yet, as I shall argue, whereas in the earlier uprisings references to Islam played a key role in claiming religious orthodoxy vis-à-vis a government made up of unbelievers, the rhetoric of the new Muslim militants is characterized by their insistence on an Islamic political order.

Historical confrontations between French colonial officials and Muslim intellectuals over the extent to which Islamic norms and precepts, as well as a centuries-old culture of Arabophone Muslim erudition, should inform the ordering of social and personal relations in public and domestic life played out mainly in the domains of education and the legal regulation and adjudication of family matters.

A cornerstone in French colonial attempts to impose their *mission civilisatrice* on the populations in the French West African territories was the firm grounding of the principle, newly institutionalized at home, of *laïcité* in the administration of its colonial subjects. This meant, among other things, that the educational system was to be administered under the exclusive control of the colonial administration and required that the political and social influence of Muslim religious scholars and the nascent presence of Christian missionaries in certain regions of the French Sudan be contained (Robinson 1988; 1992). French colonial policy vis-à-vis Muslims showed fear of a pan-Islamic resistance to European colonialism associated with reform-minded intellectuals who had close intellectual ties to the *Hijaz* (see hereafter). To stem the tide of pan-Islamic radicalism, colonial administrators supported religious authorities who, being often associated with the Islamic mystical traditions, were deemed to represent a syncretic, more tolerant "African Islam." In so doing, the colonial judicial system sidelined, at least in some areas, a former elite of Muslim legal experts (Stewart 1997; Triaud 1997).

French colonial policy relied on a dual legal system featuring two bodies of law having their own spheres of application. French positive law (*Code Napoléon*) regulated the affairs of French citizens and *assimilés*—that is, non-African foreigners and Africans who had acquired French citizenship (*citoyens*). The rest of the colonized population, the *sujets Français* ("French subjects"), was adjudicated under various "indigenous" or "customary" laws among which Islamic law held a privileged position. What colonial administrators applied as "customary" law only gradually emerged from the interplay between the colonial judiciary and local "experts" having their own agendas of maintaining or reinforcing patriarchal and political control.[4]

Customary and Islamic law was applied only to certain social domains, such as the regulation of marriage and inheritance matters. Because for decades the colonial juridical system had been consulted mostly by the urban population of *evolués* and French citizens, for the majority of the colonial subjects, the regulation of intra- and interfamilial matters remained in the hands of male family authority (Robinson 1988; 1992). Still, colonial legislation of selected aspects of family life generated much resentment on the part of family elders and politically dominant families and clans, who feared a loss of control over male juniors, daughters, and wives, as well as over families located at the lower echelons of political hierarchies (Hanretta 2009, ch. 6, 7; Roberts 2005, ch. 4–6).[5] In regions having a predominant Muslim population, as in the north, opposition by politically dominant lineages to these legal measures was cast as a rejection of reforms that contradicted local "Islamic custom" (Hall 2011a, ch. 8; Lecocq 2010, 102–3, 173).

Education emerged as another field of struggle. Since the early decades of the twentieth century, when the first reformed "Franco-Arab" schools were created, French colonial efforts to limit the influence of Islamic norms and traditions on the making of colonial subjects clashed with Muslim scholars and reformers over school curricula and over whether French or Arabic should serve as main instructional language (Brenner 2001; Villalon et al. 2012, 13–14). These confrontations generated new lines of conflict between different groups of Muslims, especially in the late 1930s, when Muslim intellectuals returned from extended stays in Egypt and Saudi Arabia and sought to counter the effects of the educational system established under French colonial rule,[6] deepen ordinary believers' religious knowledge, and purify conventional religious practices from "unlawful innovations" (*bida'*). By broadening access to Arabic literacy and religious interpretation, Muslim reformists, sometimes backed by the colonial state, challenged the foundations of established religious authority (Brenner 2001, ch. 4; 2007). In so doing, the reformists initiated religious controversies that reflected social and political transformations throughout Muslim West Africa and showed in regulations ranging from dress and prayer posture to life cycle rituals (Amselle 1985; Kaba 1974; 2000; Launay 1992; Masquelier 1999; Soares 2005;

Triaud 1986). These reforms yielded paradoxical results. By carving out a space for the transmission of Islamic knowledge, they were able to limit, and to a certain extent counter, French colonial influence on the making of colonial subjects. However, the exclusion of Islamic schools from what was officially recognized as "education" in the proper sense of the term laid the foundations for their continued exclusion in the postcolonial period.

In the run up to independence, the colonial administration's support of established religious clans translated into a broad support lent by Muslim authorities to the conservative PSP party (which was more favorable to French colonial administration). The political influence of these religious clans waned after 1956, when the competing party, US-RDA, won the French elections.

In some of Mali's northern territories, politically influential Tuareg clans capitalized on a double political legitimacy as warriors and as descendants of a Muslim nobility (Klute 2013, 53).[7] Here, too, developments in the late colonial period similarly weakened the position of established religious clans, even if their influence was to outweigh that of intellectuals pushing for a renewal of Muslim religious practices for several decades.

State Regulation of "Islam" and Moral Renewal

The first government of Modibo Keita (1960–68), with its administration of religious matters, reform of the educational system,[8] and its curtailing of opportunities for Muslim merchants through a socialist nationalization scheme, restricted the space for Muslim activities. A (heterogeneous) Muslim intellectual elite remained in charge of Islamic knowledge transmission in the form of "traditional" and reformed Qur'anic schools. But in the absence of public funding and because of the limited employment opportunities available to graduates, the "confessional schools" could not compete with regular state schools (Villalon et al. 2012, 19–21). The weak political standing of religious authorities and other Muslim intellectuals foreclosed their possibilities to prompt public debate on the integration of Islamic principles into national legislation.

At the local level, however, the endorsing in Mali's first constitution of colonial regulations regarding bride price, minimum marriage age, and the noncompulsory nature of marriage nurtured resentment of the new political order. In the region of Kidal in Mali's northeast, Kel Essuk (religious specialists) and Ifoghas (the politically dominant, noble clans of warriors) presented the "un-Islamic" nature of the new government as a reason for resisting integration into the Malian nation-state. Representatives of leading Tuareg clans (the Illelan/Tillellan) of Kidal resented the state's interference in marriage and family matters, especially in the form of the Code de Mariage et de Tutelle (CMT) of 1963, which capped the bride price and set a minimum marriage age for men and women (Lecocq 2010, 187). Other demands, such as for the segregation of boys and girls at school, an Islamic curriculum, and the use of Arabic and Tamasheq as instructional languages, challenged the educational policy of President Keita's government and its colonial *laicité* and assimilationalist agenda (Lecocq and Schrijver 2007, 155). The government's refusal to respond to these demands was one motivation for the bloodily repressed, Tuareg uprisings of 1963–64 under the leadership of Muhammad Ali Attaher. Yet, notably, even if Tuareg leaders framed their grievances as a matter of safeguarding "Islamic custom" against a government of unbelievers, at that time, the "symbolic language of Islam" (Eickelman 1987) did not mobilize broad, transethnic resistance to the central state in Bamako.

The relatively weak political position of Muslim authorities changed gradually in the 1970s, when a new generation of Muslim reformists benefited from funds of a transnational *da`wa* movement spearheaded by Saudi Arabia and expanded the local infrastructure of Islamic education and welfare (Brenner 1993b; see Otayek 1993). President Traoré (r. 1968–91) sought to control the influx of money and the attendant blossoming of an infrastructure of Muslim religiosity through a strategy of integration and cooptation. He established control over Muslim interest groups through a national association (AMUPI[9]) yet simultaneously granted these groups privileges, such as extended broadcasting periods on national radio and television. *Da`wa* funding from international sponsors diminished considerably in the 1980s. However, political changes prompted by the ouster of President Moussa Traoré in 1991 opened up new spaces for Muslim activism that illustrated a broadening consensus about the need to bring personal and social life in line with an Islamic ethics (Schulz 2006). This consensus, as well as the new challenge to *laicité* state institutions that it revealed, manifested in two main fields of activism: education and legislation (see hereafter). In both fields, arguments by state officials and by Muslim activists replayed controversies from the early twentieth century onward (Villalon et al. 2012, 12–14).

Muslim activist organizations and networks that formed the institutional basis of the Islamic renewal movement operated initially in towns of central Mali, where traditional religious authorities had limited influence on the religious field. In the late 1980s, the idiom of Islamic moral renewal also gained salience in the north at the initiative of young men who, though not of elite political or religious background, had earned an educational degree from institutions of religious learning in Libya and Algeria. These men, together with other returnees from forced exile in North Africa, launched the second "Tuareg rebellion" against "Mali," which they described as a culturally and religiously foreign government.[10] Much like the older generation of Tuareg leaders, who had justified their resistance to state encroachment in 1963 as a defense of "Islamic custom," the leaders of the armed rebellion of the early 1990s claimed a uniform northern *religious* identity for which internal social status differences and regional variation in livelihoods and historical experiences vis-à-vis the central state mattered less than an allegedly uniform practice of Islam.

The grievances formulated by leaders of the 1990s rebellion articulated the experiences of economic and political marginalization, bloody repression, and forceful displacement that had characterized the relation between certain segments of the northern population and "Mali." Repeated persecution and forced exile had made transnational mobility and the presence of nonnationals a regular feature of life in northern Mali. The gradual strengthening of an idiom of Islamic renewal was facilitated by the presence of several international actors and organizations such as the *Tablighi Jama`at* that arrived in the north in the late 1999s.[11] In Kidal, the Tablighi Jama`at was strongly backed by the Ifoghas (the politically dominant "white" Tuareg clan) for several years before it lost support in 2001 (Lecocq and Schrijver 2007, 149f).[12]

In 2006, violent opposition to the central state was relaunched by militants who had earlier played a leading role in the 1990s rebellion. Grievances were again cast as a matter of safeguarding local Islamic traditions against a government of unbelievers and transpired in demands regarding education (Lecocq and Schrijver 2007, 155), thereby taking up concerns voiced before independence and after the first Tuareg uprising. The demands, articulated by politically dominant Tuareg clans, expressed concern for state interference in the educational domain as a central site for the making of "proper Muslims." The demands, which were in line with the "erudite" version of Islam represented by the Tablighi, contrasted with the Salafi jihadist agenda of the Algerian militant organization GSPC (Lecocq and Schrijver 2007, 155).

Thus, much as with developments in Mali's south during roughly the same period, in the north, a trend toward "popularizing" and advocating Islam as a community-building idiom has emerged since the late 1980s. Still, until the mid-2000s, the tendency to politicize a northern Muslim religious identity did not manifest itself in any organized effort to establish shari`a or to make Islamic ethics the foundation of public order.

In central Mali, President Traoré's fall from power and the introduction of multiparty democracy in 1991 marked a new era for Muslim activism in national and local political arenas. A movement of Islamic moral renewal emerged, based on networks of social, logistical, and financial support by which Muslim leaders of different background and credentials mobilize followers in urban and semiurban areas. The complex structure of religious and political patronage created multiple points of articulation between society and state (Schulz 2012, ch. 4). Although operative throughout the country, the networks' ties to state institutions and officials were stronger in central Mali than in its northern territories.

Leading protagonists of the renewal movement disagree among each other over how the moral renewal of self and society should be effected. Yet they all claim that a (more or less specified) set of Islamic norms and prescriptions should reorder public and family life. Competition over access to state resources and institutions has played a role in shaping relations among these contending Muslim factions. Thus, contrary to the oppositional rhetoric employed by some Muslim groups—for instance, with regard to the family draft law (see hereafter)—their activities bolster the central role of the state in mediating relations among them.

Key elements of the "Islamic" moral order (or, respectively, shari'a) for which Muslim activists called were never spelled out.[13] The "Islamic ethics" to which the activists refer thus operates similar to a "moving target": It constitutes a shifting and hence elusive endpoint. Still, the success of the networks of Muslim activism in the 1980s and 1990s indicates a broadening social consensus about the relevance of an Islamic ethics to a reordering of social relations. The consensus is the product of historical processes that, echoing dynamics of the colonial period, have crystallized in a strong representation of women in the Islamic renewal movement since the 1980s.[14] Among the processes are the growing symbolic and pragmatic significance of education, the transformation of Muslim practice and identity from a marker of social and professional status to a matter of personal conviction and practice, a rearticulation of gender ideologies, a greater stress on individual responsibility, and transformations in domestic economies that were prompted or reinforced by the structural adjustment policy of the 1980s (see Schulz 2012, ch. 3, 4).

A New Ethics: The "Female Face" of Islamic Renewal

The strong participation of women from the urban lower and lower middle classes in the Islamic renewal movement demonstrates that the call for a new Islamic ethics resonates with their quotidian concerns, experiences, and dilemmas.[15] Although the leaders of the Muslim women's learning groups understand their teachings as an instruction in traditional Islamic prescriptions and in the "rights and duties of women in Islam," their lectures address concerns that emerge for urban women in the wake of limited income opportunities, greater responsibility for family subsistence, and a persistent patriarchal gender ideology.

Muslim women often insist that Malian society should be regulated in conformity with a more pristine Islamic moral order—that is, that Malians should "revert" to the authentic teachings of Islam (Schulz 2008a).[16] Women should bear full responsibility for their own salvation and for the moral renewal of society and should pursue these obligations in spite of opposition they encounter from family and in-laws. Their emphasis on individual responsibility is noteworthy, signaling important changes in the significance of religious observance that can be traced to the early decades of the twentieth century and that implied its resignification from an element of family affiliation, professional specialization, or "ethnic" identity to a matter of personal conviction. The particular sites where women are told to show their convictions hints at influences from Western schooling, such as an emphasis on "building one's own viewpoint."

Also characteristic of the renewal movement is supporters', both men's and women's, attribution of primary significance to a believer's immediate access to and understanding of the scriptures.[17] Among women who stress the importance of textual understanding, this hints at changes in the gender-specific structuring of Muslim knowledge transmission and interpretive authority. Until the 1970s, religious learning and sustained ritual knowledge were limited mostly to women of elite background.[18] Because most members of the Muslim women's groups are younger and come from the middle and lower-middle classes, their learning efforts cast in stark relief the broadening of access to religious instruction that has been under way for several decades. Muslim women's learning initiatives can thus be seen as a result of the educational reforms initiated by earlier generations of Muslim activists who sought to reach segments of society hitherto excluded from religious knowledge transmission.

The female leaders of the Muslim women's groups exhort women to invite others "to embark on the path to God" (*ka alasira ta*)[19] by setting a good example. Women are to excel not only in proper ritual performance but also in the cultivation of a certain sensibility characterized by *maloya* (modesty, "shame"), *sabati* (endurance, patience), and a capacity for self-control and submissiveness (*munyu*) toward husbands and seniors.[20]

Closely related to Muslim women's emphasis on personal conviction is their view that "being a proper Muslim" must manifest itself through daily public practice, as well as through one's embodied and nonargumentative "profession" of faith vis-à-vis others. Women's efforts to show their newfound faith as a means to convince others to join their moral movement have resulted in a number of activities in public and semipublic settings (Schulz 2007; 2008b). Among these practices is the choice of a "sober," "decent" apparel, one associated by members of the reform movement and by outsiders with an Islamic ethics. Muslim women also move the fulfillment of ritual obligations into spheres of greater public visibility, thereby blurring commonly accepted demarcations between public and domestic settings and between gender-specific realms of proper practice.

Muslim women's view of their own role in the Islamic renewal movement evinces a long-term transformation in the organization of religious ritual and in understandings of what it means to be a proper believer. The growing "Islamic consensus" (see Brown 2011) manifests itself in ordinary believers' efforts to make "Islamic values" binding for the regulation of interpersonal relations and public order.

Islamic Ethics and Lawmaking: The Controversy over the Family Draft Law

The effects of the invigoration of Muslim activist networks and the widening consensus over the need to reorder society and family in accordance with Islamic precepts can also be seen in the indeterminate outcome of the family law reform project. The debates surrounding the draft law also shed light on what representatives of the Muslim national organization and other Muslim opinion leaders understood by an "Islamic" reordering of family life, as well as how they defined "Islamic ethics" in substantive terms.

In 1999, President Konaré's government launched the law reform project PRODEJ (Promotion de la Démocratie et de la Justice au Mali) with the financial support of international donor organizations (mainly supplying US and European funds); in aid negotiations with the government, the latter had given this reform top priority. The official rationale given for the reform project was to eliminate inconsistencies between the constitution and the *Code du Mariage et de la Tutelle (CMT)* and the *Code de Travail* that resulted from sometimes conflicting customary, Islamic, and state legal norms. This was especially the case with regard to bride price, marriage registration, number of wives, wives' obligation to obey their husband, and wives' choice of residence. Beyond these immediate concerns, the reform project was clearly intended to minimize the influence of Islamic norms and to limit the prerogatives of Muslim religious authorities— for example, with regard to marriage validation. Within the administration, the reform project was supported most strongly by the Ministry of Women and Family and the Ministry of Justice. Within civil society, the reform project was pushed by women's rights activists.[21]

Whereas representatives of the national Muslim organization AMUPI were invited to participate in the publicly staged debates of the draft law, other prominent leaders of the Islamic renewal movement (such as Sheikh Chérif Haidara) were excluded.[22] AMUPI representatives argued that Mali was a Muslim nation (thereby disregarding the existence of non-Muslim religious minorities) and that the "Islamic values" that formed the basis of the national community should be protected against politicians attempting to impose their "culturally foreign" secularist ideas. They maintained that the regulation of family life should be done in accordance with Islamic norms and prescriptions. Yet the concrete measures and formulations these Muslims proposed revealed that their interventions were often guided by pragmatic concerns, particularly of maintaining patriarchal and gerontocratic privilege (such as, for example, in controlling marriage arrangements and in limiting women's opportunities to legal redress in case of divorce, child custody, and inheritance issues). Contrary to their claims of opposing a government seeking to impose a "culturally foreign" principle of *laicité*, these Muslim spokespersons occasionally formed strategic alliances with (male) officials from the Ministry of Justice. These officials, in turn, presented themselves as defenders of the principle of *laicité* against the onslaught of "religious fundamentalists." Yet they were similarly preoccupied with inhibiting legal changes that would have strengthened the rights and position of women in domestic affairs.

Five important insights emerge from the ways in which the draft law controversy unfolded during the early 2000s. First, far from pursuing a consistent agenda vis-à-vis Muslim interest groups, the state administration developed divergent positions and interests with regard to the regulation of family matters. Second, in spite of their claims to articulate a consistent set of Islamic principles, the positions articulated by Muslim representatives revealed a strong concern with the loss of patriarchal and gerontocratic control. Third, although Muslim interest groups and state officials and politicians clashed over certain issues, there were also significant points of interest convergence among (male) representatives of the judiciary and Muslim representatives. Fourth, these shared agendas weakened the claim of AMUPI representatives to defend a pure set of "Islamic ethics" against a secularist-minded government. Fifth, the fact that only AMUPI representatives were invited to the debate (in their role as "Muslim interest groups") revealed sharp divisions within the Islamic renewal movement.

Under the government of Alpha Toumani President Touré (2002–12), Muslim protest against the family draft law intensified.[23] In 2010, in preparation for the next presidential campaign, Touré capitalized on the unpopularity of the draft law (strongly associated with the office of his predecessor, President Konaré, and his party ADEMA) to mobilize voters against the still powerful ADEMA party networks. The bill was passed by parliament in 2009 but was signed by President Touré only in early 2012, after it had been partly revised to accommodate the demands of Muslim opponents. This outcome, as well as President Touré's reluctance to give Muslim opponents another occasion to fuel popular discontent with his government, are clear indications of the political weight that Muslim activist networks have come to carry over the past fifteen years, as well as the extent of their influence on lawmaking.

Transformations in the Field of Debate since the Coup d'État

As we have seen, since the 1990s, the governments of presidents Konaré and Touré have refrained from directly challenging the growing influence of Muslim activist groups. Some of these activists are part of the *Haut Conseil Islamique du Mali*, yet they also draw substantial social support from religious patronage networks that operate outside the state. As illustrated by the spectacular success of Sheikh Sharif Haidara and his group Ansar Dine, these patronage networks mobilize people at the neighborhood level; they provide a social infrastructure of financial support, education, and health care and thereby step into the void left by a fledgling state.[24]

The situation of political instability that followed President Touré's ouster in March 2012 only heightened people's sense of urgency and thereby strengthened the influence of Muslim activist networks.[25] The sense of precariousness did not end with the election of President Ibrahim Boubacar Keita ("IBK"), sworn into office in September 2013. President Keita's government continues with the accommodation strategy pursued by the transitional government of 2012–13 vis-à-vis Muslim interest groups that allows them greater representation in state structures and gives their interests greater consideration in policy implementation.

Thus far, the accommodation strategy has resulted in two measures. The first, diametrically opposed to the draft law, was to grant the religious marriage ceremony full legal status as civil marriage. For Muslim religious authorities, the measure implies a significant increase in autonomy to regulate family matters beyond state control. The second significant step has been the creation of a Ministry of Religious Affairs (*Ministère des Affaires Religieuses et du Culte*) in 2012.

As a consequence of the effort by the government to incorporate and contain the mounting challenge of certain Muslim interest groups, the political and administrative structures of the state have changed in ways that attenuate the principle of *laïcité*. Secularist-minded intellectuals and representatives of religious minorities (first and foremost Christians) have followed these developments, as well as the "ideological calibration" (Brown 2011, 117) they imply, with great concern. Still, as worrisome as the trend appears in critics' eyes, the cooptation strategy has thus far allowed the state to keep a hand in steering religious debate and in shaping relations between different Muslim factions. By creating new structures of representation for Muslims that promise to regulate public affairs in accordance with "Islamic values," the state has maintained a certain control over the definition of "proper Islam" and over how "Islamic values" are translated into policymaking and into the regulation of collective and family life.

The political weight and mobilizing potential of Muslim activist groups that has been bolstered by the March 2012 *coup d'état* indicates a growing consensus about the need to reform society and self in accordance with Islamic values and prescripts. However, tension has not subsided between this consensus on one side and the "growing cacophony" (Brown 2011, 110) within the field of Muslim debate on the other.

Muslim debate in the national arena (centered on southern Mali) still works as a "discourse of truth and ignorance" that strongly resembles the ways intra-Muslim debate has proceeded historically (Brenner 1993b; 2001). But several new expressions have been integrated into the older opposition between "rightful believers" and "those who do not know." The new term *Salafist* and the new significance attributed to the notion of *Sunna* show the influence of global political trends and events in northern Mali on national religious debates. This is seen in the example of Sheikh Chérif Haidara, a prominent, if controversial spokesman of the Islamic renewal movement (Schulz 2012, ch. 6, 7). For years, Haidara insisted that his defense of the *Sunna* gave him an intermediate position between, on one side, "radical" Arab Islam and, on the other, local "traditional" religious practices that have been criticized by reform-minded activists as not fully in line with Islamic injunctions. Since 2012, however, in an effort to counter the northern Ançar Dine and his "Salafist" opponents from the *Haut Conseil Islamique du Mali*, Haidara has portrayed himself as the defender of "local tolerant Islam."[26] He now vocally endorses emblematic practices of this local Islam, such as *dhikr* (Bam. *zikiri*), the celebration of the Mawlud, and saint veneration. Haidara also aligns himself with "Sufi Muslims" (a term rarely used until 2010) and sets himself apart from the "people of the *Sunna*" (*sunamogow*), whose "foreign origins," efforts to build a new politicoreligious order, as well as readiness to use the violence he denounces. To a greater extent than before, Haidara stresses his tolerance vis-à-vis Christians and other nonbelievers, who, he often insists, should not be forced to convert to Islam.[27]

Regardless of the arguments that religious leaders such as Chérif Haidara employ to position themselves vis-à-vis their opponents in the field of Muslim debate, it is evident that reference to shari`a has become commonplace practice. It remains to be seen whether the cacophony of Muslim positions will exacerbate the present politically volatile situation in southern Mali or instead help neutralize the contending Muslim factions and opinion leaders.

Shari`a Politics in the North: Social and Political Dynamics

The March 2012 coup d'état in central Mali facilitated the emergence of several military organizations in the north that challenged the legitimacy and military control of the Malian state.[28] Initially the most successful military grouping was the MLNA,[29] an organization that calls for an independent Tuareg state and that is headed by individuals who played a leading role in the Tuareg uprising of the 1990s. The MNLA soon lost out to three Muslim militant organizations—the Ançar Dine, MUJAO,[30] and MIA[31] (a splinter group of the Ançar Dine)—that emerged in response to the presence of international military forces, all of which benefit from the financial and logistical support of the al-Qaeda network,

AQMI.[32] In a series of military confrontations with the MNLA in 2012, the three groups gradually took control over the three northern regions of Gao, Timbuktu, and Kidal, where they implemented a set of "shari`a measures" ranging from strict modesty and chastity rules for women (and for men, though to a lesser degree) to the banning of music and alcohol.

After the invasion of Mali's north by French troops, and with the military and logistical support of the United Nations and of African Union member states, in January 2013 the three northern regions were wrested away from Muslim militant organizations. Still, the security situation remains precarious; missile attacks and road bombs are the order of the day in Timbuktu and Gao. Far from being under control of international military forces, Kidal still operates as a stronghold for the Ançar Dine and, by implication, for Al-Qaeda networks. What are the historical roots of these recent developments—in particular, of the growing symbolic appeal of the politicoreligious program of the Muslim militant groups? How could references to shari`a become such a powerful idiom of political mobilization?

Some conflict lines that render the current situation in Mali's northern territories so volatile have their origins in the civil war situation in the early 1990s and found a provisional end with the Flame of Peace Ceremony in March 1996. The main players in the early 1990s military confrontations were Tuareg separatist fighters, the Malian army, and, later, the paramilitary Gandakoy organization. In the late 1990s, international Islamic networks also started operating in the north. Leading members of the Algeria-based GSPC and the Tabligh al Jamaat justified their political and religious programs by referring to the Islamic traditions of the Sahara, arguing that they were merely continuing a tradition of political Islam similar to that responsible for the Islamization of the Maghreb and al-Andaluz (see Lecocq and Schrijver 2007, 161–62).

Responding to demands by leaders of the 1990 rebellion, infrastructure and economic development projects were initiated in the north with the support of Western donors. Yet a widespread sense that these measures did not benefit the majority of the population led to renewed hostilities and violent confrontations between 2006 and 2009. Those who reignited the military confrontations were the leaders of the 1990s rebellion, and their demands echoed those of the 1990s uprisings in Kidal (Lecocq and Schrijver 2007, 155). A renewed phase of militarization of the north took place in 2011 under the influence of the military confrontation between Gaddafi loyalists and rebels in Libya. The militarization resulted in a massive influx of arms, all aided by the return of (Tuareg) ex-soldiers of Gaddafi's army who joined various military groups and the Malian army.

A series of bloody confrontations between the Malian army and the MLNA in late 2011 and early 2012 resulted in Malian army defeats. These raised concerns about President Touré's failure to respond adequately to the security situation in the north. Ultimately, political destabilization and the growing presence of transnational Islamic networks in Mali's north were decisive factors in the military coup of March 2012.

By framing their struggle as a political project that cannot be realized as long as the secular principles of Mali's constitution were maintained, Muslim militants in the north clearly differ from the majority of renewal activists in Mali's south. Leading spokesmen of Muslim militancy, such as Iyad Ag Aghali, the leader of Ançar Dine and a native of Kidal, justify their breaking with the MNLA by referring to their intention to create a politicoreligious order attuned to the Islamic traditions of the Sahara. They argue that by reorienting the populations to their shared Islamic traditions, they will be able to bring moral order and bridge social and political divisions. This resonates strongly among non-Tuareg segments of the northern population (especially those residing in Gao and Timbuktu regions) who contest the ("white" Tuareg) MLNA call for an independent Tuareg nation, which rests on the claim that all northerners are Tuareg. The claims by Muslim militants to bring greater justice also significantly echoes the grievances of social groups who resent the privileges and political dominance of leading Tuareg clans. Current shari`a politics in the north, then, involve a "rebranding" (Peletz 2013, 622) of longstanding grievances in an Islamic idiom. They emerge at the interface of various moral and social concerns for which the juridical and legal regulation of social life is only one among different domains that require reform. Shari`a politics also reflect strong transnational influences.

To understand the emergence of Muslim militant groups from the interplay between transnational networks of Muslim activism and local social and moral concerns, we need to account for local social and political divisions and to consider that the social composition of local populations and sources for political conflict differ from one northern region to the other. The political divisions played an important role in the varied responses to the shari`a measures by different segments of the northern population.

Kidal and Menaka are the main areas of Tuareg settlement, where chiefly "white" and non-Tuareg lineages form the majority of the local population. The politically dominant social group in Kidal is the ("white" Tuareg) Ifoghas. Their earlier, seminomadic forms of livelihood and their position as masters of the "black" Tuareg slaves, the Ikhlan, were seriously undermined by the droughts of the 1960s and 1980s, as well as by periodic persecution at the hands of the central state. Also part of the social hierarchy are the former vassals of the Ifoghas, the Imghad, who historically depended on the Ifoghas for protection and support.

In spite of their loss in economic standing, the Ifoghas seek to hold on to their earlier privileges and prerogatives and still form the politically dominant group. Most of the members of Ançar Dine and of MIA are of Ifoghas origin, but some Ifoghas also play a leading role in the MNLA. Their former vassals, the Imghad, who outnumber the Ifoghas, are not involved in either of the three political organizations. Also resentful of the activities of the Muslim militants and of their aspirations to regulate social life in accordance with Islamic principles are the ("white" Tuareg) Kel Essuk; historically, they constituted the religious aristocracy. Until the arrival of Muslim militants, they were in charge of religious services in and around Kidal and Menaka.³³ The fourth social group, the Ikhlan, the former slaves of the Ifoghas, have also refrained from joining the political opposition.

To a significant extent, Ançar Dine regroups ex-fighters of the 1990s secessionist rebellion and formerly junior AQIM commanders. Berabish Arabs dominate the Ançar Dine in Timbuktu, whereas the Kidal groups are composed mainly of the Kel Adagh chiefly lineage. Leading figures of the MUJAO are southern Saharans, and its support base is composed of Fulbe, Songhay, and Ikhlan. The support base of Muslim militants in Menaka is very similar to that in Kidal. In Menaka, the Imochar (or Kel Talatye) are the politically dominant group and are the former masters of the Bellah (ex-slaves). They have not joined the Ançar Dine group but instead support the MNLA secessionist movement. The former vassal groups, the Imghad, outnumber the Imochar in Menaka, too. Along with the Kel Essuk (religious specialists), they refused to join either three Muslim political groups or the MNLA. Some of the Bellah, who outnumber any of the other social groups, have joined the MUJAO, in opposition to their former masters and their Ançar Dine organization. Also supportive of the MUJAO is a fifth social group, the nomadic Fulbe pastoralists, who hold grievances against the politically dominant Imochar to whose cattle raiding activities they were historically exposed.

Those who have been instrumental to the implementation of shari`a regulations at the local level were often young men who graduated from a local *medersa* (*madrasa*) in the Maghreb, Libya, or Saudi Arabia. Although their educational career does not secure them a job in the formal job market, the arrival of Muslim militants has allowed them to enter into direct competition with established clans of religious specialists (Kel Essouk, Kel Intsar, Cherifs). In Kidal, some of these young men have also joined the military wing or the Islamist vigilante forces of the Ançar Dine.

Implementing Shari`a

What reforms were introduced by the militant organizations under the heading of shari`a regulations? How did different local groups respond to them, and to what extent did their reactions reflect on, and complicate, existing divisions and contentions?

Shari'a measures imposed by the Muslim political groups that received most international and national media coverage were those that related to public conduct and gender relations in public and domestic settings. Measures that generated mixed local reactions hardly ever made it into news headlines. The regulation of gender relations in domestic and public settings involved serious restrictions on women's public visibility and prohibitions of the mixing of unrelated men and women, inflicting severe punishments for noncompliance. Courtyards were restructured to ensure a stricter separation of female and male areas within the domestic sphere. A new dress code required men to wear a combination of knee-length trousers and a blouse (*petit bubu*) or an ankle-length garment (*jellaba*); women had to don a full-body garment (called *hijab*). Also forbidden was the playing of music in the streets, during weddings or festivities, and on local radio. In addition to the punishing of extramarital sexual relations by stoning, theft and road banditry were punished by the cutting off of limbs.

For obvious reasons, opposition to these restrictions was strongest among younger Western-educated women and men, who denounced the measures as manifestations of an intolerant Islam at variance with local religious practices. In many cases, the severity of the punishment imposed by militants, not the regulation itself, generated the greatest resentment. Even here, significant differences existed between the Timbuktu and Gao regions on one side, where Muslim militants were resented by many as "foreigners," and, on the other side, Kidal and Menaka, the home base of the majority of Ançar Dine fighters. Because these fighters were and still are embedded in local kin networks, their military control found greater acceptance. By the same token, kinship ties obligated them to be more lenient toward those who transgressed shari'a restrictions.

Although the shari'a measures prompted considerable resentment among some segments of the local population, they nevertheless resonated with a widespread sense that to counter the moral degradation of society, people should live a "sober" life and free themselves from the temptations of Western culture and consumerism—and that the only way to do so was to reorder social life in accordance with local Islamic traditions and values. This widespread concern with moral reform was echoed by the slogan "let's clean up (matters) among us" ("*nettoyez chez nous*"), promulgated by Muslim militants.

To social groups who historically had little power to defend themselves against their white Tuareg masters, the arrival of the Muslim militant organizations meant a considerable improvement of a situation previously characterized by the absence of an ordering and protective state power. To these segments of the population, the enforcement of shari'a by Muslim groups guaranteed a certain measure of social justice for the first time. These and other select groups have responded favorably to shari'a measures. These measures could be labeled leveling devices because they undermine existing political hierarchies and socioeconomic inequalities. For similar reasons, the imposition of a so-called *zakat* payment has enjoyed great popularity among the poor. Ironically, the *zakat* has facilitated wider acceptance of the drug traffic by allowing those involved in the traffic to make up for their sins by distributing part of the income generated from this illicit source of income.

Another popular measure taken by the Muslim militants was to limit the bride price to the symbolic sum of 15,000 to 20,000 FCFA,[34] a rule that effectively left little room for parents to refuse their daughters for marriage. As a measure that greatly enhances younger men's chances of getting married at an age at which they were conventionally expected to marry, this reform has been extremely popular among younger men. Its popularity shows in the fact that even second-generation Malians who reside in Niamey now travel to Menaka, Timbuktu, and Gossi to find a bride for themselves, a practice commonly—and laughingly—nicknamed "jihadi marriage" (*"mariage jihadiste"*). The popularity of the capping of the bride price is significant in several respects. Apart from the regulation's not being founded on shari`a legal prescripts, it replays and inverts historical grievances, recalling a controversy in the early decades of the twentieth century that already pitted segments of the politically dominant clans against each other when the political "reformer" Muhammad Ag Attaher, backed by the colonial administration, sought to limit the bride price against the will of chiefly clans in Timbuktu (Hall 2011a, ch. 7). The measure also illustrates longstanding continuities in the social grievances of younger men and of inferior status groups vis-à-vis male seniors and politically dominant clans over their control of marriage arrangements (cf. Hanretta 2009, ch. 6). Finally, the imposition of the measure by militants in Kidal who belong to the chiefly lineage and who, through this measure, seek the support of politically less powerful men, appears almost as an inversion of the resistance by members of the same Ifoghas group to the 1963 *Code du Mariage et de Tutelle* that limited the bride price to a symbolic sum, a resistance justified as a protection of "Islamic custom" (Lecocq 2010, 105ff) at that time. Because of this complex historical legacy, the "jihadi marriage" measure illustrates that the "shari`a regulations" imposed by Muslim militants were informed by longstanding social and political divisions that have been played out in and complicated by the encounter with the colonial and postcolonial state.

Conclusion

This chapter has shown that external influences, including outside funding (notably, Saudi oil money since the late 1970s) and international Islamist networks (AQMI) that over the last two decades have expanded their influence across the Sahara and the West African Sahel, cannot fully account for the growing significance of a shari'a discourse in Malian political and social life. Nor is the Malian case an illustration of state-orchestrated shari'a politics.

Needed instead is a historical account of how, since the late 1970s, Muslim activists' references to shari'a and Islamic ethics have lent complex and changing meanings and momentum to Malian society and politics. References to Islamic ethics generate profound resonances in present-day Mali that are a function of people's quotidian aspirations, concerns, and dilemmas. These examples show that the concrete meanings of shari'a are diverse and shift over time. I have used a "bottoms-up" perspective to account for the growing appeal of the "symbolic language of Islam" (Eickelman 1987) and to explain the shifting meanings behind this apparently persistent symbolic register (see Hatem 1994; Navaro-Yashin 2002; Peletz 2002).

In tracing the "internal" mechanisms of these developments (Vogel 2011, 89), I identified the degradation of urban economies, political liberalization since the early 1990s, and a growing sense of social and moral crisis as factors lending unprecedented weight and appeal to the language and organization of Islamic moral renewal. Along with a growing consensus about the need to renew society and self according to Islamic values, references to an "Islamic ethics" became more central to political debates over collective interest and public order. It has become more difficult for secularist-minded intellectuals to challenge the new general consensus because of the malleable nature of the "Islamic" values invoked. For decades the meanings of shari'a remained vague and "plastic" (Brown 2011, 116), primarily reflecting a general appreciation of the importance of Islamic values and morals.

Only with the occupation of the north by Muslim militant groups has the meaning of shari'a become more tangible and concrete. Muslim militants defined shari'a as a set of regulations aiming at public order and domestic "stability." This particular reading of shari'a has, in turn, been adopted by Muslim opponents who promote Islamic renewal in the urban centers of central Mali. Critical of the political program of Muslim militant groups in the north, these opponents posit a contrast between themselves as "moderate" and peaceful defenders of the right path and violent "*jihadi* salafists." Yet even if these critics oppose the forceful imposition of the shari'a measures, they do not question the equation of shari'a with the regulation of public and domestic life. For both groups, then, shari'a operates as a framing device to imagine and project a range of possibilities for renewing social and moral life.

Along with the process that moved shari'a politics to the forefront of political debate, rifts within the Muslim religious field have become more pronounced. Rather than reversing this trend, the coup d'état of March 2012 has reinforced its centrifugal tendencies. By creating or rendering more apparent the vacuum at the center of the Malian state, the coup opened the way for regional and international militant Muslim forces to impose a political order that these groups claim is more consistent with Islamic norms and injunctions.

The evolving meanings of Islamic ethics, then, have moved along different trajectories in Mali's north as opposed to its south. In the northern territories, the promulgation of an Islamic ethics has been achieved by political actors who benefit from the weakness or absence of state structures. Because of the long history of persecution of the Tuareg and other groups by the central state—a history that for some time now has been framed as an opposition to a government of unbelievers—local society in the north has become a breeding ground for the spread of shari`a politics. Although the measures currently implemented as elements of shari`a have been welcomed only by certain segments of the northern populations, measures fostering a popularization of shari`a and Islamic ethics have been under way since the late 1990s in ways that resemble processes in other regions of the Muslim world (for example, Deeb 2006; Hefner 2011).

In contrast to the north, where the recent spread of shari`a worked through the *absence* of state institutions, in central Mali, state institutions and the two governments of democratic Mali have played a significant role in the promotion of shari`a politics, partly by strengthening structures and lending support to certain representatives of Islamic moral renewal in the national arena. Because of the particular ways the state has sought to contain Muslim forces (that is, by coopting and integrating them into state structures), it has strengthened the political standing and public audibility of Muslim activists calling for a stricter adherence to Islamic norms in ways that resemble the instrumental role the Egyptian state has played in according Islam a new role in national politics over the last two decades (for example, Hatem 1994; see Brown 2011, 116).

All this points to a process of mutual appropriation (similar to the notion of "mutual assimilation of elites" originating with Jean Francois Bayart [1989]) by, on one side, the political elite and current government of President Keita, and, on the other, Muslim forces who push for a stricter application of Islamic prescriptions in the public and domestic domains. Although this dynamic allows "political authority (to) shape . . . religious interpretation" (Brown 2011, 117), it implies that the political and administrative structures of the state are changing, too, in an effort to incorporate and contain Muslim forces (see Hefner 2011).

Future developments in the relationship between the state and Muslim activists, and, by implication, in shari`a politics in central Mali, will depend on two factors. The first is the power vacuum at the heart of the central state, exacerbated by the ongoing power struggle among members of the political elite on one hand and between them and certain members of the Malian military on the other. For the moment, the presence of French and other international troops in the capital and in urban areas of the north has reduced the risk of another military putsch. But it remains to be seen whether over the long run the presence of international forces will not contribute to a further loss in legitimacy of the present political regime. It also remains an open question whether the government of President Keita will come up with a viable plan to mend the fissures and address the grievances in Mali's northern territories that fuel resentment between populations of the north and of the south. It is conceivable—even likely—that Muslim activist networks will garner greater support from any continuing political and economic insecurity.

The second factor is the extreme degree of political instability, exacerbated by the involvement of a range of international players, in Mali's northern regions. Much will depend on the degree of success of the international military forces in the northern territories, as well as whether their presence leads to a containment of international and local Islamist groups and thus lessen the "pressure" on President Keita's government and the military to guarantee public order and security. At present, the trend seems to be one of growing destabilization, both in the north of the country and in central Mali—a situation that may open the door for more radical Muslim forces to take political control.

References

Amselle, Jean-Loup. 1985. *"Le Wahhabisme à Bamako (1945–1985)."* *Canadian Journal of African Studies* 19 (2): 345–57.

Bayart, Jean Francois. 1989. *L'Etat en Afrique. La Politique du Ventre.* Paris: Éditions Karthala.

Brenner, Louis. 1993a. "Constructing Muslim Identities in Mali." In *Muslim Identity and Social Change in Subsaharan Africa*, edited by Louis Brenner, 59–78. Bloomington: Indiana University Press.

———. 1993b. *"La culture arabo-islamique au Mali."* In *Le radicalisme islamique au sud du Sahara*, edited by R. Otayek, 161–95. Paris, Talence: Karthala.

———. 2001. *Controlling Knowledge: Religion, Power and Schooling in a West African Muslim Society.* Bloomington and Indianapolis: Indiana University Press.

———. 2007. "The Transformation of Muslim Schooling in Mali: The *Madrasa* as an Institution of Social and Religious Mediation." In *Schooling Islam. The Culture and Politics of Modern Muslim Education*, edited by Robert Hefner and Muhammad Qasim Zaman, 199–223. Princeton, NJ: Princeton University Press.

Brown, Nathan. 2011. "Egypt: Cacophony and Consensus in the Twenty-First Century." In *Shari`a Politics. Islamic Law and Society in the Modern World*, edited by Robert Hefner, 94–120. Bloomington: Indiana University Press.

Cooper, Barbara. 1997. *Marriage in Maradi: Gender and Culture in a Hausa Society in Niger (1900–1989).* Portsmouth, NH, and Oxford: Heinemann, James Currey.

Deeb, Lara. 2006. *An Enchanted Modern: Gender and Public Piety in Shi'i Lebanon.* Princeton, NJ: Princeton University Press.

Eickelman, Dale. 1987. "Changing Interpretations of Islamic Movements." In *Islam and the Political Economy of Meaning. Comparative Studies of Muslim Discourse*, edited by Roff, 13–30. Berkeley, Los Angeles: California University Press.

Hall, Bruce. 2011a. *A History of Race in Muslim West Africa, 1600–1960*. Cambridge, UK, and London: Cambridge University Press.

———. 2011b. "How Slaves Used Islam: The Letters of Enslaved Muslim Commercial Agents in the Nineteenth Century Niger Bend and Central Sahara." *Journal of African History* 52:279–97.

———. 2013. "Arguing Sovereignty in Songhay." *Afriques*, special issue *Histoire etarchéologie du Sahel ancien: nouveaux regards, nouveaux chantiers* 4: 1–17.

Hanretta, Sean. 2009. *Islam and Social Change in French West Africa: History of an Emancipatory Community*. Cambridge, UK: Cambridge University Press.

Harrison, Christopher. 1988. *France and Islam in West Africa, 1860–1960*. Cambridge, UK: Cambridge University Press.

Hatem, Mervat. 1994. "Egyptian Discourses on Gender and Political Liberalization: Do Secularist and Islamist Views Really Differ?" *Middle East Journal* 48 (8): 661–76.

Hefner, Robert. 2011. "Indonesia: Shari'a Politics and Democratic Transition." In *Shari'a Politics: Islamic Law and Society in the Modern World*, edited by Robert Hefner, 280–318. Bloomington: Indiana University Press.

Kaba, Lansine. 1974. *The Wahhabiyya: Islamic Reform and Politics in French West Africa*. Evanston, IL: Northwestern University Press.

———. 2000. "Islam in West Africa: Radicalism and the New Ethic of Disagreement, 1960–1990." In *The History of Islam in Africa*, edited by Nehemia Levtzion and Randall Pouwels, 189–208. Athens, Oxford, and Cape Town: Ohio University Press, James Currey, David Philip.

Klein, Martin A. 1998. *Slavery and Colonial Rule in French West Africa*. Cambridge, UK: Cambridge University Press.

Klute, Georg. 2013. "Post-Gaddafi Repercussions in Northern Mali." *Strategic Review for Southern Africa* 35 (2): 53–67.

Launay, Robert. 1992. *Beyond the Stream. Islam and Society in a West African Town*. Berkeley, Los Angeles, and Oxford: University of California Press.

Lecocq, Baz. 2010. *Disputed Desert: Decolonisation, Competing Nationalisms and Tuareg Rebellions in Northern Mali*. Leiden, Netherlands: Brill.

Lecocq, Baz, and Paul Schrijver. 2007. "The War on Terror in a Haze of Dust: Potholes and Pitfalls in the Saharan Front." *Journal of Contemporary African Studies* 25 (1): 141–54.

Lecocq, Baz, Gregory Mann, Bruce Whitehouse, Dida Badi, Lotte Pelckmans, Nadia Belalimat, Bruce Hall, and Wolfram Lacher. 2013. "One Hippopotamus and Eight Blind Analysts: A Multivocal Analysis of the 2012 Political Crisis in the Divided Republic of Mali." Extended Editor's Cut. http://media.leidenuniv.nl/legacy/lecocq-mann-et-al---one-hippo-8-blind-analysts-editors-cut.pdf.

Loimeier, Roman. 2003. "Patterns and Peculiarities of Islamic Reform in Africa." *Journal of Religion in Africa* 33 (3): 237–62.

Mahmood, Saba. 2005. *Politics of Piety: The Islamic Revival and the Feminist Subject*. Princeton, NJ: Princeton University Press.

Mann, Gregory. 2003. "Fetishizing Religion: Allah Koura and French 'Islamic Policy' in Late Colonial French Soudan (Mali)." *Journal of African History* 44:263–82.

Marshall, Ruth. 2009. *Political Spiritualities: The Pentecostal Revolution in Nigeria*. Chicago, IL: University of Chicago Press.

Masquelier, Adeline. 1999. "Debating Muslims, Disputed Practices: Struggles for the Realization of an Alternative Moral Order in Niger." In *Civil Society and the Political Imagination in*

Africa: Critical Perspectives, edited by Jean Comaroff and John Comaroff, 218–50. Chicago and London: The University of Chicago Press.

McDougall, Ann. 1986. "The Economics of Islam in the Southern Sahara: The Rise of the Kunta Clan." *Asian and African Studies* 20:45–60.

Navaro-Yashin, Yael. 2002. *Faces of the State: Secularism and Public Life in Turkey*. Princeton, NJ: Princeton University Press.

Otayek, Rene, ed. 1993. *Le radicalisme islamique au sud du Sahara*. Paris, Talence: Éditions Karthala.

Peletz, Michael. 2002. *Islamic Modern: Religious Courts and Cultural Politics in Malaysia*. Princeton, NJ: Princeton University Press.

———. 2013. "Malaysia's Syariah Judiciary as Global Assemblage: Islamization, Corporatization, and Other Transformations in Context." *Comparative Studies in Society and History* 55 (3): 603–33.

Peterson, Brian J. 2011. *Islamization from Below: The Making of Muslim Communities in Rural French Sudan, 1880–1960*. New Haven, CT: Yale University Press.

Roberts, Richard. 1991. "The Case of Faama Mademba Sy and the Ambiguities of Legal Jurisdiction in Early Colonial French Sudan." In *Law in Colonial Africa*, edited by K. Mann and Richard Roberts, 185–204. Portsmouth, NH: Heinemann and James Currey.

———. 2005. *Litigants and Households: African Disputes and Colonial Courts in the French Soudan, 1895–1912*. Portsmouth, NH: Heinemann.

Robinson, David. 1988. "French 'Islamic' Policy and Practice in Late Nineteenth-Century Senegal." *Journal of African History* 29 (3): 415–35.

———. 1992. "Ethnography and Customary Law in Senegal." *Cahiers d'Etudes Africaines* 32 (132): 221–37.

Sanankoua, Bintou. 1991. "*Les associations féminines musulmanes à Bamako.*" In *L'enseignement islamique au Mali*, edited by B. L. B. Sanankoua, 105–26. Bamako, Mali: Editions Jamana.

Schulz, Dorothea. 2006. "Promises of (Im)mediate Salvation: Islam, Broadcast Media, and the Remaking of Religious Experience in Mali." *American Ethnologist* 33 (2): 210–29.

———. 2007. "Competing Sartorial Assertions of Femininity and Muslim Identity in Mali." *Fashion Theory* 11 (2/3): 253–80.

———. 2008a. "Piety's Manifold Embodiments: Muslim Women's Quest for Moral Renewal in Urban Mali." *Journal for Islamic Studies* 28:26–93.

———. 2008b. "(Re)Turning to Proper Muslim Practice: Islamic Moral Renewal and Women's Conflicting Constructions of Sunni Identity in Urban Mali." *Africa Today* 54 (4): 21–43.

———. 2012. *Muslims and New Media in West Africa: Pathways to God*. Bloomington: Indiana University Press.

Soares, Benjamin. 2005. *Islam and the Prayer Economy: History and Authority in a Malian Town*. Ann Arbor: University of Michigan Press.

Stewart, Charles. 1973. *Islam and Social Order in Mauritania*. Oxford: Clarendon Press.

———. 1997. "Colonial Justice and the Spread of Islam in the Early Twentieth Century." In *Le temps de marabouts: Itinéraireset strategies islamiques en Afrique occidentale francaise, v. 1880–1960*, edited by David Robinson and Jean-Louis Triaud, 53–66. Paris: Éditions Karthala.

Triaud, Jean-Louis. 1986. "*Abd al-Rahman l'Africain (1908–1957), pionneur et precurseur du wahhabisme au Mali.*" In *Radicalismes islamiques*, vol. 2, edited by O. Carré and Paul Dumont, 162–80. Paris: Harmattan.

———. 1997. "Introduction." In *Le Temps des Marabouts: Itinéraires et stratégies islamiques en Afrique occidentale francaise, v. 1880–1960*, edited by David Robinson and Jean-Louis Triaud, 1–29. Paris: Karthala.

Villalon, Leonardo, Abdourahmane Idrissa, Mamadou Bodian. June 2012. "*Religion, demande sociale, et réformes éducatives au Mali.*" *Africa Power and Politics Research Report* 7:1–58. http://r4d.dfid.gov.uk/PDF/Outputs/APPP/Report07-juin-2012.pdf.

Vogel, Frank. 2011. "Saudi Arabia: Public, Civil, and Individual Shari`a in Law and Politics." In *Shari`a Politics: Islamic Law and Society in the Modern World,* edited by Robert Hefner, 55–93. Bloomington: Indiana University Press.

Notes

1. The article draws on empirical research on Islamic renewal conducted in urban areas (San Segu and Bamako) in southern Mali between February 1998 and January 2014 (thirty months total). The analysis of recent developments in Mali's northern regions is based on research conducted by Souleymane Diallo in Kidal, Niamey, and the refugee camp of Abala (Cercle de Filingué) in southwest Niger, near the Malian border, since 2010.

2. Central Mali is understood in a political, not a geographical, sense. It refers to the central state in the capital Bamako and the strong rooting of the government in the different rural and urban areas that make up Mali's southern triangle.

3. Conversion rates in French West Africa increased rapidly after the 1920s, from 3,875,000 Muslims in 1924 to 6,241,000 in 1936 (Brenner 2001, 88n5; Triaud 1997).

4. The application of "customary" law by altering relations between powerful clans and their slaves and narrowing women's chances to realize grievances strengthened patriarchal and gerontocratic power within the family (Roberts 1991; 2005; see Cooper 1997).

5. The *Decréts* Jacquinot and Mandel (1932 and 1939, respectively) prohibited the custom of levirate and made marriage conditional on the spouses' mutual consent. The elevated dowry has been a contentious issue in local arenas at least since the early twentieth century. The reform-minded Tuareg leader Muhammad Ali Ag Attaher identified the elevated dowry as an impediment to marriage for young men and for poorer families. His attempts to lower the dowry were contested by older (white) Kel Entsar, who considered the elevated dowry a means to control marriage arrangements and young men (see Hanretta 2009, ch. 6).

6. The reformers took up earlier reform initiatives by Muslims affiliated with the mystical traditions of Islam (*turuq,* see Loimeier 2003), even if they differed from their predecessors in the concrete measures and goals of reforms they developed. Some intellectuals launched reformed schools, with a curriculum and pedagogical format adapted from Western-style schools, that enabled access to education for social groups widely excluded form religious training (Brenner 2001).

7. Notable differences exist between different areas where the Tuareg make up the majority of the population. In Kidal, the Kel Adagh ground their political dominance in a Muslim religious identity, claiming sharifian descent and hence a political-cum-religious leadership. In Menaka, by contrast, the dominant political clan draws not on religious prestige and gene-alogy but instead highlights nobility and warrior identity to justify its power (Lecocq and Schrijver 2007, 149–51).

8. The different Islamic school institutions were not integrated into the state educational sector but were treated as confessional schools overseen by the Ministry of Internal Affairs (Villalon et al. 2012, 16–17).

9. Association Malienne pour l'Unité et le Progrès de l'Islam.

10. The opposition against "Mali"—that is, against the central government—was articulated most strongly by younger men of the Ifoghas clan (from the Kidal region) and by other "white"

Tuareg who belonged to the secessionist movement FIA (Front Islamique de l'Azawad) with strong roots in Algeria. A number of these Tuareg rebels had grown up in exile in Libya and Algeria (with some of them spending extended periods of time in the military training camps opened by Gaddafi as early as 1981); others had attended institutions of religious learning in Libya and Algeria.

11. Other international organizations were, first, a pan-Sahel and, after 2005, trans-Saharan counterterrorism program initiated by the United States after 2001 and, second, the Algeria-based Salafist group GSPC (Groupe Salafiste pour la Prédication et le Combat), which gave rise to AQMI (Lecocq and Schrijver 2007).

12. Iyad Ag Aghali, the founder and leader of the Ançar Dine group in Kidal and an Ifoghas, joined the Tablighi, went first to Pakistan and then to Paris for his religious studies. In Kidal, the Tablighis were opposed by the Idnan, a group that the Ifoghas considered their social inferiors, as well as by many women who resented the Tablighis' conservative gender ideology. In Menaka, the Kel Essuk, the established lineage of religious specialists, opposed the presence of Tablighis who, lacking support from the local chiefly family, were obliged to leave. In Timbuktu, Tablighi missionaries were similarly viewed as competitors to local established religious practice and as potential South Asian fundamentalists whose presence would make the locality a target of US retaliation (Lecocq and Schrijver 2007, 150).

13. Only a (political and numerical) minority of these Muslim activists (commonly referred to as *intégristes*) claimed to launch a (never specified) reform of Mali's constitution in accordance with shari`a and, after the introduction of multiparty democracy, attempted (unsuccessfully) to translate this goal into a political party program.

14. Hanretta's (2009, ch. 6, 7) insightful analysis of the widespread support that Yacouba Sylla received from women in the late 1920s shows that already at this historical juncture, similar changes in the meaning of personal religious "conviction" and in the relations between generations and men and women occurred. Still, I would argue that new circumstances, such as the accelerated, transnational movement of ideas and actors, mark a qualitative shift in the processes I describe for the 1990s.

15. The women refer to themselves as "Muslim women" (*silamemusow*), thereby marking their distance from other women who have not yet "embarked on the path to God."

16. This perception exists in tension because until the 1920s, Muslim identity and religiosity, although enjoying a certain presence in many urban areas of Mali's south, turned into the religion of the majority of the urban (and rural) population only during the course of the colonial period. In these urban areas (that is, in towns where historically, lineages associated with Muslim erudition and authoritative practice, did not have a stronghold), the renewal movement thrives. Hence the identity as "proper" Sunni Muslims these women claim for themselves does not entail a return to an older, original form, nor can many of their practices be seen as a perpetuation of traditional Muslim religiosity.

17. This emphasis on direct access to Islam's foundational texts is illustrated by Muslim women's presenting as a primary rationale for their socializing activities the objective to "learn" and their referring to their associations as "learning groups" (sing. *kalani ton*).

18. In the absence of written documentation, and drawing on Sanankoua (1991) and on my oral historical research, I surmise that until the 1970s, female erudition was primarily limited to Muslim families of traders and scribes.

19. *Alasira* is commonly translated into French as "religion" but clearly resonates with the Sufi notion *tariqa* or "path."

20. The view that the cultivation of a specific emotional disposition should serve as a starting point for personal ethical reform bears resonances with Salafi–Sunni-inspired thought articulated in female revivalist circles in Cairo (Mahmood 2005). But in contrast to female

da`wa in Cairo—where, according to Mahmood, women do not view their public profession of their faith as essential to their mission—Muslim women in Mali emphasize the public and collective significance of their daily practices (Schulz 2008a).

21. I have shown elsewhere (2003; 2012, ch. 1) that women's rights activists claimed to defend the rights of women yet clearly prioritized the dilemmas of urban intellectual middle-class women. Female AMUPI representatives, in contrast, argued from the perspective of lower-class women in town and of rural women who have little chances of accessing the court system.

22. Members of the AMUPI steering committee had a hand in the decision not to invite Chérif Haidara. Also absent during the debate were members of the AMUPI who in the early 1990s called for the introduction of shari`a (without specifying it).

23. Muslim opposition to the legal reforms was articulated in and outside the new structure Haut Conseil Islamique du Mali (HCIM), created under President Alpha Konaré in January 2001 to incorporate Muslim organizations that refused membership in the AMUPI.

24. Since 1999, Haidara has transformed his home neighborhood Bamako-Bankoni from a slum into a lively area having paved roads, electricity, a hospital, and a bakery (all of them financed through savings of his followers). More recently, Haidara has been very active in providing logistical and financial support to refugees from northern Mali who live near the Nigeria–Mali border.

25. This is illustrated by several close confidants of Sharif Haidara's having created a political party (Parti pour la Restauration des Valeurs du Mali, or Fasoko) that won considerable electoral support in the legislative elections of July/August 2013.

26. Haidara thereby reiterates the colonial distinction between a radical, foreign, "Arab" Islam and a more tolerant and malleable hybrid "African Islam" (Brenner 2001; Harrison 1988).

27. Abdoulaye Diakité, "Chérif Ousmane Madani Haidara, Guide d'ançar Dine: 'Le Prophète n'a jamais contraint un peuple à l'Islam', L'indicateur du Renouveau, February 26, 2013.

28. Muslim militants draw on a thriving transnational shadow economy of smuggling, narcotraffic, and European hostage-taking that has generated the monetary resources for armament of the zone since the early 2000s.

29. Mouvement pour la Libération de l'Azawad.

30. Movement for Divine Unity and Jihad in West Africa.

31. Mouvement Islamique de l'Azawad.

32. Al Qaida au Maghreb Islamique.

33. In Timbuktu, the association of these religious specialists (Chérifs, Kel Intsar, and Kel Essouk) with saint veneration made them primary targets of Muslim militants and their pillaging of tombs and of other sites emblematic of the rooting of Islamic mystical traditions in local religious practice.

34. Approximately $30–40.

10   Syariah, Inc.: Continuities, Transformations, and Cultural Politics in Malaysia's Islamic Judiciary

Michael G. Peletz

MALAYSIA IS A Muslim-majority nation in Southeast Asia that is sometimes referred to as "The Crossroads of Asia" or, alternatively, "Truly Asia" (as a current government slogan has it), in light of its rich ethnic and religious diversity. It is a model of success in the Muslim world, as well as the global south more generally, owing to the rapid development of its middle classes and the stunning rates of urbanization, economic growth, and educational attainment it has sustained in recent decades; indeed, during the 1980s and 1990s, it was known to leaders in many parts of the world as a beacon of moderate and progressive Islam. Malaysia is also a place where state-sponsored Islamization and analytically distinct though culturally interlocked processes of bureaucratization, rationalization, and corporatization have proceeded apace, raising questions in some quarters of the nation—especially but not exclusively among non-Muslims—about the co-imbrication of law, politics, and religion and what the expansion of state power and its sanctification via symbols, idioms, and discourses of Islam means for its citizens and the future. For reasons such as these, and because Malaysian political, economic, and religious elites have endeavored to position the nation as the global center of Islamic banking and finance, an inquiry into recent developments in Malaysian Islamic law (Mal. *syariah*; Ar. *shari`a*) should be of broad interest to scholars and policymakers alike.[1]

My understanding of syariah in Malaysia is based on more than three years of ethnographic fieldwork and archival research that I have conducted since the late 1970s. One of the research projects I undertook in the late 1980s focused on the Islamic court in the small town of Rembau, Negeri Sembilan (about sixty miles south of the nation's capital, Kuala Lumpur). Partly because I was able to return to this same court in 2011 and 2013, continuities and transformations in its discourses and practices since the 1980s serve as my point of departure for this chapter.

One assumption informing my chosen object of study and my methodological approach to it is that an ethnographically and historically oriented focus on the syariah judiciary allows us to productively contextualize and concretize a good deal of the often abstract, hypothetical, and free-floating syariah talk heard in different quarters of Malaysian society and, of course, globally—some streams of which are strongly "prosyariah" but others definitely not (few, in any case, are indifferent [see this volume, Emon, chapter 2]). The approach I adopt allows for a clear view of how the relevant discourses and social forces play out on the ground in the context of an increasingly corporate system of governance.

I organize my comments into three sections. The first focuses on historical continuities since the 1980s, with special reference to dynamics of gender, marriage, divorce, and "lawfare." The second involves transformations that have occurred since the late twentieth century. Of chief concern here are seemingly contradictory changes entailing both Islamization and the modeling of the Islamic judiciary on its more powerful and prestigious civil law counterpart, processes of bureaucratization and corporatization that include the much-celebrated implementation of Japanese systems of management and auditing, and the expanded purview of the syariah judiciary with respect to what have come to be defined as criminal offenses ("creeping criminalization"). The third and final section of the chapter addresses some of the comparative and other implications of my findings, including questions bearing on the relative uniqueness and generalizability of the Malaysian experience with state-sponsored Islamization.

Some Gendered and Other Continuities

We might begin with a brief consideration of what by many criteria is a sacred text for Malaysians of all religious orientations and from all walks of life: the federal constitution. The constitution of the Federation of Malaya, drafted by the Reid Commission on the eve of independence from the British in 1957, specifies that Malaya, which became Malaysia in 1963, is a parliamentary democracy having a constitutional monarchy, with both prime minister and king at its helm. It also stipulates (in article 3) that "Islam is the religion of the Federation." This provision was apparently intended primarily to ensure that state ceremonies and pageantry, associated with celebrations of the nation's independence and rituals of investiture and inauguration, for example, would be Islamic in character—featuring Islamic prayers (*doa*), (Malay) Muslim dress codes, and *halal* food, for example—out of respect for the nation's Malay/Muslim majority (Harding 2012, 233–36).[2] Importantly, albeit with one critical but partial exception noted hereafter, the constitution does not go on to specify that syariah is or should be *a* basis for the nation's legislation, let alone *the* main (or sole) basis for legislation—and it explicitly guarantees freedom of religion (articles 3 and 11). Indeed, the constitution and the texts to which it refers make abundantly clear that the extant, British-derived system of secular law, based on the common law, is the law of the land, except within the narrowly delimited jurisdictional domains of the nation's syariah courts, which are subject to state rather than federal control (and within "native" or "customary"/*adat* courts, which are not relevant here). According to the constitution, the syariah judiciary has no jurisdiction over the affairs of non-Muslims, who currently constitute nearly 40 percent of the nation's citizenry. Its jurisdiction over Muslims, moreover, is confined largely to "family law" and other personal status law: matters of marriage, divorce, child support, spousal maintenance, certain sexual transgressions, as well as consuming alcohol, observing Ramadan, "respecting Islam," and the like. Virtually all other offenses, including traffic violations, theft, murder, treason, and human trafficking, are dealt with in the nation's far more powerful and prestigious secular courts, generally known as civil courts (*mahkamah sivil*), in accordance with secular/civil law, regardless of the plaintiff's professed religion.[3] These are important, and in some instances intensely contested and politicized, features of the national juridical landscape to bear in mind, especially as we proceed to a consideration of the kinds of cases typically adjudicated in the Islamic court of Rembau and its counterparts elsewhere in Malaysia.

As in times past, the vast majority of plaintiffs in Islamic courts both in Rembau and in Malaysia as a whole are women, just as most defendants are men—typically plaintiffs' husbands or former husbands. Noteworthy as well are continuities in the types of cases that women (and to a lesser extent men) bring to the courts, the vast majority of which concern civil rather than criminal matters. As in previous decades, female plaintiffs typically petition the courts to help them resolve problems associated with their husbands' failure to provide spousal or child maintenance (*nafkah*) or to clarify the status of their marriages (or to seek either a *taklik* divorce, owing to violation of a stipulation in the marriage contract, or a termination of marriage via *fasakh*, "judicial voiding of the marriage contract," "annulment"). The first two sets of issues are often inextricably linked insofar as women who have not received support from husbands who have left home to seek a living are commonly uncertain whether their husbands have simply been delinquent in providing them with money or news of their whereabouts or have divorced them via the *talak*/repudiation clause, which need not be recited in their presence or the court's to effect a valid divorce (though failure to do so in the courthouse is illegal). Women seeking *taklik* or *fasakh* divorce are often in the courts for the same general kinds of reasons. Men, in contrast, usually approach the courts to obtain formal approval of their divorces or to seek the court's permission for polygynous unions, but not for clarification of ambiguity or owing to financial hardship. In this, too, we see considerable continuity with times past as well as important changes that require men to obtain the court's permission to effect a divorce or a polygynous marriage that is legal in the eyes of the state.

Relevant here are quantitative data on court use obtained by anthropologists in the late 1980s and early 1990s, as well as their congruence with material from the period 2005–10. Data I collected in the course of my study of the *kadi's* (Islamic magistrate's) office in Rembau, Negeri Sembilan, during the period 1987–88 indicated that women were plaintiffs in 67 percent (22/33) of cases (Peletz 2002, 156). Statistics from the District Religious Office in Kempas, Selangor, and Kota Jati, Kedah, obtained in 1990 and 1991 by Sharifah Zaleha Syed Hassan and Sven Cederroth (1997), indicate broadly comparable patterns: Women were the plaintiffs in 79 percent (333/420) and 92 percent (423/459) of cases, respectively.[4] There are of course many dynamics to which these data do not speak—for instance, how women have been buffeted about by the courts in ways that men have not. But I am primarily concerned with the fact that the vast majority of plaintiffs in all three states (Negeri Sembilan, Selangor, and Kedah) were women.

Aggregate data collected by the Malaysian Department of Syariah Judiciary (Jabatan Kehakiman Syariah Malaysia; JKSM) bearing on the period 2005–10 reveal profound continuities since the late 1980s. In Negeri Sembilan, women were plaintiffs in 73 percent (9,699/13,201) of cases brought to the courts; the corresponding figures for Selangor and Kedah are 69 percent (35,693/51,566) and 72 percent (4,324/5,975), respectively.[5] These statistics reveal that Malaysia's Islamic courts are still very much "women's courts" in the sense that women constitute the overwhelming majority of those who seek out the court's aid in resolving domestic problems. One set of reasons for this has to do with gender skewing in Islamic law, coupled with the way Islamic law is codified in Malaysia: Women lack the legal prerogatives to resolve marital and related domestic problems without the help of the state-backed courts. Unlike men, women thus cannot divorce their spouses unless they have obtained the assistance and cooperation of the courts—hence the state. This is an important historical continuity to bear in mind. So, too, is women's continued experience of discrimination in the workplace and continued bearing of the lion's share of the responsibility for the socialization and care of infants and children. One consequence is that compared to men, women enter and experience marriage with significantly fewer economic resources to fall back on and are thus not only much more dependent on their spouses' earnings than vice versa but also far more likely than men to seek the court's assistance when their spouses' financial contributions to the household are not forthcoming.

Other gendered continuities include the fact that in various kinds of legal proceedings, women's appearance and their bodies and bodily functions (for example, when they last menstruated, whether they are pregnant) are the subject of much greater legal concern than are men's. Consider also the gendered composition of court staff, especially judges. Before 2010, all of Malaysia's Islamic judges were men, a pattern in keeping with many other Muslim-majority nations, where prevailing sentiment has it that classical Islamic texts prohibit women from serving in this capacity. This view was virtually universal in Malaysia during my early fieldwork, but the years since then have seen a gradual loosening (though not a shattering) of the hegemony, largely thanks to the efforts of Muslim feminist activists such as Sisters in Islam (SIS; see this volume, Mir-Hosseini, chapter 3) as well as female scholars working in prestigious universities such as the University of Malaya and the International Islamic University Malaysia who do not consider themselves feminists (à la SIS) but nonetheless share SIS's general view that there is ample support for the appointment of women as syariah judges in classical Islamic texts such as the Qur'an and *hadith*.

In July 2010 the government announced, amid much fanfare, the appointment of two women as judges in the Islamic judiciary for the Federal Territories of Kuala Lumpur and Putrajaya. (Since that time three other woman have been appointed as syariah judges—two in Melaka, the other in Perlis.) In a speech announcing the decision, Prime Minister Najib Tun Razak (r. 2009–present) declared that "the appointments were made to enhance justice in cases involving families and women's rights and to meet current needs" and that "the decision was part of the Government's commitment to transform the Syariah judiciary."[6] Najib went on to say that "the Government agreed to allocate RM 15 million [around $5 million] to the Family Support Division to *help those in dire straits due to their husbands' failure to abide by Syariah Court orders*" (emphasis mine)—a significant confirmation from the highest office in the land of the view long espoused by Islamic court staff and many others (female and male alike) that (Malay) men in their roles as husbands and fathers are responsible for most of the problems associated with (Malay) marriage and divorce. Najib added that "issues such as the *fight* for custody involving couples from different religions, *battles* over the remains of deceased converts, *disputes* over property inheritance between Muslims and non-Muslims, . . . and multi-million ringgit claims . . . required a high level of expertise and wisdom to resolve" (emphasis mine).

Language highlighting the latter kinds of hot-button interfaith cases and the symbolically laden "fights," "battles," and "disputes" associated with them is in many ways out of keeping with the daily workload and tenor of Islamic courts. Statistically speaking, such cases are so rare as to barely appear in ledgers detailing the relative frequencies of the different kinds of cases that come before the courts, which are oriented toward negotiation, mediation, and compromise in any event, not zero-sum decisions such as images of "battles" and the like often conjure (Peletz 2002; Sharifah Zaleha Syed Hassan and Cederroth 1997). But they are increasingly central to highly fraught public debates and wars of position bearing on the status and scope of syariah in Malaysia. Some of these contests center on whether the ruling party, UMNO (the United Malays National Organization)—ostensibly committed to a broadly construed "civilizational

Islam" (for example, *Islam Hadhari*) that emphasizes the higher objectives and general ethical *geist* or "spirit" of the religion as distinct from the more "syariah-minded" approach associated with the Islamist opposition party, PAS (the Pan-Malaysian Islamic Party)—is doing enough to safeguard the nation's Islamic resources and identity.[7]

Media accounts the next day cited the prime minister's comments that the appointments were "a historic moment" for Malaysia, showing "that women in the country were treated equally as men," and that "Islam does not set limitation[s] for women to advance" (Roslina Mohamad 2010). In the following days, however, the media carried an announcement from Syariah Appeals Court Judge Md Yusup Che Teh that "a panel ... had been set up to discuss the jurisdiction of the two women judges."[8] "Among the concerns raised were the kinds of cases ... [they] could *not* preside over" (emphasis added). "Md Yusup ... said the demarcation of duties ... was not gender discrimination, but based on Islamic rulings that could not be disputed." Yet Md Yusup made no reference to the specific "Islamic rulings" in question: whether they might be found in the Qur'an or *hadith*, for example; in early, medieval, or subsequent Islamic history; or perhaps in recent Malaysian *fatwa*. Nor did he offer any clarification concerning his statement that the Islamic rulings at issue "could not be disputed."

This bald-faced but exceedingly ambiguous assertion was perhaps intended as a reference to passages and positions in the Qur'an and *hadith* that might be subsumed under the category of *muhkam* as distinct from *mutashabih*. *Muhkam* is usually translated as "inherently clear" and intelligible—"beyond doubt, and not susceptible to abrogation," hence "allow[ing] for only one clearly definitive interpretation" and set of juristic opinions—in contrast to *mutashabih*, which pertains to foundational textual phenomena that are "equivocal, ambiguous, susceptible to different interpretations" and a range of different juristic positions (Abou El Fadl 2001, 304, 305). At the same time, Md Yusup's assertion might have been intended (and widely interpreted) as a warning that the government would brook no debate on these matters and that anyone seeking to contest the government's position on such issues would be liable for criminal charges under the state's syariah enactments or the dreaded Internal Security Act (ISA), a thoroughly secular provision from the colonial era that allows for indefinite detention without specific charges or prospect of trial.

The state's manipulation of these kinds of ambiguities is a key component of strategies of governance involving what Comaroff and Comaroff (2005, 30) refer as to "lawfare." Lawfare is typically characterized by a regime's "use of its own rules—of its duly enacted penal codes, its administrative law, its states of emergency, its charters and mandates ... its norms of engagement—to impose a sense of order on its subordinates [and enemies] by means of violence rendered legible, legal, and legitimate by the regime's sovereign word." In Malaysia, tactics of lawfare are not confined to those who are part of the state apparatus but are also commonly deployed by conservative Muslim sectors of civil society to silence groups (such as Sisters in Islam) that are perceived as threatening their values and interests or those of the "race," nation, or global Muslim community (*umat*). Although these strategies build on important historical precedents and thus represent a significant continuity vis-à-vis earlier times, they have become particularly intense in the last decade or so.

The recent appointment of five women as Islamic judges is one of many progressive developments in the syariah juridical field that has occurred in recent years. (Others include both the creation of a Family Support Division to help women and children negotiate the trials and tribulations of divorce and changes in the substance of Islamic family law; see hereafter). The fact remains, however, that at present, women comprise a mere 3.4 percent (5/147) of the nation's Islamic judges. Corresponding estimates for the civil judiciary are far less skewed, suggesting that women comprise around 35–40 percent of the nation's civil court judges.[9] The more gender-equitable distribution of judgeships seen in the civil judiciary is likely to contribute indirectly to the increase of female judges in the Islamic judiciary in the years to come, especially because the political, religious, and specifically legal elites in charge of modernizing the Islamic judiciary are commonly inspired by civil court models and the sensibilities and dispositions associated with them. Put differently, and to underscore a point taken up in due course, the gold standard that informs much of the rationalization and reform of Malaysia's Islamic judiciary is the nation's *civil* judiciary—along with innovations in Alternative Dispute Resolution (ADR) processes, family courts, and psychological counseling from the US, Europe, Australia, and Japan—not syariah-based developments in nations such as Saudi Arabia, Pakistan, Egypt, or Indonesia. This is the case even though Islamization—construed as the heightened salience of Islamic symbols, idioms, discursive traditions, and attendant practices in specifically political arenas and in the realms of personal piety—is a goal that Malaysia's Muslim political and religious elites share with their counterparts in most other Muslim-majority nations.

Corporatization and Other Transformations

Having focused thus far on continuities in the domain of the Islamic judicial establishment since the 1980s, I want to proceed with a discussion of the flip side of the coin—namely, the transformations that have occurred during this period. (Some of the transformations considered here also entail continuities vis-à-vis earlier decades; in certain instances, the distinction between transformations and continuities is as much quantitative as qualitative.) I deal with four related sets of dynamics: the increased salience of common-law models and sensibilities, corporatization and e-governance, the embrace of Japanese systems of management and auditing, and the expanded purview of Islamic law with respect to criminal offenses.

Syariah and Common-Law Sensibilities

Perhaps the single most important point to emphasize about the relationship between syariah and common law in Malaysia is that for many decades, the political, religious, and specifically legal elites who have been centrally involved in reforming the syariah legal system have consciously endeavored to model that system on its far more powerful and eminently more prestigious secular counterpart, Malaysia's civil judiciary, and the common-law traditions inherited from the British colonial era with which that counterpart is inextricably associated (Horowitz 1994; Peletz 2002). This is not to imply that elites have abandoned efforts to enhance the operations and legitimacy of the syariah legal system in specifically Islamic terms. Far from it. Nor am I suggesting that all innovations introduced into the system in recent years, such as the formal mediation processes referred to by the Arabic-origin term *sulh* that were initiated in 2001, are of non-Islamic origin or design (Peletz 2013; Ramizah Wan Muhammad 2008; Sa'odah binti Ahmad 2010). My point about modeling needs to be understood in relative rather than absolute, mutually exclusive terms, especially because virtually all the world's major legal systems are deeply hybrid with respect to the historical origins of their characteristic features and the ways in which these features are currently configured, inflected, legitimized, and contested.[10]

This latter modeling, on the system of civil law, is evident in the Islamic court's greatly increased reliance on written evidence (as distinct from oral testimony) and in its heightened concern with written precedent, reflected partly in the rapid growth in the past few decades of Malay- and English-language academic and professional publications that the nation's Islamic judges and lawyers are expected to read, master, and respect (for example, *Jurnal Hukum, Jurnal Syariah*, the *Shariah Law Journal, Syariah Reports*, the *Malaysian Journal of Syariah and Law*, the *IIUM Law Journal*). This modeling is also apparent in the Islamic courts' tendencies toward more adversarial hearings—partly a function of the recent proliferation in the courts of lawyers—and in the augmented concerns on the part of court officials and lawyers alike with myriad procedures characteristic of the civil judiciary. Such concerns were strikingly obvious both in the nearly 140 motions and hearings that I observed in the syariah courts in Kuala Lumpur, Penang, and Negeri Sembilan during the period 2010–13 (and in the 115 or so civil court cases that I sat in on for comparative purposes in 2012 and 2013) and in the legal documents shared with me during this time. I refer here to procedures for lodging complaints; maintaining order and decorum in the courtroom; generating and handling summons, search and arrest warrants, affidavits, and appeals; discerning what constitutes fact, relevance, burden of proof, and legally salient evidence; delivering and recording judgments; and keeping records and managing paperwork and electronic files more generally. As one knowledgeable scholar recently put it on the basis of her careful study of written documents, the latter procedures "are borrowed wholly from common law, making them almost a carbon copy of laws used in civil (secular) courts" (Maznah Mohamad 2010, 516).

Recent decades have also seen significant shifts toward common-law sensibilities in the substance of family (and other personal status) law administered by Islamic courts even as they have witnessed controversial cases involving the imposition (in some instances commuted) of "Islamic punishments" such as whipping or caning for adultery and the consumption of alcohol. Many of these shifts date from the 1980s and early 1990s and could easily have been reversed since then, but they have become further entrenched. Although technical examples are provided elsewhere (Horowitz 1994; Peletz 2002, n.d.), suffice it to note that several bear on the increasingly restricted legality of men's prerogative to enter into polygynous unions and to effect extrajudicial divorce (via the *talak*/repudiation clause), the more liberal division at divorce of conjugal earnings (*harta sepencarian*), and the expanded grounds for certain kinds of divorce initiated by women, such as *fasakh* ("annulment"). Importantly, such shifts have not occurred in a simple unilinear fashion; rather, they have proceeded in fits and starts and have occasionally been temporarily or partially reversed. In certain instances, moreover, they have seen countervailing or orthogonal developments cast in Islamic frames (Kamali 2000, 12–13, 66–68, 306, 317–18 passim; Norani Othman 2008).

Consider also that in state-sanctioned parlance, Malaysia's Islamic judges are nowadays designated by the generic (Arabic-origin) term for judge or magistrate, *hakim* (sometimes by the more specific *hakim syarie*), whose primary referent in the Malaysian context has long been civil court judges. The more conventional (Arabic-origin) term for Islamic judge, *kadi* (sometimes rendered *qadi, qadzi,* and so forth), which was prevalent (indeed, the preferred signifier) in Malaysia through the 1980s and long before, is no longer in official use.

This bit of sociolinguistic engineering constitutes a striking break both with Islam's classical juridical past, which is inextricably linked with the term *kadi* and vice versa, and with the terminologies and symbolics of Islamic judiciaries in most of the contemporary Muslim world. It reflects official strategies to upgrade the status and prestige of Islamic judges *in relation to civil law judges* in the eyes of the legal–judicial profession and the populace as a whole.[11] Official thinking has it that such upgrades require "rebranding," the term half-jokingly used by a high-ranking member of the syariah judiciary with whom I discussed these matters in 2011. A key feature of this rebranding involves capitalizing on the legitimacy of the civil court system by incorporating various features of that system into the syariah judiciary and divesting Islamic judges of the negative connotations of the term *kadi*—rural, backward, capricious, and irrational— some of which were foregrounded in Max Weber's Orientalist caricatures of "*kadi*-justice" (Weber [1925] 1968).

Corporatization, E-Governance, and the E-Syariah Portal

Thoroughly resonant with the foregoing are the sartorial styles and professional activities and organizations of Islamic judges and syariah lawyers alike. Syariah lawyers (generally known as *peguam syarie*) are increasingly involved in hearings in Islamic courts, as might be expected in light of the rapid growth of the Malay middle class; the greater financial stakes in cases concerning divorce, spousal maintenance, child support, and conjugal earnings (which, taken together, dominate the docket); and the pressures toward bureaucratic specialization, rationalization, and reform spawned by these and attendant developments. Not coincidentally, both syariah lawyers and Islamic judges organize their professional practices and formal associations on civil law models, such as those of the Malaysian Bar Council and Lincoln's Inn. Even in small towns far from the capital, moreover, their professional attire is nowadays exceedingly "corporate" in the smartly tailored Western black-business-suit sense of the term, much like that worn by their colleagues in the civil judiciary, some of whom donned the long white wigs of their English counterparts and former colonizers through the early 1990s. Here, too, we see clear evidence of rebranding that capitalizes on the legitimacy of the civil judiciary.

Terms such as *Islamization*, like the kindred *syariahtization* and *desecularization*, obfuscate these dynamics. They sometimes suggest, or are interpreted to mean, certain kinds of homogeneous (or homogenizing) processes that we think we understand, perhaps out of familiarity with broadly analogous processes in other parts of the Muslim world such as Iran, Pakistan, Afghanistan, or Sudan. Moreover, considering the full range of developments—many of them mutually contradictory—that have occurred in the Islamic judiciaries and national legal systems of these latter nations in recent years (Hefner 2011b; Otto 2010), it is not clear whether Islamization or desecularization are particularly meaningful designations. In any case, they reveal very little about the actual workings of Malaysia's Islamic judiciary or, expanded jurisdictions aside—admittedly no small matter—the directions in which it is moving.

In Malaysia, the relevant dynamics have less to do with one or another variant of Islamization than with contextually variable processes of bureaucratization, rationalization, corporatization, and neoliberal globalization. In light of the scope, force, and overall salience of corporatizing developments in recent decades, I should make clear that my use of the concept of "corporatization" takes as its point of departure the hierarchically authorized models, practices, sensibilities, and dispositions, along with the pecuniary and other values and interests animating and sustaining them, that prevail in upper-level management circles in corporate/capitalist business sectors of Malaysia and beyond. More generally, I am interested in the relative permeation throughout Malaysian society of certain economistic and attendant administrative/managerial principles and ideals, once associated largely with the upper echelons of rational (industrial) capitalism, that have become increasingly hegemonic and "commonsensical," though variably so, across a wide variety of cultural–political and other domains.

In the past two decades, Malaysian authorities, in consultation with international advisors from a variety of fields, have embraced globalized forms of e-governance with a vengeance, much as Mazzarella (2006) has documented for India. Before clarifying e-governance, a fascinating example of "Islamic modern" Malaysian style, I should mention that these advisors hail from corporations such as AT&T, Hewlett Packard, IBM, Motorola, Nippon Telegraph and Telephone, and Sun Microsystems.

The term *e-governance*, like the synonym *e-government* (favored by those who authorize official Malaysian discourse), refers to the use of "high-end, state-of-the-art information and communication technologies to facilitate efficient and effective delivery of government services through . . . [densely networked] electronic delivery channels."[12] E-governance works across—and systematically integrates—the entire spectrum of state agencies; ideally it will enable "citizens to access, transact and obtain any government service via a range of multimedia portals . . . such as phone, PC, . . . and interactive TV" (Muhammad Rais Abdul Karim and Nazariah Mohd Khalid 2003, 54–55). One rationale for developing e-governance is that to remain transnationally competitive, "the business of government" must be continually reinvented, building on "forms of governance" that are "at once stable and predictable yet agile and flexible" (Muhammad Rais Abdul Karim and Nazariah Mohd Khalid 2003, 2). This move is squarely embedded in ideologies of "high modernity," which James Scott (1998, 4) characterizes in terms of "a self-confidence about scientific and technical progress" and "the rational design of social order commensurate with the scientific understanding of natural laws." According to the latter logic, "if the future is viewed as a scientific and technological puzzle, then E-Government will be the integral interlocking piece that completes the picture, at least for now" (Muhammad Rais Abdul Karim and Nazariah Mohd Khalid 2003, 3).

Malaysia's commitment to e-governance is a central entailment of former prime minister Mahathir's Vision 2020, launched in 1991, which aimed to ensure that Malaysia would join the ranks of fully industrialized nations by the year 2020. As part of this commitment, Mahathir (r. 1981–2003) poured resources into what is known as the Multi-Media Super Corridor (MSC). The MSC is a zone of high-tech development fifty kilometers long and twenty kilometers wide, extending from Kuala Lumpur's City Center in the north to the Kuala Lumpur International Airport in the south; it includes Putrajaya (the government's administrative capital, containing offices for more than 40,000 federal employees) and Cyberjaya (a massive IT-themed town with a science park and university complexes at its core). Sometimes characterized as a mélange of Silicon Valley and Hollywood, the MSC is a key component of the government's strategy to create "a technology-literate . . . workforce that can perform in a global environment and use Information Age tools to support a knowledge-based economy" (Muhammad Rais Abdul Karim and Nazariah Mohd Khalid 2003, 32). E-governance, for its part, is promoted as "the crown jewel of the MSC," though one should add that according to some scholars (Bunnell 2004), the MSC has fallen far short of government expectations.

In 2002, as part of the e-governance initiative, authorities rolled out an extremely sophisticated, visually stunning, and highly interactive E-Syariah Portal. The E-Syariah Portal was created with a number of specific goals in mind (in addition to the general objectives of e-governance noted earlier). One goal is to enable Islamic judges, lawyers, auditors, and others to code, classify, manage, and track cases and their outcomes electronically, thereby reducing the notorious backlog of suits and allaying widespread criticisms along the lines of "justice delayed is justice denied." Another objective of the E-Syariah Portal is to facilitate officials' efforts to amass reliable information on the whereabouts and financial resources of litigants and other "persons of interest" to the Islamic judiciary and to the police and others who help them develop their databases.

The E-Syariah Portal is also designed to disseminate legal forms and other information to members of the public, designated in official literature as "users," "customers," "citizen-users," and "change targets." Users can surf the sites accessible through the E-Syariah Portal to obtain details of syariah lawyers registered with the system, along with lists of the different types of civil and criminal cases handled by the Islamic judiciary. Users can also access information relevant to the state-specific statutory laws that bear on each type of case, activating links to passages from the Qur'an and *hadith* that officials have selected to provide authoritative religious rationales for the statutory laws and relevant punishments in question. In addition, the portal prominently displays the exact times at which Muslims are called to prayer each day. One of the reigning ideas is that the portal will serve modern Muslims' needs in much the same way as a "one-stop shopping center."

The E-Syariah Portal is thus equipped with critically important pedagogical, legitimizing, and regulating tools. These tools are geared, on the one hand, toward encouraging technological and digital literacy and, on the other, toward enhancing surveillance, discipline, and control. Not surprisingly, the latter goals are omitted from official pronouncements, which are cast in discourses of reform that "promise and pledge" to "revise and streamline Islamic law" and its administration, to clarify the "visions, missions, and (quality) objectives" of the courts, and to "manage complaints and advice within 14 days of their receipt." According to spokesmen in the Prime Minister's Department, the more encompassing E-Syariah Project aims to "introduc[e] administrative reforms to upgrade the quality of services of the Syariah Courts by enhancing the effectiveness of the Islamic Justice Department . . . in coordinating and monitoring its respective agencies and to improve the productivity and efficiency of the Syariah Courts management nationwide" (Muhammad Rais Abdul Karim and Nazariah Mohd Khalid 2003, 78–79). Rather hard to miss is the global management-speak suffusing these kinds of official overviews, and the fact, quite familiar to most readers in these neoliberal times, that "good governance is . . . [made] synonymous with sound development management" (Rittich 2001, 932).

Japanese Management and Auditing

More recently, we have seen evidence of an extension or revival of Mahathir's Look East policy of the early 1980s, which included government and corporate efforts to use Japanese management techniques in local industrial production so as to encourage continued Japanese investment and inculcate Malay employees with a version of the Japanese work ethic. I refer to the fact that the syariah judiciary *and the governmental apparatus in its entirety* have adopted Japanese systems of corporate management and financial auditing. This has involved launching widely advertised campaigns that emphasize the 5Ss—in Japanese *seiri, seiton, seiso, seiketsu,* and *shitsuke;* in Malay: *sisih, susun, sapu, seragam,* and *sentiasa amal;* in English *sort, set in order, shine, standardize,* and *sustain.* These euphemisms do not do justice to the goals or demands of the campaign, which, like others of its sort, aims to encourage new modalities of self-management, ethical engagement, and "social awareness" (of one's self, one's work habits, one's coworkers, and one's workplace) so as to better discipline, motivate, and govern Muslim and other Malaysian citizen–subjects; enhance their efficiency, productivity, personal accountability, and global competitiveness; and help guide the nation to a more prosperous and secure future (see also Rudnyckyj 2010).

When I visited the Islamic court in Kuala Lumpur in the (northern) summers of 2010 and 2011, the campaign was in full swing. The walls of the registrar's office, for example, were adorned not only with the usual photographs of the prime minister, the king, and the queen but also with plaques bearing beautiful calligraphic renderings of the words *Allah* and *Muhammad* and flow charts depicting the organization of the court hierarchy and the stages involved in processing cases. They also featured prominent wall hangings celebrating and explicating the new Japanese system of management and auditing, some enumerating the 5Ss in both Japanese (a language unintelligible to virtually all Malaysians) and Malay. In their backstage offices, moreover, various members of the judiciary were wearing jackets emblazoned with the 5S logo. Others thumbed through, carried around, or had within easy reach official guidebooks for implementing the 5S system, such as *Panduan Amalan 5S Sektor Awam*, the *5S Practice Guide for the Civil Service* (Government of Malaysia 2010); these included glossy color photographs illustrating the proper way to maintain one's bulletin boards, filing cabinets, surge protectors, and toilets. The more expansive goal is to ascertain how best to manage and audit the workflow, overall operations, and "outcomes" of the syariah judiciary and otherwise provide the public with the quality of service demanded by Total Quality Management (TQM) protocols and the International Organization for Standardization (ISO). The ISO is, for many Malaysian policymakers, the ultimate arbiter of an ever proliferating range of standards and more encompassing normativities for business, government, society, and culture alike, as is readily apparent to anyone who has recently spent time in Malaysian universities, government offices, bookstores, or other venues associated with the production or dissemination of official or public culture.

Because this Japanese-inflected corporatizing development dates from 2010, systematic assessment of its effects might thus be premature. Quite likely, however, it will affect employee productivity and morale, courtroom procedures, and dealings with the public in some of the same general ways as studies collected in Marilyn Strathern's edited book *Audit Cultures* (2000) described for broadly analogous dynamics in the United Kingdom, Greece, New Zealand, and elsewhere. One common theme in these cases is that they typically involve "coercive accountability" on the part of those subject to rapidly proliferating audit regimes. Limited resources (time, money, intellectual capital) associated with the provisioning of vital services are subject to compulsory reallocation so as to meet one-size-fits-all assessment protocols based on top-down corporate business models that are patently ill suited to many of the extrabusiness contexts in which they are unilaterally imposed. Another common theme is the diffuse, enduring alienation experienced by employees who feel their relative autonomy and authority to make informed judgments about the services they provide has been seriously compromised by bottom-line corporate considerations masked in discourses focusing on efficient time–space management or lofty ethical imperatives.

This is precisely what we see in Malaysia's civil courts: The fetishization of key performance indicators (KPIs) has become a tyranny for judges and lawyers alike, litigants (especially plaintiffs) being the most disadvantaged (Whiting 2011). Should we see similar developments on the Islamic side (one syariah judge told me that they are already evident in the syariah lower courts), the major losers could well be women, who, unlike men, are heavily dependent on the courts (hence the state) to negotiate their relationships with their spouses. On the other hand, the setting of timetables and other goals for the resolution of disputes may prove to be a huge plus for women, who in previous years have faced lengthy delays and other obstacles in their efforts to obtain justice.

Even if systematic assessments of the effects of runaway audit culture in the syariah judiciary are premature, the other dynamics alluded to here have been evident for decades now and merit serious consideration. Some of them raise politically sensitive questions about the ontological status of present-day Malaysian syariah. One question has to do with the bureaucratized, corporatized, positivized syariah that exists in contemporary Malaysia: Does this form of syariah have any organic or other connection with the pre- and early modern variants of syariah that, in addition to being community-based, were thoroughly grounded in local cultural conventions and "*ijtihad*ic hermeneutics," as scholars such as Wael Hallaq (2009), addressing the Muslim world as a whole, have discussed with such insight and clarity? The question is an exceedingly important one in Malaysia and elsewhere in light of heavily freighted debates bearing on what is authentically (or quintessentially) Islamic, what roles one or another conceptualization of syariah should play in the nation at present and in the years to come, and who is qualified to engage these debates (Peletz 2005; 2013; n.d.; Zainah Anwar 2001; see also this volume, chapters 1 and 2). Suffice it to add that as far as most ordinary Malays are concerned, "[e]ach of the laws and procedures applied in the [nation's] shari'a courts is clearly stated in the Qur'an," and that this kind of popular legal consciousness seriously thwarts efforts by feminists (such as SIS) and other nonstate actors to critically engage the ways in which the state has configured the syariah juridical field and the legally codified norms of the syariah courts in particular (Moustafa 2013, 179–80 passim).

Criminality and Creeping Criminalization

In addition to seeing corporatizing trends of various kinds, the past few decades have also witnessed successful efforts by Malay political and religious elites to augment the criminal jurisdiction and penal power of the Islamic judiciary to encompass nearly everything that might be construed as involving the religious or moral comportment of Muslims. A critical caveat is that this is exclusive of offenses lying squarely within the jurisdiction of the civil courts such as theft, murder, stock market fraud, drug trafficking, illegal assembly, and the like, all of which are already heavily criminalized and far more severely punishable than in times past.

This turn resonates with the popular normative and ethical trend, well documented for urban Malays, whereby concerns with the binaries of *halal* and *haram* (that which Allah permits and forbids, respectively) have increasingly filtered into all areas of public and private life, such that "more and more is taken in, valorised, and then subjected to a normative halal/haram judgment" (Fischer 2008, 30). This is not to suggest, however, that most urban (or rural) Malays necessarily lend their unequivocal support to all state strategies involving criminalization in the name of Islam. The sentiments, dispositions, and ethical orientations of ordinary Malays (as distinct from political and religious elites and those at the forefront of social movements) have long been more pluralistic than those associated with advocates of Islamization, state-sponsored or otherwise (Peletz 1997; 2002). That said, the robust (but graduated) pluralism associated with "traditional" Malay culture has become increasingly constricted, as evidenced partly by the heightened cultural centrality of *halal/haram* binaries. In short, state strategies of the sort outlined here have clearly affected the ethical imaginaries of ordinary Malays and other Muslims (even as they have built on longstanding cultural precedents), just as they have contributed to ethnic and religious polarization throughout the nation (Lee 2010; Liow 2009; Norani Othman, Puthucheary, and Kessler 2008; Peletz 2009).

Before delving into matters of criminality, it is essential to distinguish between the kinds of criminal cases (*kes jenayah*) that the syariah judiciary is currently empowered to deal with but does not engage on a regular basis, on the one hand, and those that it commonly adjudicates, on the other. Both sets of cases are important to consider, but they should not be confused. One reason for this is that the greatly expanded scope of religious, moral, and other offenses subject to the jurisdiction of the Islamic courts has not had an appreciable affect on the everyday practices, caseload, litigant base, or overall tenor of the courts, which are among my main concerns in this chapter. The enhanced purview is nonetheless significant in terms of the cultural–political atmosphere, including relations between Muslims and non-Muslims, as well as the directions that assemblages of religion, law, and governance are moving.[13] Let us first consider with what kinds of criminal cases the Islamic courts typically deal.

According to the JKSM, the vast majority (more than 98 percent) of criminal cases that came before the nation's Islamic courts during the period 2011–12 fell into one or another of fifteen official categories. In table 10.1 I present the relevant categories, followed by the number of cases and the percentage for each category in relation to the total number of these cases, listing them in descending order of frequency.

"Illicit proximity" (*khalwat*), involving a man and a woman who are not married to one another (and who are not *muhrim* [barred from intermarriage by genealogical considerations]) being alone in a secluded or confined locale, is by far the most common criminal offense handled by the syariah judiciary. Nearly 13,000 new charges of *khalwat* were lodged during the period 2011–12,

Table 10.1. Major Types and Number of Criminal Offenses Handled by Malaysia's Syariah Courts, 2011–12*

Rank	Offense	Number	Frequency
1	"Illicit Proximity" (*khalwat*)	12,740	36.9%
2	Marriage offense with respect to part II of the Islamic family law [enactment] (*berkahwin bersalahan dengan bahagian dua undang-undang keluarga Islam*)	6,520	18.9%
3	Divorce without the permission of the court (*perceraian tanpa kebenaran mahkamah*)	3,207	9.3%
4	Polygamy [polygyny] without the permission of the court (*poligami tanpa kebenaran mahkamah*)	2,282	6.6%
5	Activities that are inappropriate in public places (*perbuatan tidak sopan di tempat awam*)	2,181	6.3%
6	Collusion, being an accomplice/collaborator (*subahat*)	1,911	5.5%
7	Fornication/Adultery (*bersetubuh luar nikah*, lit. "coupling/coitus/copulation outside of marriage")	1,369	4.0%
8	Gambling (*berjudi*)	1,067	3.1%
9	Not appearing before the NCR Registrar [Registrar of Marriage, Divorce, Reconciliation] (*tidak hadir di hadapan pendaftar NCR*)	1,061	3.1%
10	Out of wedlock pregnancy (*hamil luar nikah*)	1,058	3.1%
11	Not respecting Ramadan (*tidak menghormati Ramadan*)	382	1.1%
12	[Drinking] intoxicating beverages (*minuman yang memabukkan*)	325	0.9%
13	Failing to file a report regarding the Islamic family law [enactment] (*tidak membuat laporan berkaitan undang-undang keluarga Islam*)	153	0.4%
14	Teaching [religion] without certification (*mengajar tanpa tauliah*)	152	0.4%
15	A male posing or behaving as a female (*lelaki berlagak perempuan*)	121	0.4%

* N = 34,529. Source: Malaysian Department of Syariah Judiciary.

nearly twice the number of the second most common type of criminality to come before the Islamic courts: "marriage offenses with respect to part II of the Islamic family law [enactment]," which tend to involve marriages that were "nonregisterable" either because they were not solemnized properly or because they violated the minimum age or consent requirements for one or both parties.

Consider also that cases of *khalwat* are more than nine times as frequent as those involving charges of fornication/adultery, formerly referred to as *zina*. This is partly because *khalwat* is much easier to prove and is in some ways more obvious than fornication/adultery, requiring only one or more credible witnesses to the couple's having been alone in a secluded or confined locale (or other relevant evidence), as opposed to either a witness who actually observed sexual relations of the illicit sort at issue here or evidence of other varieties, such as an out-of-wedlock pregnancy.

I was curious why the Malay expression *bersetubuh luar nikah* (coupling/copulation outside of marriage) has increasingly replaced the more conventional Arabic-origin *zina* in official discourse bearing on fornication/adultery. According to a high-ranking member of the JKSM with whom I discussed these matters in 2010, the main reason is that "We don't have *hudud* laws here." This is a shorthand reference to a complicated religious/legal/political nexus—specifically that *zina* is an offense falling under the Qur'anic rubric of *hudud* law (along with theft, highway robbery, intoxication, apostasy, and false accusations concerning *zina*); that *hudud* laws have never been implemented in Malaysia, despite efforts by political and religious elites in Kelantan, Terengganu, and elsewhere to have them introduced; and that if they had been implemented in accordance with widespread interpretations of Qur'anic jurisprudence, their infraction could result in 100 lashes for fornication that does not involve adultery and in death by stoning for adultery. Because these particular sanctions (100 lashes, death by stoning) do not exist in Malaysia, the syariah judiciary has good reasons to formally avoid using the term *zina*, even though it was the term of choice for the offenses in question until quite recently and is still found in some official publications. Significantly, although this instance of sociolinguistic engineering is motivated partly by concerns to ensure that the Islamic judiciary avoids inconsistencies with classical syariah, it nonetheless involves jettisoning a terminological cornerstone of the classical jurisprudential tradition. We have seen that a similar scrapping has occurred with the recent rebranding of Islamic judges as *hakim*, for this has entailed relegating the term *kadi*, a key symbol in and of Islamic jurisprudence since the time of the Prophet, to the dustbins of Malaysian history.

Both types of offense (*khalwat*, *bersetubuh luar nikah*) involve heterosexual couples, as do activities that are inappropriate in public places (holding hands, hugging, kissing). Same-sex couples believed to have engaged in sexual transgression are not charged with any of these offenses and do not typically come before the Islamic courts in any event. Rather, if charged with a crime, they are hauled before the *civil* courts, in some instances under Section 377 of the National Penal Code, which provides for imprisonment up to twenty years and whipping for any acts, whether or not consensual, of "carnal intercourse against the order of nature"[14]—this even though the Islamic courts are authorized to deal with cases of *liwat* (sodomy).[15]

More generally, the three types of syariah criminality that I mention at the outset of the previous paragraph represent 47.2 percent of the criminal cases heard by the Islamic courts during 2011–12. Taken collectively, cases involving marriage offenses with respect to Part II of the Islamic Family Law Enactment, divorce without the court's permission, polygamy without the court's permission, collusion, and gambling constitute another 43.4 percent of the court's workload during that period. In short, more than 90 percent of the court's criminal caseload centers on these eight categories of offense.

Two of the six infractions (illicit proximity, fornication/adultery) have long been designated as syariah crimes. Items on the top-eight list that have come to be defined as criminal behaviors since the early 1980s include activities that are inappropriate in public places, collusion (for example, in facilitating an illegal marriage or another type of criminality), divorce or polygamy without the court's permission, and gambling, the first two of which are exceedingly vague and for this reason alone of great concern to women's groups, human rights organizations, and others wary of moral policing by the state or conservative sectors of Muslim society. Items on the more expansive list of fifteen criminal offenses that are new include "a male behaving or posing as a female," which is also quite vague and problematic.

Charges against males posing or behaving as females are rarely brought before the syariah judiciary: There were only 121 newly registered lawsuits involving accusations of this sort during the period 2011–12, compared to more than 25,000 suits involving alleged infractions of heterosexual (including marriage/divorce) codes, more than 1,000 instances of reported gambling, and nearly 200,000 civil suits in the syariah courts during the same period. Such charges pertain to transgressions of gender codes (dressing as a female, for example), not those bearing on sexual activity per se, though some *mak nyah* (the general term for male-bodied individuals who consider themselves to be "females born/trapped in male bodies" and who typically dress in women's attire) sometimes engage in prostitution with normatively gendered males to support themselves and are thus involved in homosexual relations. Men who dress or behave as women are also liable to be charged in the civil judiciary (for example, for creating a public nuisance or "outraging decency"). More generally, they are more likely to encounter difficulties with the police than with authorities directly associated with the syariah judiciary, though it is also true that investigators associated with other state religious bureaucracies (such as JAWI and JAIS)[16] appear to initiate many of the cases against *mak nyah* through raids on the venues they frequent, following which they turn their investigations over to the police or to officials in the syariah judicial establishment for processing. Police, I might add, usually deal with them extrajudicially—that is, by harassing, arresting, detaining, humiliating, and sometimes assaulting them, then letting them go without bringing formal charges against them.

Alternately, feminized males who are of middle-school age might be shipped off to "reeducation centers" to be toughened up and otherwise resocialized in accordance with increasingly narrow and martial notions of Malay masculinity. Official concerns with the prevalence in high schools and college settings of "soft males" (*lelaki lembut*) are so pronounced that in the early years of the new millennium, the International Islamic University of Malaysia sponsored an elaborate research project to investigate this highly visible phenomenon on its own campus and to target those who "deliberately become effeminates" (as distinct from "genetically effeminate males," about whom much less can be done) so as to "eliminate their sexual identity confusion" and "protect society" (Noraini Mohd Noor et al. 2005). As discussed elsewhere (Peletz 1996; 2009), ordinary Malays have long been far more generous in their dealings with male-bodied gender transgression than these initiatives suggest. One of the larger issues is that ordinary Malays have long practiced and espoused a relatively inclusive and progressive Islam; another is that when it comes to gender and many other areas, there is a good deal of tension between ordinary ethical sensibilities and dispositions on the one hand and authorized or authorizing legal and ethical discourses on the other.[17]

There are currently no laws on the books stipulating that a female behaving or posing as male constitutes a syariah offense (except in the state of Perlis [Tan Beng Hui 2012, 63]). But this may not be true for long in the current cultural–political climate and considering that 2008 saw the National Fatwa Council (*Majlis Fatwa Kebangsaan*), made up of *mufti* and `ulama representing the entire federation, issue a condemnation of *pengkids* ("tomboys": females dressing or behaving like males). "Sexual relations between female persons" (*musahaqah*) is already listed as a syariah crime, having been designated as such since the moral panics of the mid-to-late 1990s. Like *liwat*, it is currently punishable in the syariah courts of some states by a fine of up to 5,000 *ringgit*, imprisonment up to three years, or whipping with up to six strokes of a rattan cane. According to my sources in the JKSM, no women have ever been charged under these provisions in Malaysia's Islamic courts. Women believed guilty of infractions of the sort at issue here are sometimes dealt with in other venues (for example, the civil courts) and, far more commonly, by other, usually less formal means—teasing, gossip, ostracism, police harassment, and the like—as are males who are held to be involved in gender transgression or same-sex relations.

As we are now addressing syariah crimes that are rarely if ever adjudicated by the Islamic judiciary but that are nonetheless of great symbolic and political import, it bears repeating that we need to distinguish between the types of infractions that commonly come before the courts, on the one hand, and those with which the courts are empowered to deal but that they do not usually address, on the other. An additional, and a twofold, point to reiterate is that the past few decades have seen vastly expanded definitions of what kinds of behavior constitute syariah criminality, something that bodes ill for Malaysians (Muslims and non-Muslims alike) as the nation's exceedingly top-heavy executive branch increasingly uses whatever resources it has available to stifle dissent and otherwise neutralize its real and imagined adversaries and critics.

The greatly augmented jurisdictions and penal powers of the Islamic courts now cover more than seventy different types of criminal offenses. This number is sure to grow in the years ahead. The sanctions the courts are empowered to impose for such crimes will in all likelihood be increased in severity as well, as has been the trend in recent decades. Some of these crimes are relatively unambiguous and are not new, such as failing to perform Friday prayers and disrespecting Ramadan. Others, many of which are of recent provenance, are highly ambiguous (or at least potentially so) thanks to the government's insistence on monopolistic definitions and "state simplifications" (Scott 1998), which are not usually explicit and which do in fact change over time—but that are not necessarily clearly broadcast in advance or even after the fact—of what constitutes acceptable Islamic doctrine and ritual practice. That said, Shi'ite, especially Iranian Shi'ite, teachings and practices are definitely out, at least for Malays (but not necessarily for Muslims of presumed Shi'ite/Pakistani background), and groups such as Darul Arqam and Ayah Pin's Sky Kingdom are banned as "deviationist," as are various Sufi *tariqat*, despite the absence in the Qur'an of any clear basis for deviationism (An-Na'im 1999).

The current list of syariah criminal offenses includes wrongful worship; teaching false doctrine; the propagation of religious doctrines other than Islam among Muslims; making false religious claims; insulting or bringing into contempt the religion of Islam; deriding Qur'an verses or *hadith*; printing, publishing, producing, or disseminating material contrary to Islamic law; instigating neglect of religious duty; teaching or professing religion without a *tauliah*; expressing contempt or defiance of religious authorities; defying a syariah court order; expressing an opinion contrary to *fatwa*; instigating a husband or wife to neglect spousal duties or to divorce; indecent acts in a public place; gender-transgressive behavior on the part of males; same-sex relations involving either males or females; and collusion, as we have seen. This list is far from exhaustive, but it should suffice to convey a sense of how political and religious elites have endeavored to position the Islamic judiciary to better discipline and control Muslims and others in Malaysia and ostensibly help guide them to a more secure and prosperous future.

There are important ironies here worthy of brief consideration. Ever since Malaysia achieved its independence in 1957, national-level political and religious elites associated with the ruling party (UMNO) have promoted what Robert Hefner (2011a) refers to as a broadly "ethicalized" Islam and have been at pains to distinguish this orientation from the more legalistic, syariah-minded policies championed by the Islamist opposition party, PAS. The UMNO approach has long been keyed to expansively cast moral principals: "faith and piety in Allah; a just and trustworthy government; a free and independent people; . . . vigorous pursuit and mastery of knowledge; . . . balanced and comprehensive economic development; . . . protection of the rights of minority groups and women; cultural and moral integrity," and so forth (see note 7). In theory, UMNO's approach contrasts sharply with that of PAS, which has tended to focus on the virtues and necessity of implementing narrowly defined legal codes (for example, *hudud* laws) and on other such legalistic fixes as revamping the federal constitution so that the Qur'an and the *Sunna* constitute its core. One irony is that UMNO's twin commitment to the instantiation of broadly construed ethical values and to being both different from and better than PAS also entails a strong commitment to syariahtization (in the form of creeping criminalization as well as landmark concessions to the syariah courts regarding their jurisdiction in hot-button cases involving the abjuration of Islam, interfaith couples, and the proper burial of those whose late-life conversion to Islam is in dispute),[18] albeit of a contrasting—"kinder, gentler," and more gradual—sort than that proposed by its nemesis. A second and related irony is that as different groups (particularly UMNO, PAS, and their respective supporters) spar over the pros, cons, and interpretations of various legal initiatives and symbolics bearing on syariah, the underlying ethical considerations and attendant political implications, including not least for the nation's non-Muslims, are sometimes eclipsed or altogether ignored, much like the situation in Pakistan described by Zaman (this volume, chapter 8). As one Chinese Malaysian lawyer commented: "PAS has put the frog into the pot of hot boiling water. UMNO put the frog in the pot and then boiled the water. Either way we're going to get burned" (cited in Lee 2010, 89).

Conclusion

In this chapter I have examined selected continuities and transformations in Malaysia's Islamic judiciary since the 1980s. Continuities in gender, power, and prestige are quite striking, as we have seen. So, too, are transformations in the discourses and practices of the courts. Bureaucratization, rationalization, and corporatization are, in my view, the most relevant glosses for these latter dynamics, particularly if we focus on the quotidian operations of the courts and the types of suits that usually come before them, the kinds of cultural logics typically at play when they dispose of cases, the manner in which they manage and audit their workload and "products," and the general directions—emphasis on the plural—in which the judiciary as a whole is moving (Peletz 2002, n.d.).

The trope of Islamization is of course highly salient as well. It is nonetheless essential to bear in mind that modeling the Islamic courts on the nation's far more powerful and eminently more prestigious system of civil courts and its common-law practices has in most contexts been seen as more pressing than the need to enhance the operations or legitimacy of the syariah judiciary in specifically Islamic terms. A partial exception to this generalization is (perhaps) the expansion of the jurisdiction and penal power of the Islamic judiciary with respect to criminal matters—which, not coincidentally, is thoroughly entangled with creeping criminalization in private and public arenas subject to civil law. The two sets of historically specific dynamics—Islamization and the increased relevance of common law in the syariah judiciary—should not be construed as mutually exclusive or inherently contradictory, though paradoxes and ironies abound. Donald Horowitz (1994) made this incisively clear based on research undertaken in the early 1990s. Others, focusing on the twenty years since Horowitz's research—a period that could have seen developments at sharp odds with Horowitz's findings but that did not—have reached broadly analogous conclusions (Maznah Mohamad 2010; Peletz 2002, n.d.).

Throughout the past few decades, Malaysia's political, economic, and religious elites have been deeply (but often ambivalently) committed to a variant of neoliberal globalization. This has necessarily entailed embracing processes of corporatization and a host of others that are not of direct concern here, such as the privatization of enterprises, activities, and resources formerly owned or managed by the state (related to healthcare, education, transportation, water supply, and the like [Jomo 1995; Tan 2008]). I have already noted that my use of the term *corporatization* draws attention to the models, practices, and sensibilities that prevail in upper-level management circles in corporate/capitalist business sectors in Malaysia and beyond. More generally, I am interested in the relative permeation throughout Malaysian society of economistic and attendant administrative/ managerial principles and ideals, once associated largely with the upper echelons of rational (industrial) capitalism, that have become increasingly hegemonic across a wide variety of social, cultural–political, and other domains. Indices of these trends include Japanese management and auditing regimes, ISO protocols, and the fetishization of KPIs in the civil judiciary, universities, and elsewhere, as well as the spectacular growth of industries centered around *halal* food and body care products (Fischer 2008), Islamic management, banking, and finance, and syariah compliance in the workplace (Sloane-White 2011a; 2011b). Worthy of mention as well is the popularity of Indonesian-origin organizations such as ESQ (Emotional and Spiritual Quotient), which meld together Islamic doctrine and spirituality, Western management sciences, and pop psychology discourses of self-development (Rudnyckyj 2010; see also Hoesterey 2008). Founded by Dr. Ary Ginanjar Agustian, ESQ regularly hosts lavishly choreographed multimedia-enhanced training sessions at upscale hotels in Kuala Lumpur and beyond, selectively targeting upper-level management personnel, parents, teens, and others; the organization boasts nearly 80,000 members ("alumni") in Malaysia and more than 1 million worldwide.

In these latter initiatives we see a clear commodification and rebranding of Islam—as procorporate/capitalist development, friendly to common-law sensibilities, and otherwise modern, progressive, and this-worldly. No "clash of civilizations" here! This rebranding is strikingly evident in the Islamic judiciary, which authorities are marketing by means of (*inter alia*) densely networked sites in cyberspace; DVDs, books, journals, and other media products; and gifts to conference attendees, visiting dignitaries, curious anthropologists, and others that include glossy brochures, notepads, ballpoint pens, traveling coffee mugs, and colorful, sturdy tote bags variably embellished with the Islamic judiciary's corporate logos and trademarks. As Malaysia further cements its ties to the "power/knowledge networks of global capitalism" (Zuern 2010, 201), it increasingly resembles a gigantic emporium where everything is being merchandized, albeit not necessarily for enhanced market share in the narrow sense of the term. Contests for legitimacy, which are never fully settled, clearly require strategic marketing as well.

I do not want to conclude this chapter on a discouraging or depressing note, especially because some readers may find certain of the foregoing perspectives to be rather dark in a Weberian or Foucauldian sense. Instead I want to stay upbeat, emphasizing an exceedingly important point taken up in more detail elsewhere (Peletz 2005) concerning the vast majority of the struggles that are currently being waged in Malaysia over Islam and other key symbols and institutional resources—including contestations between Malays and non-Malays, as well as those associated with rivalries and fault lines within the *umat*, most members of which advocate a broadly cast civilizational Islam (though not necessarily *Islam Hadhari* per se; see note 7) as distinct from a more narrow, legalistic syariah-mindedness that is popular in some quarters, especially among supporters of PAS. Indeed, in the Malaysian setting, in sharp contrast to what we have recently seen in various quarters of the Muslim world (for example, Algeria, Tunisia, Egypt, Libya, Syria, and Mali), these contests are taking place in relatively democratic and largely peaceful ways, not through disappearances, torture, assassinations, suicide or other bombings, large-scale uprisings, coups d'état, or vigilante campaigns of stoning, amputation, and maiming. More specifically, they are occurring through elections that are often (but not always) relatively free and fair; passage of constitutional amendments and other legislation; court battles (some of which clearly involve lawfare); weekly seminars and educational outreach; legitimate lobbying and merchandizing efforts; PR blitzes; letters to the editors of local newspapers; electronic media, including, of course, the largely ungovernable internet; and a myriad of academic and nonacademic seminars and public fora, some explicitly designed to make provision for disparate voices and variously defined subalterns.

It is also true that state-sponsored Islamization is by some criteria more "extreme" in Malaysia than in Saudi Arabia, Iran, Pakistan, and the Sudan, to take a handful of relatively well-studied examples. I use "extreme" not to describe state imposition of *hudud* laws or support of public executions or the obligatory seclusion of women—there is none of this in Malaysia—but in the twofold sense that the state and other institutions of governmentality have not only gone to great lengths to homogenize Islamic sensibilities and dispositions but have also been relatively (some might say remarkably) successful in doing so.[19]

Indeed, by certain measures, legal and other developments bearing on syariah in Malaysia might be said to be moving in the opposite direction as those in Saudi Arabia, widely regarded by outside observers as being far more homogenous, intolerant, and repressive than Malaysia and forever committed to staying the course. Saudi Arabia has recently witnessed a relative flowering, in legal, political, religious, and lay circles, of pluralistic sentiments and dispositions concerning beliefs and practices long considered heretical by Saudi authorities, such as those of Shi`as and Sufis. The astonishing emergence in recent years of new forms of marriage known as *misyar* and *sadiq*, the latter of which was "developed for young people not [financially] established enough for conventional marriage, . . . [enabling] them to meet for sexual relations from time to time" (Vogel 2011, 85) is also worthy of note, especially since there is nothing comparable on the horizon in Malaysia, where religious authorities invest ever greater resources in policing the boundaries of conventional (Muslim) marriage and carefully regulating all varieties of sexual relations. Frank Vogel's incisive research indicates that "Saudis appear to feel, both individually and civilly, a new sense of power and initiative to treat directly with the meanings and legitimacies of shari`a" and to do so "without waiting for or depending on the state or even establishment scholars" (Vogel 2011, 60). Dynamics such as these incline him and others (for example, Hefner 2011a, 28–29; Okruhlik 2005) to a guarded optimism concerning the development of new subjectivities in the Saudi context and perhaps "the emergence, even, of a Habermasian-type 'public sphere'" (Vogel 2011, 88).

It may seem anomalous in light of Malaysia's tremendous economic successes and its burgeoning and increasingly well-educated Malay middle classes that there has been relatively little opposition, ambivalence, or publicly elaborated alternatives vis-à-vis state-sponsored Islamization, at least among Malays.[20] The anomalies are less striking when one considers that ever since the Melaka Sultanate (1400–1511), Malays have tended to view the state as the protector of their interests, priorities, and ethical wellsprings—including, most notably, (Malayan)

Islam—in the face of real and imagined threats from rival groups of Muslims as well as Chinese, Indians, and other non-Muslims (Muzaffar 1979). Another related issue is that Malay criticism of those who cast themselves as stewards of the nation's Islamic resources and identity is often construed by fellow Malays as "letting down the [ethnic/racial/religious] side." This is a grave ethical breach akin to the offense of treason (*derhaka*), which has long been linked in Malay mythology with both incest and cannibalism, the most heinous crimes imaginable. For reasons such as these, and because so many Malays have recently attained middle-class status and are understandably reluctant to jeopardize all they have gained by their rallying against the very state whose policies have helped them garner their new class standings, Malay opposition to the homogenization entailed in state-sponsored Islamization—and to the kinds of excesses commonly associated with top-heavy executive branches—is less pronounced than one might expect, though it certainly exists. More generally, the constellation of variables outlined here makes Malaysia somewhat of a special case among other Muslim-majority nations but not at all unusual in a theme-and-variation sense.

References

Abdullah Ahmad Badawi. 2006. *Islam Hadhari: A Model Approach for Development and Progress.* Petaling Jaya: MPH Publishing.

Abou El Fadl, Khaled. 2001. *Speaking in God's Name: Islamic Law, Authority and Women.* Oxford: Oneworld.

Ahmad Hidayat Buang. 2007. "Islamic Contracts in a Secular Court Setting? Lessons from Malaysia." *Arab Law Quarterly* 21:317–40.

Ali, Kecia. 2006. *Sexual Ethics and Islam: Feminist Reflections on Qur'an, Hadith, and Jurisprudence.* Oxford: Oneworld.

An-Na'im, Abdullahi. 1999. "The Cultural Mediation of Human Rights: The *Al-Arqam* Case in Malaysia." In *The East Asian Challenge for Human Rights*, edited by Joanne Bauer and Daniel Bell, 147–68. New York: Cambridge University Press.

Bunnell, Timothy. 2004. *Malaysia, Modernity, and the Multimedia Super Corridor: A Critical Geography of Intelligent Landscapes.* Abingdon, UK: Routledge Curzon.

Comaroff, John L., and Jean Comaroff. 2005. "Law and Order in the Postcolony: An Introduction." In *Law and Disorder in the Postcolony*, edited by Jean Comaroff and John L. Comaroff, 1–56. Chicago: University of Chicago Press.

El-Rouayheb, Khaled. 2005. *Before Homosexuality in the Arab-Islamic World, 1500–1800.* Chicago: University of Chicago Press.

Farish Noor. 2005. *From Majapahit to Putrajaya: Searching for Another Malaysia.* Kuala Lumpur: Silverfish Books.

Fischer, Johan. 2008. *Proper Islamic Consumption: Shopping among the Malays in Modern Malaysia.* Copenhagen: NIAS Press.

Government of Malaysia. 2010. *Panduan Amalan 5S Sektor Awam* (5S Practice Guide for the Civil Service). Putrajaya: MAMPU.

Hallaq, Wael. 2009. *Shari`a: Theory, Practice, Transformations.* Cambridge, UK: Cambridge University Press.

Harding, Andrew. 2012. *The Constitution of Malaysia: A Contextual Analysis.* Oxford: Hart Publishing.

Hefner, Robert W. 2011a. "Introduction: Shari`a Politics—Law and Society in the Modern Muslim World." In *Shari`a Politics: Islamic Law and Society in the Modern World,* edited by Robert W. Hefner, 1–54. Bloomington: Indiana University Press.

Hefner, Robert W., ed. 2011b. *Shari`a Politics: Islamic Law and Society in the Modern World.* Bloomington: Indiana University Press.

Hodgson, Marshall. 1974. *The Venture of Islam: Conscience and History in a World Civilization,* 3 vols. Chicago: University of Chicago Press.

Hoesterey, James. 2008. "Marketing Morality: The Rise, Fall, and Rebranding of AA Gym." In *Expressing Islam: Religious Life and Politics in Indonesia,* edited by Greg Fealy and Sally White, 90–107. Singapore: Institute of Southeast Asian Studies.

Horowitz, Donald. 1994. "The Qur'an and the Common Law: Islamic Law Reform and the Theory of Legal Change." *The American Journal of Comparative Law* 42 (2/3): 233–93, 543–80.

Jomo, K. S., ed. 1995. *Privatizing Malaysia: Rents, Rhetoric, Realities.* Boulder, CO: Westview Press.

Kamali, Mohammad Hashim. 2000. *Islamic Law in Malaysia: Issues and Developments.* Kuala Lumpur: Ilmiah Publishers.

Kugle, Scott Siraj al-Haqq. 2010. *Homosexuality in Islam: Critical Reflections on Gay, Lesbian, and Transgender Muslims.* Oxford: Oneworld.

Lee, Julian. 2010. *Islamization and Activism in Malaysia.* Singapore: Institute of Southeast Asian Studies.

Liow, Joseph. 2009. *Piety and Politics: Islamism in Contemporary Malaysia.* Oxford: Oxford University Press.

Makdisi, John. 1999. "The Islamic Origins of the Common Law." *North Carolina Law Review* 77:1635–1739.

Maznah Mohamad. 2010. "The Ascendance of Bureaucratic Islam and the Secularization of the Sharia in Malaysia." *Pacific Affairs* 83 (3): 505–24.

Mazzarella, William. 2006. "Internet X-Ray: E-Governance, Transparency, and the Politics of Immediation in India." *Public Culture* 18 (3): 473–505.

Moustafa, Tamir. 2013. "Islamic Law, Women's Rights, and Popular Legal Consciousness in Malaysia." *Law and Social Inquiry* 38 (1): 168–88.

Muhammad Rais Abdul Karim, and Nazariah Mohd Khalid. 2003. *E-Government in Malaysia.* Kuala Lumpur: Pelanduk Publications.

Muzaffar, Chandra. 1979. *Protector?* Penang: Aliran.

Najmabadi, Afsaneh. 2005. *Women with Moustaches, Men without Beards: Gender and Sexual Anxieties of Iranian Modernity.* Berkeley: University of California Press.

Ng Cheng Yee. 2010. "Don't Sideline Women Judges, Syariah Court Told." *The Star,* July 16.

Noraini Mohd Noor, Jamil Farooqui, Ahmad Abd. Al-Rahim Nasr, Hazizan Bin Md. Noon, and Shukran Abdul Rahman. 2005. *Sexual Identity: Effeminacy among University Students.* Kuala Lumpur: International Islamic University Malaysia.

Norani Othman. 2008. "Religion, Citizenship Rights and Gender Justice: Women, Islamization and the Shari`a in Malaysia since the 1980s." In *Sharing the Nation: Faith, Difference, Power and the State 50 Years after Merdeka,* edited by Norani Othman, Mavis Puthucheary, and Clive Kessler, 29–58. Petaling Jaya, Malaysia: Strategic Information and Research Development Centre.

Norani Othman, Mavis Puthucheary, and Clive Kessler. 2008. *Sharing the Nation: Faith, Difference, Power and the State 50 Years after Merdeka*. Petaling Jaya, Malaysia: Strategic Information and Research Development Centre.

Okruhlik, Gwenn. 2005. "Empowering Civility through Nationalism: Reformist Islam and Belonging in Saudi Arabia." In *Remaking Muslim Politics: Pluralism, Contestation, Democratization*, edited by Robert W. Hefner, 189–212. Princeton, NJ: Princeton University Press.

Otto, Jan Michiel, ed. 2010. *Sharia Incorporated: A Comparative Overview of the Legal Systems of Twelve Muslim Countries in Past and Present*. Leiden, Netherlands: Leiden University Press.

Peletz, Michael G. 1996. *Reason and Passion: Representations of Gender in a Malay Society*. Berkeley: University of California Press.

———. 1997. "'Ordinary Muslims' and Muslim Resurgents in Contemporary Malaysia: Notes on an Ambivalent Relationship." In *Islam in an Era of Nation States: Politics and Religious Renewal in Muslim Southeast Asia*, edited by Robert W. Hefner, 231–73. Honolulu: University of Hawaii Press.

———. 2002. *Islamic Modern: Religious Courts and Cultural Politics in Malaysia*. Princeton, NJ: Princeton University Press.

———. 2005. "Islam and the Cultural Politics of Legitimacy: Malaysia in the Aftermath of September 11." In *Remaking Muslim Politics: Pluralism, Contestation, Democratization*, edited by Robert W. Hefner, 240–72. Princeton, NJ: Princeton University Press.

———. 2009. *Gender Pluralism: Southeast Asia since Early Modern Times*. New York: Routledge.

———. 2013. "Malaysia's Syariah Judiciary as a Global Assemblage: Islamization, Corporatization, and Other Transformations in Context." *Comparative Studies in Society and History* 55 (3): 603–33.

———. n.d. *Syariah Transformations*. Book ms. in prep.

Ramizah Wan Muhammad. 2008. "The Theory and Practice of Sulh (Mediation) in the Malaysian Shariah Courts." *IIUM Law Journal* 16 (1): 33–50.

Rittich, Kerry. 2001. "Who's Afraid of *Critique of Adjudication*? Tracing the Discourse of Law in Development." *Cardozo Law Review* 22 (3/4): 929–46.

Roslina Mohamad. 2010. "Syariah Breakthrough." *The Star*, July 5.

Rudnyckyj, Daromir. 2010. *Spiritual Economies: Islam, Globalization, and the Afterlife of Development*. Ithaca, NY: Cornell University Press.

Sa'odah binti Ahmad. 2010. "The Effectiveness of Mediation and *Sulh* in Resolving Family Disputes: A Study of Parties' Satisfaction with *Sulh* in the State of Selangor." PhD thesis, International Islamic University of Malaysia.

Scott, James C. 1998. *Seeing Like a State: How Certain Schemes to Improve the Human Condition Have Failed*. New Haven, CT: Yale University Press.

Sharifah Zaleha Syed Hassan, and Sven Cederroth. 1997. *Managing Marital Disputes in Malaysia: Islamic Mediators and Conflict Resolution in the Syariah Courts*. Richmond, UK: Curzon Press.

Sloane-White, Patricia. 2011a. "Beyond Islamism at Work: Corporate Islam in Malaysia." In *Whatever Happened to the Islamists?*, edited by Olivier Roy and Amel Boubekeur, 72–99. New York: Columbia University Press/Hurst.

———. 2011b. "Working in the Islamic Economy: Sharia-ization and the Malaysian Workplace." *Sojourn* 26 (2): 304–34.

Strathern, Marilyn, ed. 2000. *Audit Cultures: Anthropological Studies in Accountability, Ethics, and the Academy*. London: Routledge.

Tan Beng Hui. 2012. "Sexuality, Islam and Politics in Malaysia: A Study on the Shifting Strategies of Regulation." PhD thesis, National University of Singapore.

Tan, Jeff. 2008. *Privatization in Malaysia: Regulation, Rent-Seeking, and Policy Failure*. London: Routledge.

Vogel, Frank. 2011. "Saudi Arabia: Public, Civil, and Individual Shari`a in Law and Politics." In *Shari`a Politics: Islamic Law and Society in the Modern World,* edited by Robert W. Hefner, 55–93. Bloomington: Indiana University Press.

Weber, Max. (1925) 1968. *Economy and Society: An Outline of Interpretive Sociology,* 2 vols., Edited by Guenther Roth and Claus Wittich. Berkeley: University of California Press.

Weiss, Meredith. 2006. *Protest and Possibilities: Civil Society and Coalitions for Political Change in Malaysia.* Stanford, CA: Stanford University Press.

Whiting, Amanda. 2008. "Desecularizing Malaysian Law?" In *Examining Practice, Interrogating Theory: Comparative Legal Studies in Asia,* edited by Penelope (Pip) Nicholson and Sarah Biddulph, 223–66. Leiden, Netherlands: Martinus Nijhoff.

———. 2011. "Political Struggles and Practical Ethics: A History of Malaysian Lawyers and Lawyering." Paper presented at Workshop on Law and Society in Malaysia. University of Victoria, BC, July 14–16.

Zainah Anwar. 2001. "What Islam, Whose Islam? Sisters in Islam and the Struggle for Women's Rights." In *The Politics of Multiculturalism: Pluralism and Citizenship in Malaysia, Singapore, and Indonesia,* edited by Robert W. Hefner, 227–52. Honolulu: University of Hawaii Press.

Zuern, John. 2010. "Mind Your Own Business: Cisco Systems in the Power/Knowledge Network." In *Cultural Critique and the Global Corporation,* edited by Purnima Bose and Laura Lyons, 182–214. Bloomington: Indiana University Press.

Acknowledgments

I am grateful to Ikmal Adian Mohd Adil for research assistance. I also must express my deep gratitude to Tuan Haji Mohamad Shakir Bin Abdul Hamid of the Malaysian Department of Syariah Judiciary (Jabatan Kehakiman Syariah Malaysia) for facilitating my interactions with his colleagues and for helping me locate data relevant to this project. Earlier versions of this chapter were presented at Boston University, Free University Amsterdam, Free University Berlin, New York University, the University of Malaya, and the University of Toronto. The questions and comments I received in those settings helped me refine some of my arguments, as did written remarks provided by Robert Hefner and Tan Beng Hui. Recent research trips to Malaysia were made possible by funding from the National Endowment for the Humanities, the Koninklijk Instituut for Taal-, Land- en Volkenkunde (KITLV), Emory University, and the University of Malaya (UM). At UM, I am indebted to Ahmad Hidayat Bin Buang, Azirah Binti Hashim, Najat Binti Nabihah, and Siti Zubaidah Binti Ismail for making possible my 2013 participation in the research project entitled "Islamic Law in Practice." This chapter incorporates material adapted from Peletz 2013; I alone am responsible for any errors and shortcomings.

Notes

1. I spell Malay terms, including those of Arabic origin, in accordance with the conventions of standard Malay except when quoting published material following other guidelines. I should also note that I use the terms *Islamic law* and *syariah* (Ar. *shari`a*) interchangeably.

2. Ethnic Malays, nearly all of whom identify themselves as Sunni Muslims, constitute around 51 percent of Malaysia's population of approximately 30 million (http://www.statistics .gov.my/portal/index.php?lang=en). The two other major ethnic groupings are Chinese, the

majority of whom are Buddhists, though some are Christian; and Indians, most of whom self-identify as Hindus, the remainder being either Muslim, Sikh, or Christian. Because all Malays are Muslims, and because about 85 percent of Malaysia's Muslims are Malay, I use the terms *Malay* and *Muslim* (and *non-Malay* and *non-Muslim*) interchangeably when discussing ethnic, religious, and related phenomena in the Malaysian context.

3. That the nation's secular courts are generally referred to as civil courts even though they handle both civil *and* criminal offenses may be confusing to the uninitiated reader. Further confusion may arise because infractions handled by the syariah court system are classified as either civil cases (*kes mal*) or criminal cases (*kes jenayah*). This is to say that both the civil and the syariah judiciaries make use of the civil/criminal distinction in the infractions subject to their jurisdictions. The meanings of subsequent references to civil and criminal offenses will be clear from the context of the discussion.

4. Cited in Peletz (2002, 157–58).

5. The temporal changes with respect to any particular state—that is, the rise in the percentage for Negeri Sembilan and the declines in the percentages for Selangor and Kedah—might reflect coding procedures as much as anything else, or the small size of the samples from the 1980s and 1990s, in some instances limited to those cases involving proceedings that the anthropologist(s) actually observed.

6. All quotes in this paragraph derive from the article "First Syariah Women Judges," which appeared in *The Sunday Star* on July 4, 2010.

7. In Malaysia, the term *Islam Hadhari*, usually translated as "civilizational Islam," is widely associated with Abdullah Ahmad Badawi, Malaysia's fifth prime minister (r. 2003–9), who developed and branded the concept and sought to implement its basic features (see Abdullah Ahmad Badawi 2006). Abdullah's popularity declined precipitously during his last years in office, as did the general currency of the branded expression *Islam Hadhari*, except in certain think tanks and the publications linked with them. More important for our purposes is that the overall vision entailed in *Islam Hadhari*—"Faith and piety in Allah; A just and trustworthy government; A free and independent people; A vigorous pursuit and mastery of knowledge; A balanced and comprehensive economic development . . . The protection of the rights of minority groups and women; [and] Cultural and moral integrity" (Abdullah Ahmad Badawi 2006, 4)—was shared by Abdullah's predecessor, Mahathir Mohamad (r. 1981–2003) and also resonates deeply with the approach to Islam adopted by Abdullah's successor, Najib Tun Razak (r. 2009–present). Although they have branded themselves in different ways—Mahathir: Vision 2020; Abdullah: Islam Hadhari; Najib: 1 Malaysia—all three prime ministers have advocated what Robert Hefner (2011a) refers to as a broadly "ethicalized" Islam as distinct from the more "syariah-minded" (Hodgson 1974) platform articulated by the Islamist opposition party, PAS (the Pan Malaysian Islamic Party).

8. Quoted passages in this paragraph are taken from Ng Cheng Yee's "Don't Sideline Women Judges, Syariah Court Told," which appeared in *The Star* on July 16, 2010.

9. Catherine Eu, former executive director of the Malaysian Bar Council (personal communication, September 9, 2013).

10. Germane here is John Makdisi's (1999) argument that key features of English common law developed by Henry II in twelfth-century England, including common-law notions of contract and trial by jury, were adapted from medieval Islamic law of the Maliki tradition practiced in North Africa and Sicily, elements of which were incorporated first into the Norman law of Sicily and subsequently into both the Norman law of England and what came to be known as English common law.

11. Ahmad Hidayat Buang's (2007, 322) observation that Malaysia's "Syariah court . . . [is] seen by many as a second class, incompetent court" is clearly intended as a relative point: that

the syariah court is regarded as second-class and incompetent *in relation to the civil court,* which in many respects constitutes the gold standard. So, too, is Kamali's (2000, 312) convergent, widely shared view that "[t]he Syariah Courts and their judges and personnel . . . exist on the fringes of the system and tend to see themselves as being marginalized."

12. From Prime Minister Mahathir's foreword to *E-Government in Malaysia* (Muhammad Rais Abdul Karim and Nazariah Mohd Khalid 2003).

13. Not least because of the augmented resources thus provided to state authorities and conservative sectors of Muslim civil society inclined toward strategies of lawfare to silence and punish their adversaries and critics.

14. Section 377, often taken by outside observers as a sign of Oriental despotism and Islamic sexual repression, is of British colonial, not Islamic, origin; this is why the terminology of Section 377 has long been virtually identical across a number of former British colonies, including Malaysia, Singapore, Burma, India, and Pakistan.

15. Limitations of space preclude discussion of *liwat*; for important treatments of the subject from historical, feminist, and textual/theological perspectives, see El-Rouayheb (2005), Najmabadi (2005), Ali (2006), and Kugle (2010).

16. JAWI is the acronym for the Jabatan Agama Islam Wilayah Persekutuan (Federal Territory Department of Islamic Religion); JAIS is shorthand for the Jabatan Agama Islam Selangor (Selangor Department of Islamic Religion). These are among the state bureaucracies coordinated by JAKIM (Jabatan Kemajuan Islam Malaysia [Malaysian Department of Islamic Development]) that are involved in interpreting, safeguarding, and promoting Islam (see Liow 2009; Tan Beng Hui 2012).

17. This tension merits far more discussion than is feasible here.

18. Some of these latter cases are discussed by Whiting (2008) and Harding (2012).

19. These are of course relative points, and I am not suggesting utter uniformity in experiences, understandings or representations of Islamic ethics, law, or ritual; there is still a great deal of variation in these realms, though decidedly less than in earlier decades (Peletz 1996; 1997; 2002; 2005; 2009).

20. But see Peletz (1997; 2002), Zainah Anwar (2001), Farish Noor (2005), Weiss (2006), Lee (2010).

11 Islamic Ethics and Muslim Feminism in Indonesia

Robert W. Hefner

Although sometimes overlooked in accounts of Muslim civilizational history, the Southeast Asian nation of Indonesia offers a striking example of just how and why Islamic ethical and legal traditions can vary over time and space. The variation reflects the authorities and media through which Muslim ethical knowledge is produced, reproduced, and scaled up in state and society and through which that knowledge co-imbricates with other ethical imaginaries and aspirational projects. This chapter examines the role of Islamic social and religious movements in the production, reproduction, and change of Muslim women's ethics in Indonesia from the late nineteenth century to today. It highlights the circumstances that have favored the emergence of a relatively reformed understanding of Islamic law and ethics. Although in some ways remarkable, the Indonesian example offers general insights into the prospects for a more gender-equitable reform of Islamic ethics today.

Shari`a Ideals and Gender Ethics in Indonesia

Understanding the interplay of gender ideals and Islamic ethics in modern Indonesia requires going back in time. The ethical imbrications at work in premodern Indonesia were significantly different from those in the premodern Arab Middle East. The differences are essential for understanding why gender realities in Indonesia differed from those in the Muslim Middle East as both regions moved into the modern era.

Although Arab Muslim traders had sailed through Indonesian archipelago as early as the late seventh century, the first mass conversion to Islam did not begin until six centuries later. Rather than armies of horse-mounted warriors sweeping in from across the steppe, the primary vector for conversion to Islam was the Muslim-dominated Indian Ocean trade, linking southern Arabia and India with the Indonesian archipelago and southern China. As the trade reached its apogee from the fifteenth to seventeenth centuries, Islam spread to most coastal and interior kingdoms in the central and western archipelago, displacing once-dominant Hindu-Buddhist kingdoms (Reid 1993; Ricklefs 2012, 3–12).

Although military conflicts broke out in the course of conversion, the process was for the most part gradualist and peaceful. No less important, Islam's primary promoters were not ethnically foreign but rather were local rulers who shared language, culture, and gender norms with the subjects they brought to their new faith. The elite-mediated and coethnic nature of the conversion process meant that until the rise of Middle Eastern–influenced movements of Islamic reform in the nineteenth and twentieth centuries, there was considerable cultural continuity from the old religion to the new, including in matters of kinship and gender.

Over the centuries that followed, Southeast Asia developed an Islamic civilization, but until the modern period, it maintained many distinctive characteristics regarding women and Islamic legal traditions. As Anthony Milner (1995, 146, 217) and Jajat Burhanudin (2006) have both demonstrated, during its first centuries, Southeast Asian Islam had a "raja-centric" rather than a *madrasa*-based cast. The pomp and ceremony of a Sufi-inflected imperial Islam served as one of the primary exemplars for popular understandings of Islamic ethics (see also Pelras 1996; Woodward 1989, 164). Court arts of broadly Indic nature, including shadow theater and Ramayana-influenced dance traditions in which bare shoulders and tight bodices were the female norm, remained widespread across the central kingdoms until well into the twentieth century.

Muslim Southeast Asia did have transregional networks conveying a normative vision consonant with that of the Muslim Middle East. From the seventeenth century onward, an Arabic-language "cosmopolis" served to disseminate works of theology, grammar, Prophetic biography, and moral edification across the Indian Ocean region (Azra 1992; Ricci 2011, 262–67). However, one institution important to the Middle Eastern ethical landscape was notable by its absence: the *madrasa*. As noted in the introduction to this volume, the *madrasa* is a boarding school for intermediate and advanced study in the Islamic sciences in general and fiqh jurisprudence in particular. By the twelfth century CE, the *madrasa* had become "perhaps the most characteristic religious institution of the medieval Near Eastern urban landscape" (Berkey 2003, 187). Among lettered elites, the institution facilitated a great "recentering and homogenization" of Islamic knowledge and authority (Berkey 2003, 189; see also Bulliet 1994; Chamberlain 1994). In educated circles, too, fiqh came to be regarded as the queen of the Islamic sciences and the key to a proper Islamic normativity, not least regarding gender and sexuality.

Little of the *madrasa*'s ethical assemblage was put in place in premodern Southeast Asia. As a result, before the twentieth century, fiqh had a limited place in local ethical registers. Certainly Muslim Southeast Asia had its share of Islamic study circles and boarding residences where young men (and, more rarely, young women) came together to discuss Islamic matters, but with the possible exception of Aceh on the northern tip of Sumatra (Riddell 2001, 103–24;

but see Feener 2013, 63), these institutions devoted their pedagogical energies to Qur'an memorization, Prophetic biographies, *tasawwuf* spirituality, and moral edification of a nonjurisprudential sort. The historical record does show that some Muslim scholars owned small digests that summarized a few features of Shafi'i law (Hooker 1984), but until the rise of Islamic reform in the late nineteenth century, the careful study and robust enforcement of those legal traditions were unknown. Islamic moral registers had much less to do with scholarly fiqh, then, than they did with lessons from the life of the Prophet and a Sufi-informed concern with moving closer to God under the guidance of a living saint.

Although modern academic studies of Islamic legal texts have sometimes made it seem as if fiqh is the only fount from which Muslim ethical ideas flow, Turkish historian Ahmet Karamustafa (2007) has shown that in premodern times there was a similarly nonlegal cast to popular Muslim religious imaginaries across broad swaths of Muslim Eastern Europe and Central Asia. Muhammad Khalid Masud (2002) and Barbara Metcalf (1984) have similarly emphasized that ethical traditions in Muslim South Asia always included registers more varied than fiqh commentaries. In two important respects, however, the co-imbrications sustaining Muslim religious imaginaries in Southeast Asia were distinctive. First, as Merle Ricklefs has demonstrated with regard to Muslim central Java (which had one of the least fiqh-oriented Islamic ethical heritages in all of Indonesia; see Hooker 2008; 2013), the normative plurality allowed for the efflorescence of "mystic synthesis" that combined a commitment to Sufism and observation of the five pillars of Islam with "acceptance of the reality of local Javanese spiritual forces such as . . . the Goddess of the Southern Ocean . . . and a host of lesser supernatural beings" (Ricklefs 2012, 7). In Indonesian lands beyond central Java, the synthesis may not have been as theologically unconventional, but cosmological eclecticism was widespread (see, for example, Cederroth 1981).

The second consequence of Southeast Asia's nonfiqh Islamic normativity had to do with women. Many of the gendered categories and presuppositions of fiqh discourse in Middle East lands were absent or only partially recognized in Southeast Asia, at least until the rise of Islamic reform in the late nineteenth century—and even then they remained significantly quarantined until well into the twentieth century. Although some women wore loose-fitting headscarves (Ind. *kerudung*; Mal. *tudung*), the *hijab* was rare (see Candraningrum 2013; Smith-Hefner 2007). With the exception of a few aristocrats, female seclusion was unknown (Watson Andaya 2006, 172–78). Women were the dominant actors in local markets; men predominated only in long-distance trade (Alexander 1987; Brenner 1998; Reid 1993, 162–64). In daily life, women were free to move about villages and towns unescorted. Divorce for women (at least before bearing children) entailed little stigma. In some parts of Southeast Asia, local sexual cultures acknowledged a third sex and transgenderism (Davies 2010; Peletz 2009).

Most revealing of all with regard to the restricted influence of classical fiqh in local gender registers, many Muslim-majority communities ignored the law's rules on succession, including the provisions stipulating that a daughter's share in inheritance should be half of her brother's. In much of the region, daughters' and sons' shares were equal. Even in the more fiqh-conversant portions of the archipelago, such as Aceh (Siegel 1969; cf. for Java, see Geertz 1961; Hefner 1990), patterns of authority and affection within the family had a "matrifocal" quality, with mothers making everyday decisions and serving as the family's emotional pillar. As was (and still is) the case among the Minangkabau of West Sumatra and Negeri Sembilan in the Malay peninsula, a few Muslim populations retained a matrilineal kinship system, with the prominent place for women that such a system typically implies (Peletz 1996, 101–54). Although present in the archipelago, patrilineal kinship was not common in the more densely populated kingdoms of western and central Indonesia. Even where operative (as in Aceh; Bowen 1991; Siegel 1969), patrilineal descent did not give rise to the powerful tribes that operate in some Arab societies to this day, nor was the social organization of kinship and sexuality such that it generated severe masculinist codes of modesty, sexuality, and tribal honor such as those associated, most famously, with the *hasham* tradition in the Arab Middle East (Abu-Lughod 1986, 105). In these and other regards, Muslim Southeast Asia maintained an Islamic ethical register on gender matters that was strikingly different from the Arab Middle East.

A New Islamic Reform

Certainly Southeast Asian Islam was never a region unto itself, and in the late nineteenth century, a growing interaction with centers of pilgrimage and learning in the Middle East (see Laffan 2003; Snouck Hurgronje 1931; Vredenbregt 1962) brought about a heightened engagement with fiqh-based normativity. From the middle decades of the nineteenth century onward, the Indonesian and Malaysian equivalent of the Middle Eastern *madrasa*, known as a *pondok* or *pesantren* (see Azra et al. 2007; Dhofier 1999; Hefner 2007), became a prominent feature on the social landscape and a major influence on Muslim ethical imaginaries (see Bruinessen 1995; Ricklefs 2007, 52–72). In the last years of the nineteenth century, the rapid establishment of *pesantren* across central and western portions of the archipelago ensured that a well organized, if at first minority, wing of the Muslim community developed a lettered familiarity with fiqh (Hefner 2009; Bruinessen 1989; 1994; 1995). In the first decades of the twentieth century, this development converged with social change and anticolonial ferment to spur the rise of organized movements for the implementation of shari'a. Historical studies indicate that there was little agreement on just what shari'a entailed, not least for matters of state. The growing influence of fiqh-derived normativity in *pesantren*-linked circles did lead, however, to appeals for a "shari`a-compliant" refiguration of gender mixing and rules regarding women's dress, divorce, and inheritance (see Kartodirdjo 1972; Peletz 1996, 309–32).

This was but the beginning of more than a century of public–ethical contention in Indonesia in which questions of gender and nation have figured prominently. Although during the middle decades of the twentieth century Indonesia developed a sizable nationalist movement of a broadly "secularist" nature (see hereafter), some of the most important ethical contentions had to do not with contests between Muslims and non-Muslim or nominally Muslim secularists but with opposing *Muslim* understandings of Islamic ethics. In particular, no sooner had fiqh become a point of ethical orientation for some *pesantren*-based Muslims than for other observant Muslims, the hope for a more authentic profession of the faith imbricated with aspirational projects less exclusively grounded on classical jurisprudence (Hefner 2007).

Two developments contributed to this permutation of Islamic ethical registers. First, not long after the network of *pesantren* boarding schools had been put in place and the conditions created for what might have appeared to be an ascendant fiqh hegemony, the movement of Islamic reform known in Indonesia as Islamic "modernism" (Ind. *kaum modernis*; see Abdullah 1971; Noer 1973; Roff 1994) arose in urban areas across the region. Faced with the threat of European colonialism, modernists in groups such as the Muhammadiyah (established in Yogyakarta, Java, in 1912; see Alfian 1989; Nakamura 2012, 51–77; Peacock 1978) concluded that the most effective educational instrument for the improvement of the Muslim community was not the *pesantren* with its fiqh-centered curriculum but was the "Islamic day school" (Ind. *sekolah Islam*; Hefner 2007). With its classrooms, blackboards, and mix of general and religious instruction, the latter institution was modeled on Protestant and, especially, Catholic schools, which had been introduced by European missionaries in the early years of the twentieth century (see Kruithof 2014, 95; Steenbrink 2003, 207).

Although Indonesia's modernists publicly affirmed the importance of shari`a, they insisted that its proper understanding required believers to put aside medieval fiqh and return to the Qur'an and *Sunna*. The Muhammadiyah's founder, Ahmad Dahlan (1868–1923; see Mulkhan 2010), had studied in Mecca and there developed an interest in reformist ideas, including those of well-known Egyptian modernist Muhammad Abduh (1849–1905). Like Abduh, Dahlan and his followers stressed the importance of *ijtihad* (lit. "striving" or "self-exertion"; or, in Islamic jurisprudence, the effort by qualified religious scholars to infer the rules of Islamic law) over pious conformity (*taqlid*) to the teachings of classical jurists. The Muhammadiyah leadership also insisted that in modern times, the most effective way to perform *ijtihad* was collectively (*ijtihad jama`i*), so as to ensure that judgments drew on a balanced array of scholarly and practical experts (Djamil 1995, 59).

It is important *not* to view Muhammadiyah initiatives regarding education and law as being mere technical matters. They were key ingredients in a broader, though not yet formally rationalized, effort to develop a new Islamic ethical register capable of providing moral guidance in the modern world. In its simplest terms, this initiative was premised on the familiar modernist conviction that Islam can and should be the foundation for a far-reaching modernization of self and society (see Peacock 1978). What was distinctive about the Muhammadiyah's understanding of this well-known modernist conviction was that it was thought to require not only conformity to God's commands but also development of new forms of empirical knowledge and social activism. These were necessary if Muslims were to make good on their religion's promise not merely to enforce God's rules but also to educate youth, care for the sick, improve economic welfare, and, in short, bring about a more truly Islamic *and* modern society.

Although they never developed a full theory to explain their legal methodologies (Hosen 2003), Muhammadiyah scholars justified this expansion of ethical horizons by referring to the concept of *maslahah* or "public interest," insisting that the *maslahah* was among the "higher aims of the shari`a" (*maqasid al-shari`ah*; see Djamil 1995, 60; Masud 2005). Long recognized in the Maliki school of law, in the late nineteenth and twentieth centuries the concept of *maslahah* was invoked and expanded by Islamic reformists in many parts of the globe to justify initiatives not addressed in classical commentaries but regarded as of urgent political and ethical concern (see Hallaq 2011; Opwis 2007; see also Feener 2007, 137).

In the case of the Muhammadiyah, the principle of *maslahah* was used to justify an even broader array of activities than proposed by modernists in most other lands. No development illustrated this emphasis more clearly than that most remarkable of Indonesian achievements: the establishment and spread of Islamic welfare associations. Viewed from a comparative Islamic perspective, Indonesia has the most "associationalized" variety of Islam in the world. Today the reformist Muhammadiyah has some 25 million members. It manages 12,000 schools, 167 institutions of higher learning, 421 orphanages, 345 polyclinics and hospitals, and a nationwide bank (Bank Pengkreditan Rakyat). Here in practice is demonstrable evidence of a distinctive and *maslahah*-ized understanding of Islamic ethics.

The Muhammadiyah example also illustrates just how Islamic moral registers, including those informing understandings of shari`a, can change over time in ways at variance with the jurists' classical tradition. Although they had not yet devised an explicit rationale such as Tariq Ramadan would promote in the 2000s (Ramadan 2009; see this volume, chapter 1), what the Muhammadiyah and other Indonesian modernists were attempting from the 1920s onward was just such a fusion of *maqasid*-informed ethics with practical knowledge for understanding and changing the world. Here was a new Islamic aspirational project indeed—one initiated, so to speak, *avant la lettre* that could justify it in explicit ethicolegal terms.

Why did Muhammadiyah intellectuals and activists not take the additional step and provide such publicly reasoned rationales for their *maslahah*-based activities? In one sense, they did or they thought they did, inasmuch as—as already noted—they justified their activities with reference to *maslahah* and the higher aims of the shari'a (*maqasid al-shari'a*). However, by the standards of mainline Islamic jurisprudence, they failed to carry out the detailed normative work and public reasoning necessary to socialize this new ethical understanding to the Muslim public.

There were deeper sociological reasons for Muhammadiyah's hesitant public reasoning. At this point in history, the movement's membership was recruited primarily from ranks of the urban commercial class rather than from the rural network of fiqh scholars associated with Indonesia's *pesantrens*. Muhammadiyah long had suffered a shortage of skilled legal scholars. Buoyed by the modernist conviction that grounding one's activities on the Qur'an and *Sunna* was sufficient, and living as they did in a society in which fiqh-rulings did yet not pervade public discussions, Muhammadiyah leaders also appear to have felt that detailed jurisprudential rationales were not of immediate importance. However, the formulation of such rationales was also impeded because although its leadership was brightly modernist, the rank and file of the Muhammadiyah has always included members who have notably unreformed understandings of Islamic law (see hereafter).

Tellingly, only in 1929 did the Muhammadiyah establish a *fatwa* council (the Majlis Tarjih, or MT) for the issuance of rulings on matters of religious importance (Anwar 2005). Rather surprisingly in light of Muhammadiyah's boldness in other spheres (see Njoto-Feillard 2012), from 1929–53, the MT issued fatawa on ritual matters alone, steering clear of social, political, and educational matters (Hosen 2003, 84). In the 1950s, the MT issued rulings on the sources of Islam and a few social matters, but it began to address weighty social matters such as bank interest, interreligious marriage, and in vitro fertilization only after 1968. Although in the late 1990s the organization attempted to jumpstart a broad array of intellectual innovations by appointing young Muhammadiyah intellectuals— including a well-regarded Muslim feminist—the initiative stalled for reasons that will become clear (see also Burhani 2013).

As the chapters in this book make clear, popular Islamic moral registers change in response to broader developments in society. The changes can create pressures for new understandings and practices of Islamic law and ethics. Over the course of the twentieth century, public ethical pressures such as these grew steadily in Indonesia. However, the two obstacles discussed herein—the reluctance or inability of reformists to follow through on these changes by promoting a discursivized reinterpretation of Islamic legal traditions, as well as the reformist inability to scale these discourses into the commanding heights of state and Muslim society—were to handicap broader efforts to bring about sustainable reforms, including those of importance to Muslim women.

Nationalism and Muslim Women's Activism

One historical fact stands out in any assessment of Muslim women and the nationalist movement in Indonesia: As in the Arab Middle East (see Badran 2009), the aspiration for a new and more equitable arrangement for women originated not in the aftermath of the national awakening but from its beginning (see Robinson 2009, 34). Although the Dutch had had a colonial presence in the archipelago for some three hundred years, only during the late nineteenth century had they extended their rule across the breadth of what they called the Netherlands East Indies. The colonial expansion created the need for what Benedict Anderson (1991) has described as armies of "creole functionaries": native peoples educated in European-style schools to meet the administrative needs of the colonial state. The demand for such an educated workforce was especially strong because of the small size of the European settler population and the scale of the Dutch economic intervention—seen in the nineteenth century as one of the most extensive in the European-colonized world (see Fasseur 1992; Hefner 1990, ch. 1). However, as in other modern European colonies, the Enlightenment values of freedom, equality, and progress that European administrators cited to justify their rule were also invoked by educated indigenes to demand justice for native people.

The first movements for Indonesian national awakening arose in the 1910s. By the end of the decade, the movements had mobilized hundreds of thousands of followers across the central territories in the archipelago. Muslim-based groups such as the Association of Muslim Merchants (Sarekat Dagang Islam, est. 1911) and its larger and more deliberately anticolonial successor, the Islamic Association (Sarekat Islam, est. 1918; see Ricklefs 2007; Shiraishi 1990), were among the first to develop a mass base. The latter movement quickly split along ideological lines, however, with those committed to a socialist or Marxist vision of nationhood separating from Muslim nationalists intent on ensuring the recognition of some variety of Islamic law in an independent Indonesia. This contest between Muslim nationalists committed to state implementation of Islamic law and nationalists (including many Muslims) of a broadly "secular" or "multiconfessional" orientation remained one of the defining divides of Indonesian politics for the rest of the twentieth century.[1]

During these early years, education, colonial subjection, and new emancipatory aspirations combined to give rise to the "consciousness of the political category of 'woman'" (Robinson 2009, 34). Rather than standing in polar opposition, Islamic and secularly oriented women's movements agreed on many issues, especially those related to women's education and family welfare. However, on the delicate matter of whether the state should be used to reform private family life, the two groups parted ways. Although in 1930 a splinter group in the Muslim women's movement briefly joined with its secular nationalist counterparts in calling for reform to religious laws on marriage, divorce, polygyny, and inheritance (see Blackburn 2008, 87–88), most Muslim women's groupings rejected such proposals. However, the ethical imbrications in play here were more complicated than first meets the eye, as illustrated, once again, in the experience of the Muhammadiyah.

Muhammadiyah's founder, Ahmad Dahlan, established a women's section shortly after the organization's founding, whose leadership he gave to his wife. The section's initial aim was to promote a more pious profession of the faith among women (Doorn-Harder 2006). In 1917, the department's name was changed to Aisyiyah. In the 1920s, the women's wing expanded its range of activities to include women's education and family health. Although legitimized in generically "Islamic" rather than fiqh terms, the organization also promoted the adoption of the head scarf, which at this stage in Indonesian history consisted of the loose-fitting head cover known as the *kerudung* rather than the more encompassing headscarf common in Indonesia today and known here as the *jilbab*. Like its traditionalist rival, the Nahdlatul Ulama, Muhammadiyah also enforced gender-segregated seating at meetings where both sexes were present, using a curtain (*tabir*) to separate the two seating areas.

As Susan Blackburn (2008, 88) has noted, in the 1920s and 1930s, both the Muhammadiyah and Nahdlatul Ulama (which did not yet have a separate women's wing), "held profoundly conservative views about women's place," particularly on questions related to women's involvement in national politics. By contrast, more self-consciously anticolonial Muslim groups, such as the Indonesian Islamic Association Party (*Partai Sarekat Islam Indonesia*, or PSII), allowed women a larger public role, including speaking before mixed-sex audiences. At a PSII conference in Yogyakarta in 1930, "representatives of the women's branch spoke about raising women to a position of equality with men, and about polygyny and marriage laws" (Blackburn 2008, 87). In 1940, PSII women published a commemorative volume in which they openly lamented what they described as the male leadership's indifference to women's concerns (Blackburn 2008, 88).

Although Aisyiyah, the women's wing of the Muhammadiyah, was an ardent proponent of women's education and family health, it wanted no part of the PSII women's calls for reforms to marriage laws. Indeed, Aisyiyah's pronouncements on marriage made clear it had two priorities regarding gender ethics: that a woman's primary social role lie in the home and child-rearing (Wieringa 2002, 124) and that Muslim women not join with secular nationalists in any campaign to rewrite laws on marriage and divorce (Robinson 2008, 42; Wieringa 2002, 67).

Public statements aside, there were signs of ethical debate within Aisyiyah on just these questions. In her *Sexual Politics in Indonesia* (2002), Saskia Wieringa reports that although Aisyiyah leaders refused to join in antipolygyny campaigns "because the Qur'an accepted it, in private leaders were often unhappy about this" (Wieringa 2002, 67). One elderly Aisyiyah leader recalled in interview with Wieringa that "[p]ersonally I have never agreed with polygyny. I would never have allowed it. But it is a religious rule, so what can we say against it?" (Wieringa 2002; see also Doorn-Harder 2006).

The point here is that whether in the 1920s or several decades later, most Aisyiyah women and some Muhammadiyah men recognized that Islamic legal traditions allowed polygyny, but many activists invoked other moral registers to qualify the rule's scope of application. In this as in so many other examples, and to return to a point raised in chapter 1 of this book, a discursivized religious rule (polygyny's legality according to divine law) is rethought in light of a less formally discursivized but widely held moral register. However, the inability of gender reformists in groups such as Muhammadiyah to perform the normative work and scaling required to promote a new discourse on polygyny meant that this largely tacit consensus would be vulnerable to later challenge.

From the late 1920s onward, then, this ethical and epistemic impasse undercut the ability of the two wings of the Indonesian women's movement to coordinate their appeals. The deadlock was starkly illustrated at the first Women's Congress, which opened in Yogyakarta, Java, on December 22, 1928. At that meeting, Muslim women joined with secular nationalist colleagues to appeal to the colonial government to require that in the *nikah* marriage ceremony the presiding official explain the procedures for conditional divorce, whereby woman have the right to initiate divorce proceedings (an arrangement known in Indonesia as *taklik talak* and requiring that during the *nikah* wedding ceremony husbands be told the circumstances under which women can initiate divorce). This fleeting collaboration aside, later congresses foundered on secular nationalist proposals for additional legislation to restrict polygyny and expand women's rights in divorce and inheritance.

During the middle decades of the twentieth century, the struggle over family law took a back seat to a growing and ultimately catastrophic contest over the place of religion in the new nation. At the time of the declaration of independence in August 1945, the leaders of the young republic—Soekarno (1901–70), a Western-educated secular–socialist of Muslim background, and Mohammad Hatta (1902–80; see Rose 2010), an ethnic Minangkabau and nationalist from a distinguished Sumatran Muslim-scholar family—had pressed for and won a preamble that defined Indonesia as a nation founded on monotheistic ideals but *not* committed to state-enforced shari`a. The young republic's leaders claimed that the latter compromise was necessary to reassure Christians in eastern Indonesia, who were unwilling to join the republic if Islamic law were to be implemented.

At independence most of the new republic's civil law and court protocols were transferred from the Dutch colonial period with few changes. This did mean, however, that the Republic continued to recognize the operation of the Islamic court system that had been formally established by Dutch royal decree in 1882. Called "priests' councils" (*priesterraden*) by the Protestant Dutch, the tribunals were actually Islamic family courts. Most of their case load had to do with divorce and inheritance (although jurisdiction in matters of inheritance was moved back into civil courts in 1937). The tribunals were presided over by judges and a senior religious official appointed by native rulers. The boards had no powers of enforcement other than appeal for an executory decree from a local civil court. All these details reflected the "reception theory" emphasized by Dutch officials, according to which Islamic legal traditions were used "only insofar as they had been 'received' into the region's custom" (Cammack 2007, 148; see also Burns 2004).

Although the new Ministry of Justice had at first pressed for the absorption of the Islamic tribunals into the national court system (Lev 1972, 63–75), Muslim parties mobilized to save the Islamic system and repositioned it under the Ministry of Religion rather than the more secular–nationalist Justice Ministry. In 1951 the parliament passed a statute that authorized the extension of Islamic courts beyond their area of original operation in Java and Madura, making their territorial jurisdiction coextensive with the civil court system (Cammack 2007, 149). For matters of marriage, divorce, and inheritance, then, Muslim Indonesians went to Islamic courts, whereas non-Muslims went to civil courts. Both groups were required to register their marriages and divorces in the local office of religious affairs. The degree to which the Islamic tribunals actually applied Shafi'i law in cases of divorce and inheritance varied by region, reflecting the continuing influence of customary (Ind. *adat*) law. Otherwise, in both civil and criminal law, Islamic legal traditions had little place. Apostasy was not criminalized, and religious freedom was managed in a manner modeled on the Dutch tradition of "pillars" (*verzuilingen*) rather than Islamic legal traditions (see Hefner 2013).

During the 1950s and 1960s, however, calls again grew for a more extensive implementation of what its proponents called shari`a. Party competition pitted Muslims committed to the establishment of an Islamic state against parties of the secular left, including, most notably, the Indonesian Nationalist Party (PNI) and the Indonesian Communist Party (PKI). By the early 1960s, Indonesia was the second most populous Muslim-majority country in the world (after greater Pakistan's breakup in 1971, Indonesia would be the most populous). Indonesia also had the world's two largest Muslim social welfare associations, the Muhammadiyah and Nahdlatul Ulama. By this same period, however, Indonesia had an even more unusual claim to fame: It was home to the largest communist party outside of the Eastern Bloc (Mortimer 1974).

During these years, the Indonesian Communist Party's women's organization, known by its acronym as Gerwani (*Gerakan Wanita Indonesia*, or Indonesian Woman's Movement), grew steadily larger than its Muslim rival, reaching 4 million members by the early 1960s. Ironically, however, as the PKI grew and the Muslim–communist rivalry intensified, Gerwani's commitment to women's issues slackened. In the 1950s, Gerwani had aligned itself with secular nationalists to oppose child marriage and polygyny; it also called for legal reforms restricting a husband's right to unilateral divorce (Wieringa 2002, 238). However, "opposition to polygyny brought Gerwani into conflict with the male PKI leadership, many of whom were polygamous" (Robinson 2009, 56). The same opposition also soured Gerwani's relationship with President Sukarno, who by this time was *marxisant*-socialist in orientation. In 1954, the president offended many women in his own party by taking a second wife over the very public objections of his first wife. During these same years, the president publicly dismissed feminism as divisive, insisting that the socialist revolution was the only way to do away with gender inequalities (Wieringa 2002, 47, 116). For these and other reasons, and notwithstanding the shared commitment of Muslim and secularist women's groups to women's education and welfare, any hope of reforming Indonesian marriage laws faded.

The rivalry between Muslim and Communist organizations took a violent turn in the aftermath of an attempted left-wing officers' coup, which seems to have had the backing of some in the communist leadership, on the night of September 30, 1965. The coup collapsed in just several days, and it set in motion a conservative countercoup (Cribb 1990). Over the weeks that followed, anticommunist army generals purged their ranks of communist sympathizers, mounted a propaganda campaign against the PKI leadership, and set out with civilian vigilantes to round up and execute communist activists. The largest civilian militias were those associated with the Nahdlatul Ulama and Muhammadiyah (Hefner 2000, ch. 7). As in Hindu Bali, however, the armed forces also made common cause with anticommunist youth from other religious communities (Robinson 1998).

By the time the killing was over, some 500,000 communists had perished, and tens of thousands more had been imprisoned (Cribb 1990; Roosa 2006). Drawing on fabricated reports that Gerwani women had played a role in the killing of six army generals the first night of the coup attempt, the new regime demonized the Gerwani and other left-wing women's groups. Over the next few years, the New Order regime put in place a repressive gender ideology that defined a woman's place as in the home, subordinate to her husband. The regime justified the formulation with reference to *kodrat*—or (in the Indonesian understanding of this Arabic-derived term) women's "biological" nature (Brenner 2011, 480; Robinson 2009; Wieringa 2002, 22). This conservative gender register was supposed to serve as a model for women's roles throughout the New Order era. But the register was to prove incapable of containing the complex changes in women's roles and self-understandings set in motion, ironically enough, by the New Order's conservative modernist developmental programs.

Muslim Feminism Reborn

Looking back on the first seven decades of twentieth-century Indonesia, one might at first be tempted to speak of a legacy squandered. Coming into the new century, Indonesia had a promisingly plural variety of gender cultures and Islamic moral registers. Across the archipelago, Muslim women were notable for their prominence in the family and marketplaces. When in the 1910s and 1920s the first calls were made to open schools for girls, the initiatives were quickly taken up, first by modernist Muslims and shortly thereafter by Muslim traditionalists. Indonesian society also developed the largest Muslim social welfare organizations in the world, each having a vibrant women's wing. Although they stopped short of advocating changes to marriage laws, the women's associations took up the banner of women's education and family welfare. The range of activities promoted by Muslim associations helped nurture habits of the heart vital for the reimagining of Islamic legal traditions, in a manner responsive to *maqasid*- and *maslahah*-based ideas of the public good (see this volume, chapter 1).

Notwithstanding these pluralist legacies, in the middle decades of the twentieth century Indonesian politics descended into a zero-sum competition for control of the state. During the heyday of parliamentary politics in the 1950s, the main political parties "competed fiercely for influence in every sphere of life and on a round-the-clock basis" (Anderson 1983, 487). The political process was centrifugal and system-challenging, and there was "little acceptance of common fundamentals" (Feith 1963, 316; see also Mietzner 2008). The conflict pushed women's and gender issues to the margins. It also extinguished any hope for the scaling up of *maslahah*-based ethical practices into an explicit, discursivized, and state-promoted reformation of Islamic ethicolegal traditions. The spiral of political violence climaxed in the mass killings of 1965–66. The new regime's ideological program emphasized neoconservative patriarchy in the family.

Notwithstanding this downward spiral, a generation after the regime assaults on women's activism, Indonesia had developed one of the world's largest Muslim feminist movements (Feillard and Madinier 2006; Rinaldo 2013; Robinson 2009; Schröter 2013). By the 1990s, Indonesia had also created what was arguably the world's largest Muslim-led democracy movement (Hefner 2000). Needless to say, there was no sweeping Muslim democrat triumph. Indonesia had always had, and still has (see ICG 2002; 2008; Jones 2013), a variety of radical Islamist group-ings, the largest of which campaign in support of an etatized, positivized, and harshly populist variety of Islamic law (see Hilmy 2010, 99–134; Hooker 2008, 277–81; Lindsey and Kingsley 2008, 295–320). Notwithstanding the complexity of the political scene, however, a new Muslim women's movement emerged. No less remarkable—and far more than was the case for first-generation women's activists in the 1920s and 1930s—the new movement took aim squarely at the reformation of Islamic legal traditions on matters relevant to women (Doorn-Harder 2006).

How was this possible? A key influence on the new Muslim women's movement had to do with broad changes in education, gender, and social class unleashed by New Order development programs. Between 1965 and 1990, the per-centage of literate Indonesians jumped from 40 percent to 90 percent of the total population (Jones and Manning 1992). During the same period, the percentage of young people completing senior high school rose from 4 percent to more than 30 percent. There was also a steady growth in private and public Islamic schooling, which today educates about 15 percent of the student population (Hefner 2009). No less remarkably, by the late 1990s, the proportion of young women compris-ing the *madrasa* student body had grown to more than half the total enrollment (Jabali and Jamhari 2002, 68–69).

Young women's enrollment in the country's prestigious state Islamic University system (known by the acronym UIN-IAIN) at first lagged behind that in higher education generally. In the early 1980s, women were about 30 percent of the student body at these colleges and universities; by the 2000s, however, they were just under half. In postgraduate programs, their numbers lagged more severely, but there was steady progress nonetheless. At the two most prestigious State Islamic Universities (the Jakarta Hidayatullah and the Yogyakarta Sunan Kalijaga State Islamic University), women formed only 3 percent of the student body in 1988 and 20 percent in 1998 (Jabali and Jamhari 2002, 47). Their numbers today are estimated to be around 35 percent of the postgraduate student body.

The 1980s and 1990s, then, were a period of sustained economic growth and far-reaching educational expansion. The years also witnessed an unprecedented Islamic revival (Ind. *kebangkitan*), a key portion of which involved conservative activists' promotion of "shariatization" in gender relations. As studies by Din Wahid (2013), Farish Noor (2012), and Noorhaidi Hasan (2006) have under-scored, some among the newer normative currents had roots in transnational Islamist movements, especially the Muslim Brotherhood. The activists called for state enforcement of an unreformed and positivized variant of shari`a. Broth-erhood ideas were especially popular among the many Indonesians returning from study in Egypt, Syria, and Saudi Arabia in the 1980s and 1990s. Referred to as the *tarbiyah* ("cultivation," "education") movement (see Machmudi 2006), the Brotherhood-influenced wing of the revival went on in the 2000s to develop the most successful of post-Soeharto Indonesia's new Islamist parties, known today as the Prosperous Justice Party (PKS). The party has consistently secured 7 percent of the vote in national elections, although its long-awaited expansion beyond that figure has not materialized (see Bubalo, Fealy, and Mason 2008, 49–74; Hamayotsu 2011).

Although the *tarbiyah* movement has been supportive of women's education and participation in parliamentary politics, its transnational ties have made many among the membership *less* inclined to ground their normative imaginaries on Indonesia's own Islamic moral legacies. Indeed, the party's conservative wing has at times seemed to deny that Indonesia has any legitimately Islamic normative heritage at all. In its first years, PKS activists "viewed . . . Islamic shari'a entails a set of values and laws that must be implemented in daily life" (Octavia 2012, 16; see also Fahmi 2006). Party activists interpreted Islamic legal traditions as stipulating that women's primary role lies in the home raising children, and forbidding women's leadership in mixed-gender groupings.

But there were other transnational influences at work in late- and post-Soeharto Indonesia. From the late 1980s on, a new and theologically savvy generation of Muslim feminists arrived on the national scene. As in much of the Muslim world (Badran 2009; Mir-Hosseini 1999), the social profile of the new Muslim feminism differed from that of the first generation of women activists in the 1920s and 1930s. The latter had emerged in the context of the anticolonial struggle and was tied to mass-based social activism. As with the PKI's Gerwani or the Muhammadiyah's Aisyiyah, however, the interests of these women's organizations were often subordinated to those of a male-led, mass organization. No less important, although some Muslim women activists expressed personal reservations about Islamic legal rules for polygyny and divorce, most lacked the formal Islamic legal training to challenge these rules on scholarly grounds.

This was the critical difference with the Muslim feminists of the 1990s. The latter had both the training and the interest in working through gendered aspects of Islamic ethicolegal traditions "from within" (see this volume, chapters 1–3). Many second-generation activists had familial ties to mass-based Muslim organizations, including Nahdlatul Ulama'a Muslimat and Muhammadiyah's Aisyiyah and Nasyiah (the latter being for young Muhammadiyah women). But the critical spark for the new Muslim feminism did not *originate* in these mainline organizations. The main pathway to the new Muslim feminism was by way of small study circles and nongovernmental organizations engaged with new international currents of Islamic feminist thought, and preoccupied with formulating a scripturally defensible reform of Islamic law on matters related to women.

That second-generation Muslim feminism emerged from study circles and NGOs preoccupied with Islamic legal questions is, of course, not unique to Indonesia. The situation was similar in much of the Arab Middle East (Latte Abdallah 2010) and in neighboring Malaysia (Anwar 2001; 2013). In all these examples, one saw small circles of well-educated and religiously observant women, not tied to any particular mass movement, working through Islamic sources to devise gender-equitable readings of, foremost, the Quran, and, secondarily, the *Sunna* and fiqh.

What was unusual about Indonesia's Muslim feminists was that so many of them emerged from institutions of higher Islamic learning supported by the very same New Order state that had promoted conservative models of female domesticity. As Muhammadiyah feminist thinker Siti Syamsiyatun (2008, 144) has observed, the state Islamic educational system (UIN/IAIN) "has become a major source for women's religious empowerment." Indeed, in the Muslim feminist movement's first years in the 1990s, the ranks of both Muslim and secular feminist organizations were disproportionately filled by graduates of the State Islamic university system (see Rinaldo 2013; Robinson 2009).

The rise of Muslim feminism from within the State Islamic university sector was facilitated not only by rising women's enrollments but also by a broadening of the system's curriculum. Under the leadership of the Minister of Religious Affairs, Mukti Ali, in the mid-1970s, the ministry undertook an ambitious upgrading of the IAIN system. Reforms included the establishment of a program of faculty enhancement that sent faculty and students to universities in Canada, the United States, and Western Europe in addition to existing programs in Egypt and Saudi Arabia (Hefner 2009). The program was anchored on the special relationship between the IAIN and the program in Islamic studies at McGill University in Canada, where Minister Ali had been a graduate student in the 1960s. By 2001, ninety-nine IAIN instructors had studied at McGill; twelve had received their PhD (Jabali and Jamhari 2002, 26). On returning to Indonesia, these scholars were appointed to key administrative posts in the Ministry of Religious Affairs and the IAIN in an effort to modernize the state Islamic educational system by linking the Islamic sciences to the humanities and social sciences.

There were two other institutional developments of decisive importance for the emergence of second-generation Muslim feminists. In the late 1990s, and with the financial support of the Jakarta office of the Asia Foundation, four state Islamic colleges developed "Women's Studies Centers" (Pusat Studi Wanita) that sponsored courses, speaker seminars, and research on gender issues. The best among these centers' faculty, all women, were provided with scholarships to pursue PhDs in disciplines deemed relevant for furthering women's studies, including law, Islamic studies, and sociology. During these same years, Muslim scholars at the Hidayatullah State Islamic University in Jakarta developed a new curriculum for civic education that combined the study of Islamic ethics with curricular segments on democracy, civil society, and human rights, including women's rights (Hefner 2009). In 2003, the program was implemented across the state Islamic college and university system (Jackson 2007). In these and other respects, the state Islamic university sector became a pioneer not only in new thinking on gender matters but also in national programs of civic education (see also White and Anshor 2008).

These educational trends were complemented by important shifts in the country's two main mass-based organizations—adding to the hope that with these groups' backing, some of the normative work done by the new Muslim feminists might be scaled up into state programs and law. In the 1980s, the Nahdlatul Ulama had come under the leadership of Abdurrahman Wahid, the charismatic grandson of one of early-twentieth-century Indonesia's most distinguished traditionalist scholars (Barton 2002; Feillard and Madinier 2006). In the mid-1990s, Wahid had become a leader in the growing democracy movement. Seventeen months after Soeharto's overthrow, in October 1999, Wahid was elected president. Wahid was a well-known supporter of women's rights, and his wife, Sinta Nuriyah Abdurrahman, was a Muslim feminist in her own right. Sinta Nuriyah played a pivotal role in a campaign to introduce antiviolence and gender-equity programs into the Islamic school (*pesantren*) curriculum (Doorn-Harder 2007, 37). A network of NU-linked nongovernmental organizations was also active in the development of a gender-equitable fiqh, which drew on classical jurisprudence to provide critical arguments in support of reproductive rights and gender equality. Masdar Masudi, the founding director of the Center for Pesantren and Societal Development (Pusat Pengembangan Pesantrendan Masyarakat, or P3M), was a leading theorist in the movement (Sciortino, Natsir, and Mas'udi 1996).

But the gender-reform coalition of which many Indonesians had dreamed ultimately faltered. After Wahid's departure from the organization in 1999, the new NU leadership—pressed by conservative scholars in the provinces—balked at pressing forward with programs of gender "mainstreaming." NU has always been a complex federation of *pesantren*-based `ulama, and even in the heyday of the democracy movement in the 1990s a large wing of the organization had been skeptical of the efforts of reformists such as Wahid, Sinta Nuriyah, and Masdar. From 2001 onward, an antireform faction in NU organized a successful campaign to take the national organization in a more conservative, albeit not at all extreme, direction (Bruinessen 2013; Feillard and Madinier 2006).

The situation within Indonesia's other mass-based Muslim organization, the Muhammadiyah, showed a similar pattern of gender and pluralist progressivism on the part of the leadership in the 1990s, followed by province-led pushback in the 2000s. From 1995 to 1998, the Muhammadiyah had been under the leadership of Amien Rais (1944–), an outspoken critic of the Soeharto regime who played a pivotal role in the 1997–98 democracy movement. Although he was (and is still today) seen as moderately conservative on Muslim–Christian questions, Rais oversaw the appointment of outspoken theological reformists to Muhammadiyah's Majlis Tarjih in alliance with such leading democratic–pluralists as Syafii Maarif and Amin Abdullah. Most remarkable was his appointment of a leading Muhammadiyah feminist, Siti Ruhaini Dzuhayatin, to the Tarjih council (see Ruhaini Dzuhayatin 2001). Over the next few years, she and the Muhammadiyah intellectual Amin Abdullah worked unceasingly to encourage the organization to develop gender-sensitive programs (see Nurlaelawati 2007).

As with NU, however, the heady reformism of the early post-Soeharto era soon gave rise to an antiliberal backlash. The first hints of trouble became visible in the Muhammadiyah in the early 2000s, when regional branches signaled their unhappiness with the national leadership's mandating of affirmative action programs for women. At the forty-fifth national congress, held in Malang in 2005, officials from several districts defied the executive board by refusing to send at least one woman representative from each district, as the board—at the urging of the Aisyiyah leadership—had requested (Dewi 2008, 171). Ruhaini and several other Muhammadiyah women, along with almost all the male reformist leadership, were also voted out of office (Burhani 2013; Syamsiyatun 2008, 158–60). To many observers, the outcome showed that the demand for gender equity in the organization "is still an elite-centered issue" (Dewi 2008, 179). My own research in Yogyakarta during these years indicated that the gender issue was but one among several developments to which Muhammadiyah conservatives objected; their core objection had to do with what they regarded as the excessive influence of "liberal" currents in Muhammadiyah ranks.

Analysts differ in identifying the reasons for and depths of this "conservative turn" in Indonesia's largest Muslim organizations (Bruinessen 2013; Burhani 2013). They note that in contrast to the situation in several Middle Eastern countries, Indonesian national elections have not seen any dramatic surge in favor of Islamist parties (Aspinall 2005; Mietzner 2008; Ufen 2008). Indeed, one of the most striking features of electoral politics in the post-Soeharto era has been that Muslim parties committed to the state-enforced implementation of "shari`a law" have for the most part seen their share of the national vote plummet. Similarly, in the course of debates over constitutional reforms during 2001–2, efforts to insert a clause into the constitution requiring the state to enforce "shari`a" were repeatedly rebuffed as mainstream Muslims joined secular nationalist parties to oppose any such amendment (Hosen 2007, 201–15; Salim 2008, 79–107).

In the aftermath of these setbacks, however, Islamist parties and movements launched campaigns to compensate for their lack of power in the nation's capital by building up their influence in the provinces. Among other things, they sought to implement "regional bylaws" (*peraturan daerah*), many of which addressed issues regarded as shari'a-inspired. The most common bylaws dealt with matters of broad public concern, including prostitution and the growing availability of drugs and alcohol. But others have taken aim squarely at girls and women, requiring the wearing of the *hijab* in schools and public spaces and limiting the movement of unescorted women after dark (Robinson 2009, 172). Although the bulk of this legislation was implemented in regions long regarded as bases for Islamist movements (Bush 2008), some of the most ardent supporters of the regulations were politicians from secular nationalist parties. As political scientist Michael Buehler (2008) has shown, in several instances, these officials aimed to use the "Islamic" bylaws to curry support in the conservative wing of the Muslim community and blunt ongoing corruption investigations.

Although the heyday of shari'a bylaws seems to have passed, the trend was indicative of a rougher populist turn to Indonesian politics in the new democratic era. In the more open environment of the 2000s, politics took on a rough-and-tumble air less favorable to the scaling up of initiatives for a gender-equitable reformation of religious and state law. In short, and not unlike the situation in some Middle Eastern countries undergoing political transitions, the post-Soeharto era's openness has allowed conservatives and militants (see Wilson 2006; 2008) to exercise an influence on public debate disproportionate to their actual representation in society and, even more so, their share of the vote in national elections.

Family Law Reform Rebuffed

In this climate of democratic opening and coarsening of public contention, Muslim feminists launched their boldest attempt at legal reform—only to see the proposal fail. The initiative was the release in October 2004 of a draft bill known as the Counter Legal Draft (CLD), put forward to revise sections of the Compilation of Islamic Law used in the country's Islamic courts for matters of marriage, divorce, and inheritance (Lindsey 2012, 69–101; Mulia and Cammack 2007; Wahid 2010; see also Bowen 2003). The CLD was prepared by a seven-member team of Islamic legal scholars under the leadership of Siti Musdah Mulia, a professor at the Hidayatullah State Islamic University in Jakarta and a special assistant to the minister of religion. The recipient of numerous international awards (including, in 2007, the US government's International Women of Courage Award), Mulia was born into a traditionalist Sulawesi Muslim family and received her early training in a pesantren. Known for her staunch support of women's rights, freedom for religious minorities, and (in recent years) gay rights, Mulia was recruited by the Ministry of Religion in 2001 to lead a "Working Group for Gender Mainstreaming."

The timing seemed right. The years 2000–2002 were the peak of democratic and feminist activism in post-Soeharto Indonesia. Conservative Islamists, including those in militia groups such as the Islamic Defenders Front (Wilson 2008), had not yet finished putting in place a national network, a project they would largely complete by 2005. The celebrated Muslim democrat Abdurrahman Wahid was president (through August 2001). Under Wahid's leadership, the Ministry for the Empowerment of Women moved to implement a series of bold reforms. In 2001, in particular, the ministry announced a national policy of "zero tolerance" for violence against women. The policy's action plan singled out several provisions from the Compilation of Islamic Law as discriminatory (Mulia and Cammack 2007, 133). Mulia's team also argued that some clauses in the compilation were in violation of international laws to which Indonesia was a signatory.

At first the CLD enjoyed the support of high-ranking officials in the Ministry of Religion. But even some Western scholars of Islamic law were surprised by the scope of the CLD reforms. The senior Australia-based scholar of Indonesian fiqh, M. B. Hooker, described the CLD as "a surprising document which . . . absolutely rejects the established principles of fiqh in favour of a purely secular scheme of family law" (Hooker 2008, 25). Mulia and her team, however, rejected such characterizations, insisting that the CLD "embraces the . . . Qur'anic commitment to equality and freedom in a thoroughgoing and uncompromising way" (Mulia and Cammack 2007, 128). In these and other statements, Mulia justified the draft by citing the higher aims of the shari'a (*maqasid al-shari'a*) to relativize and displace long-established fiqh rulings. More specifically, Mulia argued that "the principle of the equality of human beings before God" flows from the core Islamic principle of God's unicity (*tawhid*; Mulia and Cammack 2007, 137).

Five of the CLD's proposals proved especially controversial. These were the draft's proposal to ban polygyny outright, to allow interreligious marriages (forbidden under the existing Compilation of Islamic Law), to do away with the requirement that a women be represented by a male guardian (*wali nikah*) in the marriage ceremony, to equalize inheritance shares for sons and daughters, and to make disobedience (*nusyuz*) a moral failing for which husbands as well as wives can be faulted. All these provisions were at variance with the Compilation of Islamic law used in Indonesia since 1991. The proposed reforms amounted to a high-stakes gamble to replace existing fiqh traditions with a contextual, *maqasid*-based program premised on the notion that "the purpose and goal of Qur'anic text . . . is the eventual emancipation of humanity from all forms of bondage and oppression" (Mulia and Cammack 2007, 138).

Australian legal scholar Tim Lindsey has noted an additional contextual dimension to the timing of the CLD's presentation. The draft was "a conscious response by progressive Muslim intellectuals to the legal Islamisation agenda pushed by conservative Muslims, in particular through . . . Regional Regulations (Peraturan Daerah) based on moral norms derived from conservative understandings of Islamic legal traditions." In short, the CLD was intended as a broadside "defence against resurgent Islamist moral conservatism" (Lindsey 2012, 80).

In the end, however, the gamble proved ill timed. In the interim between 2001 and 2004, the circumstances of Indonesian democracy had changed. After a bitter dispute with former allies, President Wahid was ousted from office in August 2001 (Feillard and Madinier 2006). At first startled by the boldness of Muslim progressives in the early years of the post-Soeharto era, by 2002 conservative Islamists had rebounded and begun to stage well-coordinated demonstrations against Muslim democrats and feminists. The largest groups, including the Islamic Defenders Front, the Hizbut Tahrir Indonesia, and the Council of Indonesian Mujahidin (MMI; see Hefner 2012; Hilmy 2010), put in place a media-savvy network for countering liberal initiatives, combining social media blitzes with noisy street demonstrations (Hefner 2003; Wilson 2008). Although the militants were unable to translate their protests into electoral gains, their ability to intimidate state and private officials and disseminate their message through a network of mosque preachers proved brilliantly effective at shifting public opinion just enough to scuttle efforts at legal reforms.

Two weeks after its introduction, the minister of religion withdrew the CLD from legislative discussion. Lindsey captures well the emotional tenor in the aftermath of the bill's withdrawal: "The authors of the Counter Legal Draft now see it as a failure" (Lindsey 2012, 92). Muslim intellectuals whom I interviewed over the following three years bemoaned their failure to realize that the CLD draft had poured fuel on the fire of a neoconservative backlash, not least in semigovernmental 'ulama bodies such as the Majelis Ulama Indonesia (MUI; see Hasyim 2011). In 2005, just a year after the Counter Legal Draft controversy, the MUI issued a *fatwa* declaring that "secularism, pluralism, and liberalism" were contrary to Islam (Gillespie 2007; Ichwan 2013; Olle 2009). Over the following months, Islamist vigilantes cited the *fatwa* to justify attacks on liberal Muslims and Muslim nonconformists (Crouch 2014; Hefner 2012; ICG 2008). The heyday of feminist and democratic pluralism in Indonesia had, it seemed, passed.

Although the situation of Muslim gender reformists seemed to have darkened in 2004, things were not quite as dire as they at first appeared. Although it remains a regular target of neoconservative criticisms, the state Islamic university system continues its programs in civic education and "gender mainstreaming." In the face of a rash of terrorist bombings in the early 2000s, many of them targeting the Christian minority, the Indonesian state launched one of the most even-handed and successful antiterrorism campaigns in the entire world (Jones 2013). In 2014, Indonesia elected a new president, Joko Widodo, a pluralist Muslim who, though not an intellectual, has long shown a generous hand on matters of interreligious relations, women's issues, and, above all, the rights and dignity of ordinary citizens.

Although there seems little possibility any time soon of any bold reform of Indonesia's marriage laws, Muslim feminist ideas on sexual trafficking, violence against women, and male abuse of *talaq* divorce continue to make legislative headway (Robinson 2009). The reform of Indonesian marriage laws remains a distant dream, but Indonesian democracy has defied its skeptics, and the movement of Indonesian women into higher education, employment, and the Islamic sciences also continues unabated. The alternative ethical sensibilities to which the latter changes give rise are alive and well and are likely to continue to create alternate ethical imaginaries and pressures for Islamic ethical reform for some time to come.

Conclusion: Islamic Law and New Gender Ethics

Although in many regards the Indonesian case is distinctive, there are comparative lessons to be learned as to the conditions of the possibility of modern Islamic ethical reform on gender matters. The first and most basic insight has to do with the strengths and vulnerabilities of today's gender reformists by comparison with those of the first generation of Muslim women activists in the early years of the twentieth century. That first wave drew much of its political energy from the movements of anticolonial liberation taking shape in lands such as Egypt, Tunisia, and Indonesia. As Badran (2009) shows for Egypt and Robinson (2009) has demonstrated for Indonesia, the interplay between national liberation and women's emancipation was as much ethical as it was organizational: Ideas of modernist–Islamic reform and post-Enlightenment natural rights co-imbricated to legitimate aspirations for women's dignity and equality. In this manner, first-wave Muslim feminism was able to borrow political energy and intellectual capital from the growing public commitment to nationalist ideals. When some among this first generation of women's activists pressed for reforms of marriage laws and customs, they did so most commonly on the basis of arguments grounded on post-Enlightenment ideals rather than on an explicitly reformed fiqh.

On this latter point, however, things have changed greatly over the past generation. Although citizen ideals of Enlightenment derivation continue to figure in Muslim feminism, the rise of Islamist movements demanding state enforcement of a positivized and codified "Islamic law" has moved questions of Islamic legal traditions to the center of political debate. In these circumstances, the Muslim proponents of gender equality have little choice but to engage Islam's legal traditions in an effort to devise a gender-equitable alternative.

Far more systematically than their early-twentieth-century predecessors, then, Muslim feminists today take aim directly at the legacy of unreformed fiqh, as well as other popular practices and commentaries, to provide an *internal* religious critique of gender inequality and social injustice (see this volume, Emon, chapter 2, and this volume, Mir-Hosseini, chapter 3). As Ziba Mir-Hosseini (2003; 2009) has emphasized, some among these women reformers have sought to carry out a critical exegetical reading of scripture. Others, including Mir-Hosseini herself, as well as Kecia Ali (2006; 2010) and, much earlier, Fatima Mernissi (1991), have taken an even bolder tack: advancing the cause of gender equity by engaging "with juristic constructs and theories, to unveil the theological and rational arguments and legal theories that underlie them," so as to demonstrate that these theories, rather than being eternal and divine truths, are varieties of "social construction, like other laws in the realm of mu'amalat . . . shaped in interaction with political, economic, social and cultural forces" (Mir-Hosseini 2009, 28).

In Indonesia and many other Muslim lands, the intellectual complexity of these reform efforts poses challenges. New Muslim feminists have been able to avail themselves of new social and communications media to weave together a global network of like-minded reformers. This has been important not only for creating a sense of transnational solidarity but also for gaining access to scholars better versed in religious reasoning in contexts in which local activists lack such skills. Although there was no shortage of qualified religious exegetes in the late 1980s in Iran or Morocco, or in the 1990s in Indonesia, in Malaysia, organizations such as Sisters in Islam (SIS) did not have the depth of scholarly expertise required to prepare detailed and credible reform arguments. They have been able to compensate for their comparative disadvantage, however, by reaching out to international scholars such as Amina Wadud, Abdullahi Ahmed An-Na'im, and, most recently, Ziba Mir-Hosseini. All three scholars have provided sophisticated theoretical counters to conservative Islamist pushback on SIS's proposals (see Anwar 2001; 2013; Lindsey and Steiner 2012, 297–320).

In the heyday of *Reformasi* democracy in the early 2000s, Indonesia's gender reformers were confident that that they would succeed in their campaign to push through gender reforms, relying on a coalition of liberal-minded reformists in the Ministry of Religion and democracy activists in society. They had seemingly good reasons for their confidence. Parliament had just turned back efforts to introduce constitutional amendments that would have required the state to implement an unreformed variety of Islamic law (Salim 2008). The bureaus of the Ministry of Religion that were responsible for gender sensitization included many reform-minded individuals having ties to the Muhammadiyah and Nahdlatul Ulama. However, even before presentation of the proposed Counter Legal Draft to Parliament in 2004, there were signs that the initiative was in trouble. The drafters' decision to include provisions allowing interreligious marriage provided Islamist opponents with the chance to portray the bill as an assault on the integrity of the Muslim community itself. Well-coordinated demonstrations followed, and the inclusion of mainline

Muslims as well as radical Islamists in the ranks of the protestors signaled that the draft bill was about to lose its way.

The Indonesian example has parallels in other Muslim societies. In many national settings, a more open politics allows populists and militants to use demonstrations and threats to intimidate party and government officials, mobilizing enough public opinion to raise the costs of liberalizing reforms higher than most politicians are willing to pay. If this situation applies to post-Soeharto Indonesia, it applies all the more to countries where the political transition moved from simple regime change to violent social upheaval, such as Libya, Egypt, and Syria.

Together these examples indicate that in the aftermath of the Muslim world's varied transitions, there will be no one-size-fits-all model for gender-sensitive ethical reform. But the examples demonstrate some common prerequisites. First, when some variety of Islamic awakening has given rise to calls for the "shariatization" of state and society (Tibi 2013), successful reform will require leaders who have the intellectual wherewithal to engage Islamic ethical and legal traditions on their own terms. Second, after having engaged these traditions, the leadership will have to work to organize alliances willing and able to scale up the products of such efforts into programs for ethical "hegemonization" in state and civil society (Hefner 2000, 25).

A third and final prerequisite for sustainable gender reform concerns changes in popular and elite understandings of shari'a and Islamic ethics. When popular society equates the historical fiqh with an unchanging and unquestionable shari'a, Muslim feminists and others proposing changes to family laws risk being accused of apostasy. Seen from this angle, the rise of campaigns for the implementation of an unreformed shari'a may well put the proponents of gender-reform on the defensive. But it is precisely this challenge that has spurred a new generation of Muslim women to work to change Islamic ethical traditions from within. As in Indonesia, the result is still very much a work in progress—but it is a task made all the more imperative and promising as a result of the great changes taking place in modern Muslim women's lives.

References

Abdullah, Taufik. 1971. *Schools and Politics: The Kaum Muda Movement in West Sumatra (1927–1933)*. Ithaca, NY: Modern Indonesia Project, SEAP, Cornell University.

Abu-Lughod, Lila. 1986. *Veiled Sentiments: Honor and Poetry in a Bedouin Society*. Berkeley and Los Angeles: University of California Press.

Alexander, Jennifer. 1987. *Trade, Traders and Trading in Rural Java*. Singapore: Oxford University Press.

Alfian. 1989. *Muhammadiyah: The Political Behavior of a Muslim Modernist Organization under Dutch Colonialism*. Yogyakarta, Indonesia: Gadjah Mada Press.

Ali, Kecia. 2006. *Sexual Ethics and Islam: Feminist Reflections on Qur'an,* Hadith*, and Jurisprudence.* Oxford: Oneworld.

———. 2010. *Marriage and Slavery in Early Islam.* Cambridge, MA: Harvard University Press.

Anderson, Benedict. 1983. "Old State, New Society: Indonesia's New Order in Comparative Historical Perspective." *Journal of Asian Studies* 42 (3): 477–96.

———. 1991. *Imagined Communities: Reflections on the Origin and Spread of Nationalism.* London and New York: Verso.

Anwar, Syamsul. 2005. "Fatwâ, Purification and Dynamization: A Study of Tarjîh in Muhammadiyah." *Islamic Law and Society* 12 (1): 27–44.

Anwar, Zainah. 2001. "What Islam, Whose Islam? Sisters in Islam and the Struggle for Women's Rights." In *The Politics of Multiculturalism: Pluralism and Citizenship in Malaysia, Singapore, and Indonesia,* edited by Robert W. Hefner, 227–52. Honolulu: University of Hawaii Press.

———. 2013. "From Local to Global: Sisters in Islam and the Making of Musawah: A Global Movement for Equality in the Muslim Family." In *Gender and Equality in Muslim Family Law: Justice and Ethics in the Islamic Legal Tradition,* edited by Ziba Mir-Hosseini, Kari Vogt, Lena Larsen, and Christian Moe, 107–24. London and New York: Tauris.

Aspinall, Edward. 2005. "Elections and the Normalization of Politics in Indonesia." *South East Asia Research* 13 (2): 117–56.

Azra, Azyumardi. 1992. "The Transmission of Islamic Reformism to Indonesia: Networks of Middle Eastern and Malay Indonesian Ulama in the Seventeenth and Eighteenth Centuries." PhD dissertation, Department of History, Columbia University, New York.

Azra, Azumardi, Dina Afrianty, and Robert W. Hefner. 2007. "*Pesantren* and *Madrasa*: Muslim Schools and National Ideals in Indonesia." In *Schooling Islam: The Culture and Politics of Modern Muslim Education,* edited by Robert W. Hefner and Muhammad Qasim Zaman, 172–98. Princeton, NJ: Princeton University Press.

Badran, Margot. 2009. *Feminism in Islam: Secular and Religious Convergences.* Oxford: Oneworld.

Barton, G. 2002. *Abdurrahman Wahid: Muslim Democrat, Indonesian President; A View from the Inside.* Honolulu: University of Hawaii Press.

Berkey, Jonathan. 2003. *The Formation of Islam.* Cambridge, UK: Cambridge University Press.

Blackburn, Susan. 2008. "Indonesian Women and Political Islam." *Journal of Southeast Asian Studies* 39 (1): 83–105.

Bowen, John R. 1991. *Sumatran Politics and Poetics: Gayo History, 1900–1989.* New Haven, CT: Yale University Press.

———. 2003. *Islam, Law and Equality in Indonesia: An Anthropology of Public Reasoning.* Cambridge, UK: Cambridge University Press.

Brenner, Suzanne. 1998. *The Domestication of Desire: Women, Wealth, and Modernity in Java.* Princeton, NJ: Princeton University Press.

———. 2011. "Private Moralities in the Public Sphere: Democratization, Islam, and Gender in Indonesia. *American Anthropologist* 113 (3): 478–90.

Bruinessen, Martin van. 1989. "*Kitab Kuning*: Books in Arabic Script Used in the *Pesantren* Milieu." *Bijdragen tot de Taal-, Land-, en Volkenkunde* 146 (2/3): 225–69.

———. 1994. "*Pesantren* and *Kitab Kuning*: Maintenance and Continuation of a Tradition of Religious Learning." In *Texts from the Islands: Oral and Written Traditions of Indonesia and the Malaya World,* edited by Wolfgang Marschall, 121–45. Berne, Switzerland: University of Berne Press.

———. 1995. "Shari`a Court, *Tarekat* and *Pesantren*: Religious Institutions in the Banten Sultanate." *Archipel* 50:165–200.

———. 2013. "Introduction: Contemporary Developments in Indonesian Islam and the 'Conservative Turn' of the Early Twenty-First Century." In *Contemporary Developments in Indonesian Islam: Explaining the "Conservative Turn,"* edited by Martin van Bruinessen, 1–20. Singapore: ISEAS.

Bubalo, Anthony, Greg Fealy, and Whit Mason. 2008. *Zealous Democrats: Islamism and Democracy in Egypt, Indonesia, and Turkey.* Double Bay, Australia: Lowy Institute for International Policy.

Buehler, Michael. 2008. "The Rise of Shari`a Bylaws in Indonesian Districts: An Indication for Changing Patterns of Power Accumulation and Political Corruption." *South East Asia Research* 16 (2): 255–85.

Bulliet, Richard W. 1994. *Islam: The View from the Edge.* New York: Columbia University Press.

Burhani, Ahmad Najib. 2013. "Liberal and Conservative Discourses in the Muhammadiyah: The Struggle for the Face of Reformist Islam in Indonesia." In *Contemporary Developments in Indonesian Islam: Explaining the "Conservative Turn,"* edited by Martin van Bruinessen, 105–44. Singapore: ISEAS.

Burhanudin, Jajat. 2006. "*Kerajaan*-Oriented Islam: The Experience of Pre-Colonial Indonesia." *Studia Islamika* 13 (1): 33–66.

Burns, Peter. 2004. *The Leiden Legacy: Concepts of Law in Indonesia.* Leiden, Netherlands: KITLV Press.

Bush, R. 2008. "Regional Sharia Regulations in Indonesia: Anomaly or Symptom?" In *Expressing Islam: Religious Life and Politics in Indonesia*, edited by Greg Fealy and Sally White, 174–91. Singapore: Institute of Southeast Asian Studies.

Cammack, Mark. 2007. "The Indonesian Islamic Judiciary." In *Islamic Law in Contemporary Indonesia: Ideas and Institutions*, edited by R. Michael Feener and Mark E. Cammack, 146–69. Cambridge, MA: Harvard University Press.

Candraningrum, Dewi. 2013. *Negotiating Women's Veiling: Politics and Sexuality in Contemporary Indonesia.* Bangkok, Thailand: Research Institute on Contemporary Southeast Asia.

Cederroth, Sven. 1981. *The Spell of the Ancestors and the Power of Mekkah: A Sasak Community on Lombok.* Göteborg, Sweden: Universitatis Gothoburgensis.

Chamberlain, Michael. 1994. *Knowledge and Social Practice in Medieval Damascus, 1190–1350.* Cambridge, UK: Cambridge University Press.

Cribb, Robert. 1990. *The Indonesia Killings, 1965–1966: Studies from Java and Bali.* Monash Papers on Southeast Asia, No. 21. Clayton, Australia: Centre of Southeast Asian Studies, Monash University.

Crouch, Melissa. 2014. *Law and Religion in Indonesia: Conflict and the Courts in West Java.* London and New York: Routledge.

Davies, Sharyn Graham. 2010. *Gender Diversity in Indonesia: Sexuality, Islam and Queer Selves.* London and New York: Routledge.

Dewi, Kurniawati Hastuti. 2008. "Perspective versus Practice: Women's Leadership in Muhammadiyah." *Journal of Social Issues in Southeast Asia* 23 (2): 161–85.

Dhofier, Zamakhsyari. 1999. *The* Pesantren *Tradition: The Role of the* Kyai *in the Maintenance of Traditional Islam in Java.* Tempe: Monograph Series, Program for Southeast Asian Studies, Arizona State University.

Djamil, Fathurrahman. 1995. "The Muhammadiyah and the Theory of Maqasid al-Shari`ah." *Studia Islamika* 2 (1): 53–67.

Doorn-Harder, Nelly van. 2006. *Women Shaping Islam: Indonesian Muslim Women Reading the Qur'an.* Urbana-Champaign: University of Illinois Press.

———. 2007. "Reconsidering Authority: Indonesian Fiqh Texts about Women." In *Islamic Law in Contemporary Indonesia: Ideas and Institutions*, edited by R. Michael Feener and Mark E. Cammack, 27–43. Cambridge, MA: Harvard University Press.

Fahmi, Nashir. 2006. *Menegakkan Syariat Islam ala PKS*. Solo, Indonesia: Era Intermedia.

Fasseur, Cornelis. 1992. *The Politics of Colonial Exploitation: Java, the Dutch, and the Cultivation System*. Ithaca, NY: Cornell University, SEAP Publications.

Feener, R. Michael. 2007. *Muslim Legal Thought in Modern Indonesia*. Cambridge, UK: Cambridge University Press.

———. 2013. *Shari'a and Social Engineering: The Implementation of Islamic Law in Contemporary Aceh, Indonesia*. Oxford: Oxford University Press.

Feillard, Andrée, and Rémy Madinier. 2006. *La Fin de l'Innocence? L'Islam Indonésien Face à la Tentation Radicale de 1967 à Nos Jours*. Paris: Les Indes Savantes.

Feith, Herbert. 1963. "Dynamics of Guided Democracy." In *Indonesia*, edited by Ruth T. McVey, 309–409. New Haven, CT: Human Relations Area Files.

Geertz, Hildred. 1961. *The Javanese Family: A Study of Kinship and Socialization*. Prospect Heights, IL: Waveland.

Gillespie, Piers. 2007. "Current Issues in Indonesian Islam: Analysing the 2005 Council of Indonesian Ulama Fatwa No. 7 Opposing Pluralism, Liberalism, and Secularism." *Journal of Islamic Studies* 18 (2): 202–40.

Hallaq, Wael B. 2011. "*Maqāsid* and the Challenges of Modernity." *Al-Jami'ah* 49 (1): 1–31.

Hamayotsu, Kikue. 2011. "The End of Political Islam? A Comparative Analysis of Religious Parties in the Muslim Democracy of Indonesia." *Journal of Current Southeast Asian Affairs* 30 (3): 133–59.

Hasan, Noorhaidi. 2006. *Laskar Jihad: Islam, Militancy, and the Quest for Identity in Post-New Order Indonesia*. Ithaca, NY: Southeast Asia Program, Cornell University.

Hasyim, Syafiq. 2011. "The Council of Indonesian Ulama (Majelis Ulama Indonesia, MUI) and Religious Freedom." Bangkok: IRASEC.

Hefner, Robert W. 1990. *The Political Economy of Mountain Java: An Interpretive History*. Berkeley and London: University of California Press.

———. 2000. *Civil Islam: Muslims and Democratization in Indonesia*. Princeton, NJ: Princeton University Press.

———. 2003. "Civic Pluralism Denied? The New Media and *Jihadi* Violence in Indonesia." In *New Media in the Muslim World: The Emerging Public Sphere*, edited by Dale F. Eickelman and Jon W. Anderson, 158–79. Bloomington: Indiana University Press.

———. 2007. "Introduction: The Culture, Politics, and Future of Muslim Education." In *Schooling Islam: The Culture and Politics of Modern Muslim Education*, edited by Robert W. Hefner and Muhammad Qasim Zaman, 1–39. Princeton, NJ: Princeton University Press.

———. 2009. "The Politics and Cultures of Islamic Education in Southeast Asia." In *Making Modern Muslims: The Politics of Islamic Education in Southeast Asia*, edited by Robert W. Hefner, 1–54. Honolulu: University of Hawaii Press.

———. 2012. "Islamic Radicalism in a Democratizing Indonesia." In *Routledge Handbook of Political Islam*, edited by Shahram Akbarzaden, 105–18. New York and London: Routledge.

———. 2013. "The Study of Religious Freedom in Indonesia." *Review of Faith and International Affairs* 2 (2): 18–27.

Hilmy, Masdar. 2010. *Islamism and Democracy in Indonesia: Piety and Pragmatism*. Singapore: ISEAS Press.

Hooker, M. B. 1984. *Islamic Law in South-East Asia*. Singapore: Oxford University Press.

———. 2008. *Indonesian Syariah: Defining a National School of Islamic Law*. Singapore: Institute of Southeast Asian Studies.

———. 2013. "Southeast Asian Shari'ahs." *Studia Islamika* 20 (2): 183–242.

Hosen, Nadirsyah. 2003. "Revelation in a Modern Nation State: Muhammadiyah and Islamic Legal Reasoning in Indonesia." *Studia Islamika* 10 (1): 65–96.

———. 2007. *Shari`a and Constitutional Reform in Indonesia.* Singapore: ISEAS Press.

ICG. 2002. "Al-Qaeda in Southeast Asia: The Case of the 'Ngruki Network' in Indonesia." Jakarta and Brussels: Asia Briefing No. 20.

———. 2008. "Indonesia: Implications of the Ahmadiyah Decree." Jakarta and Brussels: Asia Briefing No. 78.

Ichwan, Moch Nur. 2013. "Towards a Puritanical Moderate Islam: The Majelis Ulama Indonesia and the Politics of Religious Orthodoxy." In *Contemporary Developments in Indonesian Islam: Explaining the "Conservative Turn,"* edited by Martin van Bruinessen, 60–104. Singapore: ISEAS.

Jabali, Fuad, and Jamhari, eds. 2002. *IAIN & Modernisasi Islam di Indonesia* [The State Islamic Institutes and the Modernization of Islam in Indonesia]. Jakarta: Logos Wacana Ilmu.

Jackson, Elizabeth. 2007. "Crafting a New Democracy: Civic Education in Indonesian Islamic Universities." *Asia Pacific Journal of Education* 27 (1): 41–54.

Jones, Sidney. 2013. "Indonesian Government Approaches to Radical Islam since 1998." In *Democracy and Islam in Indonesia,* edited by Mirjam Künkler and Alfred Stepan, 109–25. New York: Columbia University Press.

Jones, Gavin W., and Chris Manning. 1992. "Labour Force and Employment during the 1980s." In *The Oil Boom and After: Indonesian Economic Policy and Performance in the Soeharto Era,* edited by Anne Booth, 363–410. Kuala Lumpur: Oxford University Press.

Karamustafa, Ahmet T. 2007. *Sufism: The Formative Period.* Berkeley and Los Angeles: University of California Press.

Kartodirdjo, Sartono. 1972. "Agrarian Radicalism in Java: Its Setting and Development." In *Culture and Politics in Indonesia,* edited by Claire Holt, 71–125. Ithaca, NY: Cornell University Press.

Kruithof, Maryse. 2014. "'Shouting in a Desert': Dutch Missionary Encounters with Javanese Islam, 1850–1910." PhD thesis, Department of History, Erasmus University, Rotterdam, Netherlands.

Laffan, Michael Francis. 2003. *Islamic Nationhood and Colonial Indonesia: The Umma below the Winds.* London and New York: Routledge Curzon.

Latte Abdallah, Stéphanie. 2010. "Introduction: Féminismes Islamiques." *Revue des mondes musulmans et de la Méditerranée* No. 128, 13–31.

Lev, Daniel. 1972. *Islamic Courts in Indonesia: A Study in the Political Bases of Legal Institutions.* Berkeley: University of California Press.

Lindsey, Tim. 2012. *Islam, Law and the State in Southeast Asia,* vol. 1, *Indonesia.* London and New York: Tauris.

Lindsey, Tim, and Jeremy Kingsley. 2008. "Talking in Code: Legal Islamisation in Indonesia and the MMI Shari`a Criminal Code." In *The Law Applied: Contextualizing the Islamic Shari`a,* edited by Peri Bearman, Wolfhart Heirichs, and Bernard G. Weiss, 295–319. London and New York: Tauris.

Lindsey, Tim, and Kerstin Steiner. 2012. *Islam, Law and the State in Southeast Asia,* vol. 3, *Malaysia and Brunei.* London and New York: Tauris.

Machmudi, Yon. 2006. Islamizing Indonesia: The Rise of Jemaah Tarbiyah and the Prosperous Justice Party (PKS)." PhD dissertation, Faculty of Asian Studies, Australian National University, Canberra.

Masud, Muhammad Khalid. 2002. "The Scope of Pluralism in Islamic Moral Traditions." In *Islamic Political Ethics: Civil Society, Pluralism, and Conflict,* edited by Sohail H. Hashmi, 135–47. Princeton, NJ: Princeton University Press.

———. 2005. *Shâtibî's Philosophy of Islamic Law*. Kuala Lumpur: Islamic Book Trust.

Mernissi, Fatima. 1991. *Women in Islam: An Historical and Theological Enquiry*. Oxford: Basil Blackwell.

Metcalf, Barbara Daly, ed. 1984. *Moral Conduct and Authority: The Place of Adab in South Asian Islam*. University of California Press.

Mietzner, Marcus. 2008. "Comparing Indonesia's Party Systems of the 1950s and the Post-Soeharto Era: From Centrifugal to Centripetal Inter-party Competition." *Journal of Southeast Asian Studies* 39 (3): 431–53.

Milner, A. C. 1995. *The Invention of Politics in Colonial Malaya: Contesting Nationalism and the Expansion of the Public Sphere*. Cambridge, UK: Cambridge University Press.

Mir-Hosseini, Ziba. 1999. *Islam and Gender: The Religious Debate in Contemporary Iran* Princeton, NJ: Princeton University Press.

———. 2003. "The Construction of Gender in Islamic Legal Thought and Strategies for Reform." *Hawwa: Journal of Women of the Middle East and the Islamic World* 1 (1): 1–28.

———. 2009. "Towards Gender Equality: Muslim Family Laws and the Shari`ah." In *Wanted: Equality and Justice in the Muslim Family*, edited by Zainah Anwar, 23–63. Petaling Jaya, Malaysia: Musawah.

Mortimer, Rex. 1974. *Indonesian Communism under Sukarno: Ideology and Politics, 1959–1965*. Ithaca, NY: Cornell University Press.

Mulia, Siti Musdah, and Mark E. Cammack. 2007. "Toward a Just Marriage Law: Empowering Indonesian Women through a Counter Legal Draft to the Indonesian Compilation of Islamic Law." In *Islamic Law in Contemporary Indonesia: Ideas and Institutions*, edited by R. Michael Feener and Mark E. Cammack, 128–45. Cambridge, MA: Harvard University Press.

Mulkhan, Abdul Munir. 2010. *Kiai Ahmad Dahlan: Jejak Pembaruan Social dan Kemanusiaan*. Jakarta: Kompas Books.

Nakamura, Mitsuo. 2012. *The Crescent Arises over the Banyan Tree: A Study of the Muhammadiyah Movement in a Central Javanese Town, c. 1910s–2010*, 2nd enlarged ed. Singapore: ISEAS Press.

Njoto-Feillard, Gwenaël. 2012. *L'Islam et la réinvention du capitalisme en Indonésie*. Paris: Karthala.

Noer, D. 1973. *The Modernist Muslim Movement in Indonesia, 1900–1942*. Kuala Lumpur: Oxford University Press.

Noor, Farish. 2012. *Islam on the Move: The Tablighi Jama`at in Southeast Asia*. Amsterdam, Netherlands: Amsterdam University Press.

Nurlaelawati, Euis. 2007. "Modernization, Tradition, and Identity: The *Kompilasi Hukum Islam* and Legal Practice in the Indonesian Religious Courts." PhD thesis, Department of Religious Studies, Utrecht University.

Octavia, Lanny. 2012. "Islamism and Democracy: A Gender Analysis on PKS's Application of Democratic Principles and Values." *Al-Jami`ah* 50 (1): 1–21.

Olle, John. 2009. "The Majelis Ulama Indonesia versus 'Heresy': The Resurgence of Authoritarian Islam." In *State of Authority: The State in Society in Indonesia*, edited by Gerry van Klinken and Joshua Barker, 95–116. Ithaca, NY: Cornell Southeast Program Publications.

Opwis, Felicitas. 2007. "Islamic Law and Legal Change: The Concept of *Maslaha* in Classical and Contemporary Islamic Legal Theory." In *Shari`a: Islamic Law in the Contemporary Context*, edited by Abbas Amanat and Frank Griffel, 62–82. Stanford, CA: Stanford University Press.

Peacock, James L. 1978. *Muslim Puritans: Reformist Psychology in Southeast Asian Islam*. Berkeley and Los Angeles: University of California Press.

Peletz, Michael G. 1996. *Reason and Passion: Representations of Gender in a Malay Society*. Berkeley and Los Angeles: University of California Press.

———. 2009. *Gender Pluralism: Southeast Asia since Early Modern Times*. London and New York: Routledge.

Pelras, Christian. 1996. *The Bugis*. Oxford: Blackwell.

Ramadan, Tariq. 2009. *Radical Reform: Islamic Ethics and Liberation*. Oxford and New York: Oxford University Press.

Reid, Anthony. 1993. *Southeast Asia in the Age of Commerce, 1450–1680*, vol. 2, *Expansion and Crisis*. New Haven, CT: Yale University Press.

Ricci, Ronit. 2011. *Islam Translated: Literature, Conversion, and the Arabic Cosmopolis of South and Southeast Asia*. Chicago: University of Chicago Press.

Ricklefs, M. C. 2007. *Polarising Javanese Society: Islamic and Other Visions (c. 1830–1930)*. Honolulu: University of Hawaii Press.

———. 2012. *Islamisation and Its Opponents in Java: c. 1930 to the Present*. Singapore: NUS Press.

Riddell, Peter. 2001. *Islam and the Malay-Indonesian World*. London: Hurst and Company.

Rinaldo, R. 2013. *Mobilizing Piety: Islam and Feminism in Indonesia*. New York: Oxford University Press.

Robinson, Geoffrey. 1998. *The Dark Side of Paradise: Political Violence in Bali*. Ithaca, NY: Cornell University Press.

Robinson, Kathryn. 2008. "Islamic Cosmopolitics, Human Rights and Anti-Violence Strategies in Indonesia." In *Anthropology and the New Cosmopolitanism: Rooted, Feminist and Vernacular Perspectives*, edited by Pnina Werbner, 111–33. Oxford and New York: Berg.

———. 2009. *Gender, Islam and Democracy in Indonesia*. London and New York: Routledge.

Roff, William R. 1994. *The Origins of Malay Nationalism*, 2nd ed. Kuala Lumpur: University of Malaya Press.

Roosa, John. 2006. *Pretext for Mass Murder: The September 30th Movement and Suharto's Coup d'État in Indonesia*. Madison: University of Wisconsin Press.

Rose, M. 2010. *Indonesia Free: A Political Biography of Mohammad Hatta*. Singapore: Equinox Publishing.

Ruhaini Dzuhayatin, Siti. 2001. "Gender and Pluralism in Indonesia." In *The Politics of Multiculturalism: Pluralism and Citizenship in Malaysia, Singapore, and Indonesia*, edited by Robert W. Hefner, 253–67. Honolulu: University of Hawaii Press.

Salim, Arskal. 2008. *Challenging the Secular State: The Islamization of Law in Modern Indonesia*. Honolulu: University of Hawaii Press.

Schröter, Susanne. 2013. "Gender and Islam in Southeast Asia: An Overview." In *Gender and Islam in Southeast Asia: Women's Rights Movements, Religious Resurgence and Local Traditions*, edited by Susanne Schröter, 7–52. Leiden and Boston, MA: Brill.

Sciortino, Rosalia, Lies Marcoes Natsir, and Masdar F. Mas'udi. 1996. "Learning from Islam: Advocacy of Reproductive Rights in Indonesian *Pesantren*." *Reproductive Health Matters* 4 (8): 86–96.

Shiraishi, Takashi. 1990. *An Age in Motion: Popular Radicalism in Java, 1912–1926*. Ithaca, NY, and London: Cornell University Press.

Siegel, James T. 1969. *The Rope of God*. Berkeley: University of California Press.

Smith-Hefner, Nancy J. 2007. "Javanese Women and the Veil in Post-Soeharto Indonesia." *The Journal of Asian Studies* 66 (2): 389–420.

Snouck Hurgonje, C. 1931. *Mekka in the Latter Part of the 19th Century*. Leiden, Netherlands: Brill.

Steenbrink, Karel. 2003. *Catholics in Indonesia: A Documented History 1808–1900*. Leiden: KITLV Press.

Syamsiyatun, Siti. 2008. "Women Negotiating Feminism and Islamism: The Experience of Nasyiatul Aisyiyah, 1985–2005." In *Indonesian Islam in a New Era: How Women Negotiate*

Their Muslim Identities, edited by Susan Blackburn, Bianca J. Smith, and Siti Syamsiyatun, 139–65. Clayton, Australia: Monash University Press.

Tibi, Bassam. 2013. *The Shari`a State: Arab Spring and Democratization*. London and New York: Routledge.

Ufen, Andreas. 2008. "From *Aliran* to Dealignment: Political Parties in Post-Suharto Indonesia." *South East Asia Research* 16 (1): 5–41.

Vredenbregt, Jacob. 1962. "The *Haddj*: Some of Its Features and Functions in Indonesia." *Bijdragen tot de Taal-, Land- en Volkenkunde* 118 (1): 91–154.

Wahid, Marzuki. 2010. "Reformation of Islamic Family Law in Post-New Order Indonesia: A Legal and Political Study of the Counter Legal Draft of the Islamic Law Compilation." In *Islam in Contention: Rethinking Islam and State in Indonesia*, edited by Ota Atsushi, Okamoto Masaaki, and Ahmad Suaedy, 77–120. Jakarta: Wahid Institute.

Wahid, Din. 2013. "Nurturing the Salafi *Minhaj*: A Study of Salafi *Pesantren* in Contemporary Indonesia." PhD thesis, Department of Religious Studies, Utrecht University.

Watson Andaya, Barbara. 2006. *The Flaming Womb: Repositioning Women in Early Modern Southeast Asia*. Honolulu: University of Hawaii Press.

White, Sally, and Maria Ulfah Anshor. 2008. "Islam and Gender in Contemporary Indonesia: Public Discourses on Duties, Rights and Morality." In *Expressing Islam: Religious Life and Politics in Indonesia*, edited by Greg Fealy and Sally White, 137–58. Singapore: ISSEAS Press.

Wieringa, Saskia. 2002. *Sexual Politics in Indonesia*. New York: Palgrave MacMillan.

Wilson, Ian Douglas. 2006. "Continuity and Change: The Changing Contours of Organized Violence in Post-New Order Indonesia." *Critical Asian Studies* 38 (2): 265–97.

———. 2008. "'As Long as It's *Halal*': Islamic *Preman* in Jakarta." In *Expressing Islam: Religious Life and Politics in Indonesia*, edited by Greg Fealy and Sally White, 192–210. Singapore: Institute of Southeast Asian Studies.

Woodward, Mark R. 1989. *Islam in Java: Normative Piety and Mysticism in the Sultanate of Yogyakarta*. Tucson: University of Arizona Press.

Notes

1. Scholars of Indonesian political history have long hesitated to describe the non-Islamist wing of the Indonesian nationalist movement as "secular" or "secular nationalist." Statistically speaking, the majority of these nationalists were of Muslim background, and some, such as Mohammad Hatta (1902–80), the country's first vice president, came from pious families and recognized the importance of religion in public life even while taking exception to proposals to make a codified and positivized variety of Islamic shari`a the law of the land. Because most "secular" nationalists in Indonesia have long agreed on the importance of religion in public life, some scholars of Indonesia prefer to call these actors "multiconfessional" nationalists rather than "secular" nationalists (see Hefner 2000; Noer 1973).

Contributors

A graduate of the University of Chicago Law School, **Connie J. Cannon** is a Detroit-based lawyer and a researcher on Islamic law.

Professor and Canada research chair in religion, pluralism, and the rule of law, **Anver M. Emon** is an internationally recognized scholar of Islamic and comparative law. His many books include *Islamic Natural Law Theories* (Oxford) and *Religious Pluralism and Islamic Law: Dhimmis and Others in the Empire of Law* (Oxford).

Robert W. Hefner is director of the Institute on Culture, Religion, and World Affairs and serves as a professor of anthropology and a professor of international relations at the Pardee School for Global Affairs at Boston University. He is the author of eighteen books and is currently working on a comparative project on Muslim, Christians, and pluralist citizenship.

Ahmet T. Kuru is an associate professor of political science at San Diego State University. He is the author of several books, including the award-winning *Secularism and State Policies toward Religion: The United States, France, and Turkey*.

Clark B. Lombardi is the director of Islamic legal studies and a professor of law at the University of Washington Law School. He is the author of several acclaimed works, including *State Law as Islamic Law in Modern Egypt: The Incorporation of the Shari`a into Egyptian Constitutional Law* (Brill).

A leading scholar of women and Islamic law, **Ziba Mir-Hosseini** is a legal anthropologist and professorial research associate at the Centre for Middle Eastern and Islamic Law at the University of London. Her many books include *Marriage on Trial: A Study of Islamic Family Law in Iran and Morocco* (Tauris), *Islam and Gender: The Religious Debate in Contemporary Iran* (Princeton), and *Islam and Democracy in Iran: Eshkevari and the Quest for Reform* (Tauris). She has also codirected two award-winning documentary films, *Divorce Iranian Style* and *Runaway*.

Michael G. Peletz is a professor of anthropology at Emory University and is an internationally prominent scholar of Islamic law, gender plurality, and governance.

He is the author of many books, including *Islamic Modern: Religious Courts and Cultural Politics in Malaysia* (Princeton) and *Gender Pluralism: Southeast Asia Since Early Modern Times* (Routledge).

A professor of sociology at Rutgers University, **Zakia Salime** is the author of *Between Feminism and Islam: Human Rights and Sharia Law in Morocco* (Minnesota). A leading scholar of Islam and feminism, she writes on states, gendered subjectivities, and the interplay of global regimes of rights and local alternatives.

A leading scholar of Islam in West Africa, **Dorothea E. Schulz** is a professor of anthropology with the Institute for Ethnology at the University of Cologne. Her books include *Muslims and New Media in West Africa: Pathways to God* and *Culture and Customs of Mali.*

A specialist of religious and political institutions in medieval and modern Islam, **Muhammad Qasim Zaman** is the Robert H. Niehaus Professor of Near Eastern Studies and Religion at Princeton University. He is the author of many books, including *The Ulama in Contemporary Islam: Custodians of Change* and *Modern Islamic Thought in a Radical Age: Religious Authority and Internal Criticism.*

The Prince Alwaleed Bin Talal professor in contemporary Islamic thought and life at Harvard University, **Malika Zeghal** is a political scientist who studies Islamist movements in the Middle East and North Africa. Her award-winning books include *Gardiens de l'Islam: Les oulémas d'al-Azhar dans l'Egypte contemporaine* and *Islamism in Morocco: Religion, Authoritarianism, and Electoral Politics.* A forthcoming book examines states, secularity, and Islam in the contemporary world.

Index

Abduh, Muhammad, 15, 139, 264
Abdullah, Amin, 277
Abu-Lughod, Lila, 7, 9, 78–79
Abu Zayd, Nasr Hamid, 20, 145–49
adab (culture, ethico-cultural refinement), 8
ahkam (legal rules, as derived in fiqh), 6, 15, 24, 47, 65, 72, 75; categories of, 72; classical, on family, 67, 224; Muslim feminist, by comparison with classical, 66, 75–76, 279; Ottoman, with regard to women, 68; patriarchal influences on, 73, 27–76; reformist approaches to, 28, 266. *See also* family law; feminism, Muslim; fiqh; Qur'an; shari'a; Sunna
Ahmadis, 186–87
Aisyiyah (Indonesian Muslim modernist women's association), 268–69, 274, 277; views on women's roles, 269, 277. *See also* Indonesia; Muhammadiyah
AKP (political party). *See* Justice and Development Party (Turkey)
Algeria, 22
al-Haqq, Zia, 12, 185–192, 193, 194
Ali, Afrasheem, 50
Ali, Kecia, 7, 12, 14, 75, 282
Ali, Mukti, 275
Ali Agrama, Hussein, 145–47
al-Mahdi, Rabab, 45–46
al-Nahdha (Tunisian political party), 19, 39, 46, 109–11, 131n5, 132n11; debate shari'a as source of legislation, 109–120; renunciation of state-based shari'a, 113–115. *See also* Tunisia
al-Qa'ida, 22, 228n32
al-Qaradawi, Yusuf, 150, 157n9, 163
al-Shatibi, Abu Ishaq, 12, 162, 164. *See also maqasid al-shari'a*
Anderson, Benedict, 267
An-Na'im, Abdullahi Ahmed, 282
anthropology of morality, 4–5, 7, 10–11
apostasy, 10, 20, 43, 122, 127–28, 129, 145–46, 246, 270, 283. *See also* freedom; *takfir*
Arab Spring, 1, 2, 17, 19, 39; Morroccan, 19, 84, 91; shari'a in, 1, 39; Tunisian, 19; Turkish views of, 166

'Askari, Muhammad Hasan, 189–91, 195, 196, 200n11
assertive secularism. *See* secularism
Averroes. *See* Rushd, Ibn
Azar Moin, A., 8

Badran, Margot, 25, 82n6, 281. *See also* feminism
Barkey, Karen, 56
Barth, Fredrik, 5
Baudrillard, Jean, 172
Bayat, Asef, 12, 92
Bernard-Maugiron, Nathalie, 157
Bhutto, Benazir, 191–92
Bhutto, Zulfikar Ali, 185–89
Binder, Leonard, 187
Blackburn, Susan, 268
blasphemy laws, 43; Egyptian, 145–46; Pakistani, 194, 196. *See also* hisba; pluralism; shari'a; toleration
Boko Haram, 26; understanding of shari'a, 1, 2, 3, 13, 16. *See also* shari'a
Bourguiba, Habib, 114, 115, 118, 121, 131n5, 159, 171
Boykin, Lt. General William, 40–41
Buehler, Michael, 278
Burak, Guy, 33n4
Burhanudin, Jajat, 261

Canada, 39, 53–54, 122, 133n4, 275
Cantwell Smith, Wilfred, 199n2
Catholicism, 190–91, 264. *See also* Christianity
Center for Security Policy, 40–41
Christianity, 51, 64n1, 190; Enlightenment and, 44–46; Indonesia, 270, 277, 280; Malaysia, 257n2; Mali, 205, 214, 215; Pakistan, 178; Western social imaginary and, 44–46. *See also* Catholicism; Enlightenment; social imaginary
citizenship, 1, 17, 20, 60; Egyptian, 20, 139–40, 142–53, 157n11; hisba (forbidding wrong) and, 20, 139–40, 142–53, 157n11; Indonesian Muslim curriculum for, 276; "lawfare" and, 23; Maldives, 7, 50–51, 54; Mali, 206; modern states and, 65, 96, 138, 139; premodern, 60–61; Pakistan, 178–79, 180, 187, 194; state regulation of religion and, 1, 7, 119, 120, 128, 130, 178,

CPSIA information can be obtained
at www.ICGtesting.com
Printed in the USA
FSOW01n2258131216
28562FS